Table of Contents

Foreword

Drupal's modular architecture and open source nature make it a popular PHP application framework and content management system for hundreds of thousands of web developers around the world. More than 900 people contributed code and ideas to the Drupal 6 release and even more are responsible for developing and maintaining more than 2,000 contributed modules that can be used to extend Drupal's functionality.

The size, passion, and velocity of the Drupal community, combined with Drupal's strength as a platform, allow incredible things to happen. Every day new modules are contributed and existing modules are improved upon. Whether these modules are created to catch up with the latest trends on the Web or to invent completely new paradigms, the Drupal project continues to expand in many different directions.

The beauty of all these modules is that they empower website builders to assemble rich and powerful websites quickly and easily without having to be a programmer. Millions of people are using Drupal to build personal blogs, corporate websites, intranets, online photo galleries, wikis, job posting boards, conference websites, and more.

Unfortunately, the challenge for many of these site administrators, and even seasoned Drupal developers, is to try and make sense of all these modules and the ever-expanding Drupal universe. What modules should you use to build a newspaper website? What modules should you use to build an intranet? What modules are best avoided because they are being deprecated by better ones? What modules can be used on really big websites that serve millions of pages a day? Navigating your way through the Drupal world can be daunting.

This book cuts out a lot of the research time and helps you dive headfirst into Drupal. It does an excellent job explaining how to rapidly assemble a wide variety of websites using some of Drupal's most commonly used modules. Whether you're new to building websites or an experienced programmer, this book is full of useful information. I promise that by the end of this book, you'll be much more prepared to build the Drupal site of your dreams.

—Dries Buytaert
Drupal founder and project lead
July 2008

Preface

Audience

Who is this book written for?

- If your lead developer can't seem to shut up about this weird "Drupal" thing, and you want to figure out what on earth she's talking about, this book is for you.

- If your boss has approached you and said, "We need to build a site that has X, and fast!" and "X" is a photo gallery, or a product review website, or an e-commerce site, or any of the other projects covered in this book, this book is for you.

- If you know your way around Drupal, but have found yourself paralyzed by the sheer volume of contributed modules, and need help figuring out which ones are worth looking at, this book is for you.

- If you consider yourself well versed in Drupal already, but want to broaden your horizons by learning about some of its more esoteric modules, and learn best practices for building powerful Drupal websites, this book is for you.

If you're completely new to creating websites and installing web-based scripts, this book probably *isn't* for you, yet. We assume that goofy acronyms like PHP, FTP, URL, ZIP, and HTML are in your working vocabulary. Likewise, if you're interested in hardcore, nitty-gritty details about Drupal's API functions, this book *isn't* for you: our focus here is on combining *existing* modules to build out functionality, rather than creating new ones.

If you're one of the rest of us, who fall somewhere between total newbie and computer science professor, we hope that this book provides you with an invaluable reference to building practical websites with Drupal.

Assumptions This Book Makes

You'll need access to a computer or server running PHP, along with a web server (Apache preferred) and database (MySQL recommended). For local development, there are several all-in-one Apache/MySQL/PHP packages available such as WAMP for Windows (*http://www.wampserver.com*) or MAMP for Macs (*http://www.mamp.info*).

Visit *http://drupal.org/hosting* for a list of Drupal-friendly web hosting companies, and visit *http://drupal.org/requirements* to read more about Drupal's system requirements.

You will also need to install Drupal, and the hands-on chapters assume that you're using the book's source code. Appendix A provides some basic instructions, but if you run into trouble or want to read more detailed instructions, see the Drupal 6 installation guide at *http://drupal.org/getting-started/6/install*. If you are not using the source code provided with the book, Appendix C contains a list of all of the modules and themes that are used for each chapter so you can re-create them.

A Note About the Modules Used in This Book

Drupal is constantly moving and its community-contributed module world is constantly shifting. The source code for the book provides the versions that the chapters were written with, and as time moves on, the versions available on Drupal.org (*http://drupal.org*) will most likely change. Sometimes changes don't dramatically affect how things work, but other times they do. For many chapters, the hands-on sections will apply for a very long time or change so little that they will still be quite easy to follow. Even if the user interface for a module changes, after using this book and walking through various configurations, you should be equipped to explore modules on your own. In addition to the specific hands-on "recipes," you will also learn tips and best practices for how to "cook" generally, that is, how to learn about modules on your own.

Also keep in mind that the Spotlight sections, which discuss module features and comparing modules, along with Appendix B, which discusses how to evaluate modules, provide a good foundation for you to make these evaluations on your own. You can do your own comparisons as newer modules come out and make the best decisions for your use. This book is intended to not only be a guide but also a springboard for your own mastery of the Drupal contributed project world.

Contents of This Book

Beyond the initial chapters that set the stage, this book is organized as a series of recipes, each of which consists of the following structure:

Introduction
> The introduction gives an overview of what modules are covered, as well as the overall goal of the chapter.

Case study
> The case study describes the needs of a fictitious client who requires a website that can be a wiki, or have product reviews, or an image gallery. We describe some background information about the client, and go into more detail about their specific requirements.

Implementation notes

Here we discuss various solutions within Drupal to solve the client's requirements, and go into detail about which modules we've selected and why. This section compares and contrasts modules and when it's appropriate to use module A or why module B is a dead end.

Spotlight

Each chapter introduces one or more major modules or Drupal concepts, and the Spotlight sections provide a "bird's-eye view" of what each specializes in and how it works. Think of this section as a miniature "product sheet" that highlights features of a given module and what it can do.

Hands-on

After describing what a module can do in the general case, the hands-on sections will show you how to configure them by providing step-by-step "recipes" to build out the precise functionality the client requires.

Taking it further

There are a lot of helpful add-on modules that can be introduced to a particular use case to make it even more powerful. This section provides references to additional modules that enhance the functionality built out in the hands-on sections.

Summary

This section wraps up what we've learned over the course of the chapter, and provides links to the modules used, and other resources that provide more information.

Here is a list of the chapters this book covers. The first three chapters are considered "required reading" if you haven't used Drupal before. The rest of the chapters will assume knowledge of the basics of Drupal, and the Views and CCK modules. If you've used Drupal 5 but haven't yet used Drupal 6, you may also want to skim these chapters (particularly Chapter 3, as Views has changed significantly in Drupal 6).

Chapter 1, *Drupal Overview*

This chapter answers the main "need to know" questions about Drupal: what's Drupal, who's using it, why are they using it, and how does it work? It also provides some historical context to Drupal, introduces essential terminology, and everything else you need to get up to speed.

Chapter 2, *Drupal Jumpstart*

The first hands-on chapter hits the ground running, and will show you how to use Drupal's core functionality, as well as a few contributed modules, in order to build a basic business website. By the end of this chapter, you should feel comfortable in Drupal's administrative section, and also know how to create basic content through a WYSIWYG interface with the FCKeditor and IMCE modules. We'll also discuss Drupal modules that can help handle inevitable abuse, including Mollom.

Chapter 3, *Job Posting Board*
> This chapter introduces the Content Construction Kit (CCK) and Views modules by walking through the construction of a job-posting website. By the end of this chapter, you'll understand how to create custom content types and add form fields, as well as how to click together lists of any type of website content, which are the basis of all the other chapters in the book.

Chapter 4, *Product Reviews*
> In this chapter, you will build a community product review website, with the Amazon module providing the product data, and the Voting API and Fivestar modules providing a rating widget.

Chapter 5, *Wiki*
> This chapter covers several tools that can be used to create a wiki in Drupal, among other uses. The node revisions system (coupled with the useful Diff module), the Markdown filter for easy HTML entry, the Freelinking module to automatically create and link wiki pages, and the Pathauto module for automatically creating search engine-friendly URLs are all discussed in detail.

Chapter 6, *Managing Publishing Workflow*
> This chapter talks all about implementing custom publishing workflows with Drupal's Actions system combined with the Workflow module, and the Views Bulk Operations and Workspace modules for creating custom administration screens.

Chapter 7, *Photo Gallery*
> This chapter helps you build a family photo gallery using the ImageField module, along with ImageCache to automatically generate sized thumbnails.

Chapter 8, *Multilingual Sites*
> This chapter describes how to build a multilingual site using the Locale, Content Translation, and Internationalization suite of modules.

Chapter 9, *Event Management*
> This chapter's all about how to do event management in Drupal, featuring the Date and Calendar modules for storing and displaying event information, and the Flag module for keeping track of who's coming.

Chapter 10, *Online Store*
> Use the powerful Ubercart suite of modules to build a T-shirt store that includes such features as a product catalog, shopping cart, and payment processing.

Chapter 11, *Theming Your Site*
> This chapter provides some overview information about Drupal's theming system, and some basic tricks you can use to override the look and feel of Drupal. By reading this chapter, you can start modifying template files and start to give Drupal your own look and feel!

Appendix A, *Installing and Upgrading Drupal*
> If you're new to Drupal, this appendix will get you up to speed on how to install it, as well as how to do upgrades down the road.

Appendix B, *Choosing the Right Modules*
> Evaluating modules is often the biggest hurdle to building a Drupal site. This appendix is a breakdown of strategies and tips for figuring out which module will work for your site.

Appendix C, *Modules and Themes Used in This Book*
> This appendix lists the modules and themes used in each chapter to re-create the hands-on sections.

Conventions Used in This Book

The following typographical conventions are used in this book:

Italic
> Indicates filenames, directories, new terms, URLs, and emphasized text.

`Constant width`
> Indicates parts of code, contents of files, commands, and output from commands.

 This icon signifies a tip, suggestion, or general note.

 This icon indicates a warning or caution.

Any navigation around Drupal pages is displayed as follows:

> Administer→Site building→Modules (admin/build/modules).

This is an instruction to click the Administer link in the navigation block, then Site building, then Modules. As a shortcut, you can also enter the path indicated in parentheses into your browser: *http://www.example.com/admin/build/modules*.

Using Code Examples

This book is here to help you get your job done. In general, you may use the code in this book in your programs and documentation.

All Drupal code, including the Drupal 6 code that you can access through the O'Reilly website (as described shortly) is subject to the GNU General Public License, version 2. Your use of Drupal code, including copying, modification, and distribution, is subject to the license. Also, "Drupal" is a registered trademark of the founder of the Drupal project, Dries Buytaert. Information about permitted uses of the code and the trademark can be found at the Drupal website (*http://drupal.org*), where you can also find information about how the GNU General Public License affects your use of the code. More information about the license is available at *http://www.gnu.org/licenses/old-licenses/gpl-2.0.html#SEC3*.

With respect to other code examples in this book, you do not need to contact us for permission unless you're reproducing a significant portion of the non-Drupal code. For example, writing a program that uses several chunks does not require permission. Selling or distributing a CD-ROM of examples from O'Reilly books does require permission. Answering a question by citing this book and quoting example code does not require permission. Incorporating a significant amount of example code from this book into your product's documentation does require permission.

We appreciate, but do not require, attribution. An attribution usually includes the title, author, publisher, and ISBN. For example: "*Using Drupal* by Angela Byron, Heather Berry, Nathan Haug, Jeff Eaton, James Walker, and Jeff Robbins. Copyright 2009 Angela Byron, Heather Berry, Nathan Haug, Jeff Eaton, James Walker, and Jeff Robbins, 978-0-596-51580-5."

If you think that your use of code examples falls outside fair use or the permission given above, feel free to contact us at *permissions@oreilly.com*.

Downloading Drupal 6

This book's website contains a link to a downloadable copy of of Drupal 6, along with all of the modules covered in the book, and the themes used in the example websites for each hands-on chapter at *http://usingdrupal.com/source_code*. Each hands-on chapter also has an "installation profile" (a set of starter scripts that configure default options) that bootstraps a starter site for each hands-on chapter. These installation profiles may be selected at the beginning of the Drupal installation process; for example, "Chapter 4: Job Posting."

Switching between one chapter's hands-on examples and another's requires making a new site while using the same source code. You can do so with minimal fuss using the following steps:

1. Either create a new database for the chapter's installation of Drupal, or delete and re-create the existing database.
2. Copy *sites/default/default.settings.php* to *sites/default/settings.php*, overwriting the existing *settings.php* file.
3. Change the permissions on *sites/default/settings.php* so that the file is writable.
4. Rerun the installation at *http://www.example.com/install.php*.

More information on how to install Drupal is available in Appendix A.

In addition to configuring some basic settings such as the site name, the theme, and so on, for each chapter, the installation profiles (with the exception of Chapter 2) also set up the following users:

username: *admin*, password: *oreilly*
> The first user, who is in the "site administrator" role; can do everything on the site

username: *editor*, password: *oreilly*
> A user in the "editor" role; used for chapters that require users with elevated permissions

username: *user*, password: *oreilly*
> A normal user in only the "authenticated user" role

It is these users the chapters refer to when the instructions reference logging in as the "editor" user, or similar. Unless otherwise specified, it is assumed that steps are completed as the "admin" user.

Safari® Books Online

Safari
Books Online

When you see a Safari® Books Online icon on the cover of your favorite technology book, that means the book is available online through the O'Reilly Network Safari Bookshelf.

Safari offers a solution that's better than e-books. It's a virtual library that lets you easily search thousands of top tech books, cut and paste code samples, download chapters, and find quick answers when you need the most accurate, current information. Try it for free at *http://safari.oreilly.com*.

Comments and Questions

Please address comments and questions concerning this book to the publisher:

> O'Reilly Media, Inc.
> 1005 Gravenstein Highway North
> Sebastopol, CA 95472
> 800-998-9938 (in the United States or Canada)
> 707-829-0515 (international or local)
> 707-829-0104 (fax)

We have a web page for this book, where we list errata, examples, and any additional information. You can access this page at:

> *http://www.oreilly.com/catalog/9780596515805*

To comment or ask technical questions about this book, send email to:

> *bookquestions@oreilly.com*

For more information about our books, conferences, Resource Centers, and the O'Reilly Network, see our website:

http://www.oreilly.com

Acknowledgments

Team Lullabot would like to thank the book's technical reviewers, including Robert Douglass, Ajay Gallewale, Jeffrey MacGuire, David Moore, and Matt Westgate. Thanks to Tatiana Apandi and Julie Steele from O'Reilly, who helped guide us through our first collective book authoring adventure. We'd also like to thank our business folks, Liza Kindred, Haley Scarpino, and Tim McDorman, for helping juggle schedules so that we could get this book completed. Jeff Eaton gets thanks for supplying photos for the image gallery chapter. Also, thanks to Lullabot's Kent Bye for working his visualization mojo on the Views module, and John VanDyk for his extremely helpful feedback on some of the biggest chapters in the book. And a special thanks goes out to Ivan Zugec, who graciously transferred ownership of the *http://usingdrupal.com* domain to us. And of course thanks to Dries Buytaert for inventing and open-sourcing Drupal; without him, none of this would have happened.

Angela Byron would first like to give a huge shout-out to her wife, Marci McKay, who was tremendously patient and understanding with all the late nights, and is in general extremely tolerant, even supportive, of Angie's insatiable Drupal obsession. A huge thanks also to her family—in particular, her mom and dad, Jeanne and Mike, and her siblings, Keith and Sara, for their support through the authoring process. John Wait and Debra Williams-Cauley also deserve thanks for their part in helping Angie realize her dream of authoring a book. Michelle Cox and Matthew Harrison helped provide early "sanity checks" for the book outline. Moshe Weitzman, Brandon Bergren, and Dries Buytaert provided technical review of some early versions of chapters, and Dries in particular offered thoughtful input and support throughout.

Addison Berry would like to thank her partner, Colleen McGraw, who was extremely patient about the lost weekends and neglected house chores, for pushing Addi onward when mired, and being an inspiration through all the ups and downs of life. Richard Burford, Alex Dergachev, Joel Farris, Jay McDonald, Don Palmer, Jose Reyero, and Brian Vuyk graciously gave feedback on her chapters, and Wim Leers supplied an emergency Dutch translation. The entire Drupal community has been amazingly supportive in her Drupal journey and of this book. None of this would have happened were it not for them. Lastly, thanks to my parents, Joan and Merlin Berry, for supporting all of the crazy things she's done in her life and never failing to believe in her.

Nathan Haug would like to thank his amazing parents, James and Aleda Haug, as well as his inspirational grandfather, Tom Arnberg. Thanks go to his technical reviewers, David Moore and John VanDyk. Extra thanks go to all of the authors of the Drupal platform and add-on modules. Nate thanks Earl Miles for Views and Jonathan Chaffer,

Karen Stevenson, and Yves Chedemois for CCK. The Drupal platform would never be what it is without the amazing cooperation between so many individuals.

Jeff Eaton would like to thank his wife, Catherine, for her deep well of patience and encouragement. Romantic dinners should not include module testing and trouble-shooting, and Catherine's good humor when technology intruded was instrumental in seeing this project through. Doug Green, Earl Miles, and countless other members of the Drupal community gave excellent feedback and pointed out complexities that could easily trip up new users. Jason Scott and Jeff Benson provided endless late-night and early-morning commiseration, and Jeff's parents, Doug and Cindi, spent the better part of two decades encouraging his geeky adventuring.

James Walker would like to thank his two children, Andrew and Camryn, for their love, patience, and trips to the park. Karen Stevenson, Ryan Szrama, Earl Miles, and Nate Haug provided code that made his chapters possible and were extremely helpful in answering questions and providing insight. Thanks to his mom, Linda, who has always believed in him and who has always provided excellent housing for Lullabot retreats.

Jeff Robbins would like to thank his wife, Jennifer Niederst Robbins, for her love, support, and copyediting prowess, and his son, Arlo, for reminding him to keep things fun. Thanks to O'Reilly Media, which has felt like an extended family since the early 1990s, when he and Jennifer worked and met there. Jeff would like to thank Matt Westgate for being the best business partner he could imagine and for providing the stable, serene, and happy atmosphere in which Lullabot, the company, and Lullabot, the individuals, have thrived. Jeff also sends thanks and appreciation to Liza Kindred, for keeping the company running; to the rest of the team, for keeping him constantly amazed; and to the Drupal community at large, for all of the generous and astounding code that we call Drupal.

## CHAPTER 1

Drupal Overview

This book will show you how to build many different types of websites using the Drupal web publishing platform. Whether you're promoting your rock band or building your company's intranet, some of your needs will be the same. From a foundational perspective, your site will have *content*; be it audio or text or animated GIF images, a website communicates its content to the world. You will also need to *manage* this content. Although it's possible to roll your own system with enough knowledge of the underlying web technologies, Drupal makes creating your website; adding new features; and day-to-day adding, editing, and deleting of content quick and easy. And finally, your website will have *visitors*, and this book will show you many different ways in which you can engage and interact with your community using Drupal.

This chapter will begin by providing the hard facts about Drupal: what it is, who uses it, and why they chose it. It will then dive into a conceptual overview, starting with what this ambiguous term "content management" actually means, and how we arrived at building websites this way. And finally, we'll define and explain the core Drupal concepts that are necessary to understand how Drupal handles its content.

What Is Drupal?

Drupal is an open source *content management system* (CMS) being used by hundreds of thousands of organizations and individuals to build engaging, content-rich websites.[*] Building a website in Drupal is a matter of combining together various "building blocks," which are described later in this chapter, in order to customize your website's functionality to your precise needs. Once built, a Drupal website can be maintained with online forms, and without having to change code manually. Drupal is free to use; it has an enormous library of constantly evolving tools that you can use to make your website shine.

---

[*] For more on the open source software movement, please see *http://opensource.org*—which, incidentally, is also a Drupal site.

Drupal is also a *content management framework* (CMF). In addition to providing site-building tools for webmasters, it offers ways for programmers and developers to customize Drupal using plug-in modules. Almost every aspect of Drupal's behavior can be customized using these modules, and thousands of them exist that add features from photo galleries to shopping carts to talk-like-a-pirate translators. Most modules have been contributed to the Drupal community and are available for download and use on your Drupal-based website, too. All of the functionality that we'll be discussing in this book is built using a combination of "core" Drupal and these community-created modules.

It's noteworthy to acknowledge Drupal's *community*; the wetware element of Drupal is often cited as one of Drupal's biggest assets. When Drupal 6 was released in February 2008, more than 700 members of the community contributed code to the core component of the software. More than 2,000 developers maintain contributed modules, with countless more helping with testing, documentation, user support, translations, and other important areas of the project. Those familiar with evaluating open source platforms will attest to the importance of a thriving community base.

Who Uses It?

Over the last couple of years, the popularity of Drupal has exploded, to the point where some pretty big names have taken notice. Media companies such as MTV UK, Lifetime, and Sony BMG Records are using Drupal as a means of building loyal communities around their products. Print publishers such as the *New York Observer*, *The Onion*, *Popular Science* magazine, and *Fast Company* magazine use Drupal to provide interactive online content to their readers. Amnesty International, the United Nations, and the Electronic Frontier Foundation use Drupal to coordinate activism on important issues. Ubuntu Linux, Eclipse, Firefox, and jQuery are open source projects that employ Drupal to nurture their contributor communities. Bloggers such as Tim Berners-Lee, Heather B. Armstrong (a.k.a. Dooce), the BlogHer community, and Merlin Mann use Drupal as their publishing platform. Figure 1-1 shows some of these high-profile Drupal websites.

What these websites have in common is a need for powerful publishing options and rich community features.

There are several places to obtain more information online about who is using Drupal out there today. Dries Buytaert, the Drupal project founder, maintains a list of high-profile Drupal websites on his blog at *http://buytaert.net/tag/drupal-sites*. The Drupal website has a section containing detailed case studies and success stories (*http://drupal.org/cases*). Additionally, *http://www.drupalsites.net* is a directory containing thousands of Drupal websites found across the Internet, from small hobby websites to large social networks with millions of active users.

Figure 1-1. Screenshots of several high-profile Drupal websites

What Features Does Drupal Offer?

Drupal provides a number of features, which are explained in greater detail in Chapter 2. These include:

Flexible module system
> Modules are plug-ins that can modify and add features to a Drupal site. For almost any functional need, chances are good that either an existing module fits the need exactly or can be combined with other modules to fit the need, or that whatever existing code there is can get you a good chunk of the way there.

Customizable theming system
> All output in Drupal is fully customizable, so you can bend the look and feel of your site to your will (or, more precisely, to your designer's will).

Extensible content creation
> You can define new types of content (blog, event, word of the day) on the fly. Contributed modules can take this one step further and allow administrators to create custom fields within your newly created content types.

Innate search engine optimization
> Drupal offers out-of-the-box support for human-readable system URLs, and all of Drupal's output is standards-compliant; both of these features make for search-engine friendly websites.

Role-based access permissions
> Custom roles and a plethora of permissions allow for fine-grained control over who can access what within the system. And existing modules can take this level of access control even further—down to the individual user level.

Social publishing and collaboration tools
> Drupal has built-in support for tools such as group blogging, comments, forums, and customized user profiles. The addition of almost any other feature you can imagine—for instance, ratings, user groups, or moderation tools—is only a download away.

A Brief History of Content Management

Before looking any closer at Drupal, let's take a brief trip back in time to the days before content management systems. To understand how Drupal and other CMS packages simplify your work, we'll take a look at how things worked when the Web was young.

A Historical Look at Website Creation

Back in the dim recesses of time (the 1990s, for those who remember zeppelins and Model T cars), web pages were nothing more than simple text files nestled comfortably into folders on a server somewhere on the Internet. With names like *index.html*, *news.html*, *about_us.html*, and so on, these files were viewable by anyone with a web browser. Using the HTML markup language, these files could link back and forth to each other, include images and other media, and generally make themselves presentable. A *website*, as the hipsters of that day would explain, was just a collection of those files in a particular folder, as pictured in Figure 1-2.

This system worked pretty well, and it made sense. Every URL that a user on the Internet could visit corresponded to a unique *.html* file on the web server. If you wanted to organize them into sections, you made a folder and moved the files into that folder; for example, *http://www.example.com/news/* would be the address to the "News" section of the site, and the 1997 newsletter would be located at *http://www.example.com/news/fall_1997_products.html*. When the webmaster (or the intern) needed to fix a problem, they could look at the page in their web browser and open up the matching file on the web server to tweak it.

Unfortunately, as websites grew in size, it was obvious that this approach didn't scale well. After a year or so of adding pages and shuffling directories around, many sites had dozens, hundreds, or sometimes even thousands of pages to manage. And that, friends, caused some serious problems:

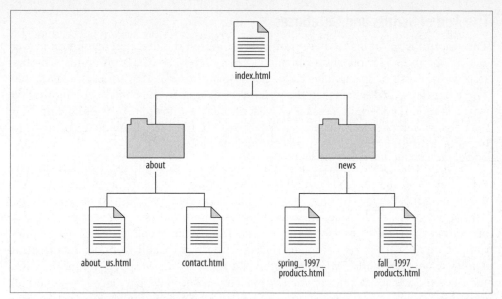

Figure 1-2. A historical look at website structure

Changing the site's design required an enormous amount of work

Formatting information, layout, and other site design was done individually on every single page. Cascading Style Sheets (CSS) hadn't yet taken the web world by storm, so tasks as simple as changing the site's default font required (that's right) editing *every single file*.

The site structure resulted in massive duplication of content

Most designs for websites included a standard footer at the bottom of the page with copyright and contact information, a header image or some kind of recurring navigation menu, and so on. If anything changed, every file had to be updated. If you were very, very lucky, all the webmasters before you had been very conscientious about making sure that there were no layout variations and this would be a scriptable change. Most webmasters weren't lucky, and to this day mutter darkly about sites built using FrontPage, PageMill, Dreamweaver, and Notepad—all at once.

Websites were impossible to keep consistent and up-to-date

Most complex sites were already organized into directories and subdirectories to keep things reasonably tidy. Adding a news story in the *news* directory meant that you also had to update the "overview" page that listed all news stories, perhaps post a quick notice on the front page of the website, and (horror!) remember to take the notice down when the news was no longer "fresh." A large site with multiple sections and a fair amount of content could keep a full-time webmaster busy just juggling these updates.

The Age of Scripts and Databases

The search for solutions to these problems prompted the first real revolution in web design: the use of scripts and *Common Gateway Interface* (CGI) programs. The first step was the use of special tags called *Server-Side Includes* (SSI) in each HTML file. These tags let web designers tell the web server to suck in the contents of another file (say, a standard copyright message or a list of the latest news stories) and include it in the current web page as if it were part of the HTML file itself. It made updating those bits much easier, as they were stored in only one place.

The second change was the use of simple databases to store pieces of similar content. All the news stories on CNN.com (*http://www.cnn.com*) are similar in structure, even if their content differs. The same is true of all the product pages on Apple.com (*http://www.apple.com*), all the blog entries on Blogger.com (*http://www.blogger.com*), and so on. Rather than storing each one as a separate HTML file, webmasters used a program running on the web server to look up the content of each article from the database and display it with all the HTML markup for the site's layout wrapped around it. URLs such as *http://www.example.com/news/1997/big_sale.html* were replaced by something more like *http://www.example.com/news.cgi?id=10*. Rather than looking in the *news* directory, then in the *1997* directory, and returning the *big_sale.html* file to a user's web browser, the web server would run the *news.cgi* program, let it retrieve article number 10 from the database, and send back whatever text that program printed out.

All these differences required changes in the way that designers and developers approached the building of websites. But the benefits were more than worth it: dozens or even hundreds of files could be replaced with one or more database-driven scripts, as shown in Figure 1-3.

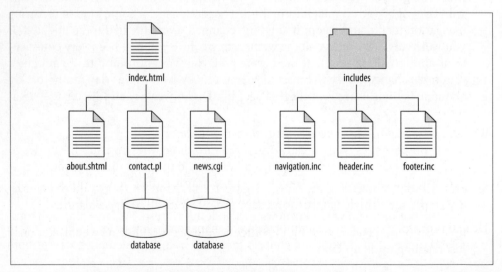

Figure 1-3. The move from individual files to database-driven scripts

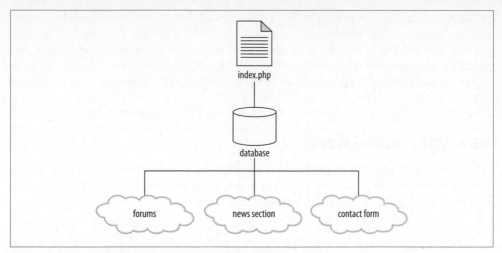

Figure 1-4. The structure of an integrated, database-driven website

Even with those improvements, however, there were still serious challenges:

Where do I change that setting again?
> Large sites with many different kinds of content (product information, employee bios, press releases, free downloads, and so on) were still juggling an assortment of scripts, separate databases, and other elements to keep everything running. Webmasters updating content had to figure out whether they needed to change an HTML file, an entry in a database, or the program code of the script.

Too many little pieces were cobbled together
> Dynamic content—such as discussion forums or guestbooks where visitors could interact—required their own infrastructure, and often each of these systems was designed separately. Stitching them together into a unified website was no simple task.

The Content Revolution

Slowly but surely, programs emerged to manage these different kinds of content and features using a single, consistent user interface. The older generation of software focused on a particular task or application, but newer CMS implementations offered generalized tools for creating, editing, and organizing the information on a website. Most systems also provided mechanisms for developers to build add-ons and new features without reinventing the wheel. Figure 1-4 illustrates how a content management system uses a single database and script to integrate all of these features.

Drupal is one of these next-generation content management systems. It allows you to create and organize many kinds of content, provides user management tools for both the maintainers of and the visitors to your site, and gives you access to thousands of third-party plug-ins that add new features. Dries Buytaert, the founder of the Drupal project, said in a speech to the 2007 Open Source CMS Summit that his goal for Drupal was to "eliminate the webmaster." That might sound a bit scary if you *are* the webmaster, but after that first thought, the implications are exciting. Using Drupal, the grunt work of keeping thousands of pages organized and up-to-date vanishes: you can focus on building the features that your site needs and the experience that your users want.

How Does Drupal Work?

At a conceptual level, the *Drupal stack* looks like Figure 1-5. Drupal is a sort of middle layer between the backend (the stuff that keeps the Internet ticking) and the frontend (what visitors see in their web browsers).

In the bottom layers, things like your operating system, web server, database, and PHP are running the show. The *operating system* handles the "plumbing" that keeps your website running: low-level tasks such as handling network connections, files, and file permissions. Your *web server* enables that computer to be accessible over the Internet, and serves up the correct stuff when you go to *http://www.example.com*. A database stores, well, *data*: all of the website's content, user accounts, and configuration settings, in a central place for later retrieval. And *PHP* is a programming language that generates pages dynamically and shuffles information from the database to the web server.

Drupal itself is composed of many layers as well. At its lowest layer, it provides additional functionality on top of PHP by adding several subsystems, such as user session handling and authentication, security filtering, and template rendering. This section is built upon by a layer of customizable add-on functionality called modules, which will be discussed in the next section. Modules add features to Drupal and generate the contents of any given page. But before the page is displayed to the user, it's run through the *theme system*, which allows modification and precise tweaking for even the pickiest designers' needs. The theme system is covered in detail in Chapter 11.

The theme system outputs page content, usually as XHTML, although other types of rendering are supported. CSS is used to control the layout, colors, and fonts of a given page, and JavaScript is thrown in for dynamic elements, such as collapsible fieldsets on forms and drag-and-drop table rows in Drupal's administrative interface.

We've talked about the "old" way of building websites using static HTML files, the transition to collections of scripts, and the "new" way: full-featured web applications that manage the entire website. This third way—Drupal's way—requires a new set of conceptual building blocks. Every website you build with Drupal will use them!

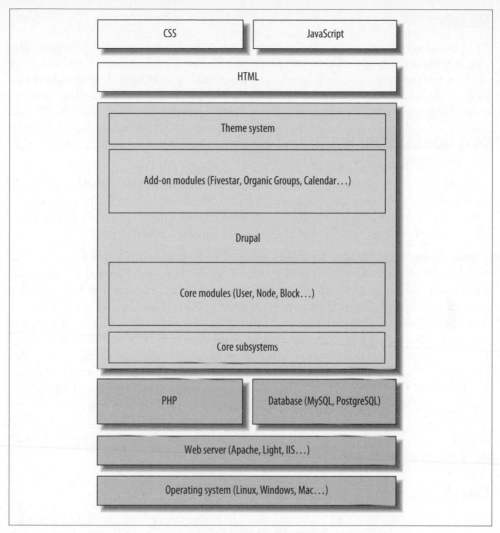

Figure 1-5. How Drupal and its conceptual layers fit with other layers of a website

Modules

Just about everything in Drupal revolves around the concept of *modules*, which are files that contain PHP code and a set of functionalities that Drupal knows how to use. All of the administrative- and end-user-facing functionality in Drupal, from fundamental features such as ability to log in or create content to dynamic photo galleries and complex voting systems, all come from modules. Some examples of modules are the Contact module, which enables a site-wide contact form, and the User module, which handles user authentication and permission checking. In other CMS applications, modules are also referred to as *plug-ins* or *extensions*.

There are two types of modules: "core" modules, which are included with Drupal itself, and "contributed" modules, which are provided by the Drupal community and can be separately downloaded and enabled. Apart from a few required core modules, all modules can be turned on or off depending on your website's precise needs.

Though there are contributed modules that offer "drop in and go" functionality, over the years the Drupal community has generally focused on modules that do one thing well, in a way that can be combined with other modules. This approach means that you have almost limitless control over what your website looks like and how it behaves. Your image gallery isn't limited by what the original developer thought an image gallery ought to look and act like. You can drop in ratings or comments and sort the pictures by camera type rather than date if you'd like. In order to have this flexibility, however, you have to "build" the functionality in Drupal by snapping together various modules and twiddling their options, rather than just checking off a checkbox for "image gallery" and leaving it at that. Drupal's power brings with it a learning curve not encountered in many other CMS packages, and with the plethora of available modules, it can be daunting trying to determine which to use. Appendix B is dedicated to tips and tricks on how to determine module quality and suitability for your projects.

Users

The next building block of a Drupal website is the concept of *users*. On a simple brochure-ware website that will be updated by a single administrator and visited only by potential customers, you might create just a single user account for the administrator. On a community discussion site, you would set up Drupal to allow all of the individuals who use the site to sign up for the site and create their own user accounts as well.

The first user you create when you build a new Drupal site—User 1—is special. Similar to the root user on a UNIX server, User 1 has permission to perform any action on the Drupal site. Because User 1 bypasses these normal safety checks, it's easy to accidentally delete content or otherwise break the site if you use this account for day-to-day editing. It's a good idea to reserve this account for special administrative tasks and configuration, and create an additional account for posting content.

Every additional user can be assigned to configurable *roles*, like "editor," "paying customer," or "VIP." Each role can be given *permissions* to do different things on the website: visiting specific URLs, viewing particular kinds of content, posting comments on existing content, filling out a user profile, even creating more users and controlling their permissions. By default, Drupal comes with two predefined roles: *authenticated user* and *anonymous user*. Anyone who creates a user account on the site is automatically assigned the "authenticated user" role, and any visitors who haven't yet created user accounts (or haven't yet logged in with their username and password) have the "anonymous user" role.

Content (Nodes)

Nodes are Drupal's next building block, and one of the most important. An important part of planning any Drupal site is looking at your plans and deciding what specific kinds of content (referred to by Drupal as "content types") you'll be working with. In almost every case, each one will be a different kind of node.

All nodes, regardless of the type of content they store, share a handful of basic properties:

- An author (the user on your site who created the content)
- A creation date
- A title
- Body content

Do you want to create a page containing your company's privacy policy? That's a node. Do you want users to be able to post blog entries on the site? Each one is a node. Will users be posting links to interesting stories elsewhere on the Web? Each of those links is stored as—you guessed it—a node.

In addition to nodes' basic, common properties, all nodes can take advantage of certain built-in Drupal features, like flags that indicate whether they're published or unpublished and settings to control how each type of node is displayed. Permissions to create and edit each type of node can also be assigned to different user roles; for example, users with the "blogger" role could create "Blog entry" nodes, but only "administrator" or "editor" users could create "News" nodes.

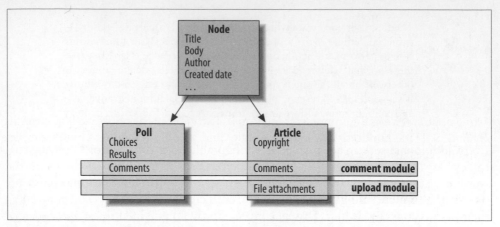

Figure 1-6. All nodes in the system share a basic set of properties; nodes may define additional, specific fields, and modules can add extra features to nodes as well

 Nodes can also store revision information detailing each change that's been made since they were created. If you make a mistake (deleting an important paragraph of the "About Us" page, for example), this makes it easy to restore a previous version.

Drupal comes preconfigured with two types of nodes: "Page" and "Story." There's nothing special about them—they offer the standard features all nodes share and nothing more. The only differences between those two types of nodes are their default configuration settings. "Page" nodes don't display any information about the author or the date on which they were posted. They're well suited to content like "About Us" and "Terms of Service," where the original author is irrelevant. "Story" nodes do display that information, and are also set to appear on the front page of the site whenever they're posted. The result is a blog-like list of the latest stories on the site.

You can use Drupal's content administration tools to create other "simple" node types yourself. Many administrators create a "news" or "announcement" node type to post official announcements, while other contributors can post story nodes. What happens, though, if you need to store more information than "title" and "body content?" Plug-in modules can add to Drupal's content system new kinds of nodes that offer more features. One example (which comes with Drupal) is the "Poll" module. When users create new "Poll" nodes, they create a list of poll questions rather than the usual "body" content. Poll nodes, when they're displayed to visitors, appear as voting forms and automatically tally the number of votes for each question.

Additionally, other modules can add to nodes' properties such as comments, ratings, file upload fields, and more. From the control panel, you can specify which types of nodes receive these features. Figure 1-6 illustrates this concept.

The idea that new modules add properties and build on top of the node system means that all content in Drupal is built on the same underlying framework, and therein lies one of Drupal's greatest strengths. Features like searching, rating, and comments all become plug-and-play components for any new type of node you may define, because under the hood, Drupal knows how to interface with their base elements—nodes.

Using plug-in modules to add new types of nodes—or to add additional fields to existing node types—is a common task in Drupal. Throughout the book, we'll be covering a handful of the hundreds of plug-in modules and you'll learn how to build complex content types using these basic tools.

Ways of Organizing Content

Another important building block is really an entire toolbox of techniques for organizing the nodes that make up your site's content. First-generation websites grouped pages using folders and directories. Second-generation sites use separate scripts to manage and display different kinds of content. Drupal, though, maintains almost everything as a node. How can you break your site up into separate topical sections, user-specific blogs, or some other organizational scheme?

First, each individual node on your site gets its own URL. By default, this URL is something like *http://www.example.com/node/1*. These URLs can be turned into user-friendly paths like *http://www.example.com/about* using Drupal's built-in Path module. For organizational purposes, all of these nodes are treated as a single "pool" of content. Every other content page on your site—topical overviews, recent news, and so on—is created by pulling up lists of nodes that match certain criteria and displaying them in different ways. Here are a few examples:

The front page
> By default, the front page of a Drupal site is a blog-like overview of the 10 most recently posted stories. To build this, Drupal searches the pool of content for nodes with the "Published" flag set to true, and the "Promote to front page" flag set to true. In addition, it sorts the list so that nodes with the "Sticky" flag are always at the top; this feature is useful for hot news or announcements that every user should see.

The Taxonomy module
> We mentioned earlier that plug-in modules can add new pieces of information to nodes, and that's exactly what Taxonomy does. It allows the administrator of a site to set up categories of topics that nodes can be associated with when they're created, as well as blog-style free-tagging keywords. You might use this module to create a predefined set of "Regions" for news stories to be filed under, as well as "Tags" for bloggers to enter manually when they post. The Taxonomy module calls all of these things "terms," and provides a page for each descriptive term that's used on the site. When a visitor views one of these pages, Drupal pulls up a list of all the nodes that were tagged with the term.

The Blog module

Drupal's built-in Blog module implements a multiuser blogging system by doing just three things. First, it adds a new node type called "Blog post." Second, it provides a listing page at *http://www.example.com/blog* that displays any nodes of type "Blog" that also have their "Published" flag set to `true`. (If a blog post has its "Published to front page" flag set to `true`, it will show up on the front page as well; Drupal never hides content on one page just because it appears on another.) Third, it provides a custom page for each user on the site that displays only blog posts written by that user. *http://www.example.com/blog/1*, for example, would display all blog post nodes that are published and were written by User 1—the administrator.

Drupal comes with several other modules that provide different ways of organizing nodes, and hundreds of plug-in modules can be downloaded to organize your site in a variety of ways. The important thing to remember is that almost all "pages" in Drupal are one of two things: a specific content node, or a list of nodes that share a particular set of properties.

Types of Supporting Content

In addition to content and listings of content, there are also various ways to supplement the content on the page. Two such types of supporting content included with Drupal core are comments and blocks.

Comments are merely responses by a user to a piece of content, and exist only in relation to that content. Users may post comments to add their thoughts to the subject matter within a node, as they often do when a particularly controversial subject comes up on a blog entry or forum topic. Like nodes, but to a lesser extent, comments can be expanded with contributed modules to have additional features such as ratings or file upload fields.

Comments provide a large number of options to tweak: comments can be displayed in a threaded or flat list, comments can be sorted with the newest or oldest on top, anonymous users can be allowed to or prevented from leaving comments, and if anonymous comments are enabled, contact details can be required or optional.

Blocks are widgets that fit into areas such as the sidebars, footers, and headers of a Drupal site. They're generally used to display helpful links or dynamic lists such as "Most popular content" or "Latest comments" and similar items. The users building block controls information about and access for your site's visitors; nodes take center stage displaying content; and blocks help give a single piece of content some context in the structure of your site.

Many times, blocks will display different content, depending on which user is currently logged in: a "Comments by your buddies" block, for example, might display a list of posts by users that the current visitor has added to their Buddies list. Each user who logs in will obviously see a different list. Additionally, blocks may be configured to show up only on certain pages, or to be hidden only on certain pages.

Getting Help

It's easy to focus only on the functionality you get for free with an open source application. But it would be a mistake to forget that the Drupal community itself is another vital building block for your website!

As you go through the hands-on examples in this book, you might run into some issues particular to your installation. Or, issues might be created as new versions of modules are released. Fortunately, the Drupal community has a wealth of resources available to help troubleshoot even the nastiest error you might encounter:

- The Drupal handbooks at *http://drupal.org/handbooks* contain a wealth of information on everything from community philosophies to nitty-gritty Drupal development information.
- The Getting Started guide at *http://drupal.org/getting-started* contains some particularly useful information to help get you through your first couple of hours with Drupal.
- The Troubleshooting FAQ at *http://drupal.org/Troubleshooting-FAQ* has useful tips and tricks for deciphering error messages that you might encounter.
- For more one-on-one help, try the Support forums at *http://drupal.org/forum/18* for everything from preinstallation questions to upgrade issues.
- If your question is about a specific module, you can post a "support request" issue (or a "bug report" if it's a blatant problem) to the module's issue queue, which reaches the module's maintainer. A helpful video on how to maneuver around the Drupal.org issue queues is available from *http://drupal.org/node/273658*, and issue queues are also discussed in Appendix B.
- There's a #drupal-support IRC channel on *irc.freenode.net* if you're more of the chatty type.

 Unlike #drupal-support, the #drupal channel on *irc.freenode.net* is *not* a support channel. This channel is a place for developers to get coding help and for other contributors to actively brainstorm and discuss improving the Drupal project as a whole. By all means, participate here to get involved in the community, and ask your coding-related questions, but remember that questions like, "Where is the option I toggle to do this?" and "What module should I use for that?" will make people a bit cranky.

When asking for help, it's always best to do as much research as you can first, and then politely ask direct, to-the-point questions. "Foo module is giving me the error 'Invalid input' when I attempt to submit 'Steve' in the name field. I tried searching for existing solutions, and found an issue at *http://drupal.org/node/1234* filed about it, but the solution there didn't fix it for me. Could anyone give me some pointers?" will get far better, faster, and more meaningful responses than, "Why doesn't Foo module work? You developers are useless!" or "How can I build a website with Drupal?" Oftentimes, you'll probably find that during the process of typing out your question in enough detail for someone else to answer it, you come up with the solution yourself!

Conclusion

In this chapter, you've learned what Drupal is. You have seen the history of websites and content management to better understand the challenges inherent in keeping a growing site healthy. We've examined the conceptual building blocks that Drupal uses when building next-generation sites, as well as how they fit together. We've also seen numerous ways to get help if you're stuck. In the following chapter, we'll put these pieces together to make your first Drupal website!

## CHAPTER 2

Drupal Jumpstart

This chapter, intended for readers who are new to Drupal, provides a tour of its capabilities, as well as definitions for its sometimes obscure terminology, by demonstrating how Drupal can be used to build a simple website. Readers who are familiar with Drupal already may still want to skim this chapter, as later chapters will assume knowledge of all content covered here. By the end, you'll understand how to perform administrative tasks in Drupal, such as configuring modules, working with content types, and setting up site navigation.

This chapter assumes that you already have Drupal up and running. For assistance, check out Appendix A, as well as the helpful online Getting Started guide at *http:// drupal.org/getting-started*

This chapter introduces the following modules:

Node (core)
> Allows you to post content and create your own content types

Comment (core)
> Allows users to create replies to node content

User (core)
> Handles allowing users to log in, as well as Drupal's robust roles and permissions systems

Block (core)
> Adds dynamic sidebars and other supplementary content

Menu (core)
> Handles management of a Drupal website's navigation

Path (core)
> Allows entry of friendly URLs such as *http://www.example.com/about* rather than *http://www.example.com/node/1*.

Administration Menu (http://drupal.org/project/admin_menu)
> Provides a dynamic drop-down navigation menu to speed administrative tasks

Contact (core)
> A simple form that site visitors may use to send inquiries to website owners

Blog (core)
> Provides quick and easy multiuser blog functionality

Taxonomy (core)
> A powerful classification and categorization system

Filter (core)
> An important and often misunderstood module that is key to Drupal security

FCKeditor (http://drupal.org/project/fckeditor)
> A "What You See Is What You Get" (WYSIWYG) editor that allows people without HTML knowledge to create rich website content

IMCE (http://drupal.org/project/imce)
> An add-on module that can work with editors such as FCKEditor to make it easy to add images to website content

The completed website will look as pictured in Figure 2-1 and at *http://jumpstart.using drupal.com.*

Figure 2-1. The completed Mom and Pop, Inc., website

Case Study

Mom and Pop, Inc., is a small organic grocery store in the midwestern United States run by its co-owners, Jeanne and Mike. Their current web presence is a long, endlessly scrolling static HTML page that lists general information such as the background of the company, its hours and location, and what promotions are currently running.

Neither Mike nor Jeanne is comfortable editing the code in the page by hand, so in order to update the web page content each week, they currently pay their next-door neighbor Goldie to hand-edit the page. Because this sort of manual labor is tedious, it usually takes a long time for her to get around to doing it. As a result, the site is frequently out of date and not doing much other than costing money to keep it online.

Mike and Jeanne would like to have a new, fresh site that they can manage themselves by filling out web forms rather than editing code. They need some static pages, such as a Home and an About page, along with a place to showcase special weekly deals. They would also like a contact form to receive inquiries from customers.

Mike and Jeanne also would like a blog where they can talk about things like in-store events or general goings-on in the community. Visitors to the site should be able to comment on blog entries, with anonymous visitors' comments going into an approval queue first.

Neither Mike nor Jeanne is a coder, so it's important that the content be easy to edit for someone without knowledge of HTML. And finally, the site should have some basic branding—site logo and colors—so that the site "feels" like their own.

Goldie's been hearing a lot about this "Drupal" thing lately, so she decides to give it a shot for this project.

Implementation Notes

The "Implementation Notes" section of each chapter will discuss, compare, and contrast various options for fulfilling the client's needs in Drupal, and how the authors came to decide on the solutions selected in the chapter.

Basics

Almost all of the functionality required by Mom and Pop, Inc., is provided by the bundle of features that comes as part of the main Drupal software download, called the Drupal "core." Drupal's Node module has the built-in ability to create various types of content on the site, including static pages, which work great for the Home and About pages. We'll use the core Path module to give these pages nice and descriptive URLs such as http://www.example.com/about.

Drupal also provides a robust roles and permissions system, which we can use to separate Goldie's tasks (website maintenance) from Mike and Jeanne's tasks (managing the daily website content) and from the customers on the site (who can do only things such as leave comments).

Drupal provides a built-in Blog module, which will be perfect for Jeanne and Mike to use for talking about cool new things happening in the store. And the Comment module will allow visitors to enter into discussions.

Drupal also comes with a module called Contact, which can be used to build a simple contact form for any website. Different categories may be set up, and each one can optionally send mail to a different email address. This feature is useful if you have different support personnel for different departments, for example.

Easy content editing and image handling

Out of the box, all content in Drupal is entered as HTML, with some security filtering provided courtesy of the built-in Filter module. Although entering HTML tags by hand is fine for a typical webmaster who's fluent in HTML, most "normal" users (particularly nontechnical users) usually don't want to enter a bunch of strange-looking code in order to do things like make a simple list.

It's also only natural that in addition to posting content on their site, Mike and Jeanne will want to post images: of the store, of coupons for a given weekly promotion, or of their kids. Drupal core has no built-in image handling, so how will we solve this problem?

The fix for both issues is Drupal's rich library of contributed add-on modules. Later in this chapter in "Spotlight: Content Editing and Image Handling," we'll discuss solutions in depth. But first, let's get started with some basics.

Spotlight: Content Management

Drupal's primary function is to enable website administrators to manage their own content. This section offers a tour of some of the most basic tools for content management in Drupal.

Content

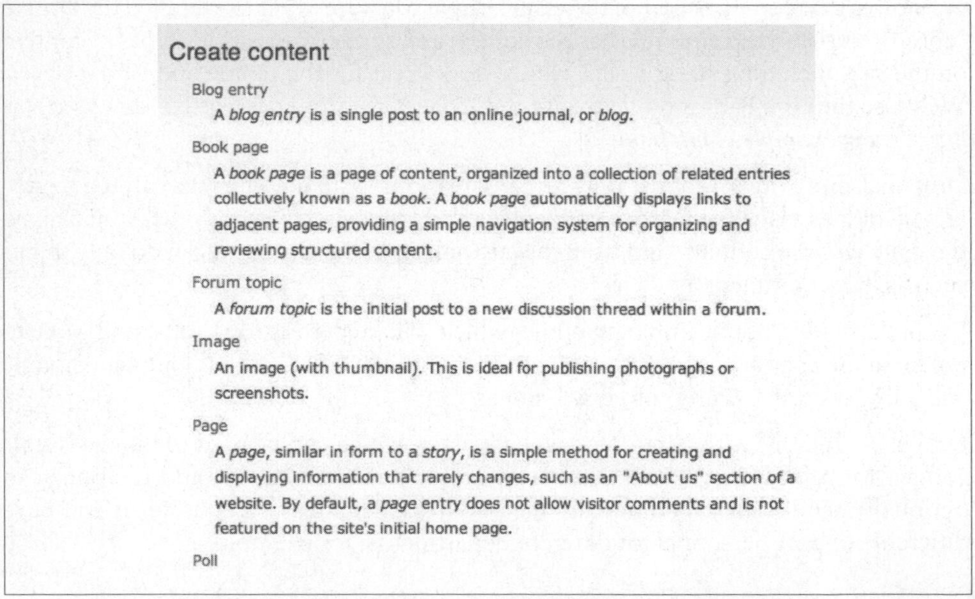

Create content

Blog entry
  A *blog entry* is a single post to an online journal, or *blog*.

Book page
  A *book page* is a page of content, organized into a collection of related entries collectively known as a *book*. A *book page* automatically displays links to adjacent pages, providing a simple navigation system for organizing and reviewing structured content.

Forum topic
  A *forum topic* is the initial post to a new discussion thread within a forum.

Image
  An image (with thumbnail). This is ideal for publishing photographs or screenshots.

Page
  A *page*, similar in form to a *story*, is a simple method for creating and displaying information that rarely changes, such as an "About us" section of a website. By default, a *page* entry does not allow visitor comments and is not featured on the site's initial home page.

Poll

Figure 2-2. A list of available content types

As discussed in Chapter 1, each piece of content in Drupal, from a static page to a blog entry or a poll, is called a *node*. Drupal comes with two content types by default: Page, intended for static content such as an "About Us" page, and Story, intended for content that will be frequently posted, such as news articles. But like most things in Drupal, content types are fully configurable. Figure 2-2 shows the "Create content" page on a typical Drupal site with several content types available. This page is found under the path "node/add" (*http://www.example.com/node/add*).

 As mentioned in the Preface, future navigation instructions within Drupal will use the shorthand "Create content" (node/add).

Figure 2-3 shows an example of a typical node form, which is used to add or edit a piece of content. Each node has a Title, which identifies the node in content listings and controls the title of the web page it's on, and most nodes also have a Body field, which holds its primary content. Although the extensive options at the bottom of this form may seem daunting, don't worry. A general site visitor won't have permissions to change Menu settings, Authoring information, or other settings, so they simply do not show up on the form for these users.

Home › Create content

Create Page

Title: *
[This is a page.]

▷ Menu settings

☑ Show summary in full view   (Join summary)

Body:
[Here is the "teaser" content. This is a short version of the content, and will appear in content listings, RSS feeds, etc. Typically, this is worded in such a way that it encourages the reader to click into the full body.]

[Here is the full body, which contains the "meat" of the content. This can be as long as you want!]

▷ Input format

▷ Revision information

▷ Comment settings

▷ Authoring information

▽ Publishing options

☑ Published

☐ Promoted to front page

☐ Sticky at top of lists

(Save) (Preview)

Figure 2-3. A typical node form in Drupal

People coming to Drupal with web development experience with a tool such as Dreamweaver often get confused by Drupal's notion of a "Page." Web development tools refer to the contents of an entire browser window from the logo in the upper-left corner down to the copyright notice in the lower-right as a "page," but in Drupal creating a new "Page" node only affects the *content* of a given web page: its title, its body, and any additional properties such as a byline or rating.

The Body field on a node can be split into a *summary* or *teaser*, which is a short blurb that entices people to read further, and the *full view*, which contains the full content. Teasers are displayed in most content listings, in RSS feeds, and in other places. The full body is only displayed when looking at a piece of content directly. You may specify whether to include the teaser as part of the full view with the "Show summary in full view" checkbox.

Nodes can have a variety of options applied to them, including the ability to track and revert revisions (this is covered in Chapter 5), and the ability to default to "Unpublished" so they're not immediately visible on the site. These options may be set on a per-node basis, or you may specify the defaults for these options for all nodes of this type in the Administration section for content types at Administer→Content management→Content types (admin/content/types) and pictured in Figure 2-4.

Page

Identification

Name: *

Page

The human-readable name of this content type. This text will be displayed as part of the list on the *create content* page. It is recommended that this name begin with a capital letter and contain only letters, numbers, and **spaces**. This name must be unique.

Type: *

page

The machine-readable name of this content type. This text will be used for constructing the URL of the *create content* page for this content type. This name must contain only lowercase letters, numbers, and underscores. Underscores will be converted into hyphens when constructing the URL of the *create content* page. This name must be unique.

Description:

If you want to add a static page, like a contact page or an about page, use a page.

A brief description of this content type. This text will be displayed as part of the list on the *create content* page.

▷ Submission form settings

▽ Workflow settings

Default options:

☑ Published

☐ Promoted to front page

☐ Sticky at top of lists

☐ Create new revision

Users with the *administer nodes* permission will be able to override these options.

Figure 2-4. The content type administration form

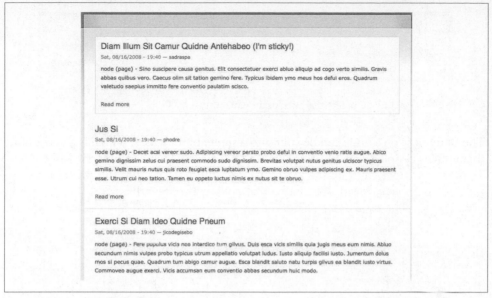

Figure 2-5. The default front page view

When default options for content types are switched, these settings are *not* retroactively applied to content that's already been created. It pays to spend some time thinking about what settings you'd like on each content type before you begin creating lots of content on your site.

Nodes that have the "Promoted to front page" publishing option checked appear on the default front page listing, available via the path *http://www.example.com/node*, as pictured in Figure 2-5. Nodes are displayed one after another, with "Sticky at top of lists" nodes on top, and the rest of the list ordered chronologically starting with the most recent.

"Front page" is a bit of a misnomer; the listing at */node* is the front page only by default; you can change the home page to whatever page you'd like, which we'll be doing later this chapter in the "Hands-On: Content Management" section.

Although this default view of content is very basic, you can create almost any type of content listing imaginable with the Views module (*http://drupal.org/project/views*), discussed in depth in the next chapter and used extensively throughout the rest of the book.

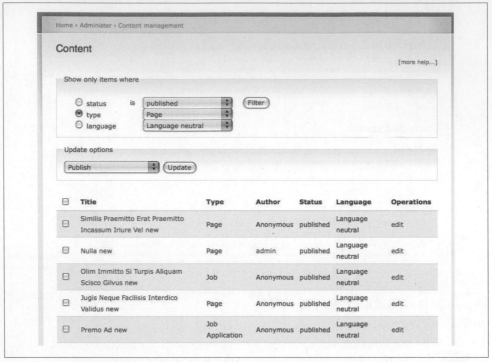

Figure 2-6. Content administration page

Making changes to content workflow once it's created is done either on the node itself, by editing it directly, or in bulk through the Administer→Content management→Content (admin/content/node) page, pictured in Figure 2-6, where content may be deleted, published, or unpublished, or have various workflow options set.

Comments

The core Comment module allows website visitors to post replies to the content within a node, which allows a discussion on the topic at hand directly with the author as well as with one another. Figure 2-7 shows commenting in action.

Most content types have comments enabled by default, although the Page type has commenting turned off initially (as it doesn't make much sense for users to discuss your "About Us" page). A veritable smorgasbord of comment settings may be configured per content type at Administer→Content management→Content types (admin/content/types), ranging from how and where comments are displayed to whether anonymous users may/must leave their contact details along with their comments. We'll cover a few of these settings later in the chapter.

Comments may also optionally be placed in a moderation queue rather than being immediately posted on the site, which can be useful as a basic spam deterrent.

Figure 2-7. The Comment module allows visitors to discuss a piece of content

 Drupal offers a number of modules that help ease the burden of dealing with spam and abusive content. We'll discuss some of the options later in this chapter in the "Spotlight: Content Moderation Tools" section.

Navigation

Hand-in-hand with creating content is being able to find it on the site. Drupal provides a built-in module called Menu for this purpose. Menus hold the navigation links to various web pages on a Drupal site. Drupal comes with three default menus:

Navigation
> The main system menu. In practice, this menu is the default "dumping ground" of links offered by modules, including administrative tasks.

Primary links
> An empty menu provided for custom navigation needs, typically displayed very prominently in the site's design. Major sections of the site such as "Home" and "Blog" tend to be placed in the Primary links menu.

Secondary links
> Another empty menu provided for custom navigation needs, but more subdued in presentation. As a general rule, more supplementary pages such as "Terms of Service" or "FAQ" are placed in the Secondary links menu.

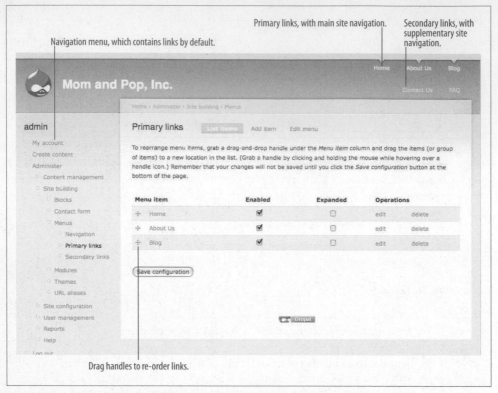

Navigation menu, which contains links by default.

Primary links, with main site navigation.

Secondary links, with supplementary site navigation.

Drag handles to re-order links.

Figure 2-8. Menu administration page showing Navigation, Primary, and Secondary link menus

 As with the Page and Story content types, you don't *have* to use the premade Primary and Secondary link menus. They are merely a potential starting point that can help you get your site up and running quickly.

Figure 2-8 shows an example of all three menus in the default core "Garland" theme. Themes will be discussed in more detail later in the "Spotlight: Themes" section of this chapter. Also note that you can easily rearrange menu items by dragging them with the gray cross-handles.

 Although under normal conditions, Primary and Secondary links are two different menus, there's also a setting under Administer→Site building→Menus→Settings tab (admin/build/menu/settings) to make the same menu contain both the primary and secondary links. This creates a sort of "drill-down" effect in which the top-level items are displayed as the primary links, and any subitems are displayed as secondary once the main section is clicked on.

Blocks

Blocks are smaller chunks of content that you can place in your pages. Examples of some default blocks provided are "Who's online," which shows a listing of users currently logged in; the "User login" block, which displays a login form to anonymous users; and "Recent comments," which shows a list of the newest comments on the site. Even the Navigation menu and "Powered by Drupal" button in the footer shown in Figure 2-8 are blocks! You can also make your own custom blocks: for example, you might create a block to display an announcement about an upcoming event.

Figure 2-9 shows the block administration page at Administer→Site building→Blocks (admin/build/block). Blocks are placed within a *region* of a page. Examples of regions are "left sidebar," "footer," and "content." Region names, and exactly where they appear on a page, can vary from theme to theme; some may define additional regions such as "Banner ad" or remove or change some of the default regions. Therefore, blocks must be configured on a per-theme basis. We'll discuss more about regions later in the "Spotlight: Themes" part of this chapter when we talk about themes. As with menus, the handles here may be used to drag blocks to different regions.

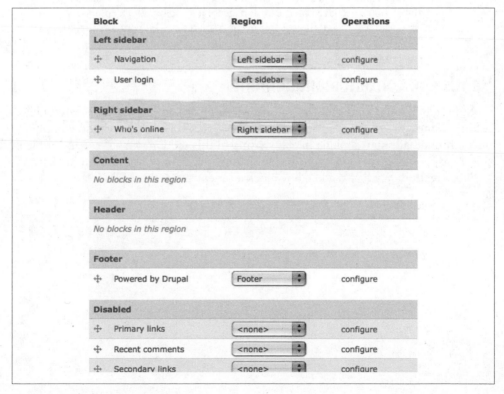

Figure 2-9. Block administration page

Be careful with using and giving access to use PHP on a Drupal site. Although an extremely powerful tool, the ability to work with PHP within a web application like Drupal opens the door for security problems and site crashes. We'll harp on this point again later in the "Hands-On: Configuring Permissions" section when we talk about access permissions.

You can customize the visibility of blocks, as well: for example, to show blocks on only certain pages or only to users with certain roles. You may also optionally use PHP to specify complex visibility settings—for example, to display a "Help" block to any users who have been members for less than a week. There is also an option to let users control the visibility of certain blocks themselves, so they have more control over their browsing experience.

 One frequently asked question is how blocks and nodes differ, as both display content. One general rule of thumb is that blocks are typically supplementary information to the actual content on the page. Blocks' content is also usually either constantly changing (in the case of the "Who's online" block), or consists of temporary information such as a blurb that's displayed on the front page for a few days. Block content is not searchable, so if the content needs to be referenced permanently, a node is a much better choice.

Hands-On: Content Management

Out of the box, our wonderful Drupal site, pictured in Figure 2-10, looks pretty bare. Adding some content with information about Mom and Pop, Inc., will do wonders to make this actually start looking like a website. In this section, we'll create a couple of simple pages—the About Us page and the Home page—and begin to build our website's navigation. We'll also add a few blocks, for extra pizzazz.

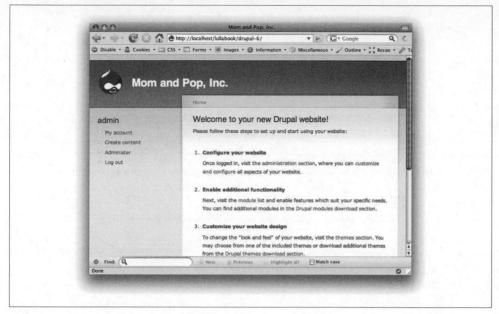

Figure 2-10. Drupal, after a fresh install

Creating Content

1. First, we'll create the site's Welcome page, which we'd like to use as the home page of the site. Go to Create content→Page (node/add/page).

2. Enter the settings provided here in Table 2-1 and Figure 2-11. Because this is a static page, we'll also place it into our primary navigation menu using the settings provided by the Menu module.

Table 2-1. Home page values

Setting	Value
Title	Welcome to Mom and Pop, Inc.
Menu settings	
• Menu link title	Home
• Parent item	<Primary links> (default)
• Weight	0 (default)
Body	Welcome to our website! We hope you enjoy your stay!

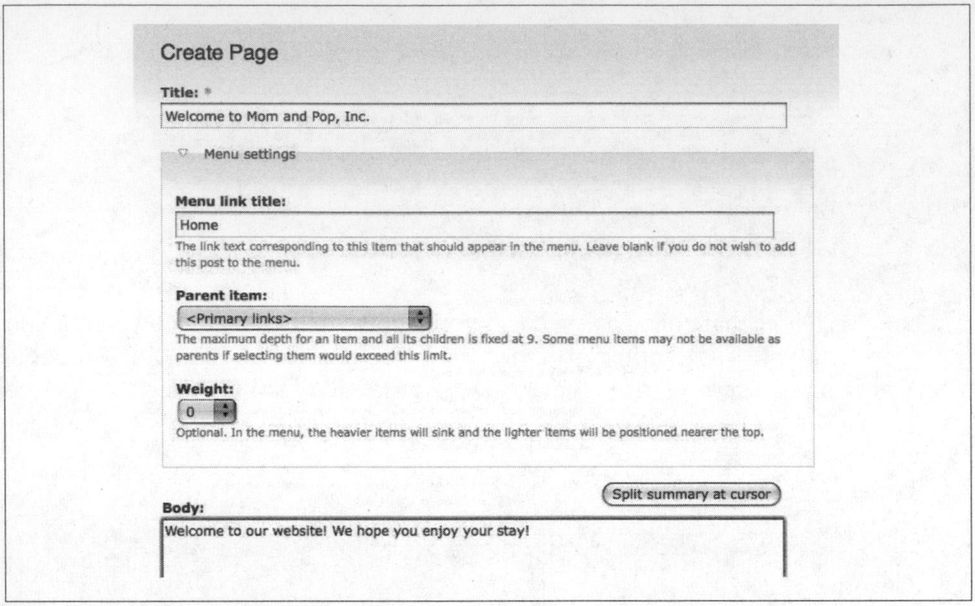

Figure 2-11. Creating the site's home page

3. Click Save to create the page. Once the page is created, make note of the path in your browser's address bar. It should look like *http://example.com/node/1*. Write down the part that comes after the *http://www.example.com/*, which should be *node/1*. This is the node ID of our page—we'll need it later.

4. Next, we'll make our About Us page, which uses the same steps. Go to Create content→Page (node/add/page).

5. As with any node we create in Drupal, we'll enter a title and a body. Enter the settings from Table 2-2 and then click Save.

Table 2-2. About page values

Setting	Value
Title	About Us
Menu settings	
• Menu link title	About Us
• Parent item	<Primary links> (default)
• Weight	0 (default)
Body	Our store has been providing organic food to the community since 1978. Come and see us at: 123 Main Street Home Town, MN Store hours: 12pm–12am

6. When completed, you should see the new page appear. Note that we have two menu items in the upper-right corner now, as shown in Figure 2-12.

 If you forgot to enter a menu item and navigate away from a page, it can be tricky to find it again without manually going to a path like *http://www.example.com/node/1*. The Content administration page at Administer→Content management→Content (admin/content/node) can help you track down straggler pages.

Now you'll see that our two new pages both appear in the menu. However, if you click on the site's title at the top of the screen, you'll be back at that old "Welcome to your new Drupal website" page, which is not quite what we want. We want the Welcome page to be the page that people are forwarded to when they initially hit the site. So let's fix that.

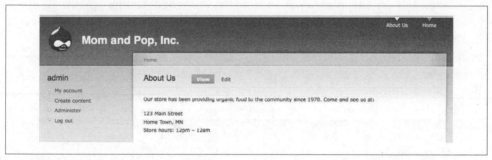

Figure 2-12. The completed About Us page

7. Head to Administer→Site configuration→Site information (admin/settings/site-information).

8. Scroll to the bottom and find the "Default front page" setting. Pull out that node ID that you wrote down earlier when we created the Home page. Replace the contents of the field with that text, which should be **node/1**. Click "Save configuration."

9. Now, if you click on the site's title once more, you should arrive at your new Home page, as pictured in Figure 2-13.

Figure 2-13. Completed Home page

10. There's one other minor content-related thing we should do before we move on. As you know, Drupal comes with both a Page and Story type. However, we're not planning to use Stories on this website. Removing the content type will reduce clutter and lessen potential confusion for Mike and Jeanne. Go to Administer→Content management→Content types (admin/content/types) to reach the content type administration page pictured in Figure 2-14.

11. Click the Delete link next to Story and click the Delete button when prompted to confirm.

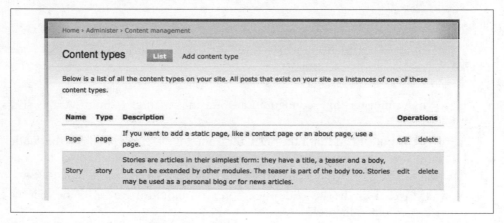

Figure 2-14. Content type administration page

Managing Site Navigation

Great! We now have a couple pages on the site and our navigation menu is starting to come together. However, there's something a little funny going on: our menu items in the top righthand corner are displayed in alphabetical order, which puts "About Us" before "Home." It would make a lot more sense for "Home" to come first, so let's fix that by reordering the items listed in the menu.

1. Go to Administer→Site building→Menus (admin/build/menu) and click Primary links (admin/build/menu-customize/primary-links).
2. Using the handles on the left side, drag the Home item above the About Us item, as shown in Figure 2-15.
3. Make sure to click "Save configuration" to save your menu settings.

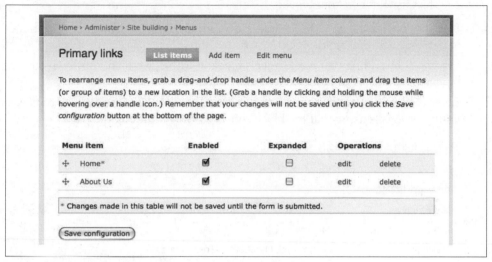

Figure 2-15. Menu administration

Now our menu should look like Figure 2-16, with Home listed first. That's more like it!

Figure 2-16. Reordered navigation menu

Configuring Blocks

Now, let's start to play around a bit with blocks on the site. Mike and Jeanne don't know what Drupal is, which is going to result in all sorts of awkward questions about that "Powered by Drupal" block in the footer. So let's remove it. Additionally, they want to be able to show off the latest weekly deal prominently on the home page, which is the perfect use for a custom block:

1. Begin by navigating to the block administration page at Administer→Site building→Blocks (admin/build/block).

2. Let's start by adding that weekly deals block. For this, we'll add our own custom block. Click the "Add block" tab (admin/build/block/add).

3. Enter the settings from Table 2-3 as shown in Figure 2-17. The "Page-specific visibility settings" ensure that the block shows up only on the home page.

Table 2-3. Settings for weekly deals block

Field	Value
Block-specific settings	
Block description	Weekly deals
Block title	This week's deals!
Block body	New this week: Oranges! Only 42 cents each. Yum!
User-specific visbility settings	
None (default)	
Role-specific visibility settings	
None (default)	
Page-specific visibility settings	
Show block on specific pages	Show on only the listed pages.
Pages	<front>

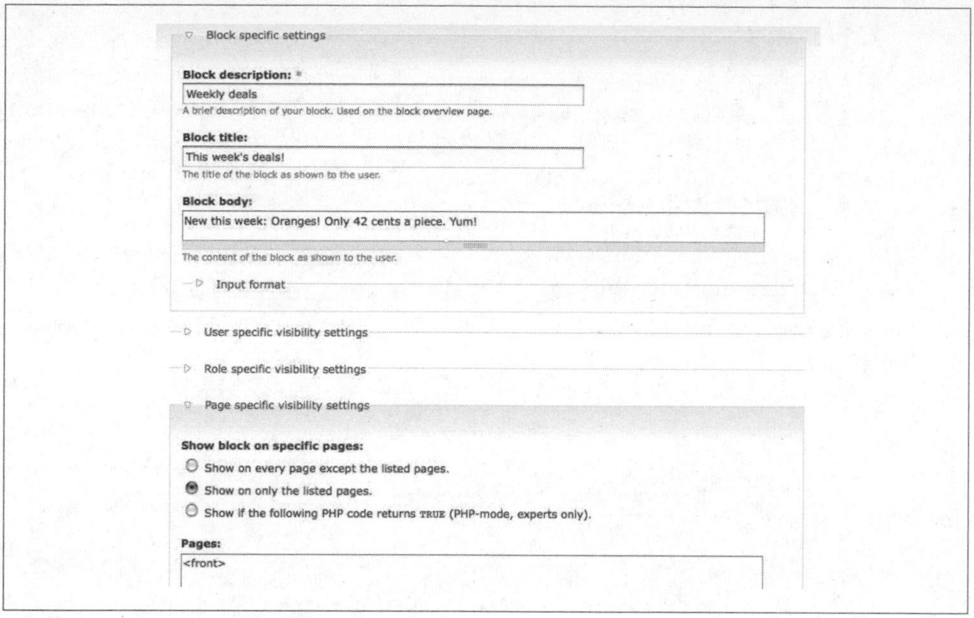

Figure 2-17. Block configuration forms

4. After saving this form with the "Save block" button, you'll return to the main block administration page.

5. Let's get our new block on the page. Click the handle next to the "Weekly deals" block and drag the table row up to the Header region. As we saw with menus, the block's table row will be highlighted in yellow, indicating that it was the most recently moved item, and it will receive an asterisk next to it to indicate that it has changed and needs to be saved.

> In addition to being able to drag and drop the blocks into the region of your choice, you can also use the drop-down select list in the Region column to choose the region.

6. While we're in here, let's remove that Powered by Drupal block, too. Click the handle next to the block and drag it from the Footer region to the Disabled region at the bottom. Now this block becomes the highlighted row, and the asterisk remains on both modified blocks. When finished with these steps, your page should look as pictured in Figure 2-18.

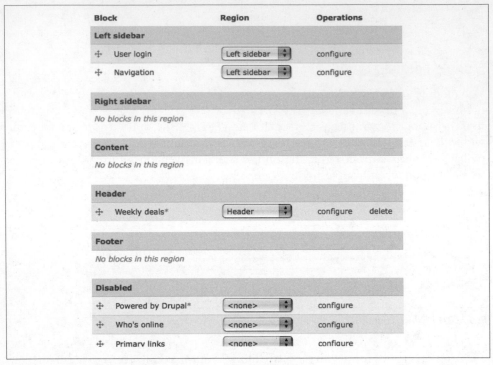

Figure 2-18. Block administration page after reordering blocks

7. Finally, click "Save blocks" to save the form, and navigate back to the home page to see your block changes in actions, as shown in Figure 2-19.

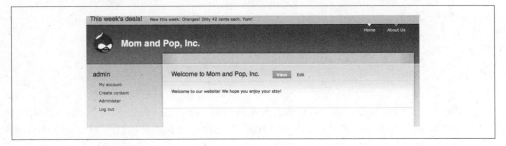

Figure 2-19. "Weekly deals" block

Spotlight: Modules

As discussed in Chapter 1, modules allow you to turn on and off functionality within your Drupal website. There are two types of modules: "core" modules, which come with Drupal itself, and "contributed" modules, which are provided for free by the

Drupal community and available for download from Drupal.org. This section discusses everything you need to know about modules.

Module Administration Page

The module administration page, available from Administer→Site building→Modules (admin/build/modules) and depicted in Figure 2-20, is where Drupal provides configuration options for your website's functionality. Related modules are grouped together within fieldsets, and each module entry contains a description and an indication of which version is currently running on the site. This version information can be extremely useful when troubleshooting problems.

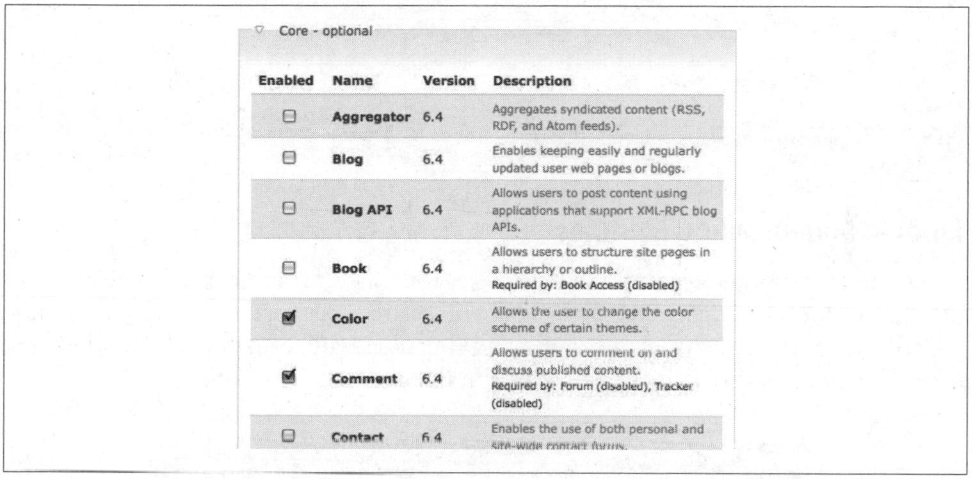

Figure 2-20. Module administration page

Modules may be switched on and off by toggling their Enabled checkboxes, which allows you to custom-tailor the functionality of any Drupal site to its unique needs, without bogging it down with needless overhead.

A module might also have *dependencies*. That is, it might require one or more other modules in order to work properly. For example, the Forum module requires both the Comment and Taxonomy modules to be enabled before it can be enabled. If you forget to do this, a confirmation screen will appear asking you whether to enable the required modules in order to proceed.

Nearly all modules also have one or more administration pages associated with them for configuring various settings. Most often, these are found under Administer→Site configuration (admin/settings) or Administer→Site building (admin/build). Because modules can easily add additional administration pages, we recommend navigating to the Administration (admin) main page and clicking the "By module" tab (admin/by-module), as pictured in Figure 2-21, to view all administrative options broken down module by module. This is a best practice to follow after installing a new module.

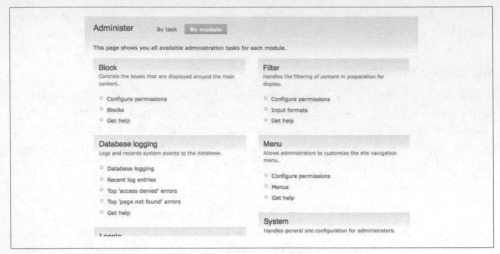

Figure 2-21. Viewing administrative tasks by module

Finding and Installing Modules

Although core modules can provide the basics for your site, and can in some cases get you pretty far, the real power in Drupal comes from its vast array of community-contributed modules. You can browse and download all contributed modules from *http://drupal.org/project/Modules*, pictured in Figure 2-22.

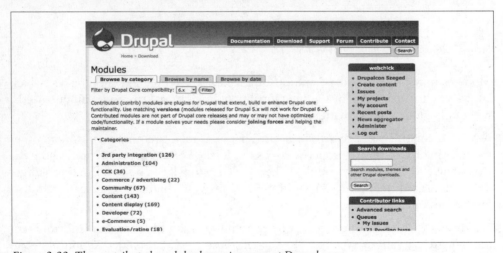

Figure 2-22. The contributed modules browsing page at Drupal.org

Note that Drupal 5.x modules are not compatible with Drupal 6.x, and vice versa. It's very important to use the "Filter by Drupal Core compatibility" selection at the top of this screen to display modules only for the Drupal version that you are using. To display modules compatible with Drupal 6, change the drop-down to 6.x, and for Drupal 5-compatible modules, select 5.x. You can use the filter only if you are logged in to Drupal.org. An account is free, and can be handy in a number of ways, so creating one is highly recommended.

Each module has its own project page on Drupal.org, as indicated in Figure 2-23. Here you'll find the name of the chief maintainer of the project; a description; and often a screenshot showing what the module does, a table containing releases that you may download, and links to other areas below, such as a module's issue queue or documentation. The version of the module you should download is the one that says "Recommended for 6.x" next to it and whose version starts with "6.x-" (unless you're using Drupal 7, in which case you'd look for "Recommended for 7.x," and so on). Visit *http://drupal.org/handbook/version-info* for much more information on Drupal's version naming conventions.

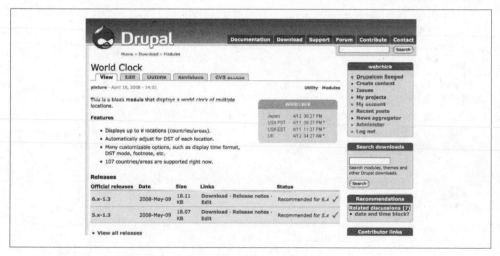

Figure 2-23. The project page for the World Clock module

 One of the most challenging aspects of using Drupal is determining which modules to use for a given task at hand. There are many modules that appear to cover similar ground, and the quality of modules can vary greatly. Appendix B is devoted entirely to the topic of tips and tricks for selecting the right modules for your project. But it's not enough to find the modules you're looking for; you also have to keep them up-to-date. We talk more about upgrading modules in Appendix A.

Once you've found your module, download it to your local drive. Like Drupal, modules downloaded from Drupal.org come with the suffix *.tar.gz*, which means that this file has been archived using tar (these files are commonly referred to as "tarball" files) and compressed using gzip. Most drag-and-drop file extraction applications, such as the free StuffIt Expander (*http://my.smithmicro.com/*) for Mac and Windows, can expand the archive and create a directory containing the original files.

Once you've extracted the module directory, place it into the *sites/all/modules/* directory and your new module should appear on the Module administration page, discussed previously.

Detailed instructions on how to install modules are available in the Getting Started handbook at *http://drupal.org/node/258*.

Removing Modules

If you decide that you no longer want to use a module, you have two choices:

Disable
> Disable a module by unchecking the Enabled checkbox and saving the form. This action switches the module off temporarily, which can be useful when troubleshooting. You can re-enable the module at any time and your website will function exactly the same, as disabling a module does not remove the module's data from your database. You may disable a module only if no other enabled modules require it.

Uninstall
> Uninstalling a module removes the module permanently. In order to uninstall a module, it first must be disabled, and then may be checked off from the Uninstall tab (admin/build/modules/uninstall). Note that many but not all modules have an uninstall function.

 Uninstalling a module will delete *all data* associated with that module, possibly including content on your website. Be *very* careful when using this option, and be sure to back up your database first. Note that uninstalling a module does not remove it from the filesystem; you still have to do this manually.

Hands-On: Working with Modules

The easiest way to wrap your head around how modules work is to try installing and configuring a couple of them. This section will cover how to install, enable, and configure two modules: Path, a module that's built into Drupal core, and Administration Menu, which is a contributed module that may be downloaded from Drupal.org.

Path Module

In the earlier hands-on section ("Hands-On: Content Management"), we created an "About Us" page and a "Home" page and added them to our site's menu. But if you return to those pages, you'll see that the URL is something like *http://www.example .com/node/1*. Wouldn't it be great if we could instead give these pages nice search engine–friendly URLs like *http://www.example.com/about*? We can, with Drupal core's Path module.

The Path module allows us to specify human-readable URLs, referred to as *URL aliases*, which mask Drupal's default way of naming paths:

1. Begin by navigating to the modules administration page at Administer→Site build-ing→Modules (admin/build/modules).

2. Under the Core – optional package, check the Enabled checkbox next to the Path module, as pictured in Figure 2-24, and click the "Save configuration" button at the bottom of the form.

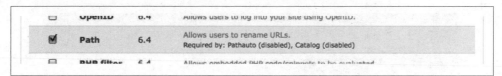

Figure 2-24. Enabling the Path module

3. Click on the About Us page in the menu, and click the Edit tab.

4. Toward the bottom of the form, you'll see a new fieldset called "URL path settings," as pictured in Figure 2-25. Enter **about** as the path, and click Save.

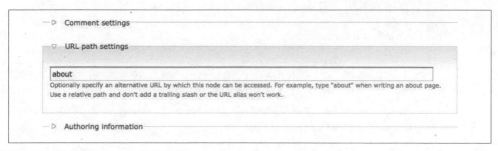

Figure 2-25. Entering a path alias for a node

5. Now, if you click on the About link in the menu once more, you should see the URL change to *http://www.example.com/about*.

6. Repeat the previous steps to add a URL alias for the Home page as well, using **home** for the "URL path settings."

Setting URL aliases by hand can be tedious. The Pathauto module (go to *http://drupal.org/project/pathauto*), covered in Chapter 5, allows you to set up customized rules that automatically generate friendly URLs for all of your website content (*http://example.com/content/about*), users (*http://example.com/user/admin*), and more.

Administration Menu Module

You've probably noticed that moving around in the Drupal administration pages gets a little tedious. For example, getting to the modules administration page requires clicking on Administer, then Site building, then Modules. Wouldn't it be nice if there were a faster way to move around? Luckily, there is: the Administration Menu module (*http://drupal.org/project/admin_menu*), pictured in Figure 2-26. This module places a dynamic drop-down menu bar for administrative users at the top of all pages, allowing quick and easy navigation around the site. This module does not come with the core, so we will need to download it first.

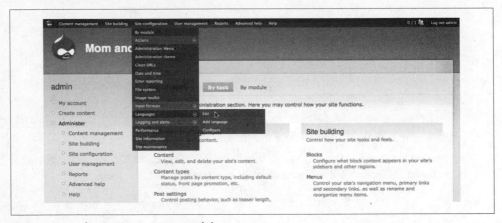

Figure 2-26. Administration Menu module

1. Go to the Administration Menu module's project page at *http://drupal.org/project/admin_menu*. Look for its table of releases, pictured in Figure 2-27.

2. Look for the release marked as "Recommended for 6.x" (in Figure 2-27, this would be 6.x-1.0) and click its Download link.

Releases

Official releases	Date	Size	Links	Status
6.x-1.0	2008-Jun-26	25.43 KB	Download · Release notes · Edit	Recommended for 6.x ✓
5.x-2.6	2008-Jul-15	28.04 KB	Download · Release notes · Edit	Recommended for 5.x ✓
4.7.x-1.4	2007-Sep-06	11.17 KB	Download · Release notes · Edit	Recommended for 4.7.x ✓

Development snapshots	Date	Size	Links	Status
7.x-1.x-dev	2008-Aug-16	26.35 KB	Download · Release notes · Edit	Development snapshot ✕
6.x-1.x-dev	2008-Aug-08	26.32 KB	Download · Release notes · Edit	Development snapshot ✕
5.x-2.x-dev	2008-Aug-13	29.22 KB	Download · Release notes · Edit	Development snapshot ✕

Figure 2-27. Administration Menu module's releases

3. Once downloaded, the file name will be something like *admin_menu-6.x-1.0.tar.gz*. Extract this file using your tool of choice, such as WinZip or StuffIt Expander. When finished, the module's files should appear in a folder called admin_menu.

4. Within your operating system, navigate to Drupal's *sites/all* folder. If it's not already there, create a *modules* subdirectory so that your path looks like *sites/all/modules*.

5. Move the *admin_menu* folder into Drupal's *sites/all/modules* folder. When finished, your site's directory should look as pictured in Figure 2-28.

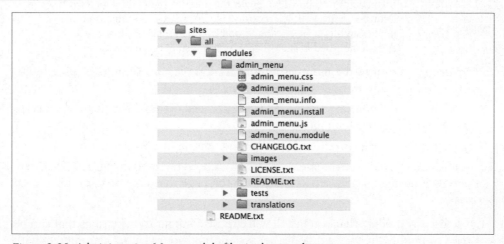

Figure 2-28. Administration Menu module files in the sites directory

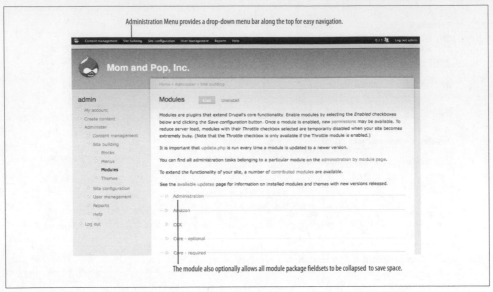

Figure 2-29. Effects of the Administration Menu module

6. With the module files in place, we can now begin the next step: installing them from the Drupal side.

> From here on out, any hands-on sections that require contributed modules will assume that these steps have been taken, and that the module files are already in place in Drupal's *sites/all/modules* directory. The book's source code comes with all of the modules necessary to build the websites in future chapters already in place. If you want to follow along with the other chapters on your own Drupal website, you'll need to download and extract each required module in this same fashion. A quick reference list of the modules and themes used in each chapter is supplied in Appendix C.

7. In Drupal, return to the modules administration page at Administer→Site building→Modules (admin/build/modules).

8. Find the Administration package fieldset and check the Enabled checkbox next to the Administration Menu module.

9. Click the "Save configuration" button at the bottom of the form.

10. Immediately, you'll see the effects of this module, as pictured in Figure 2-29. There is now a navigation bar across the top of the page that contains administration tasks.

11. Almost any module that you install will expose configuration settings that can be used to modify the way a module behaves or how your visitors can interact with it, and Administration Menu is no exception. Go to Administer (admin) and click

the "By module" tab (admin/by-module) to view a list of all enabled modules and the administrative features they expose to Drupal. As you can see in Figure 2-30, the Administration Menu module exposes a few different options: we can configure permissions for the module (which we will do in the next hands-on section), we can read help information, or we can go to the Administration Menu module settings page.

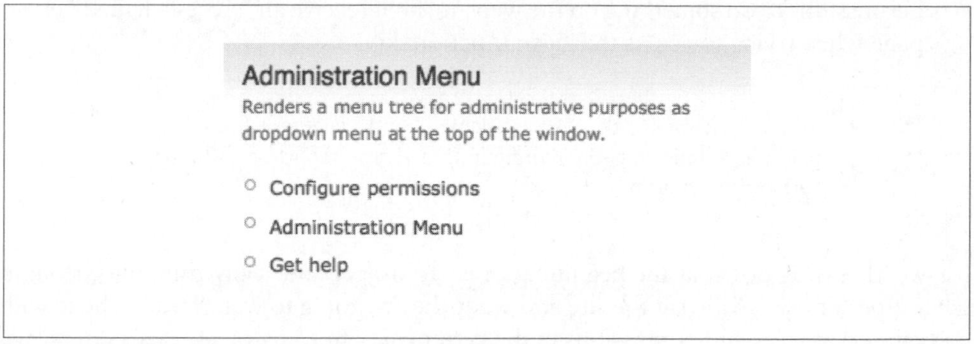

Administration Menu

Renders a menu tree for administrative purposes as dropdown menu at the top of the window.

○ Configure permissions

○ Administration Menu

○ Get help

Figure 2-30. Administration options exposed by the Administration Menu module

12. Click on Administration Menu's "Get help" link (admin/help/admin_menu) to be taken to a help page about the module. Here are some additional details about the module and a link to its settings page.

13. Click the "Administration menu" link (admin/settings/admin_menu) and take a look at the options offered there. Among other things, you can choose to collapse all module package fieldsets on the module administration form, which can help save space after you are familiar with the packages in which all the various modules live.

Now that we've seen how to install, enable, and configure a module, let's delve into detail about how to control who has access to use it.

Spotlight: Access Control

One of the most powerful features of Drupal is its rich, fine-grained access control system, based around the concept of users, roles, and permissions.

User

A visitor to the website. A user can be anyone: a casual visitor to the website, your company's president who's blogging on the site every day, your system administrator, or someone who doesn't work for your company at all but is still adding content (as with a social networking site).

Role

A group to which users can be assigned. Roles can be something like "administrator" or "sales team member." Drupal comes with two roles by default—"anonymous user" (for all users who have not logged in) and "authenticated user" (for all logged-in users)—but you can create as many different roles as you want.

Permission

Something that users within a role can (or can't!) do on the website. Each module can specify its own list of permissions that may be assigned. Examples of permissions are "access site content" and "edit own blog." If a user does not have proper permissions to do something on the website, he'll receive an "Access denied" error page when trying to access the given functionality.

 You can customize the "Access denied" and "Page not found" error pages at Administer→Site configuration→Error reporting (admin/settings/error-reporting).

It's worth sitting down at the beginning of each project and really thinking through what types of users will visit the site and what they're going to want to do. Those will correspond to roles and permissions in the system. Try to think of your users in terms as broad as possible. Particularly on small sites and at small organizations, you might be tempted to create a role for each person (e.g., "Greg's role"). But this gets extremely cumbersome, not to mention confusing, when Susan later replaces Greg. Rather, think of what Greg will be doing on the website, such as site configuration, upgrades, and backups, and name the role after those tasks (e.g., "site administrator") instead.

Configuring User Access

Controlling user access consists of two parts: (optionally) creating one or more roles to match the types of visitors your website needs to support, and assigning permissions to those roles.

Under Administer→User management→Roles (admin/user/roles), pictured in Figure 2-31, you may create, edit, or remove roles. At this stage, there's nothing more to a role than a name. Individual users may be assigned to roles either via their user profiles or from the user administration page at Administer→User management→Users (admin/user/user). Both creating and assigning roles requires the "administer users" permission.

 Clicking the "edit permissions" link next to a role on this screen will display the matrix of permissions for only that role. This feature can be useful if you need to set several permissions for only a single role.

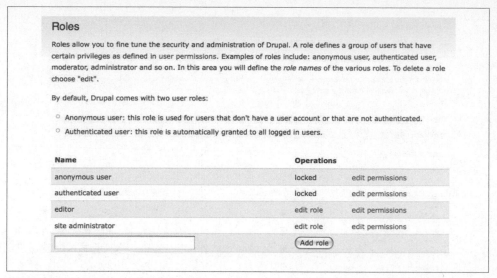

Figure 2-31. The Roles administration page

When you first create a role, it won't be assigned any permissions. Site administrators are initially responsible for defining permissions and assigning users to the new role.

At Administer→User management→Permissions (admin/user/permissions), individual permissions may be assigned to roles, as shown in Figure 2-32. Access to this screen is controlled by the "administer user permissions" permission, so different users can take care of day-to-day user-related administrative tasks without requiring an escalation of their privileges in the system.

All roles apart from "anonymous user" receive the permissions of "authenticated user" plus any other roles they're assigned. In Figure 2-32, editors and site administrators inherit the "access comments" permission because they are by nature logged in (authenticated users) in order to use the site. However, because "administer comments" is an elevated permission not given to authenticated users, it needs to be checked for both editors and site administrators so that both roles receive the permission.

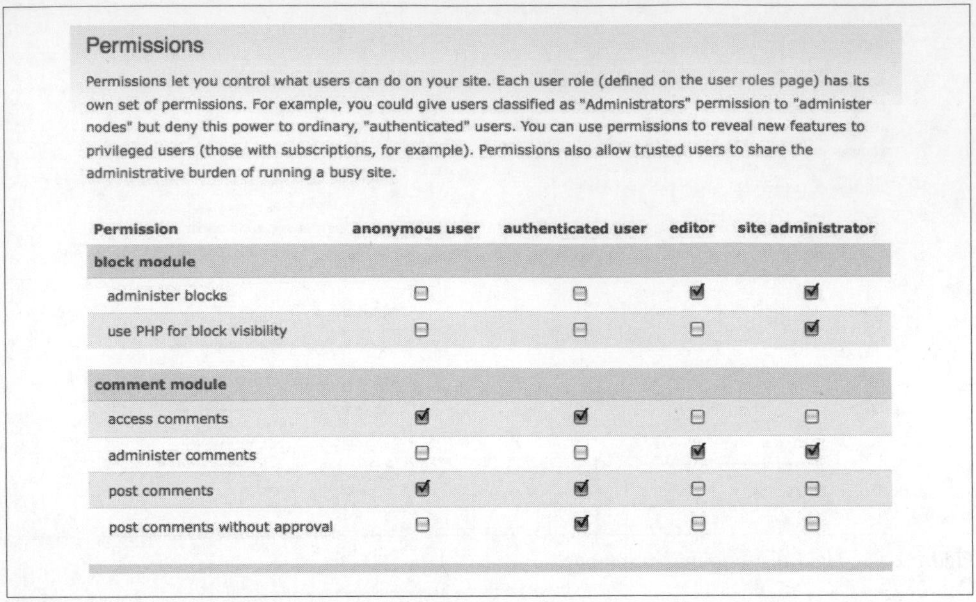

Permissions

Permissions let you control what users can do on your site. Each user role (defined on the user roles page) has its own set of permissions. For example, you could give users classified as "Administrators" permission to "administer nodes" but deny this power to ordinary, "authenticated" users. You can use permissions to reveal new features to privileged users (those with subscriptions, for example). Permissions also allow trusted users to share the administrative burden of running a busy site.

Permission	anonymous user	authenticated user	editor	site administrator
block module				
administer blocks	☐	☐	☑	☑
use PHP for block visibility	☐	☐	☐	☑
comment module				
access comments	☑	☑	☐	☐
administer comments	☐	☐	☑	☑
post comments	☑	☑	☐	☐
post comments without approval	☐	☑	☐	☐

Figure 2-32. The Permissions administration page

The Importance of Testing Access Control

Make sure that you create at least one "test" user for each role that you've defined and click through the site as those users as you complete sections of it. The account created during installation, also known as "User 1," bypasses all permission checks in the system. Though this feature is very handy when initially building the site, testing as User 1 will mask situations that will yield "Access denied" errors for your "mere mortal" visitors.

To test as a new user, log out and log back in as a different user with the role you wish to test. You can also keep multiple browsers open, logged in as a different test user in each. To switch between several accounts without having to log out between, the Devel module's (*http://drupal.org/project/devel*) "Switch user" block is very helpful.

Also note that each time you enable or disable a module, the available user permissions will most likely change, so always revisit the permissions page after installing or updating a module. In addition, you want to make sure that someone doesn't have more permissions than they should!

User Profiles

Each user has a special page in Drupal called their *user profile*. This is the page that you see when clicking the "My account" link after you have logged in. Other users might visit your user profile page by clicking your name next to a blog entry or comment you

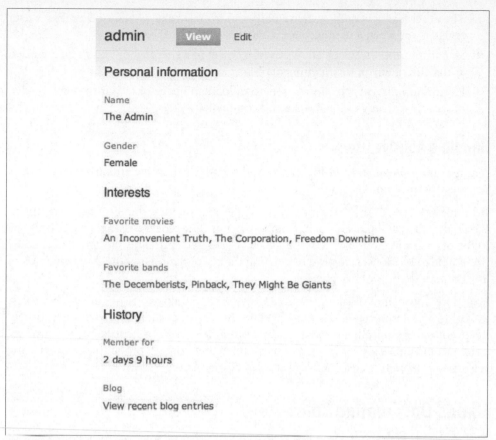

Figure 2-33. A sample user profile

have authored on the site. By default, the user profile page lists some simple information about the account, such as the username and the length of time that the user has been registered on the site. However, using add-on modules, including the core Profile module, you can add additional fields such as those in Figure 2-33, or even change the way this page looks entirely. Users may change basic settings in their user profile, such as their password and their time zone, and other modules can add additional features here as well, such as a language selection or a field to upload a picture to be displayed along with each of your user's posts.

User Settings

Under Administer→User management→User settings (admin/user/settings), there are many customizable user options, including:

- Various registration options, including whether users may create accounts themselves or this function is restricted to administrators only

- The exact text of various system emails sent from Drupal when, for example, a user registers, or when a user account is blocked
- Signature support, which allows users to enter in a small bit of text to be included at the end of any of their comments
- Picture support, which allows users to upload an image or avatar that will be displayed next to any of their posts and comments

Handling Abusive Users

A community site of any reasonable size and popularity may eventually attract visitors with less-than-honorable intentions.

Administrators with the "administer users" permission may change a user's status to Blocked, which will prevent them from logging in. The blocked user then has only the rights of an anonymous user. Users may also be deleted entirely, although it's generally preferable to block users instead of deleting them, so that their name stays attached to any content that they have posted.

For more automated blocking, Drupal provides the ability to configure access rules, available at Administer→User management→Access rules (admin/user/rules), to help keep out (or specifically allow) users by username, email, or hostname. A couple of common examples are blocking any usernames that contain profanity, or preventing registration from free email services such as Hotmail.

Hands-On: Creating Roles

Earlier, we talked about Drupal's access control system, and how it's composed of users, roles, and permissions that map to who is going to use the site and what they're going to want to do on it. Let's spend a moment brainstorming about Mom and Pop, Inc.'s needs in this area.

This site will have four types of users:

- *Passing visitors*, who will basically only be able to read and search content, comment on news items once their content has been approved, and send mail with the contact form. This will map to the built-in "anonymous user" role in Drupal.
- *Customers*, who will log into the site and can comment on content, but aren't able to actually post news items themselves. Because they will be logged in, we'll use the built-in "authenticated user" role for customers.
- The *store owners* Mike and Jeanne themselves, who will handle writing content and some of the smaller day-to-day administration of the website. They'll need to be able to create and manage content, view logs and statistics, and change certain website settings when required. However, because they're not extremely

technically savvy, the more advanced options should be hidden. We're going to call this role "editor," as they will be largely adding and editing content on the site.

- Finally, Goldie is the *webmaster*, who will actually build the site, as well as look after the more technical details for Jeanne and Mike. This will entail things like installing and upgrading modules, and configuring advanced website settings. Although she could just do everything as User 1, at some point she might want to bring on another family member to take over her duties, so it pays to be forward-thinking and make a role for this purpose. We'll call this role "site administrator."

 These standard four roles are the same ones we'll use in all future chapters. On your own Drupal site, you can have as many or as few roles as you'd like.

With that, we can begin setting up our access control:

1. Begin by creating the two additional roles—the ones for Mike and Jeanne and for Goldie, who will build the site. Go to Administer→User management→Roles (admin/user/roles).

2. Enter **editor** as a role name and click "Add role."

3. Enter **site administrator** as a role name and click "Add role." Your roles page should now look like Figure 2-31, shown earlier.

4. After setting up roles, it's always a good idea to set up some test users as well. Go to Administer→User management→Users, and click the "Add user" tab (admin/user/user/create).

5. Enter in the settings from Table 2-4 and Figure 2-34 and click "Create new account."

Table 2-4. Values for initial website users

Setting	Value
Username	Jeanne
Email address	jeanne@example.com
Password	Your choice, but try to pick something secure; perhaps "Mom-O-Rama"
Status	Active (default)
Roles	authenticated user (default) editor

6. Repeat the above step for Mike, and repeat it again for Goldie, but add her to both the editor and site administrator roles.

7. Also create a user called Random Customer, but note that Random Customer should not be assigned any special roles.

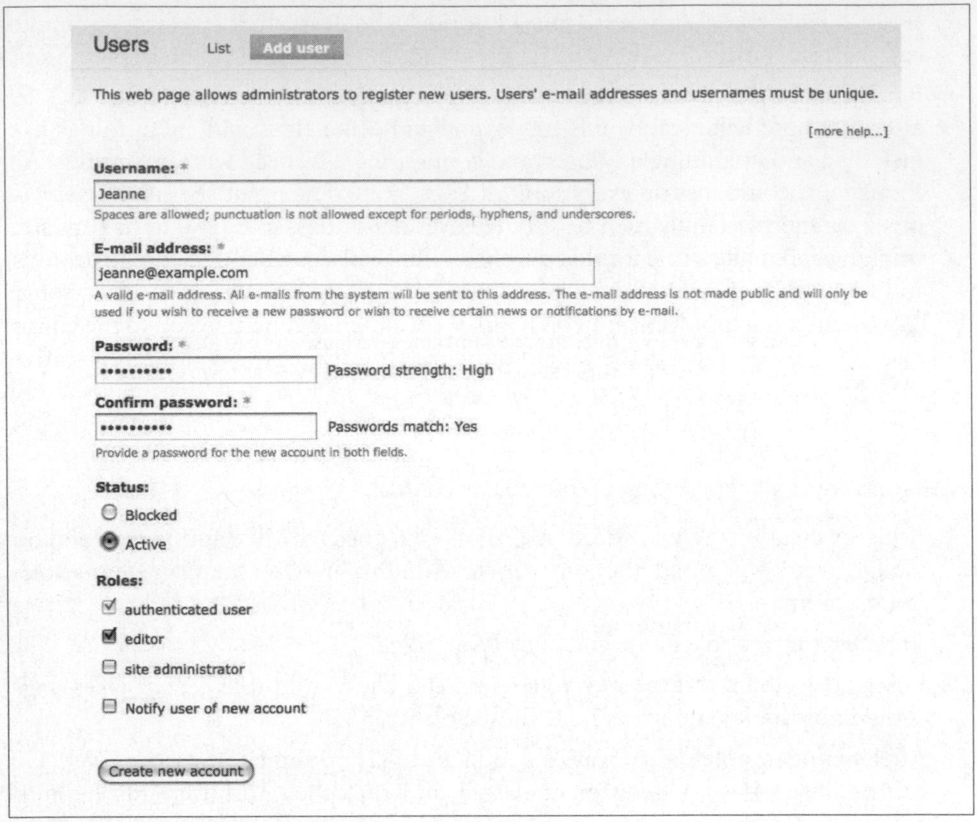

Figure 2-34. New user account form

Hands-On: Configuring Permissions

Now that we have roles in place, let's assign some permissions to control who can do what on the site:

1. Head to Administer→User management→Permissions (admin/user/permissions).

2. This screen, as seen earlier in Figure 2-32, is massive, and there's a lot to do here. We'll break this enormous table down one module at a time.

3. Remember when we enabled the Administration Menu module in the previous section? Right now, User 1 is the only person who can see the useful drop-down navigation bar at the top. Let's enable this feature for both site administrators and editors, using the settings in Table 2-5. The "access administration menu" permission controls visibility of the admin bar, and the "display drupal links" permission specifies whether resources on Drupal.org should also be part of the menu. This is a useful permission for Goldie, but not so much for Mike and Jeanne, as they won't be troubleshooting site administration issues.

Table 2-5. Permissions for the Administration Menu module

Permission: admin_menu module	anonymous user	authenticated user	editor	site administrator
access administration menu			Checked	Checked
display drupal links				Checked

4. Table 2-6 shows the permissions for the Block module, which defines two permissions: "administer blocks" and "use PHP for block visibility." The administer blocks permission allows the users within a role to select which blocks are enabled and where they appear on the page, as well as to create new blocks. As this would be a useful thing for Mom and Pop to do, we'll assign that permission to the editor role. We'll also assign it to the site administrator role, because it is an administrative task. However, we are not going to assign the use of PHP block visibility to *any* role. This is an advanced feature with security implications and only User 1 should be able to access it.

Table 2-6. Permissions for the Block module

Permission: block module	anonymous user	authenticated user	editor	site administrator
administer blocks			Checked	Checked
use PHP for block visibility				

 Whenever you see "PHP" in a permission name, think *very* carefully about whether you trust each and every one of the people within a given role before you check it. A malicious user with PHP access can wreak all sorts of havoc, from deleting all of the content on your website to spamming all of your users, or potentially interfering with other applications outside of Drupal. Beware.

5. The Comment module's permissions, listed in Table 2-7, are more straightforward. We want all users to be able to access comments, so we check that permission for both anonymous and authenticated users. Only site administrators and editors should be able to administer comments, however. This permission gives them access to an administration panel where comments may be published, unpublished, approved, deleted, and so on. Both anonymous and authenticated users should be able to post comments; however, we want anonymous users' comments to go into a moderation queue first, so we only give "post comments without approval" permission to authenticated users.

Table 2-7. Permissions for the Comment module

Permission: comment module	anonymous user	authenticated user	editor	site administrator
access comments	Checked	Checked		
administer comments			Checked	Checked
post comments	Checked	Checked		
post comments without approval		Checked		

6. Filters are another place with security implications, so we'll only give out "administer filters" permissions to the site administrator role, as indicated in Table 2-8.

Table 2-8. Permissions for the Filter module

Permission: filter module	anonymous user	authenticated user	editor	site administrator
administer filters				Checked

7. The Menu module allows you to customize your site's navigation menus. This would be a handy thing for Mike and Jeanne to be able to do, so we'll enable "administer menu" permissions for both editor and site administrator, as shown in Table 2-9.

Table 2-9. Permissions for the Menu module

Permission: menu module	anonymous user	authenticated user	editor	site administrator
administer menu			Checked	Checked

8. With the Node module's permissions, shown in Table 2-10, we're going to do something a little different. The Node module exposes lots of permissions for each content type in the system: create, edit own, edit any, delete own, and delete any. Normally, you would assign these per-node-type permissions for your users to only have access to their own content or limited number of content types. Node module also exposes a "special" permission called "administer nodes." This permission gives users rights to bypass permissions around creating, editing, deleting, and viewing any content on the site. As such, it should only be given out to trusted users. We are going to give this permission to Jeanne and Mike's editor role, as well as the site administrator role. This will not only let them create, edit, and delete all of the content on the site, but will also give them access to the main content administration page at Administer→Content management→Content (admin/content/node). All users should be able to access content, however, so we'll give that permission to both anonymous user and authenticated user. As content types are relatively advanced to configure, we'll assign the "administer content types" permission only to the site administrator role. Also check "revert revisions" and "view revisions" permissions for editor and site administrator. We'll talk more about revisions in Chapter 5.

Table 2-10. Permissions for the Node module

Permission: node module	anonymous user	authenticated user	editor	site administrator
access content	Checked	Checked		
administer content types				Checked
administer nodes			Checked	Checked
revert revisions			Checked	Checked
view revisions			Checked	Checked

By default, the "access content" permission enables access to *all* content on the entire site. However, Drupal can also be extended by numerous contributed modules to provide more fine-grained control over exactly who can access a particular node. Examples include the Node Privacy By Role module (*http://drupal.org/ project/node_privacy_byrole*), which can limit access based on a user's role, and the Organic Groups module (*http://drupal.org/ project/og*), which can limit access based on collections of related content. A complete list of access control modules is available from *http://drupal.org/project/Modules/category/74*.

9. Remember the Path module from the previous section? It'd be nice if Jeanne and Mike could also add aliases to pages that they create. We'll enable the ability to create and administer URL aliases for both editor and site administrator, as shown in Table 2-11.

Table 2-11. Permissions for the Path module

Permission: path module	anonymous user	authenticated user	editor	site administrator
administer url aliases			Checked	Checked
create url aliases			Checked	Checked

10. The System module primarily controls access to the administration section of the site. As indicated in Table 2-12, we'll give the site administrator role access to do everything on the site, but limit the editor role to accessing the administration pages without delving deeper.

Table 2-12. Permissions for the System module

Permission: system module	anonymous user	authenticated user	editor	site administrator
access administration pages			Checked	Checked
access site reports			Checked	Checked
administer actions				Checked
administer files				Checked
administer site configuration				Checked
select different theme				Checked

11. Although we haven't covered the Taxonomy module yet—we'll do so in the "Spotlight: Taxonomy" section—it counts as content; therefore, we'll give access to both editors and site administrators, as demonstrated in Table 2-13.

Table 2-13. Permissions for the Taxonomy module

Permission: taxonomy module	anonymous user	authenticated user	editor	site administrator
administer taxonomy			Checked	Checked

12. Finally, we come to the User module's permissions, shown in Table 2-14. We want everyone to access user profiles, and editors to be able to manage accounts, but we'll leave the ability to change usernames and administer the permissions to site administrators only.

Table 2-14. Permissions for the User module

Permission: user module	anonymous user	authenticated user	editor	site administrator
access user profiles	Checked	Checked		
administer permissions				Checked
administer users			Checked	Checked
change own username				Checked

13. After double-checking the permissions one more time, click the "Save permissions" button to save your work.

14. Now it's time for the final step: testing! Click "Log out" and notice that there is no navigation menu in the sidebar at all, and while you can view the contents of the site, if you try to go to a page like *http://example.com/admin*, you'll receive an "Access denied" error.

15. Log in as "Jeanne." You should have the ability to create content or administer the site.

16. Log out and then log in as "Random Customer." You should be able to see the "My account" and "Log out" links, but that's about it.

17. When finished experimenting, log back in as the first user account you created when you installed Drupal.

 Future chapters (and the book's source code) will call the users for each role user, editor, and admin, respectively, and give each account the password "oreilly."

Hands-On: Contact Form

Let's put together everything we've learned so far and get that contact form, pictured in Figure 2-35, set up.

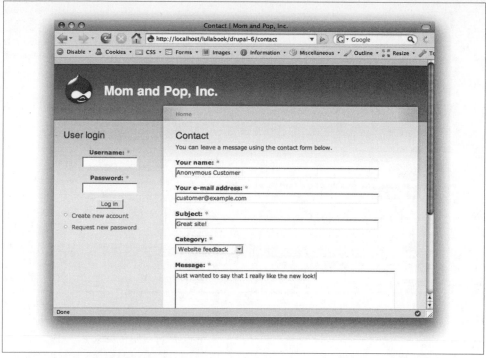

Figure 2-35. A contact form for the website

1. First, enable the Contact module. Go to Administer→Site building→Modules (admin/build/modules), check the box next to "Contact module" under the "Core – optional" package, and click "Save configuration."

2. Next, we need to set up the contact form's settings. Go to Administer→Site building→Contact form (admin/build/contact).

3. Click "Add category" (admin/build/contact/add), enter the settings from Table 2-15 as pictured in Figure 2-36, and click Save.

Table 2-15. Contact category settings

Setting	Value
Category	Website feedback
Recipients	(enter your email address)
Auto-reply	Thanks for sending feedback about our website! We will respond to your inquiry shortly.

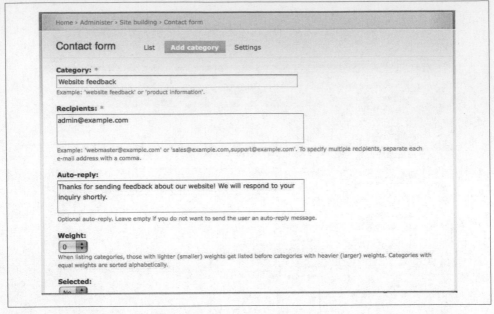

Figure 2-36. Settings for the website feedback contact form category

4. Repeat the previous steps to enter another category for "Sales opportunities." You can set this category to go to a different email address, if you'd like.

5. Next, we'll want to add a link in the website navigation to the contact form for visitors. This module happens to conveniently provide us with a menu item all ready to use, but it is not enabled by default. Anytime a module provides a menu item for you, it will always appear in the Navigation menu by default. We can easily move it to wherever we want, though. Go to Administer→Site building→Menus→Navigation (admin/build/menu-customize/navigation).

6. Find the "Contact (disabled)" menu item in the list (it will be grayed out). Click the "edit" link for it.

7. Enter the settings from Table 2-16, and click Save.

Table 2-16. Contact menu item settings

Setting	Value
Menu link title	Contact (default)
Description	Get in touch with us
Enabled	Checked
Expanded	Unchecked (default)
Parent item	<Primary links>
Weight	10

8. Finally, we need to configure permissions on the contact form so that visitors may use it. Head to Administer→User management→Permissions (admin/user/permission) and enable the permissions listed in Table 2-17. Click "Save permissions" when finished.

Table 2-17. Permissions for the Contact module

Permission: contact module	anonymous user	authenticated user	editor	site administrator
access site-wide contact form	Checked	Checked		
administer site-wide contact form			Checked	Checked

9. Finally, visit *http://www.example.com/contact* to view your shiny new contact form!

 The Contact module also provides each user on the site with her own private contact form, which is accessible from her user profile. This is a useful means of allowing users to talk to one another without exposing their email addresses.

Spotlight: Taxonomy

We have now played around with almost all of Drupal's basic site-building tools. There's just one more concept to cover in order for us to complete the functionality of Mom and Pop, Inc.: *Taxonomy*.

If you're new to Drupal, you've probably wondered what "Taxonomy" is—the word pops up all over the place, and it can sound a bit mysterious. Have no fear! It's just a technical term for a way of organizing and classifying things. If you've sorted your family photo album, filed your email in folders, or argued with a friend about whether a band is punk or ska, you've already worked with taxonomies!

Creating a taxonomy for your site starts when you identify what kinds of content you'll have, and how it can be described. Photographs, for example, might be classified by the subject matter, the location in which they were taken, or even the predominant color in the picture. In Drupal, these categories are called *vocabularies*. Each vocabulary contains specific *terms* (like Mountains or Automobiles or Pets) that can be used to describe content. Whenever you post a photograph, a music review, or a blog entry, you can select the terms that match it.

Drupal supports three kinds of vocabularies: simple lists of terms, organized hierarchies of terms, and "free tagging" vocabularies that allow you to define new terms as you post new content. Each is useful in different situations. Figure 2-37 shows an example of how each type of vocabulary might be used on a product content type.

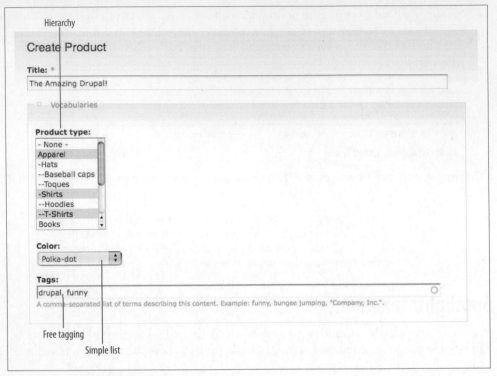

Figure 2-37. Examples of taxonomy types

 For the librarians in the house, Drupal's taxonomy system also supports more advanced features of taxonomies such as synonyms, related terms, and multiple parent hierarchies. Whew!

After submitting a piece of content, any terms it has attached will appear as links on the node page, as displayed in Figure 2-38. Each of these links displays a page listing all content to which that term has been applied, along with an RSS feed that visitors can subscribe to in order to receive notifications whenever new content with that term attached is posted.

The taxonomy system is incredibly powerful, and is one of Drupal's greatest assets as a content management system. In addition to the features provided out of the box, several contributed modules also make use of taxonomy in interesting ways, such as Taxonomy Menu module (*http://drupal.org/project/taxonomy_menu*), which turns a vocabulary into a Drupal menu that can be placed in Primary or Secondary links.

Figure 2-38. An example of taxonomy assigned to a node

Each term has a unique ID that maps to its own dedicated URL in the system, such as *http://example.com/taxonomy/term/3*. These term listings can also be combined; for example if "political" were term 3, and "humor" were term 4, the URL *http://example.com/taxonomy/term/3,4* would display all content that was both political *and* humorous, and *http://example.com/taxonomy/term/3+4* would display content that was either political *or* humorous. A book that was tagged only "humor, romance" would not show up in the first listing but would in the second.

Hands-On: Blog

It's time to put the last piece of site functionality in place: setting up blogs for Jeanne and Mike. We want blog posts to be categorized according to broad topics: is the blog post about in-store events, special deals, or general community information? But blogs should also allow "tagging"—attaching free-form keywords that don't fit in well with the major topics.

To Blog or Not to Blog?

When new site builders want to set up a personal journal or blogging site, they often turn to the Blog module that comes with Drupal. However, sometimes that's not the best choice. To understand whether the module is right for your needs, we'll take a quick look at what features it adds:

- A new content type, called "Blog"
- An overview page of all the blog posts on the site, at *http://www.example.com/blog*
- An overview page of all the blog posts by each user, at *http://www.example.com/blog/1*, where 1 is the user's account ID
- Links at the bottom of each blog post to the author's list of posts
- A filtered RSS feed for each user's blog list of blog posts
- A private "My Blog" link in the navigation menu for each user who has permission to create blog posts

    If you're building a site where one user's posts will be the primary content, all the extra pages and links from the Blog module are a distraction. It's simpler and less cluttered to create a custom content type called "Blog post" and leave the module turned off. If you're setting up a site where those posts are just one of several kinds of content, and multiple users will be posting entries, it's a great choice. That's why we'll be using it on Mom and Pop, Inc.'s site!

1. Go to Administer→Site building→Modules (admin/build/modules) and enable the core Blog module. Click "Save configuration" when finished. This will add a new content type called "Blog entry" for Mike and Jeanne to post.

2. As a general best practice, anytime we enable a new module, we should go to the Administer→User management→Permissions (admin/user/permissions) screen to configure the module's access control. We can take a look to see what permissions have been added to the list, but in our case we don't need to set any of the new permissions here. Both Jeanne and Mike already have the "administer nodes" permission, which automatically grants them the rights provided by the Blog module, so we can leave it alone.

3. Before creating any blog entries, let's set up our site's taxonomy. Go to Administer→Content management→Taxonomy (admin/content/taxonomy).

4. First, let's create a vocabulary for classifying the type of news item that's being posted. Click Add vocabulary (admin/content/taxonomy/add/vocabulary), enter the settings from Table 2-18 as shown in Figure 2-39, and click Save.

Table 2-18. "Category" vocabulary settings

Setting	Value
Identification	
Vocabulary name	Category
Description	(blank; default)
Help text	(blank; default)
Content types	
Content types	Blog entry
Settings	
Tags	Unchecked (default)
Multiple select	Unchecked (default)
Required	Checked

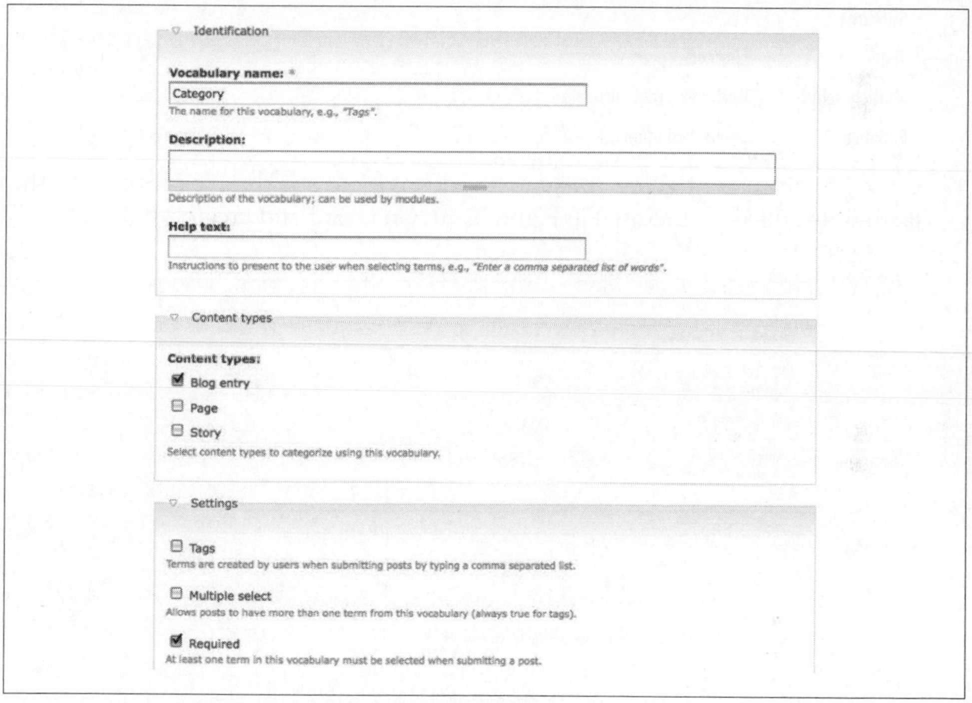

Figure 2-39. Taxonomy settings for the Category vocabulary

5. After saving the vocabulary form, you will be taken back to the main Taxonomy administration page. Click the "add terms" link next to Category, and add a few terms such as "In-Store Event," "Special Deals," "Community," and "Website Information."

6. Next, let's add vocabulary for "Tags," to add additional, ad hoc information, such as what specific products are featured. Just as before, return to Administer→Content management→Taxonomy (admin/content/taxonomy) and click the "Add vocabulary" tab (admin/content/taxonomy/add/vocabulary). Enter the settings in Table 2-19, and click Save.

Table 2-19. "Tags" vocabulary settings

Setting	Value
Identification	
Vocabulary name	Tags
Description	(blank; default)
Help text	(blank; default)
Content types	
Content types	Blog entry
Settings	
Tags	Checked
Multiple select	Unchecked (default)
Required	Unchecked (default)

7. Click Create content→Blog entry (node/add/blog) to see the blog form with the taxonomy added, as pictured in Figure 2-40. Go ahead and create a blog entry.

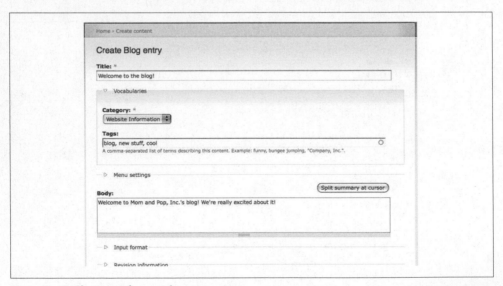

Figure 2-40. Blog entry form with taxonomy

8. The completed blog entry will look something like Figure 2-41. You'll see links there to post a comment, and to view a list of all blog entries, only those written by admin, or any post on the site assigned to a given term.

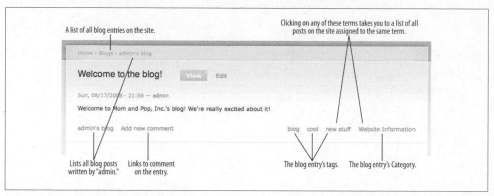

A list of all blog entries on the site.

Clicking on any of these terms takes you to a list of all posts on the site assigned to the same term.

Home › Blogs › admin's blog

Welcome to the blog!   View   Edit

Sun, 08/17/2008 - 21:58 — admin

Welcome to Mom and Pop, Inc.'s blog! We're really excited about it!

admin's blog   Add new comment   blog   cool   new stuff   Website Information

Lists all blog posts written by "admin."

Links to comment on the entry.

The blog entry's tags.   The blog entry's Category.

Figure 2-41. A completed blog entry

9. Now that we have a blog going, let's set up a link to the blog in the primary navigation. Just like the Contact module, the Blog module provides a default menu item for us. Go to Administer→Site building→Menus→Navigation (admin/build/menu-customize/navigation), locate the "Blogs (disabled)" item and click the "edit" link.

10. Enter the settings in Table 2-20 and click Save.

Table 2-20. Settings for the Blog menu item

Field	Value
Menu link title	Blog
Description	View our blog
Enabled	Checked
Expanded	Unchecked (default)
Parent item	<Primary links>
Weight	0 (default)

11. There are a couple minor changes we can make so that the commenting experience is improved for site visitors. To change the comment options, go to Administer→Content management→Content types (admin/content/types) and click "edit" next to "Blog entry" (admin/content/node-type/blog/edit).

12. Expand the "Comment settings" fieldset. Yowza! Lots of options. Although most of these are extraneous options having to do with comment display, a couple are more useful. For example, we can allow anonymous users to leave a name and website with their comments, we can make previewing comments optional (just as it is with nodes), and we can display the comment form directly on each blog

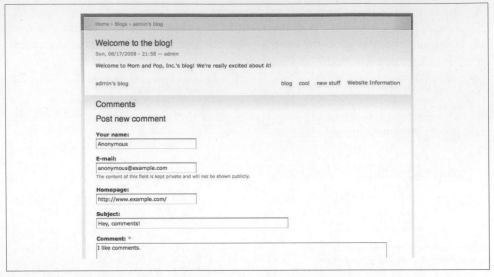

Figure 2-42. Comment form for anonymous users, after configuration

entry rather than on a separate page. Enter the settings from Table 2-21 to do so, and then click "Save content type."

Table 2-21. Comment settings for Blog entry

Field	Value
Anonymous commenting	Anonymous posters may leave their contact information
Preview comment	Optional
Location of comment submission form	Display below post or comments

13. Return to the blog listing by clicking the Blog link in the site navigation that we created earlier.

14. Click the "Log out" link to become anonymous, then click on Blog in the menu, and then click the post title to go into your full Welcome blog post. The comment form should be immediately visible, along with fields for name, email address, and website, as pictured in Figure 2-42. When submitting the comment, you will receive a notice that the comment has been queued for approval.

15. Log back in as the admin user when you're finished experimenting, and you can publish the comment from Administer→Content management→Comments under the "Approval queue" tab (admin/content/comment/approval).

Spotlight: Content Moderation Tools

When opening the floodgates for your users to become active participants in content creation, one of the inevitable things that comes up is how to handle the issue of content moderation, that is, ensuring that abusive, vulgar content and unsolicited advertising or spam is kept off the site and stays off.

You can help prevent this type of content using a two-tiered approach: automated spam detection and manual spam prevention.

Automated Spam Detection Tools

There are multiple tools that specialize in automated spam detection, but two in particular are worthy of mention in a Drupal site context: Akismet and Mollom. Each of these tools is a web service and requires an "API key," a specific random string of characters, to communicate between a website and the central reporting server.

Akismet (*http://akismet.com*) is a service created by Matt Mullenweg, creator and project lead of the blogging platform WordPress. It scans through the content of your site's comments and "trackbacks" (excerpts of posts on other blogs that link to yours), and based on its analysis of millions of other blogs' content, will either delete the content if it's spam, or send it on through if it's clean (or "ham"). Installing the Akismet module allows you to tap into the collective intelligence of millions of other blogs using the service. Chances are good that by the time a spammer trains its automated posting scripts on your website, Akismet already knows how to fingerprint the attacker and will delete the comment before it's seen by anyone on your site. And if not, Akismet provides the ability to manually mark the content as spam, and uses that data to learn from its mistakes. Akismet has been around since 2005 and has captured over seven billion spam comments, making it a tried and tested solution. The Akismet module is available from *http://drupal.org/project/akismet*, and an API key for the service may be obtained from *http://wordpress.com/api-keys/*.

Mollom (*http://mollom.com*) is a newer service started by Benjamin Schrauwen and Dries Buytaert, creator and project lead of Drupal. It performs a very similar service to Akismet by automatically scanning the content of comments and preventing obvious spam from even being posted to the website. Like Akismet, your website benefits from the collective intelligence of every other website that has a Mollom plug-in installed, and Mollom is also compatible with many different content management systems and programming languages.

However, Mollom attempts to overcome some of Akismet's shortcomings in the following ways:

- Supports blocking not just comment spam, but also spam from the contact form, node forms (blog entries, forum topics, and so on), user registration and password request form, and others. This is a unique feature to Mollom not found in competing solutions, which makes it a "one-stop solution" rather than having to use one tool for handling comments and another for handling registration forms.

- Discerns between "spam" and "ham," and displays a CAPTCHA (Completely Automated Public Turing test to tell Computers and Humans Apart), a scrambled image of letters that the user must manually enter, for those posts that are on the "borderline." This test allows humans to proceed while blocking spam robots. CAPTCHAs are displayed as both an image and an audio file for maximum accessibility. Unlike Akismet, Mollom removes the need for moderation queues and thus reduces the moderation burden for site administrators; spam is blocked before it hits the site at all.

- Allows deletion not only of spam, but also of low-quality and off-topic content or violent and abusive content. Mollom also returns a quality score for each post, based on spelling, language, and punctuation, which can be used to maintain a minimal level of professionalism on your site.

- Leverages the power of OpenID by assigning a "reputation score" to OpenID accounts across all websites. This ensures that humans' posts are let through instantly, while spammers' posts are blocked across any site they attempt to post to via an OpenID account.

- Generates graphs showing overall spam content, as pictured in Figure 2-43.

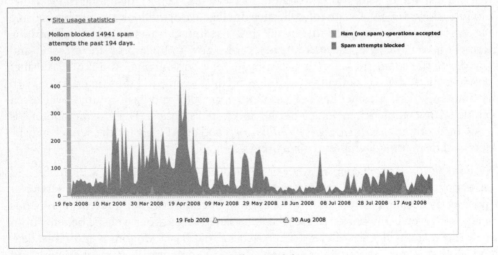

Figure 2-43. Example spam reporting from Mollom module

Mollom's goal is to eliminate the need to do any manual intervention of content moderation, by passing the "gray area" validation to the posters themselves via the conditional CAPTCHA. And, unlike the CAPTCHA provided by most websites, users are only confronted by the scrambled character challenge if their post is "borderline"—not for every single form submission, unlike other solutions such as the CAPTCHA module (*http://drupal.org/project/captcha*).

The Mollom module is available from *http://drupal.org/project/mollom* and an API key may be obtained by creating an account on *http://mollom.com.*

Manual Content Moderation Tools

Automated tools are perfect for blocking obvious spam and robots, but what do you do to prevent trolls on your site from posting pornography or other offensive content? Mollom has the ability to flag content this way, but some websites prefer a more "hands-on" approach, particularly if there are legal ramifications to offensive content appearing on the website even for a second.

Drupal core includes some basic content moderation tools, such as the ability to set any content type as "unpublished" by default (hiding it entirely from everyone but the original author and administrators), and revision control so that further edits can be "rolled back" to one that was approved. But many Drupal sites employ the one-two punch of the modr8 module (*http://drupal.org/project/modr8*), which adds a "moderation queue" status to content and some nice previewing options, as well as the Revision Moderation module (*http://drupal.org/project/revision_moderation*), a simple utility module that ensures that the approved version of a node stays published when subsequent edits are made.

Spotlight: Themes

Themes control the look of your Drupal site. It's not enough to get a site functionally working—it also has to *feel* like your own, and has to be distinguished from other sites out there.

Finding a Theme

Drupal.org has a large repository of free themes that have been uploaded by contributors. You can find a listing of these themes at *http://drupal.org/project/Themes*, or you can try them out "live" at *http://themegarden.org*.

The quality of the themes in the Drupal repository varies greatly. These themes have been created for a wide variety of purposes and needs by contributors with a broad range of programming and design skills. Download several themes and be sure to read their *README.txt* files to determine how to best use them. Many of these themes can be used as a starting point from which site administrators can customize their own site-specialized presentation.

Several companies offering for-purchase themes have also emerged in the Drupal ecosystem. These themes tend to be higher quality, a bit more "bullet-proof," and may allow for easier customization by administrators.

Theme Installation

Installing a theme requires almost exactly the same process as installing a module. Download the theme's *.tar.gz* file from its project page and extract it. Place the theme's directory into the *sites/all/themes* directory, and your new theme should appear on the Themes administration page in your Drupal installation, as shown in Figure 2-44.

 As with modules, themes written for Drupal 5 are not compatible with Drupal 6 and vice versa. Drupal 5 themes will not appear on this page if you are running Drupal 6.

Theme Configuration

Themes can be switched on from the Themes page at Administer→Site building→Themes (admin/build/themes), shown in Figure 2-44.

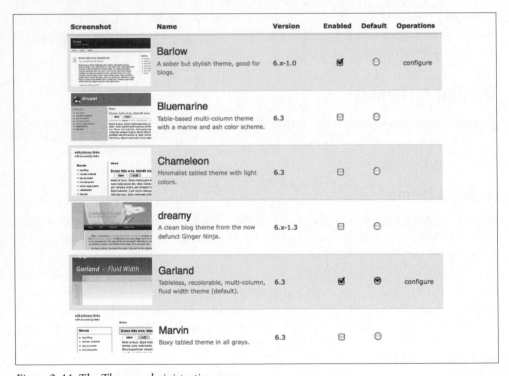

Figure 2-44. The Themes administration page

Most administrators can just ignore the "Enabled" column—the "Default" column is what actually defines the theme that all users without permission to select themes will see. Enabling our new theme is as simple as selecting it in the Default column and hitting the "Save configuration" button at the bottom of the form. The new default theme should affect the site design immediately.

The Enabled column allows the administrator to select multiple themes to be available for users with the "select different theme" permission enabled to choose from. Figure 2-45 shows a user account page for such a user when multiple themes are marked as enabled. Without this permission, which is not enabled by default, users will not actually see any of these choices. Not many sites enable this permission for users because, after all, your theme usually reflects your branding and hard design work.

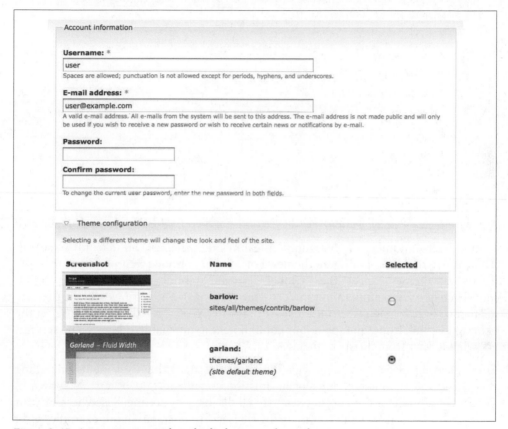

Figure 2-45. A user account with multiple themes to choose from

 The "select different theme" permission can be a useful debugging tool. A site administrator can enable both the site's normal theme and a core theme such as Garland, and switch between them if the site encounters errors. If the error happens only in the site's normal theme, then the theme is the first place to look for the problem. If it happens in both themes, it's a deeper problem, such as a database problem or configuration issue.

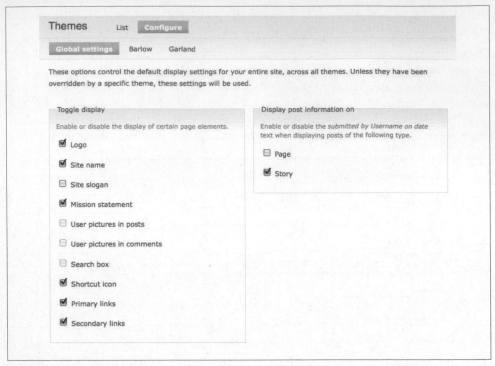

Figure 2-46. The theme configuration page allows customization of which page elements are displayed

Drupal offers a number of configuration features that themes can take advantage of. There are two ways to configure themes. For "global" options that you want to apply across all themes, select the "Global settings" tab at Administer→Site building→Themes→Configure (admin/build/themes/settings). For settings specific to a single theme, or to configure settings that are only offered on a per-theme basis, select the "configure" link from the Operations column next to an enabled theme. The settings shown will vary from theme to theme.

On the settings pages, you can toggle the display of many theme elements, including the logo image, site name, site slogan, mission statement, and others, as shown in Figure 2-46. Some of the checkboxes may be disabled by settings elsewhere in your installation. Drupal doesn't give you many clues in this area, but in our example "User pictures in posts" and "User pictures in comments" are disabled because "Picture support" has not been enabled on the Administer→User management→User settings (admin/user/settings) page. "Search box" is disabled because the Search module has not been enabled.

Settings such as site name, site slogan, and mission statement are configurable at Administer→Site configuration→Site information (admin/settings/site-information).

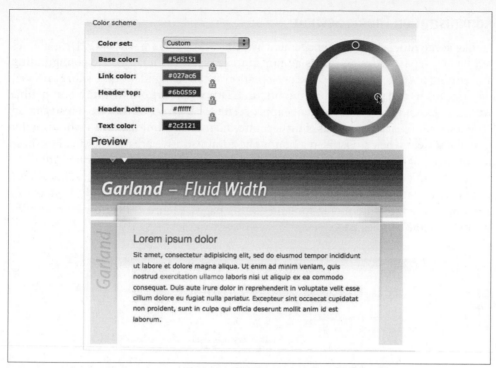

Figure 2-47. The Color module, supported in some themes, offers customization of the site's colors

The theme configuration page also allows administrators to upload their own site logo image and shortcut icon (also known as the favicon or bookmark icon, which appears in the browser's address bar) or simply point to one elsewhere on their server.

Some themes, such as the core Garland theme, also take advantage of the Color module, which allows site administrators to configure its color scheme using a handy JavaScript-based color picker. Figure 2-47 shows the Color module in action.

Blocks and Regions

It's important to remember that block regions are defined by the theme, and different themes may offer different regions. If you have blocks assigned to a region in one theme and you switch to another theme that does not offer a region with the same name, these blocks will disappear from your site. After enabling a new theme, visit the blocks administration page at Administer→Site building→Blocks (admin/build/block) and see what regions are available in your theme. You may need to reassign blocks to another region to take full advantage of the new theme.

Administration Theme Setting

Unlike some other content management systems and blogging software, Drupal does not have a separate design for its administration pages by default. Site configuration and editing of content use the same presentation as the remainder of the site. However, the large forms and tables needed to configure a Drupal site are often quite incompatible with the design and layout elements appropriate for the rest of the site—resulting in "broken" administration pages. Furthermore, many site administrators would prefer to make it clear when a user is in a nonpublic administrative area of the site. For these reasons, Drupal allows for an administration theme to be chosen by visiting Administer→Site configuration→Administration theme (admin/settings/admin). This theme will be used for all administration pages (those starting with "admin" in the URL path), and optionally for content creation and editing pages. Figure 2-48 shows the Administration theme settings page.

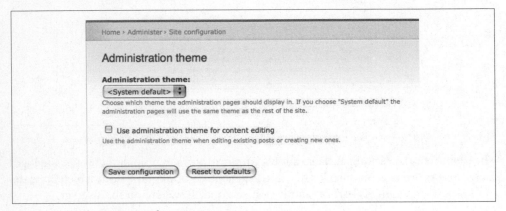

Figure 2-48. Administration theme settings page

Hands-On: Branding the Site

Now, it's time to make the site look less like Drupal and more like Mom and Pop, Inc. This section will walk through configuring a theme in order to customize the look and feel of a site.

1. Head to Administer→Site building→Themes (admin/build/themes), and ensure that the Default radio button is selected for the Garland theme. Click the "Save configuration" button. You should see your site switch to the Garland theme, if it wasn't using it already.

If the newly selected theme does not appear immediately, here are a couple of things to check:

- Is the site using an administration theme? If so, *all* administration pages will show up in the administration theme. You'll need to click to something like your site's home page to see the changed theme.

- Are there multiple themes enabled on the site, and does your user account have "select different theme" permissions? If so, either uncheck the "Enabled" checkboxes for unused themes on the Themes page or visit the "Edit" tab on the "My account" page and select the new theme.

2. Click the Configure tab (admin/build/themes/settings) to configure the Global settings, which apply to all themes.

3. Under "Logo image settings," upload the *mom_and_pop_logo.png* image in the *assets/ch02-basic* folder in the book's source code. Upon saving the form with the "Save configuration" button, you should see the new logo appear in the upper-left corner. But it looks absolutely horrendous on that blue background!

4. Click the Garland tab (admin/build/themes/settings/garland) to access the Garland-specific theme settings, which include an integrated color-picker from the Color module.

5. Choose a color scheme that is pleasing to the eye and complements the logo. Be creative! When you're happy with the results, click "Save configuration."

6. The page looks a little cluttered now with both the site logo and the "Mom & Pop, Inc." site name at the top. Let's turn off the visibility of that feature. Uncheck "Site name" in the "Toggle display" fieldset, and click "Save configuration" again.

When finished, you should have a site that now boasts Mom and Pop, Inc.'s slick Web 2.0 logo, along with a color scheme that's all their own, as shown in Figure 2-49.

Figure 2-49. Website bearing new logo and colors

Spotlight: Content Editing and Image Handling

We now have a site with all the functionality that Jeanne and Mike asked for, access control configured properly, and a slick new look, complete with a custom color scheme and fancy new logo. However, one final piece remains: streamlining the content editing process, and allowing easy image uploads.

Content Editing

As mentioned previously in the chapter, by default Drupal's content entry is done with HTML. Like most earthlings, Mike and Jeanne aren't fluent in code, so it's important that they be able to format their content and add images without it. Not surprisingly, a number of community solutions to this issue have cropped up over the years:

Toolbars
> Some users can use HTML fine if they're given a toolbar that inserts the tags on their behalf. The BUEditor module (*http://drupal.org/project/bueditor*), pictured in Figure 2-50, is an example of a module that provides such a toolbar.

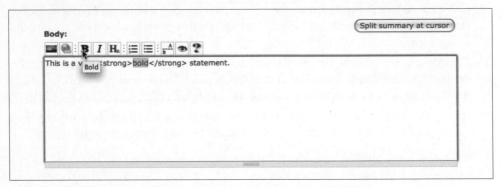

Figure 2-50. The BUEditor module provides a toolbar to assist with HTML

Text-to-HTML translators
> Modules such as Textile (*http://drupal.org/project/textile*) or Markdown Filter (*http://drupal.org/project/markdown*), covered in Chapter 5, provide the ability to take simple text such as **bold** and transform it into its HTML equivalent (bold). This syntax, once learned, is much easier and faster to type in than raw HTML.

What You See Is What You Get (WYSIWYG) editors
> WYSIWYG editors not only provide a toolbar, but also display the formatting directly in the text area, looking similar to a word processor, as pictured in Figure 2-51. There are several Drupal modules that offer integration with WYSIWYG editors, but the most popular are TinyMCE (*http://drupal.org/project/tinymce*) and FCKeditor (*http://drupal.org/project/fckeditor*).

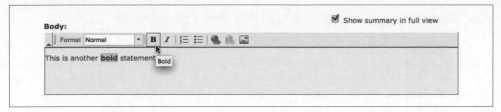

Figure 2-51. FCKeditor module displaying an editing form

The further away from raw HTML entry you go, the greater chance there is that the "smart" WYSIWYG editing plug-in will get confused and choke on complex formatting. Subtle differences between web browsers, incompatibilities with the CSS that you're using to customize your site, and other problems are all possible—if not common. Many times, the trade-off is still worth it, because the users of your site aren't interested in learning the subtleties of HTML to make something bold or italic. But due to the pitfalls, it's often best to ask, "Does my site need this?" before dropping in a "pretty" HTML editor module.

For Mike and Jeanne, we'll be using the WYSIWYG editor option. Although TinyMCE and FCKeditor are nearly functionally equivalent, the FCKeditor module has an edge, in that more Drupal 6 sites use it and the developers are much more active in maintaining it. We've therefore chosen FCKeditor for this site, although there are many other modules to choose from. The Filters/editors module category at *http://drupal.org/ project/Modules/category/63* has a list of all filter modules, including WYSIWYG editors.

It's worth keeping an eye on the WYSIWYG API module (*http://drupal .org/project/wysiwyg*). The goal of this module is to provide a single module that can support any number of WYSIWYG editors and is a likely place for future innovation for Drupal in this space.

Image Handling

One of the biggest criticisms of Drupal, apart from the fact that it does not come with a WYSIWYG editor built in, is that it has no built-in image handling. Out of the box, Drupal's built-in Upload module allows anyone with "upload files" permissions to attach image files to content they create. It's then possible for them to manually insert `<img>` tags linking those image files into the content they're writing. However, that's a pretty cumbersome process for many users, especially those attaching many images to a long post, like a magazine article.

The good news (and bad, actually), is that contributed modules provide a plethora of available options, the full extent of which is apparent in the list of Media modules at *http://drupal.org/project/Modules/category/67*. Over the past several years, quite a few

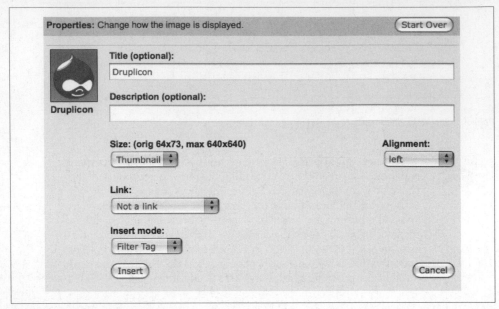

Figure 2-52. The Image Assist module

solutions to this problem have been proposed and several have been around long enough to become popular.

The Image Assist module (*http://drupal.org/project/img_assist*), pictured in Figure 2-52, takes Drupal's ability to manage different kinds of content to the extreme: it forces every image attached to a piece of content to be its very own "image" node. That makes it easier to leverage other Drupal features, like posting comments on each image or assembling galleries of images used in other posts. And before the ImageAPI module (*http://drupal.org/project/imageapi*) and the ImageCache module (*http://drupal.org/ project/imagecache*) emerged (as covered in Chapter 7), this approach was also the only easy way to automatically generate thumbnails of large images.

A more recent solution—the one that we'll be looking at in this chapter—is the IMCE module (*http://drupal.org/project/imce*), pictured in Figure 2-53. It works together with our WYSIWYG editor, giving people the opportunity to upload images in a pop-up window while they write their post. Once it's uploaded, users can insert an image into their post using the WYSIWYG editor's normal tools. IMCE also keeps track of all the images a user has uploaded in the past. It can be configured to keep each user's images in his own directory or put them all in one location. Giving each user his own directory lets each user accumulate his own library and keeps him out of other users' files. IMCE also lets you restrict things like file size and resolution, and set quotas on total space a user may take up on the server.

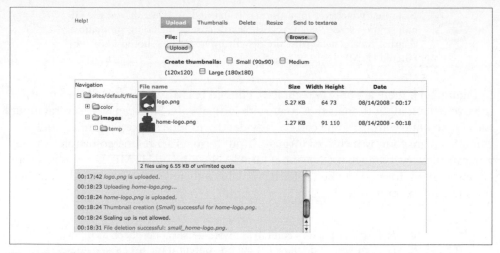

Figure 2-53. The IMCE module

Spotlight: Input Formats and Filters

You may have noticed this funny fieldset on node and block body fields that we keep ignoring called "Input formats," pictured in Figure 2-54. The *input format* that is selected for the content will affect how that content is displayed on the site. Input formats are an important security feature of Drupal, so it pays to understand them. An input format will "scan" your content and make HTML formatting changes to it before sending it to the browser for display. Each piece of content will be associated with an input format so that Drupal always knows what it is looking for and modifying, on a case-by-case basis.

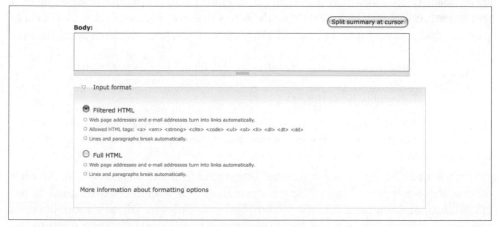

Figure 2-54. Input formats attached to a node body

Note that whichever input format is marked as "Default" on the administration screen will be accessible to *all* users, including anonymous visitors. As a general rule, the default input format should *always* be Filtered HTML.

In Figure 2-54, there are only two choices, Filtered HTML and Full HTML. These are the two default input formats that come with Drupal core. Sites can have several input formats to choose from; some can be provided by modules, like PHP filter, and you can also create your own custom formats. Input formats are restricted by roles so that you can allow everyone to use one input format, like Filtered HTML, but also make an advanced input format, like Full HTML, available only to your most trusted users, like the site administrator role.

 If a user reports a node's edit tab as mysteriously gone, check its input format. Drupal will disallow editing on content if the user's role does not have access to the input format of the content. This behavior can be used to your advantage if you want to protect certain pages from editing by users who would otherwise have access to do so.

Input formats are composed of *filters*. Figure 2-55 shows the list of filters that are used in the Filtered HTML input format. The filters are doing the real work; the input format is simply a group of filters. A filter modifies content and outputs the proper HTML for display. Examples of filters include "Line break converter," which transforms new lines (carriage returns) into `<br />` and `<p>` tags, and "URL filter," which transforms a text URL such as *http://www.example.com* into a clickable link, like `<a href="http://www.example.com">http://www.example.com</a>`. Filters can be used to do useful or fun things with your content (like the Pirate module [*http://drupal.org/project/pirate*], which transforms your text into pirate talk), but they are really important when talking about security on your site. People can do all kinds of malicious things when given a text entry box in a web browser. Using the filters that are specifically designed to help strip out malicious content, like the HTML filter, can save your site from being hacked.

 The most important filter of all is "HTML filter," which strips out dangerous HTML tags and protects your site from various sneaky attacks that could trick a browser into embedding malicious JavaScript or other executable code. This filter is enabled by default only on the Filtered HTML input format. Make sure that you implicitly trust anyone who has access to a format without this filter included, such as Full HTML.

Filters are ordered within input formats by assigning them "weights," and the filter modifications happen in that sequence. You can see the default order for the Filtered HTML format in Figure 2-56. Many contributed modules let you add more filters to your site, and you can mix and match them as you like, either adding them to the

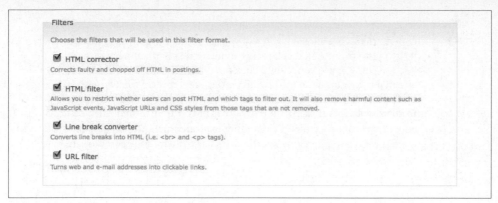

Figure 2-55. Filters for the filtered HTML input format

existing input formats or making your own. This feature will be covered in more detail in Chapter 5 when we discuss adding filters.

Name	Weight
⊹ URL filter	0 ▲▼
⊹ HTML filter	1 ▲▼
⊹ Line break converter	10 ▲▼
⊹ HTML corrector	10 ▲▼

Figure 2-56. Reordering filters for the Filtered HTML input format

A very important point to understand about formats is that they are applied only when the content is leaving the database and about to be displayed on the page. When a user enters content into a form and saves it, that content is stored in the database exactly the way it was written. When someone visits the page to view it, Drupal retrieves the raw information from the database, applies the format that is associated with it, running through each filter in turn, and then displays the final result to the browser. You can see a visual representation of this workflow in Figure 2-57. You should note that each filter is applying its own rules, in turn, to get to the finished display. If we had set this particular piece of content to use the Full HTML input format, instead of Filtered HTML, then the end result would be a bit different. With Filtered HTML, the text "alert('I cAn pwn U');" is printed out to the screen because the "script" tags are removed prior to display. With Full HTML, these tags would not be stripped and the script in the text would be *executed* rather than displayed as plain text. In this example that script would cause a harmless JavaScript window to pop up that says "I cAn pwn U" in it, but it could just as easily be a malicious script that could wreak havoc.

Because Drupal strips only on output, if you are using something in your content that is not allowed, you will still see it there when you go to edit it; it is just stripped on display. If you notice this happening and think you are going crazy, you should check the input format for the content and make sure it is not set to one that is designed to strip what you want to display. The most common instance of this behavior is when trying to display an image using the Filtered HTML input format. You can extend the tags that the HTML Filter will allow at Administer→Site configuration→Input formats (admin/settings/filters) to accommodate your tags.

Hands-On: Setting Up FCKeditor

Before we dig into the editor's setup, we will need all of the modules and requirements. You should download the latest versions of the FCKeditor and IMCE modules as you did earlier for the Administration Menu module in the "Hands-On: Working with Modules" section. The project page for FCKeditor is located at *http://drupal.org/project/ fckeditor* and the project page for IMCE is at *http://drupal.org/project/imce*. Once you have the modules in place, we still aren't quite done yet, because the FCKeditor module doesn't actually contain the FCKeditor software itself. This is because the FCKeditor software comes from its own, external open source website and community that develops and maintains it, outside of the Drupal community.

1. Go to *http://www.fckeditor.net* and click the Download link in the upper-right navigation area on the site, as shown in Figure 2-58.

2. The first version listed in the Download section will be the latest version of FCKeditor. In Figure 2-59, this is FCKeditor 2.6.3. Under the version listed are two links that you can use to download. The only difference is in the type of compression used, zip or tar, so you can use either. Click the link listed for the version you want. In Figure 2-59, this would be *FCKeditor_2.6.3.zip* or *FCKeditor_2.6.3.tar.gz*.

3. Once you have the file downloaded, go ahead and extract it. You should be presented with a folder named *fckeditor*.

4. You need to copy this folder into your FCKeditor module folder. There is already an empty folder with this name in there, so you want to *replace* that folder with the new one you just extracted. All of the similar names can get quite confusing, so make sure that your finished result has the following directory structure leading down to the FCKeditor software's main PHP file (also shown in Figure 2-60): *sites/ all/modules/fckeditor/fckeditor/fckeditor.php*.

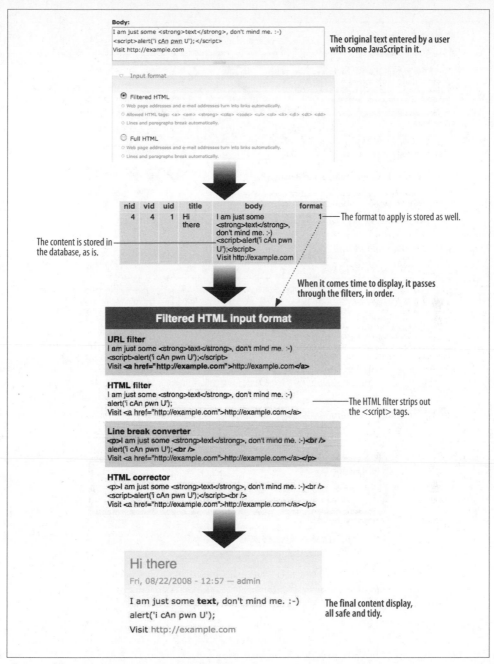

Figure 2-57. Input format workflow from page creation to display

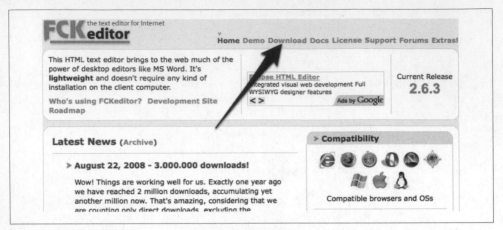

Figure 2-58. The Download link on the FCKeditor website

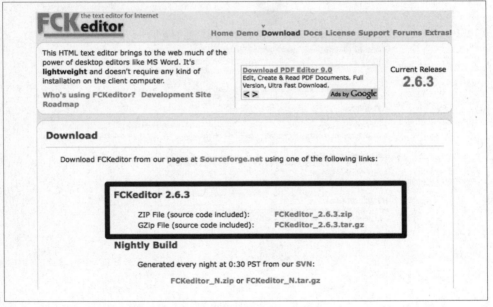

Figure 2-59. File download links for FCKeditor

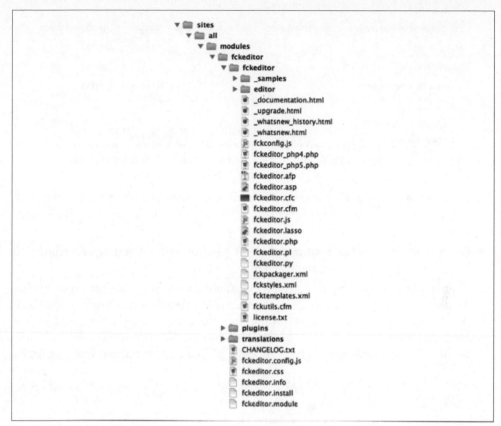

Figure 2-60. Directory structure for the FCKeditor module

Now that we have our modules and the FCKeditor package itself, we can continue with installation and configuration.

1. Head to Administer→Site building→Modules (admin/build/modules), and enable the following modules:
   - Other package
     — FCKeditor
     — IMCE

2. Go to Administer→User management→Permissions (admin/user/permissions) and check off the permissions shown in Table 2-22. Click the "Save permissions" button when done.

Table 2-22. FCKeditor module permissions

Permission: fckeditor module	anonymous user	authenticated user	editor	site administrator
access fckeditor	Checked	Checked	Checked	Checked
administer editor				Checked
allow fckeditor file uploads			Checked	Checked

> Normally, we could get away with just checking off anonymous and authenticated users, as all roles are also authenticated users. However, FCKeditor profiles are based only on the roles with the "access fckeditor" permission explicitly checked.

3. Because User 1 is initially not assigned to any roles beyond authenticated user, click "My account," and then the Edit tab (user/1/edit), and check the site administrator role.

4. Go to Administer→Site configuration→FCKeditor (admin/settings/fckeditor) to bring up the FCKeditor settings screen.

5. There are two profiles already created for us, but they don't quite line up with what we need. Let's repurpose those and change a few settings to match our needs. Click the "edit" link for the Default profile and make the changes indicated in Table 2-23. When you're done, click the "Update profile" button to save your new profile. This step will provide some nice, simple formatting options for most users.

Table 2-23. Settings for the Default FCKeditor profile

Field	Value
Basic setup	
Roles allowed to use this profile	anonymous user
	authenticated user
File browser settings	
File browser type	IMCE

6. We are returned to the FCkeditor settings page at Administer→Site configuration→FCKeditor (admin/settings/fckeditor). Our editors, Mike and Jeanne, will need more formatting options when creating their content, so we will use the Advanced profile for them along with Goldie. Click the "edit" link for the Advanced profile and match the settings shown in Table 2-24. Click the "Update profile" button when you are finished.

Table 2-24. Settings for the Advanced FCKeditor profile

Basic setup	
Roles allowed to use this profile	editor
	site administrator
	(Note: you should uncheck the authenticated user checkbox.)
File browser settings	
File browser type	IMCE

 FCKeditor provides a selection of toolbars from which you can choose. If you want to modify which buttons appear on the toolbar or create a new toolbar, you can do so by editing a configuration file that comes with the module. You can find the *fckeditor.con fig.js* file inside the *sites/all/modules/fckeditor* directory. Once you open it, you will see the toolbars with the buttons listed underneath them. Make sure that you make a copy of the original file before making any edits, so you can go back to it if you need to.

We now have some nice toolbars, but we have a small problem with our input formats. FCKeditor will add the HTML we want behind the scenes, but Drupal will strip quite a lot of it out using our default Filtered HTML format. We are using two different toolbars and they have different format needs.

The editor toolbar has many buttons and will be using all kinds of HTML. It is also used by only our most trusted users: the site administrator and the owners. Because this toolbar is used by trusted users only, the easiest thing to do is to simply give them access to the Full HTML filter so they have the freedom to use what they need to make their posts look good.

The toolbar for regular and anonymous users has only a few options on it, and these users are definitely not trusted. We need to let them use a few more HTML tags than the default Filtered HTML format will give them, but we most certainly don't want them to have Full HTML access. To get that toolbar working smoothly, we will need to modify the Filtered HTML format to accommodate the extra tags we need.

1. Go to Administer→Site configuration→Input formats (admin/settings/filters), where you will see our two default formats listed.

2. Click the configure link for the Full HTML format (admin/settings/filters/2).

3. We see a list of roles that may use this format; currently none are selected. Check off the editor and site administrator roles and then click "Save configuration" to finish.

4. Our Advanced profile will work properly now. Let's turn our attention to the Default profile. Click the configure link for the Filtered HTML format (admin/settings/filters/1).

5. To actually edit the HTML filter that is determining which tags we can and cannot use, click the Configure tab (admin/settings/filters/1/configure).

6. You will see a list of HTML tags under the "HTML filter" section in the "Allowed HTML tags" field. We need to add the following list of tags to the end of the existing list: `<img> <div> <pre> <address> <h1> <h2> <h3> <h4> <h5> <h6>` (note the spaces between each tag). These tags will allow the image button and the list of formats in the Format drop-down to display properly. Click the "Save configuration" button when done.

We now have a nice toolbar for our users that will format things and play nicely with Drupal's formats, as pictured in Figure 2-61.

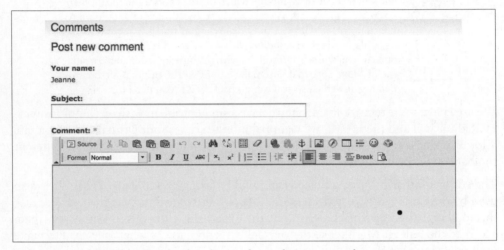

Figure 2-61. Advanced toolbar for the editor and site administrator roles

However, if you play with the toolbar a bit, you will notice that although it is nice to have the image button, it requires us to insert a URL for the image. Well, Mike and Jeanne don't know much about that. They need to be able to browse, upload, and insert images from their computers. To make that image button provide us with a way to upload, let's set up the IMCE module.

1. Go to Administer→Site configuration→IMCE (admin/settings/imce).

2. We see two premade profiles that we can use. The User-1 profile is obviously designed for User 1, but will also nicely suit our needs for the editors and the site administrator. We can use the Sample profile for the regular site users. Click the Edit link for the User-1 profile.

3. We want to tweak a few settings here. Change the Profile name to **Advanced** to match the FCKeditor profile name. This is a way for us to know that these are related in terms of how we are setting up our site, but isn't necessary for any of this work.

4. We should also change the Maximum image resolution size to **800x600**, as that is sufficiently large for their needs and 1200×1200 has the potential to break the layout of our site.

5. Click the "Save configuration" button.

6. To be consistent with naming, we'll rename the other profile too. Return to Administer→Site configuration→IMCE (admin/settings/imce) and this time click the Edit link for the Sample profile.

7. Change the "Profile name" to **Default**. The rest of the default settings should be fine, so click "Save configuration" to finish.

8. The last thing we need to do is make sure that we assign the correct profiles to the correct roles. Return to Administer→Site configuration→IMCE (admin/settings/imce) and under the "Role-profile assignments" section, set the assignments in Table 2-25. (Note that we don't need to change the weights.) We aren't going to use any profile for anonymous users, so they will be able to link to images but not upload images to the Mom and Pop server.

Table 2-25. Role-profile assignments for IMCE

User role	Assigned profile
site administrator	Advanced
editor	Advanced
authenticated user	Default

9. Click "Save configuration" and we are done!

Now, if you go to create new content, you will see a nice toolbar on your screen that looks like Figure 2-61.

Summary

This chapter provided an overview of the major functionality of Drupal by building a small website. We installed Drupal, we created some simple content and content types, we got a taste of the taxonomy system, we set up a contact form, we worked on how to configure Drupal's theme settings to customize a site to a particular look and feel, and we set our editors up with a WYSIWYG editor and image handling so that they can make their posts look just the way they want without knowing HTML.

Here is a list of modules we referenced in this chapter:

- Administration menu: *http://drupal.org/project/admin_menu*
- FCKeditor: *http://drupal.org/project/fckeditor*
- IMCE: *http://drupal.org/project/imce*

Here is a list of links that we referenced in this chapter:

- Drupal core download: *http://drupal.org/download*
- Module downloads: *http://drupal.org/project/Modules*
- Theme downloads: *http://drupal.org/project/Themes*
- FCKeditor website: *http://fckeditor.net*
- Drupal system requirements: *http://drupal.org/node/270*
- Drupal version information: *http://drupal.org/handbook/version-info*
- Drupal.org handbooks: *http://drupal.org/handbooks*
- Getting Started guide: *http://drupal.org/node/258*
- Troubleshooting FAQ: *http://drupal.org/Troubleshooting-FAQ*
- Support forum: *http://drupal.org/forum/18*
- XAMPP (local web server): *http://www.apachefriends.org/en/xampp.html*
- MAMP (local web server): *http://mamp.info/en/download.html*
- StuffIt Expander: *http://my.smithmicro.com/mac/stuffitexpander*

## CHAPTER 3

Job Posting Board

This chapter outlines the two most powerful features in Drupal. Yes, we're saying outright that the two most powerful features are the Content Construction Kit and Views. The *Content Construction Kit* (commonly abbreviated CCK) allows you to create forms containing a variety of fields—such as checkboxes, select lists, image uploads, and many others—all without writing a line of code. The *Views* module is the natural counterpart to CCK, letting you get data out of your site rather than into it. Views allows you to create pages and blocks that pull data back out and display it to your visitors. Want a paged table showing product details that can be sorted by price or manufacturer? You can build it with CCK and Views. Want to display a block that lists the albums of a particular artist in a grid as a set of album cover thumbnails? You can build it with CCK and Views. Anywhere there's a list of content on your website (and most websites are almost *all* just lists of content in one form or another), CCK and Views are the two key modules you need.

CCK and Views form the foundation of nearly every other project in this book and most of the Drupal-powered websites on the Internet. We'll cover how to set up a new content type and customize the node form so that you can add any type of field for inputting data. We'll configure a site that allows the creating of job openings, and then we'll build an interface for browsing though available jobs.

This chapter introduces the following modules:

CCK *(http://drupal.org/project/cck)*
    Adds fields to content types

Views *(http://drupal.org/project/views)*
    Creates lists of content and users

FileField *(http://drupal.org/project/filefield)*
    Adds a field for uploading files to content types

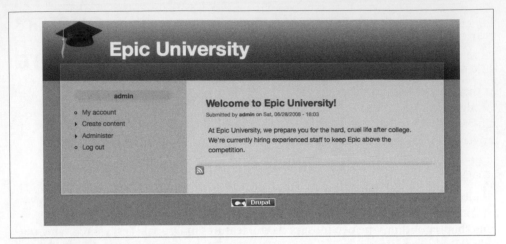

Figure 3-1. The Epic University site after installation

If you would like to participate in the hands-on exercises in this chapter, you should install Drupal using the *Job Posting* installation profile from the book's sample code. Doing this will create the example website on your web server. The website will look as pictured in Figure 3-1 and at *http://jobs.usingdrupal.com*. For more information on using the book's installation profiles, see the Preface.

Case Study

Several students on work-study at Epic University have been tasked with building a job posting website for their school. The university needs to have the site built in a short amount of time on their internal servers. Because students are building the site, it's also obviously on a tight budget. Because of its flexible node system, user management, and low cost, the students chose to download Drupal and get started building a site.

The Human Resources department requires that university faculty be able to post job openings, which include a description, department, contact person, and salary information. Users should be able to sign into the site and view both lists of all available openings and lists of openings within a single specific department. Additionally, users should be able to apply for a specific position, and to view a record of all positions to which they've applied.

Implementation Notes

Drupal core provides this site with a good starting point. It provides the needed user authentication and allows the creation of several different types of content, such as "job" and "application" types. Drupal's out-of-box functionality gives each one of these new types only a "Title" and "Body" field. We'll need quite a few more fields so that users can enter data into different fields, and so that we can pull out information from certain fields to make listings of content.

Custom input forms

At the heart of the requirements for this website, textual data will need to be inserted through a variety of forms. CCK provides the means to enter data into the site. CCK can provide several different kinds of fields needed, like a drop-down select list for the university department, or simple text fields for phone numbers and addresses.

Listings

Besides entering data into the website, job applicants and employers will want to view lists of potential jobs and applicants. For nearly any purpose of displaying content, the Views module can provide a listing of content in a variety of ways: a table, a list of full nodes or teasers, an RSS feed, a list of individual fields, and more. We'll build all the necessary lists for this chapter as views, including special views that can take a user ID or department and filter down to include only relevant content.

File uploads

Although Drupal core provides the Upload module for attaching files to content, it suffers from the following drawbacks:

- Upload functionality gets turned on by default for all content types. Most of the time, you want files attached to only one or two content types.
- All files get uploaded into the "root" of your files directory, which can become messy when you have several hundred files.
- The Upload module provides the ability to upload an unlimited number of files per node. Sometimes you want to allow users to upload only a single file per node, or a maximum of three (for example).
- Uploading a file with the Upload module requires expanding a "File attachments" fieldset, but often a file is a prominent part of a piece of content, so this "digging down" requirement is not desirable.
- The Upload module enforces a site-wide size quota and list of allowed file extensions for all users in a particular role; often, you need more flexibility in assigning these types of settings.
- The Upload module does not allow you to have more than one file browse field or to name it something specific.

Fortunately for us, the FileField contributed module for CCK helps get around each of these drawbacks. File fields may be added and configured on a per-content-type basis, and offer much more fine-grained configuration.

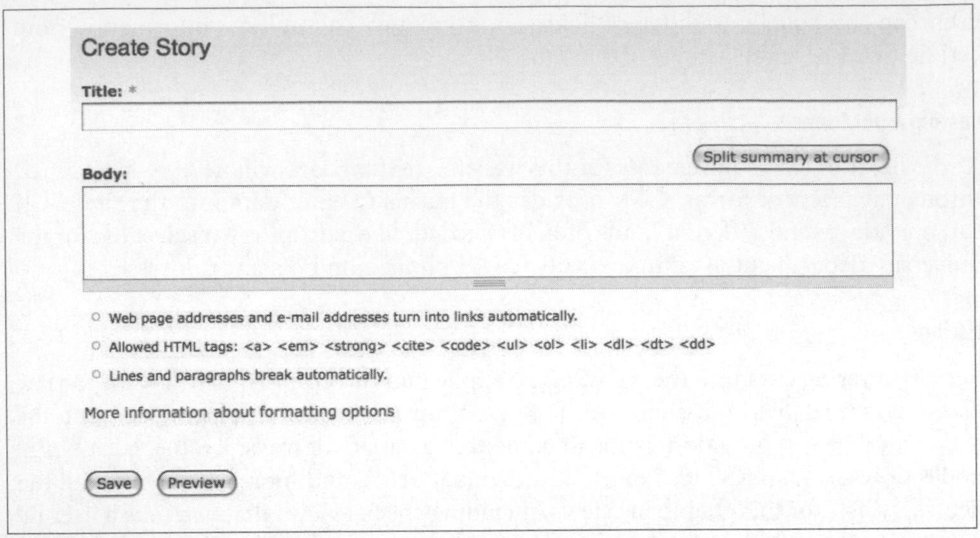

Figure 3-2. The Story content form, as presented to an authenticated user on a new Drupal site

Spotlight: CCK

CCK is an extremely flexible framework for creating forms to enter content. Although the Drupal core provides the ability to create different content types (such as a Job Opening or Application), it does not yet provide a mechanism for adding fields to the newly created types. Until CCK fields become integrated into Drupal core (which is expected in future releases), installing CCK should be the first step in nearly any Drupal website.

Upon installing a new copy of Drupal, there are two content types provided: Story and Page. Both are fundamentally the same thing—a form that contains a Title field and a Body field. Any additional content types that are created will also contain a Title field and (optionally) a Body field; it takes an add-on module like CCK to add additional fields to a content type. Figure 3-2 depicts the Story content type as it appears prior to adding fields with CCK.

After enabling the CCK module, any number of custom fields may be added to any content type. Combined with Drupal core's ability to create any number of custom content types, CCK lets you create any number of completely customized forms for adding content. Figure 3-3 shows the same form after adding a few custom fields, such as an additional text field, an image field, and a set of radio buttons.

After adding the fields, CCK can automatically handle saving information to the database, and after data is submitted, presenting this information in a variety of ways.

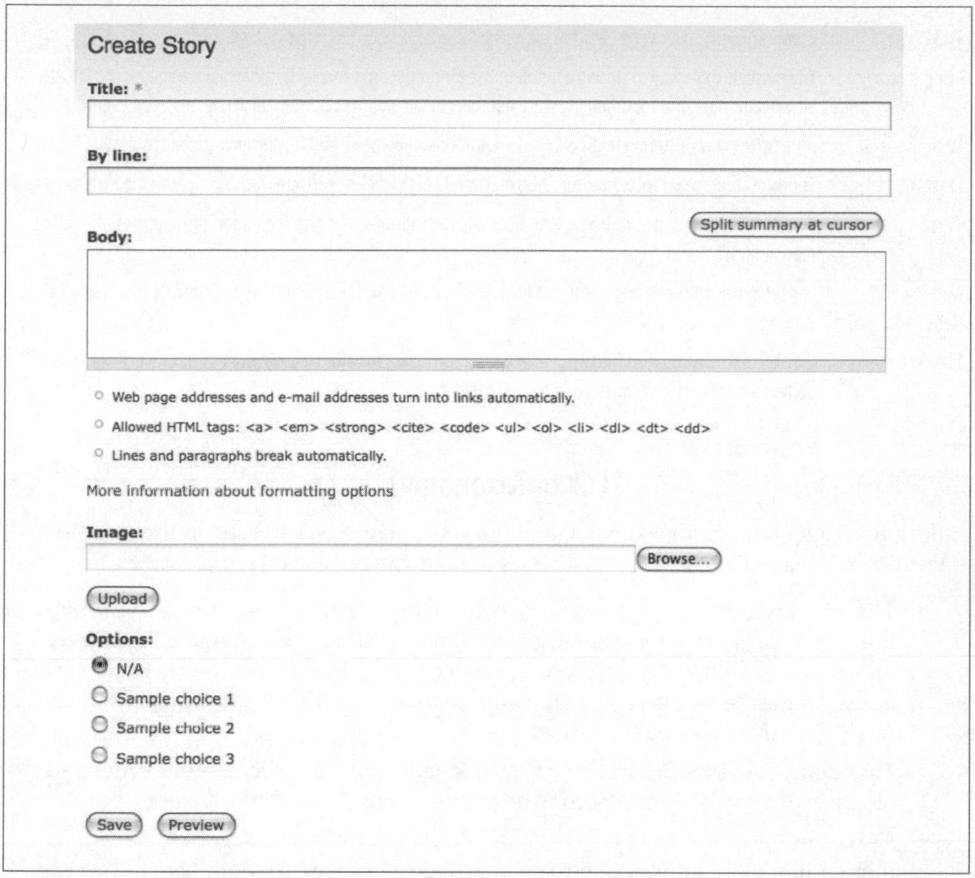

Create Story

Title: *

By line:

Body:

[Split summary at cursor]

- Web page addresses and e-mail addresses turn into links automatically.
- Allowed HTML tags: <a> <em> <strong> <cite> <code> <ul> <ol> <li> <dl> <dt> <dd>
- Lines and paragraphs break automatically.

More information about formatting options

Image:

[Browse...]

(Upload)

Options:

- ● N/A
- ○ Sample choice 1
- ○ Sample choice 2
- ○ Sample choice 3

(Save) (Preview)

Figure 3-3. The Story content type form, after adding custom fields

Fields

Functionally, CCK is set up into two end-user pieces. The first of these are *fields*, which allow a user to save data into your site. Fields represent the type of data that needs to be saved, such as integer, decimal, or text. When choosing a field to add to a content type, the first decision you need to make is what kind of data is being stored "behind the scenes" in the form. Will the information entered into the form be something basic like text or numbers, or something more special like a relationship to another node or user? The field types included in CCK "core" are displayed in Table 3-1. Other modules, such as Fivestar (*http://drupal.org/project/fivestar*), ImageField (*http://drupal.org/project/imagefield*), and Date (*http://drupal.org/project/date*), add more field types to CCK. These CCK field modules are covered later in the book, in Chapters 4, 7, and 9, respectively. A full list of available CCK field types is available at *http://drupal.org/taxonomy/term/88*.

Table 3-1. Built-in CCK field types

Field type	Common uses
Integer	The most efficient way of storing a number. Use for product numbers, identifiers, or whenever you'll have an exact number of something, like track numbers on an album or number of attendees at an event.
Decimal	An efficient way of storing numbers to a certain decimal point. Useful for currency amounts.
Float	The most accurate way of storing numbers that need a high level of precision, such as scientific measurements.
Text	Can store any string of text. Useful for names and descriptions, and also for longer full-text content such as biographies.
Node Reference	Can reference any node on the site in a field. Useful when one piece of content is related to another piece of content.
User Reference	Can reference any user on the site in a field. Useful when associating a user with a certain piece of content, such as a coordinator or contact person for an event.

CCK or Taxonomy?

Both the Taxonomy module and CCK allow you to create select lists on the form for creating content. Here are a few guidelines to help you choose one or the other:

- The primary purpose of Taxonomy is to create categories, so if you're putting things into categories, you should generally use the Taxonomy module. If you ever make a CCK field called "Category," think twice. The Taxonomy module was made for that exact purpose, and many existing modules provide integration directly with the Taxonomy module.

- Taxonomy provides hierarchies of categorization that are very easy to order and organize. If your categories need to be put into a tree, Taxonomy is a good choice.

- Taxonomy provides only a "Title" and "Description" for categories. Situations that require more information to be attached to categories would benefit by creating a content type for the category, then creating a CCK node reference field to select nodes in that category.

- A general rule of thumb is that if you can remove the field and the content type still makes sense, use Taxonomy. An article filed under a "Technology" category is still an article if you remove the category association, so Taxonomy is a good fit. If the field is *part* of a piece of content, such as an album's recording artist, then CCK is generally a better choice.

Widgets

Once the type of data is determined, then it's time to think about how it should look in the form. In CCK lingo, the form elements are called *widgets*. Do you want a dropdown select list, or a group of radio buttons? Checkboxes or an autocomplete text field? Choose the widget that makes the most sense for the user entering the data. Note that the widgets available will vary based on the field type chosen.

The widget types included in CCK core are displayed in Table 3-2. As with fields, add-on modules often expose additional widget choices.

Table 3-2. Built-in CCK widget types

Widget type	Common uses
Text field	This widget allows a single line of text to be entered, such as a name or phone number. Either plain text or formatted text entry is supported.
Text area (multiple rows)	Use this widget for entering a larger paragraph of text, such as a biography or a product description. Either plain text or formatted text entry is supported.
Single on/off checkbox	Use when something can only be answered "yes" or "no"; for example, a field that asks whether a user would like to be added to a mailing list.
Checkboxes/Radio buttons	Use when there are multiple options to select from; checkboxes will be used for fields that support selecting multiple values, radios for a single value only. In most cases, a "Gender" field makes sense as a radio button selection, whereas a "Favorite colors" field makes sense as a collection of checkboxes.
Select list	An alternative to checkboxes and radio buttons is a drop-down select list. Useful when there are many different options to choose from and it would be cumbersome to display each inline as a separate choice.
Autocomplete text field	This widget displays a text field that, as it's typed into, displays results that start with the letters entered. Typing "st" would bring up terms like "Stewart," "Studebaker," and "Style." Useful when there are a huge number of options to choose from and displaying them all in a select list would be too much to sort through. However, it requires users to have an idea of what they're searching for.

Formatters

Complementing the configuration of field input, *formatters* allow you to adjust how the data will be output when it is displayed to the users of your site. For example, decimals could be displayed with or without commas to indicate thousands, such as in Figure 3-4.

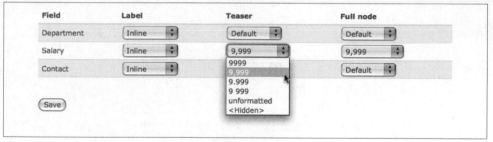

Figure 3-4. Configuring the display of a field formatter

Other modules may add additional formatters, giving you a plethora of ways of displaying information. The ImageCache module, covered in Chapter 7, is an example of such a module; it allows the display of resized images.

Keep in mind that the formatters available depend on the type of the data, making it very important to set up a field as an integer, decimal, or float if you'll be displaying numbers. CCK won't let you change the data type after the field has been set up, so if you need to change the type of field from text to integer (or any other conversion), you'll need to delete the field and add a new one with the desired type.

Hands-On: CCK

To get started with our Job Posting website, let's think about the different content types needed to build all the functionality that we require. The site requires two different types:

Job Type
: Description and details of a particular job opening.

Job Application Type
: An application ties together an individual and a particular job.

We will need to relate job applications back to the appropriate job openings, as well as relate jobs back to the appropriate contact person. The node reference and user reference fields mentioned earlier in the chapter will be an essential tool.

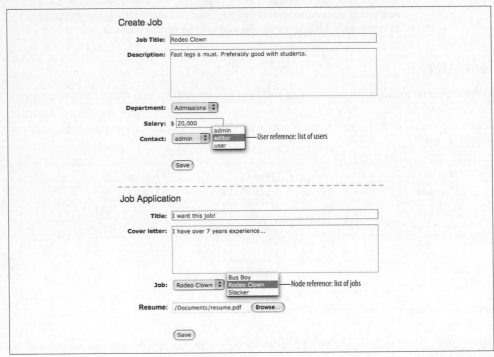

Figure 3-5. A mock-up of the forms required for the job website

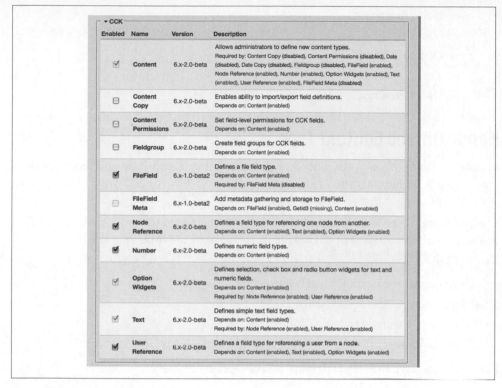

Figure 3-6. Enabling CCK modules

When building out content types in Drupal, it's best to start with a mental picture of what the form looks like that you're trying to build. Figure 3-5 shows a sketch of both the job and job application forms that we're shooting for.

1. To enable CCK, go to Administer ›Site building→Modules (admin/build/modules). Enabling CCK involves two parts: enabling the Content module, which is the "core" of CCK, and enabling one or more "field" or "widget" modules.

 The FileField module is a separate module that is not included as part of the default CCK installation. It may be downloaded from *http://drupal.org/project/filefield*, and is also included in the book's source code.

2. Enable the following modules and click "Save configuration." After the modules are enabled the page should look like Figure 3-6:

   • CCK package:
     —Content
     —FileField

—Node Reference

—Number

—Option Widgets

—Text

—User Reference

Hands-On: Job Content Type

In order to build this site, we'll need to go beyond the default Page and Story content types offered by Drupal core. This section will cover how to add your own custom content type, as well as add custom fields to it with CCK.

The Job content type will contain all the information we need to store about a particular position that's available at Epic University. It will need the following fields:

- Job Title (the normal node title)
- Description (the normal node body)
- Department (a text select field)
- Contact (a user reference field)
- Salary (an integer field)

Let's walk through the steps to create this new content type:

1. Start by visiting the main content type settings page under Administer→Content management→Content types (admin/content/types). Click the "Add content type" tab at the top of the page (admin/content/types/add).

2. Using the settings indicated in Table 3-3, create a new content type called Job. We repurpose the Title and Body fields for Job title and Description, respectively, simply by changing their labels. Be sure to expand the fieldset for "Submission form settings" to enter the title and body field labels. When completed, your screen should look similar to Figure 3-7.

Table 3-3. Settings for the Job content type

Field	Value
Identification	
Name	Job
Type	job
Description	A currently available job position
Submission form settings	
Title field label	Job title
Body field label	Description

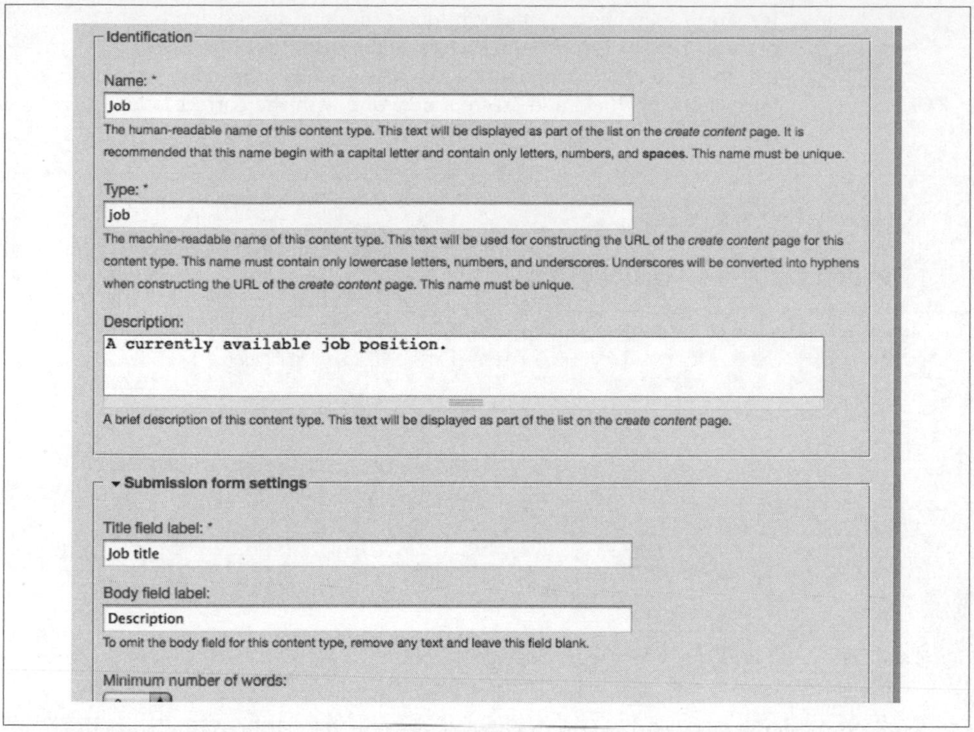

Figure 3-7. Adding a new "Job" content type

3. After submitting the form with the "Save content type" button, the new content type will be created. Click the "manage fields" link for the Job content type (admin/content/node-type/job/fields) to add our first custom field.

4. Use the settings from Table 3-4 and pictured in Figure 3-8 to complete the New field form to add a new select list for the Department field. Choose Text as the field type, as the field will be used to store text values. Once you've selected the field type, the widget type selection will appear.

Table 3-4. "New field" settings for Department option

Field	Value
Label	Department
Field name	department
Select a field type	Text
Select a widget	Select list

It's worth spending a couple of minutes thinking about what type of data a field will store before selecting the field type. Once selected, the field type can't be changed. If you make a mistake, you must delete the field and create a new one with the correct field type.

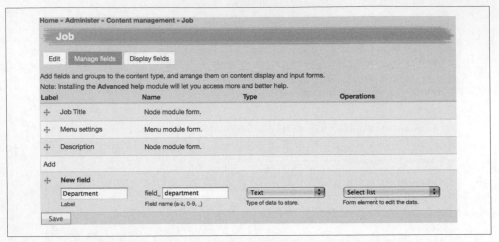

Figure 3-8. The "Add field" form for the Department field

5. After clicking the Save button, on the next page, you'll be able to fine-tune the new select list. Use the values from Table 3-5 and pictured in Figure 3-9 to give this select list a description and populate the options a user may select.

Table 3-5. Configuration for the Department field

Field	Value
Job settings	
Help text	Select the department in which this job belongs.
Global settings	
Allowed values list	Administration
	Arts
	Athletics
	Business
	Education
	Health Sciences
	Sciences

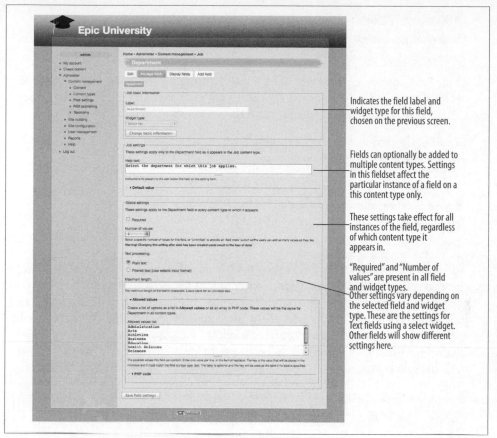

Indicates the field label and widget type for this field, chosen on the previous screen.

Fields can optionally be added to multiple content types. Settings in this fieldset affect the particular instance of a field on a this content type only.

These settings take effect for all instances of the field, regardless of which content type it appears in.

"Required" and "Number of values" are present in all field and widget types. Other settings vary depending on the selected field and widget type. These are the settings for Text fields using a select widget. Other fields will show different settings here.

Figure 3-9. CCK field configuration form

 If you've accidentally made a mistake on the CCK field configuration form, don't worry. Click the "configure" link from the "Manage fields" tab (admin/content/node-type/job/fields) at any time, and you can alter the field's settings.

6. After the new field is saved by clicking the "Save field settings" button, you should be returned to the "Manage fields" tab (admin/content/node-type/job/fields). We can now add the Salary field. Fill in the settings for the new field from Table 3-6. We'll add the salary as an integer, but if you want to include cents in the salary, you can use a decimal field instead.

Table 3-6. Settings to create the Salary field

Field	Value
Label	Salary
Field name	salary

Field	Value
Select a field type	Integer
Select a widget	Text field

7. Click Save to create the Salary field. Finish setting up the content type with the options from Table 3-7 to prefix the salary with a $ sign and give it a description. Click "Save field settings" when finished.

Table 3-7. Configuration for the Salary field

Field	Value
Job settings	
Help text	Enter a yearly salary for this position.
Global settings	
Prefix	$

8. Add a primary Contact for this job position. This will usually be the person creating the entry, but we'll allow the user to enter any of the possible faculty members on the site. This will be done as a "User reference" field, which can be displayed as a link to another user on the site. If the site grew to include hundreds of faculty members, switching the field type from a Select List to an Autocomplete Text Field might be a good idea. Enter the values from Table 3-8 into the "New field" form, and then click Save.

Table 3-8. Settings to create the Contact field

Field	Value
Label	Contact
Field name	contact
Select a field type	User reference
Select a widget	Select list

9. Configure the user reference field so that only users of the "editor" role (to which faculty members are assigned) can be referenced as indicated in Table 3-9. We'll also leave the "Reverse link" setting unchecked. A reverse link will display a link from the contact's user profile back to each of the jobs for which she's a contact. Leaving this setting unchecked will help reduce the likelihood that she is spammed by people applying for multiple jobs at once. This narrows down the list of potential users that can be selected. Click "Save field settings" when you are done.

The "editor" user role was set up for you in the Job Website install profile, along with the "editor" user and several other sample faculty members. You can assign the "editor" role to additional users via Administer→User management→Roles (admin/user/roles).

Table 3-9. *Configuration for the Contact field*

Field	Value
Job settings	
Reverse Link	Unchecked
Help text	Select the faculty member who is the primary contact responsible for hiring this position.
Global settings	
User roles that can be referenced	editor
User status that can be referenced	Active

10. Finally, before any users can actually create pieces of Job content, they'll need to have permission to create and edit this new content type. Add permissions for the new content type at Administer→User management→Permissions (admin/user/permissions). Check the options shown in Table 3-10 and click the "Save permissions" button.

Table 3-10. *Permissions for the Job content type*

Permission: node module	anonymous user	authenticated user	editor	site administrator
create job content			Checked	Checked
delete any job content				Checked
delete own job content			Checked	Checked
edit any job content				Checked
edit own job content			Checked	Checked

Hands-On: Customizing Field Display

For usability, it's often important to display forms and page contents in a specific order, and to add formatting so that it's more clear what data is being presented. The following take you through some minor customizations to the way fields are displayed:

Before testing our form out, we should reorder the fields on the form so that they make more logical sense. Click through Administer→Content management→Content types and click "manage fields" next to the Job type (admin/content/node-type/job/fields), where you can arrange the fields however you like. Drag the handle on the left side of each row and arrange the table so that it is in the order shown in Figure 3-10, and click the Save button when finished:

- Job title
- Department
- Description
- Salary

- Contact
- Menu settings

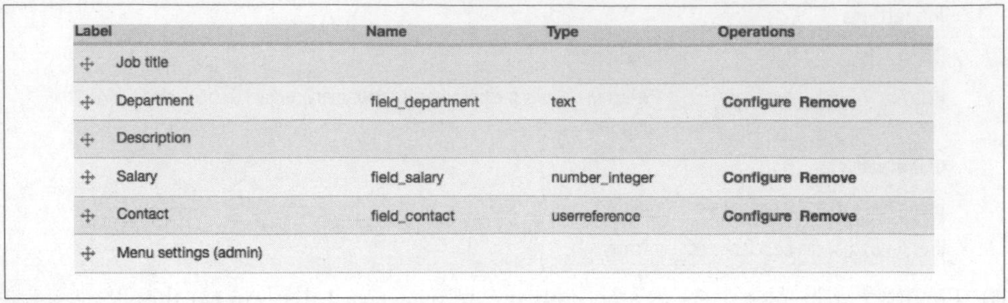

Label	Name	Type	Operations
⊹ Job title			
⊹ Department	field_department	text	Configure Remove
⊹ Description			
⊹ Salary	field_salary	number_integer	Configure Remove
⊹ Contact	field_contact	userreference	Configure Remove
⊹ Menu settings (admin)			

Figure 3-10. Field order for the Job content type

The Job content type is now nearly complete. Let's take a look at what our form currently looks like. Log in as *editor*, password *oreilly*, and create a new Job piece of content at Create content→Job (node/add/job). The form should look similar to Figure 3-11 (as *admin* user, you'll see several more options that are hidden from other users). Click Save when you're finished filling in the fields.

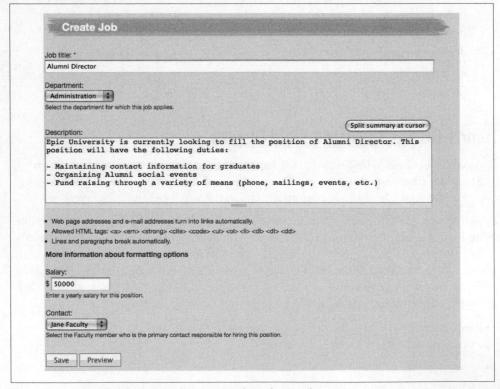

Figure 3-11. The Job form as seen by a user in the "editor" role

Taking a look at content after it's created, we'll see that it's not entirely pretty. Figure 3-12 shows the default output of our Job type when viewing the content. The labels are included above each of the fields, making the page longer than it needs to be, and the salary could really use a comma.

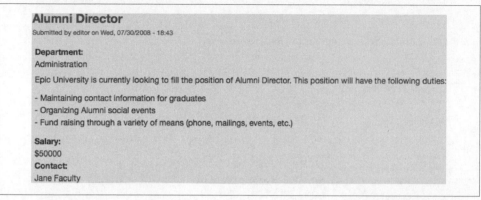

Figure 3-12. Default output of the Job content type

Fortunately, CCK provides several different ways of changing the default content, the easiest of which is CCK Formatters. Any module in Drupal is allowed to create formatters for displaying various fields, and CCK provides a few that will work in most situations. Follow these steps to change the display of the Job content to be a bit more appealing:

1. Log back in as user *admin*, password *oreilly*, go to Administer→Content management→Content types and click "edit" on the "Job type" (admin/content/node-type/job). Clicking on the "Display fields" tab will take you to the display options for the fields in the Job type. Update the form to use the values presented in Table 3-11.

Table 3-11. Display field settings for the Job content type

Field	Label value	Teaser value	Full node value
Department	Inline	Default	Default
Salary	Inline	9,999	9,999
Contact	Inline	<Hidden>	Default

2. After making the changes, your form should appear similar to the one shown in Figure 3-13.

3. After saving the changes, take a look at the Job piece of content a second time. The new, cleaner look is shown in Figure 3-14.

Now you can see that our labels are displayed next to the values, rather than on a separate line. Commas are automatically placed in the correct location for the Salary field.

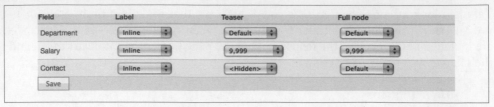

Field	Label	Teaser	Full node
Department	Inline	Default	Default
Salary	Inline	9,999	9,999
Contact	Inline	<Hidden>	Default
Save			

Figure 3-13. Display field settings for the Job content type

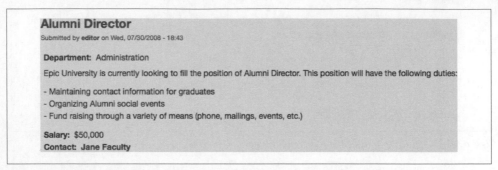

Alumni Director
Submitted by **editor** on Wed, 07/30/2008 - 18:43

Department: Administration

Epic University is currently looking to fill the position of Alumni Director. This position will have the following duties:

- Maintaining contact information for graduates
- Organizing Alumni social events
- Fund raising through a variety of means (phone, mailings, events, etc.)

Salary: $50,000
Contact: Jane Faculty

Figure 3-14. Job content after configuring the field display

 If PHP doesn't scare you (too much), and you want much more fine-grained control over the look of your website's content types, check out the Content Templates (Contemplate) module (*http://drupal.org/project/contemplate*). Contemplate is an alternative to theming (see Chapter 11 for an introduction) that provides a web-based interface for editing the display code for content types, so you can control exactly what appears, how, and where.

Hands-On: Job Application Type

Now that the university is able to create job positions, it would be helpful if users could submit résumés to the positions in which they're interested. We'll create another content type called "Job Application" or just "application" for short, using the following fields:

- Title (the normal node title)
- Introductory message (the normal node body)
- Job (node reference field)
- Résumé (file field)

1. Return to the main content type settings page under Administer→Content management→Content types (admin/content/types). Add another content type by clicking on the "Add content type" tab at the top of the page.

2. On the "Add content type" page, fill in the form with the values from Table 3-12. Again, we'll easily create the first two fields (Title and Introductory message) by reusing the Title and Body fields provided by Drupal core.

Table 3-12. Settings for the Job content type

Field	Value
Identification	
Name	Job Application
Type	application
Description	An application for a job position
Submission form settings	
Title field label	Title
Body field label	Introductory message

3. After submitting the form with the "Save content type" button, the new content type will be created. Click the "manage fields" link for the "Job application" type (admin/content/node-type/application/fields). Use the settings from Table 3-13 to add a node reference field for the job type. This will connect a particular "Job application" node with the Job node.

Table 3-13. Add field settings for Job node reference

Field	Value
Label	Job
Field name	Job
Select a field type	Node reference
Select a widget	Select list

4. Click Save and configure the Job node reference field with the values from Table 3-14.

Table 3-14. Settings for the Job node reference field

Field	Value
Global settings	
Required	Checked
Content types that can be referenced	Job

5. The last thing required for our job application type is to allow users to upload a résumé or some other file with their application. We could potentially use the core Upload module, but to gain the configuration flexibility of CCK, we'll use a file field, provided by the FileField module. Click "manage fields" (admin/content/node-type/application/fields) to add the file field using the settings from Table 3-15 and then click Continue.

Table 3-15. Add field settings for the Résumé file field

Field	Value
Label	Résumé
Field name	resume
Select a field type	File
Select a widget type	File Upload

6. On the next screen, continue to fill in the details with the settings from Table 3-16 and click the "Save field settings" button. We want to restrict the types of file extensions that may be uploaded to just document files, and also specify that all files uploaded through the widget reside in a "files" subdirectory. FileField also allows control over the visibility of the file on the application node. The provided settings will force the file to always be listed, without the possibility to override that setting. However, the options here allow for cases that require that sort of flexibility.

Table 3-16. Field settings for the Résumé file field

Field	Value
Job Application settings	
Permitted upload file extensions	pdf doc txt rtf pages odf
Path settings > File path	Resumes
Global settings	
Required	Checked
Default list value	Listed
How should the list value be handled?	Enforce Default
Description Field	Disabled

 The list of supported file extensions is included automatically below the file field when it is displayed, so there's no need to duplicate that information in the field help text.

7. Now we've added all the fields needed. Order the fields on the "Manage fields" tab as follows:

- Title
- Job
- Introductory message
- Résumé
- Menu settings

8. Finally, add permissions for the new content type at Administer→User management→Permissions (admin/user/permissions). We want logged-in users to be able to manage their own job applications, and for editors to be able to manage any of the applications. Check the options shown in Table 3-17 and then click "Save permissions."

Table 3-17. Permissions for the Job Applications content type

Permission: node module	anonymous user	authenticated user	editor	site administration
create application content		Checked		
delete any application content			Checked	Checked
delete own application content		Checked		
edit any application content			Checked	Checked
edit own application content		Checked		

That finishes the configuration of the form for the Job Application content type. Let's take a look at the finished form as a user in the "authenticated user" role. After logging in with the username *user* and password *oreilly*, the form at Create content→Job Application (node/add/job) should look as shown in Figure 3-15.

The *user* user was created for you automatically when you ran the Job Posting install profile.

Because job applications won't be as important visually as job listings, we'll skip configuring of the display options for this content type. You can still make these changes at Administer→Content management→Content types→Job Application→Fields (admin/content/node-type/application/fields). After a user creates a new job application, it should look something like Figure 3-16.

An important thing to note in this figure is how our node reference field (Job) appears when given a value. The default behavior is a link to the original piece of content that is referenced. Clicking on the Alumni Director link from this application will take us back to the Alumni Director job. There are other ways to display node reference fields as well, which can be explored in the "Display Fields" tab on the Job Application type (admin/content/node-type/application/display).

At this point, it'd be a good idea to populate your site with some content. Log in as either *admin* or *editor* with the password *oreilly* and create several pieces of Job content at Create content→Job (node/add/job). It's also a good idea to create a few posts as *user* applying for a few different positions. Having several pieces of content will help with the next section.

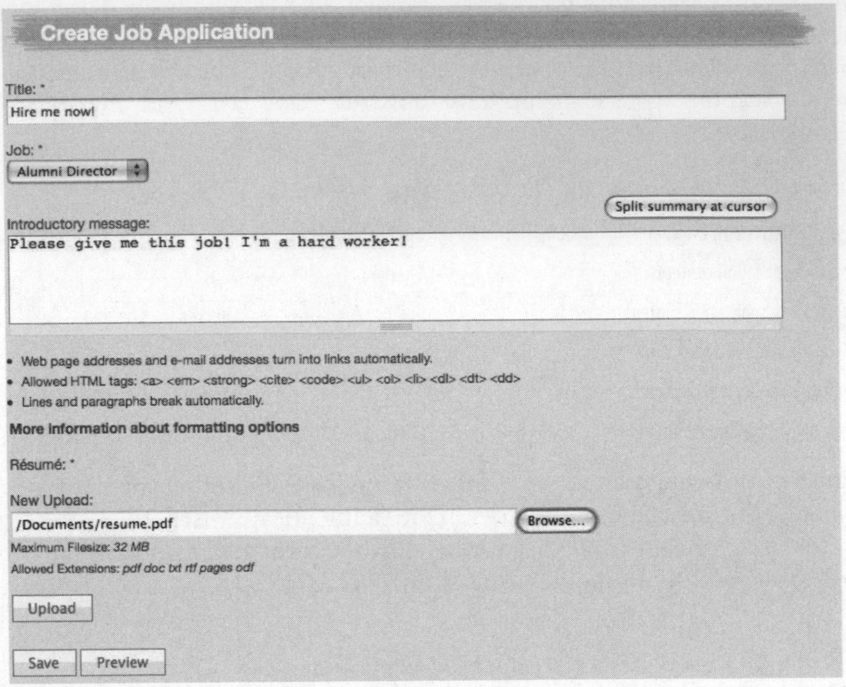

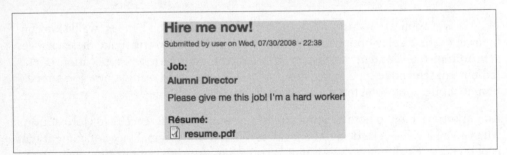

Figure 3-15. The job application form, as seen by any authenticated user

Hire me now!
Submitted by user on Wed, 07/30/2008 - 22:38

Job:
Alumni Director
Please give me this job! I'm a hard worker!

Résumé:
resume.pdf

Figure 3-16. A job application piece of content

Spotlight: Views Module

The Views module provides listings of data on your site: users, comments, nodes, and more. Any listing of data provided by the Views module is called a *view*, which we'll always refer to in all lowercase to distinguish it from the Views module, which is capitalized. Figure 3-17 shows examples of some of the listings that can be built with the Views module.

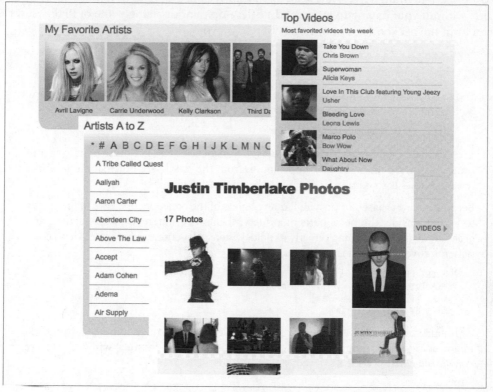

Figure 3-17. Examples of views created by the Views module

Creating a basic view entails selecting the *fields* you would like displayed (node title, author name, and images, etc.), how you would like that list to be *filtered* (only display "story" node types that are published), how you would like the listing to be *sorted* (newest stories on top), and what you would like the list to look like when it's *displayed* (a block showing a bulleted list of headlines).

In more technical terms, Views is a visual SQL query builder. When you build a view, you are essentially constructing a query that Views will pull from your site database. The Views module has significant advantages over a handcoded query. Some examples:

- You don't have to write any code just to make a listing of content.

- Modules will tell Views about their fields; you don't need to know anything about the underlying database structure, and you are insulated in case this structure should change behind the scenes between module updates.

- The same view can be used in several places on the site, as both blocks and pages.

- Results can be split into multiple-page listings, use sortable table columns, AJAX pagers, or filtering drop-downs to allow visitors to "drill down" to the content they want.

More than anything else, Views can significantly speed up the development of your site, without your having to learn module development or a single line of PHP. Views can form the backbone of outputting content on your site.

SQL and Views

SQL is a computer database language that allows for retrieval of data from a database. SQL is made up of simple commands such as:

```
SELECT title FROM node WHERE nid = 10
```

Each of these commands is called a *query*. These queries can get quite a bit longer in order to retrieve the necessary information from the database, but that's one of the reasons Views is so helpful: it can build the queries for you.

Because a view is based upon a SQL query, many of the concepts in Views map directly to SQL. Consider the basic parts of a query: the `select` statement, `where` clause, and `order by` clause. These map directly to fields, filters, sort criteria, and other views components covered later in this chapter.

```
SELECT [fields]
FROM [view type and any relationships]
WHERE [filters or arguments]
ORDER BY [sort criteria]
```

Although you don't need to know SQL to use Views, the correlation is very strong and might help you to understand Views more easily if you're familiar with SQL or are converting existing code to views.

Unlike the configuration of a new content type, the creation of a view is done entirely on a single page. Figure 3-18 depicts the main portion of the view-building interface.

Displays

A *display* determines how a view will be presented to the user. A view can have multiple displays, and can even create several pages listing the same content in different ways. The leftmost portion of the Views interface lets you choose which display you are editing. Figure 3-19 shows adding a new display to a view.

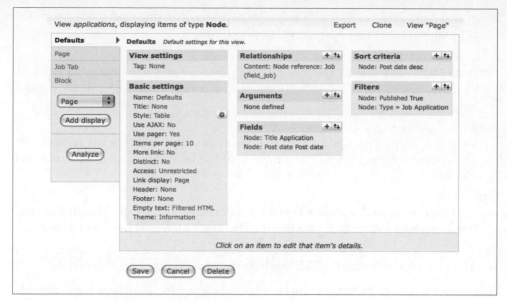

Figure 3-18. The interface for building a view

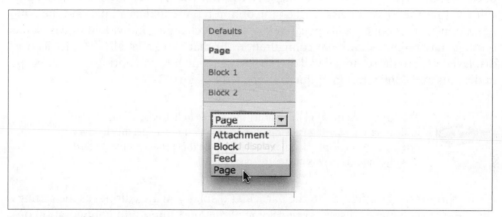

Figure 3-19. Adding a new display

By default, there are four different kinds of displays, each serving a particular purpose. Other modules may also add additional display types:

Attachment

A supplementary display that can be attached above and/or below other types of displays. This can be helpful when giving a view context or adding a glossary when your view is being filtered.

Block

Creates a compact list display that can be positioned in sidebars or any region from the Blocks configuration page at Administer→Site building→Blocks (admin/build/block).

Feed

Creates a customizable RSS feed to which users may subscribe using an RSS reader. Feeds can both receive their own URL and be attached to any block or page display.

Page

Makes a page with its own URL in which the view occupies the main content.

Views provides many exciting options to easily configure the display of your content. The settings for each view display can be configured all at once using the Defaults tab, or each display can have its own settings that override the view defaults. To change any value within the Views interface, click the option represented as a link, and the configuration for that option will appear below. Besides changing individual values, some settings may require additional configuration. In that case, a small ⚙ (gear) icon is displayed next to the setting; it will display further configuration options. The concept of defaults and configuration options is depicted in Figure 3-20.

Pay *very* close attention to whether the font is italicized, as lack of italic indicates that a setting is being overridden. You must specifically override settings on displays; otherwise, they will affect the defaults, regardless of which display is currently selected.

It's important to pay attention to the particular display you are editing, as the settings change slightly between display types. Some of the most important configuration options for a view are available only when you are configuring a particular display. For example, to set a URL for a view, you have to be configuring a Page display. The URL is presented as an option within the Page settings, displayed in the lower left of the interface. The available options for each of the different display types are shown in Figure 3-21.

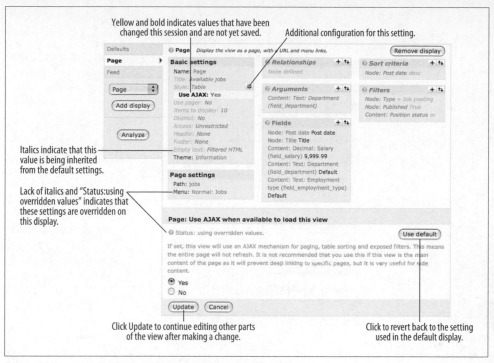

Yellow and bold indicates values that have been changed this session and are not yet saved.

Additional configuration for this setting.

Italics indicate that this value is being inherited from the default settings.

Lack of italics and "Status:using overridden values" indicates that these settings are overridden on this display.

Click Update to continue editing other parts of the view after making a change.

Click to revert back to the setting used in the default display.

Figure 3-20. Configuration when overriding a default value

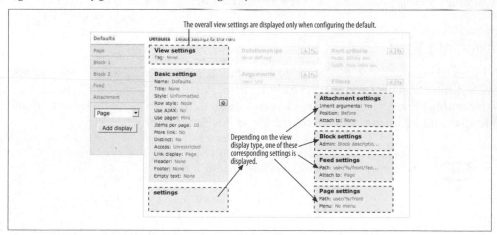

The overall view settings are displayed only when configuring the default.

Depending on the view display type, one of these corresponding settings is displayed.

Figure 3-21. The available settings may change, depending on the display type that is being edited

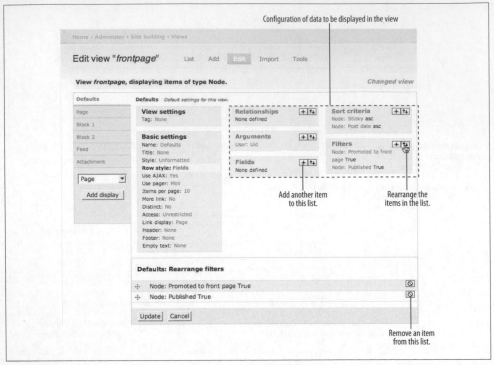

Figure 3-22. Configuration of the pieces to be included in a view

Pieces of a View

The actual meat-and-potatoes of view configuration is determining what content needs to be displayed. This configuration includes fields, filters, arguments, sort criteria, and relationships. Each piece is covered in more detail in the next section. These options are all displayed on the right side of the Views interface, as shown in Figure 3-22.

 If the Fields set of options isn't shown, it's because the "Row style" for the display needs to be set to Fields instead of Node.

Fields

A field represents a piece of data that needs to be displayed. Some examples of fields are the node title, a user's email address, a CCK field value, a taxonomy term, or pretty much any piece of data within Drupal. An alternative to selecting individual fields is to use the Node row style for a view, which will display the view's selected nodes in a listing much like Drupal's default home page.

Building Efficient Views

A view that uses the Node row style is usually less efficient than a view that uses Fields. This is because Views is able to collect all the needed data directly when using fields, but a node listing loads every field for every node that is displayed. For example, a view that needs to display only the title and author of a node should be displayed using Fields, preventing the unnecessary loading of taxonomy terms, CCK fields, or any other data added by additional modules.

Even when loading a large number of fields, using the Fields display type will often be more efficient, because Views can pull in all the data at once in a single query, rather than individually loading nodes (loading a single node will usually take at least 10 queries, or more depending on how many modules you have enabled).

The Views module includes some handy developer information at the bottom of the interface, including the SQL query that it is generating and how long the view takes to generate. The Analyze button will also alert you to any obvious things you've missed. You can use this information to make adjustments and see how they affect performance.

Filters

By default, the Views module will show all of the available users, comments, or nodes on your website. Filters are used to restrict the content list by various criteria. Some common filters include showing only nodes that have their Published flag turned on, or only nodes of a particular type, such as our Job or Job Application nodes.

Arguments

Arguments are a dynamic version of filters. In a scenario where you want to make a listing of content that is owned by a specific user, you wouldn't want to make a separate view for every user on your site. The Views module instead allows you to create a single view, and filter the results based on the user ID that is specified through an argument.

Arguments usually come from the URL. If your view is displayed at the URL *http://example.com/my_view*, directories after *my_view* would be taken as arguments. In the URL *http://example.com/my_view/10*, the number *10* would be the first argument. You can have as many arguments as you want in your view.

In addition to arguments that are at the end of the URL, you can also place arguments in the middle of a URL by using the % symbol in the argument configuration. This feature can be helpful when you want to utilize some of the existing paths in Drupal, such as user paths that might look like *http://example.com/user/10/my_view*. We still want 10 to be the first argument, but it's now in the middle of the URL. By specifying a URL path for the view as *user/%/my_view*, the symbol is swapped with the contents of the URL and passed into the view as the first argument. If this is over your head right now, don't worry—we're going to walk you through an example of this kind of argument next in the section, "Hands-On: The Views Module."

Sort criteria

Once you've narrowed down results from your database and have the fields you want to display, you can use sort criteria to determine the order in which those results show up. Some examples are sorting by the created date, author username, or by taxonomy terms.

Relationships

Relationships are new in the Drupal 6 version of Views. When you need to include data from an object that's not directly available (like a user's information) inside a listing of content (which is based on nodes), a relationship lets you retrieve the object information that is related to the listed content. In relational databases, a view relationship could be considered the equivalent of doing a JOIN in SQL.

We'll set up an example of a relationship where a job application is related to a particular piece of job content. The user creates a piece of content (an application) that is related to another piece of content (the job). Using a Views relationship, we can create a listing of content that includes information from both the application and the job itself.

Hands-On: The Views Module

The requirements of our site include two particular views. One view is frontend-facing, showing all the available jobs to users of the site. Faculty users (more specifically, users in the "editor" role) will use the second view to review the list of applicants who have applied to various jobs.

The first step to using the Views module is to enable it. The Views module has two parts: the Views module itself, which handles the low-level "plumbing," and the Views UI module, which presents the screens used to configure them. Additionally, the Advanced Help module is an optional module that provides useful inline help for modules such as Views.

1. Go to Administer→Site building→Modules (admin/build/modules) and enable the following modules:
   - Other package
     — Advanced Help
   - Views package
     — Views
     — Views UI
2. Configure the module permissions at Administer→User management→Permissions (admin/user/permissions), using the values listed in Table 3-18. As administrators

will be the only people configuring the Views module, the Advanced Help features need to be enabled for them only.

Table 3-18. Permissions for the Views module

Permission	anonymous user	authenticated user	editor	site administrator
advanced_help module				
view advanced help index				Checked
view advanced help pop-up				Checked
view advanced help topic				Checked
views module				
administer views				Checked
views_ui module				
access all views				Checked

 Be very cautious with the "access all views" permission; users with this permission will bypass any access restrictions you place on views, so all views are visible.

Jobs View

The "jobs" view will provide a listing of jobs at Epic University, categorized by department. The completed view will be similar to the one pictured in Figure 3-23.

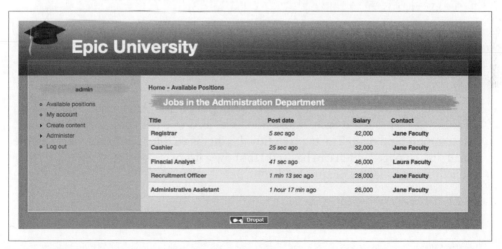

Figure 3-23. A sample page from the jobs view, listing jobs in the Administration department

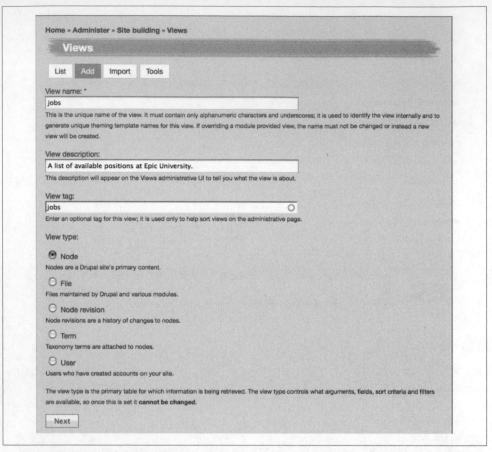

Figure 3-24. Initial view information

1. Get started by visiting the Views configuration page at Administer→Site build-ing→Views (admin/build/views).

2. Click the Add tab at the top of the page and populate the form with the values from Table 3-19. This is the basic information we need to enter for any view: a name, description, and type. The tag is optional; it helps us filter the list of views on the main listing page, which can be useful to show a list of custom views quickly. Your screen should look as pictured in Figure 3-24.

Table 3-19. Settings for adding the jobs view

View setting	Value
View name	jobs
View description	A list of available positions at Epic University
View tag	jobs
View type	Node

Figure 3-25. Basic settings for the Available Positions view

3. After clicking the Next button, Views takes you to the main view-building interface, where we will set up how this view is to be displayed by default. Ensure that the Basic Settings table is configured with the values from Table 3-20, as pictured in Figure 3-25. For each field, scroll down for the interface to configure each setting, and click Update to save.

The indicated settings create a view that shows its information in a table, with a pager to move from one page of results to another. If no jobs are found, it displays a message to that effect.

Table 3-20. The basic settings for the jobs view

Defaults: Basic settings	Value
Title	Available Positions
Style	Table
Use pager	Yes
	Full pager
Empty text	There are currently no positions available.

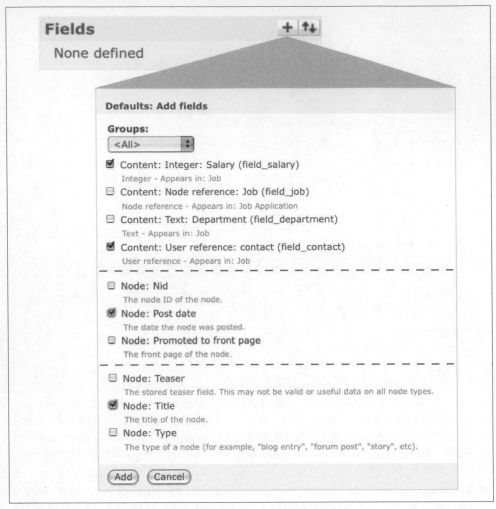

Figure 3-26. Fields for the Available Positions view

4. At this point, you may receive the error message "Display Defaults uses fields but there are none defined for it or all are excluded." Let's correct this problem by adding a few fields to the view. We'll want to display the Title, Post date, Salary, and Contact for each job.

Click the + (plus) icon within the Fields area to start adding new fields. Include the fields from Table 3-21, as pictured in Figure 3-26. To speed up entry, you can select "Node" and "Content" from the Groups selection to filter the list of available fields by only those pertaining to that group.

Table 3-21. Defaults view for the job view

Defaults: Add Fields	Value
Node:Title	Checked
Node: Post date	Checked
Content: Integer: Salary	Checked
Content: User Reference: Contact	Checked

 Fields in the Node group are those properties that are common to all types of nodes, such as the node's author or its creation date. Fields in the Content group are additional fields that were added with CCK.

5. After you click the Add button, Views will display the configuration form for each field, one by one, to allow you to configure each field's options. When you're finished entering each of the values from Table 3-22 and pictured in Figure 3-27, click the Update button.

Table 3-22. Individual field configuration for the job view

Defaults: Configure field setting	Value
Content: Integer: Salary	Format: 9,999
Content: User Reference: Contact	(leave default settings)
Node: Post date	Date format: Time ago
Node: Title	Link this field to its node: Checked

6. Click the rearrange icon in the Fields section and put the fields in the following order:

- Node: Title
- Node: Post date
- Content: Integer
- Content: User reference

7. Now that our view has fields, you should save the view by clicking the Save button. If this button is grayed out, be sure to finish editing whatever field you're editing; then the button will be activated again.

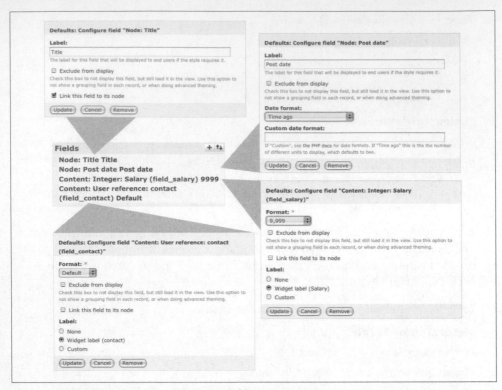

Figure 3-27. Field configuration for the Available Positions view

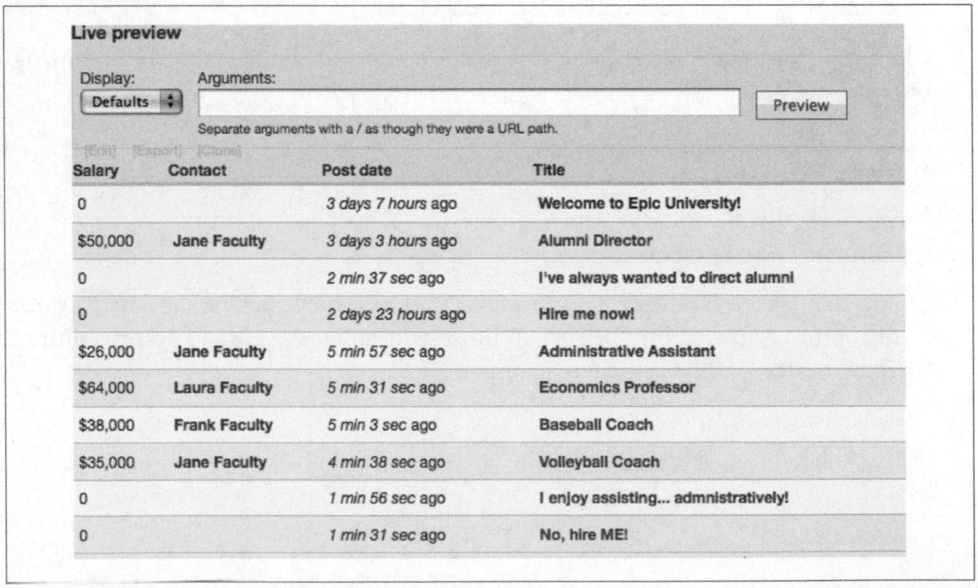

Salary	Contact	Post date	Title
0		3 days 7 hours ago	**Welcome to Epic University!**
$50,000	**Jane Faculty**	3 days 3 hours ago	**Alumni Director**
0		2 min 37 sec ago	**I've always wanted to direct alumni**
0		2 days 23 hours ago	**Hire me now!**
$26,000	**Jane Faculty**	5 min 57 sec ago	**Administrative Assistant**
$64,000	**Laura Faculty**	5 min 31 sec ago	**Economics Professor**
$38,000	**Frank Faculty**	5 min 3 sec ago	**Baseball Coach**
$35,000	**Jane Faculty**	4 min 38 sec ago	**Volleyball Coach**
0		1 min 56 sec ago	**I enjoy assisting... admnistratively!**
0		1 min 31 sec ago	**No, hire ME!**

Figure 3-28. Our view so far, with no filtering in place

8. Our view is now displaying the data we want, but it doesn't have any restrictions as to what kinds of content are being displayed, and it is not in any kind of order. Scroll down below the view configuration area and you'll see a "Live preview" of the view as it is currently configured; it should be similar to Figure 3-28.

As you can see, the view isn't being filtered to include only "job" content. It also includes our welcome post (which is a piece of Page content) and any application content on the site.

No problem! Click the + (plus) icon within the Filters area to start adding some new filters to the view. As with fields, you can use the Groups select list to filter the list down by a particular group, and after checking the correct options and clicking Add, configuration pages for each will appear below, and may be cycled through with the Update button. Add the filters and settings contained in Table 3-23 and pictured in Figure 3-29.

Table 3-23. Default filters for the jobs view

Defaults: Add filters	Value
Node: Published	Published: Checked
Node: Type	Operator: Is one of
	Node type: Job

9. Returning to the preview will show the irrelevant results now removed from the view.

 Unless you are building an administrative view purely for the purpose of viewing and moderating unpublished content, you nearly always want the Node: Published filter in place so that the view shows only content that is intended to be seen by site visitors. Clicking the Analyze button when you're finished with your view "live" is a best practice; it will warn you of this and other common issues.

10. Additionally, we'll want to set up sort criteria to put these items in some sort of logical order. Click the + (plus) icon within the "Sort criteria" area to add a sort like the one in Table 3-24, as pictured in Figure 3-30, and click Update to save the settings.

Table 3-24. Default sort criteria for the jobs view

Defaults: Sort criteria	Value
Node: Post date	Sort order: Descending
	Granularity: Second

The Granularity settings are a convenient way to make all items posted within a single time frame be sorted equally. This feature could allow you to sort new jobs by the day they were posted, then alphabetically by node title within that day. However, we leave the granularity at the Second value, simply because it is the most efficient method, as post dates are stored as seconds in the database.

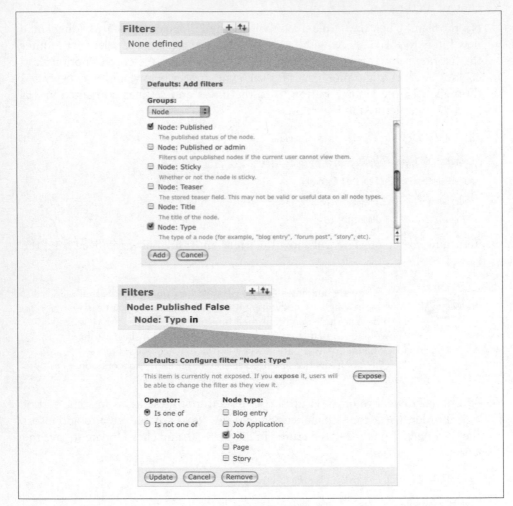

Figure 3-29. Filter configuration for the Available Positions view

11. Our view is nearly usable. It's displaying the information we want in a nice table, sorted by the time the job was posted. However, to actually make this view visible by any users, we need to add a new Display. On the left side of the interface, select Page from the list of display options, and click "Add display."

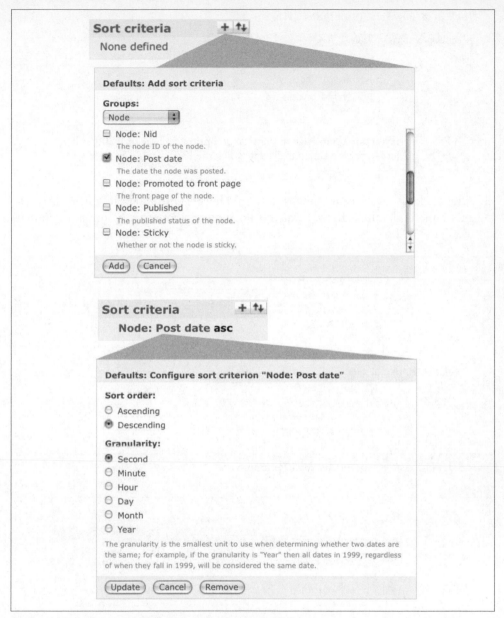

Figure 3-30. Sort criteria configuration for the Available Positions view

12. Upon adding the new display, the "Basic settings" area changes to settings specific to that display. Any settings that we specify here are added to or replace the default settings that we've already created.

In the "Page settings" area, configure the settings to those used in Table 3-25 and pictured in Figure 3-31.

Table 3-25. Page settings for the jobs view

Page: Page settings	Value
Path	jobs
Menu	Type: Normal menu entry
	Title: Available positions

If you don't see "Page settings" as an option, you are probably still looking at the Defaults display. Click the Page display instead.

13. After clicking Save for the View, you should have a convenient link in your Navigation menu that links to the Available Positions on your site. It should be similar to Figure 3-32.

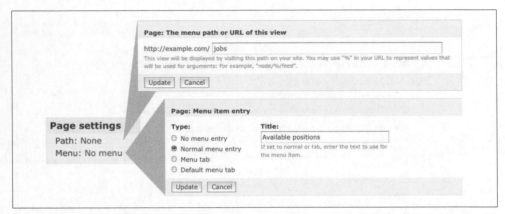

Figure 3-31. Page settings for the Available Positions view

Figure 3-32. The new jobs view, with a link in the Navigation menu

14. You'll notice that we didn't include a Department field in this listing, because our requirements actually call for a directory-type listing. That is, the first page of our jobs view should display a list of departments, and then clicking on the department

should provide a list of jobs inside. Because it would be tedious to create a view like this for each department, we'll accomplish this requirement with an *argument*, a very powerful Views feature.

To get started implementing this directory-type listing, head back to your view configuration screen at Administer→Site building→Views (admin/build/views) and click the "edit" link for the jobs view. Click the + (plus) icon in the Arguments area to add a new argument to the Page display. As before, click Add to add the Department argument, and enter the settings from Table 3-26 and Figure 3-33.

Table 3-26. Page arguments for the jobs view

Page: Arguments	Values
Content: Text: Department	Title: Jobs in the %1 Department
	Action to take if argument is not present: Summary, sorted ascending
	Case: Capitalize each word
	Case in path: Lowercase
	Transform spaces to dashes in URL: checked
	Summary style (after clicking Update): List

The "%1" in the Title looks a bit funny; this will be replaced by the name of the Department dynamically when the page is viewed. The "Action to take if argument not present" indicates what the view should do when the URL *http://www.example.com/jobs* is accessed, rather than *http://www.example.com/jobs/athletics*. Here, we are asking it to display a list of department names in ascending order. The "Summary" style will display the titles of the various departments, along with the number of jobs within that department next to it. This type of view can be very useful for directory listings. The Views module also allows you to control how the dynamic URL and title is displayed.

15. Click "Update" and you will be presented with a series of options to configure the argument options. Accept the default options for each by clicking the Update button.

Be sure to save the view when you're done.

 We add only one argument in our jobs view. But you can add as many arguments as you like. They don't even have to be the same type. This way you can get multipage structures, each drilling down additionally on the items that should appear in a list.

We're now complete with the jobs view! The final view screen should look as pictured in Figure 3-34. Take a look at our view, either by clicking the new "Available positions" link in the Navigation sidebar block, or by clicking the View "Page" link from the Views interface. After adding this argument, our view contains a nice hierarchical structure! It should be similar to Figure 3-35.

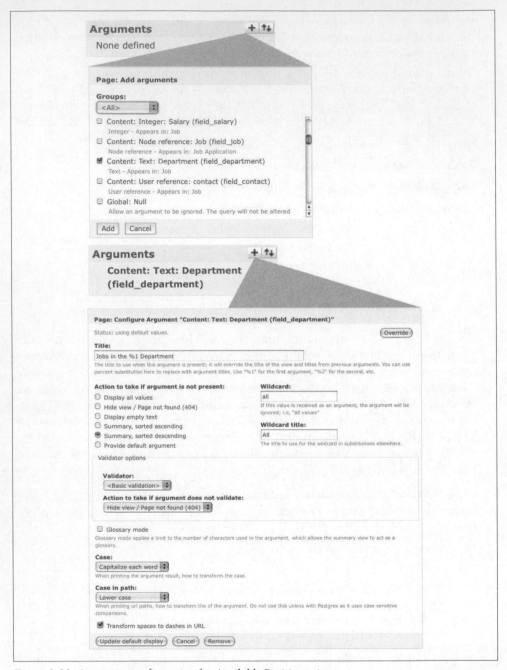

Figure 3-33. Argument configuration for Available Positions view

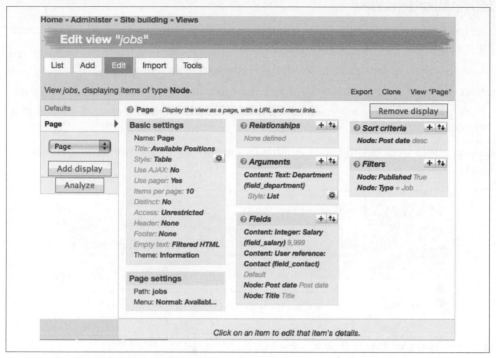

Figure 3-34. Completed Available Jobs view configuration

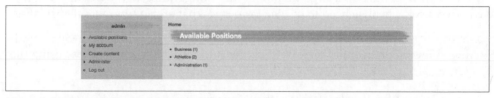

Figure 3-35. The root level of the Jobs view, after adding an argument

Clicking on any of the options will take you to a filtered listing within that category, such as in Figure 3-36. Pay attention to the URL also as you move between pages. It should be similar to *http://www.example.com/jobs/administration* or *http://www.example.com/jobs/athletics*. This is the way arguments work in Views: the path we specify displays the summary view, then any "directories" (such as administration) under that URL are taken as arguments.

This concludes our introductory view, where we've used several of the features of Views. This example included only a single display (of type Page), and we used arguments in a simple manner. In our next example, we'll create a view that uses multiple displays, and gets a little trickier with arguments.

Job Applications View

The Job Applications view will serve both as a tool for administrators and as a reference for users. It will provide the following displays:

- A listing of all job applications in the entire system as a single page
- A listing of all applications for a particular job, displayed as a tab on the job page
- A listing of applications filled out by the currently logged-in user, displayed as a block in the sidebar

Taking all these pieces together, the final view should display something similar to Figure 3-37.

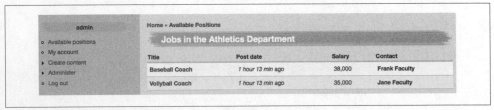

Figure 3-36. Inside the Filtered view, when the argument "athletics" is passed in

Create the View and Defaults displays

In this view, we'll be setting up several displays and then overriding the defaults within each display. By setting up a large amount of the configuration in the Defaults display, we'll save work when we need to change properties that are common to all displays.

1. Start by getting to the Views administration area at Administer→Site building→Views (admin/build/views). Click the Add tab to add a new view, using the settings from Table 3-27, then click Next.

   Table 3-27. Add view settings for the applications view

Field	Value
View name	applications
View description	A list of submitted applications for a job or by a user
View tag	jobs
View type	Node

2. Once the view has been created, set the Defaults for the view settings to be the same as Table 3-28. After configuring each setting, click Update.

Table 3-28. View basic settings for the applications view

Defaults: Basic settings	Value
Style	Table
Use pager	Yes
	Full pager
Empty text	No applications yet.

3. Now we'll set up each of the default fields, sort criteria, and filters. Click the +
(plus) icon in the Fields area. Check off the fields described in Table 3-29 and click
Add, then configure each of their settings, clicking Update after each one.

Table 3-29. Default fields for the applications view

Defaults: Fields	Values
Content: Node reference: Job	Link this field to its node: Checked
Node: Post date	Date format: Sunday, May 4, 1978 – 05:00
Node: Title	Label: Application
	Link this field to its node: Checked
User: Name	Label: Applicant

4. Click the ↑↓ (rearrange) icon in the Fields section to put the fields in the following
order:
   - Node: Post date
   - Node: Title
   - User: Name
   - Content: Node Reference: Job

5. Click the + (plus) icon in the "Sort criteria" area and add the Post date sort. Configure using the criteria from Table 3-30 and click Update.

Table 3-30. Default sort criteria for the applications view

Defaults: Sort Criteria	Values
Node: Post date	Sort order: Descending

6. Click the + (plus) icon in the Filters area and check the Node: Published and Node:
Type filters and click Add. Configure each filter with the criteria from Table 3-31, clicking Update after each filter.

Table 3-31. Default filters for the applications view

Defaults: Filters	Values
Node: Published	Published: Checked
Node: Type	Operator: Is one of
	Node type: Job Application

7. Save the progress on the applications view, pictured in Figure 3-38, by clicking the Save button.

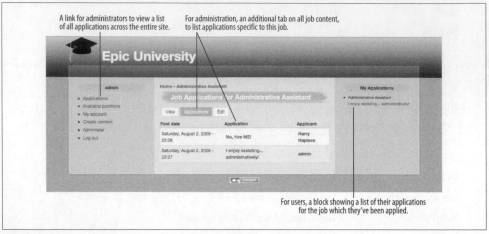

Figure 3-37. The multiple displays of the Job Applications view

This concludes the default configuration of the applications view. It isn't yet displayed anywhere on the site, but next we'll configure a simple page display to go with these defaults.

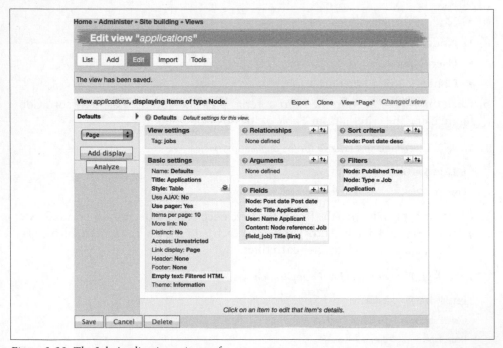

Figure 3-38. The Job Applications view so far

Create the page display

The first display that we'll create will simply use the default configuration to print out a list of all applications that have been submitted to the entire site. We'll make this page accessible only by users in the "editor" role, and give it a menu item so that it displays in the main navigation. The finished page will be similar to Figure 3-39.

If you've left the view configuration screen, return to it at Administer→Site building→Views→Applications→Edit (admin/build/views/edit/applications).

1. Select Page from the display select list and click "Add display."
2. Now we'll override our first setting. The default access to this view is set to Unrestricted, but we want to allow only "editor" members on the site to have access to review all the applications. Click on the Access: Unrestricted setting under Basic Settings.

   You'll see a notice that this setting is currently using the defaults. Click the Override button in the setting configuration, then use the settings from Table 3-32 to restrict access to this display and click Update. When finished, the settings should look as pictured in Figure 3-40.

Table 3-32. Page display access restrictions for the applications view

Basic settings	Values
Title	Click "Override"
	Applications
Access	Click "Override"
	Type: By role
	If by role: editor

 Restricting access to the view only prevents unprivileged users from accessing the view display at *http://www.example.com/applications*; it does *not* prevent an unprivileged user from typing in *http://www.example.com/node/4*, where node 4 is a job application that is not theirs. Protecting this kind of node-level access control requires the use of a *node access* module, such as Taxonomy Access Control (*http://drupal.org/project/taxonomy_access*) or Organic Groups (*http://drupal.org/project/og*).

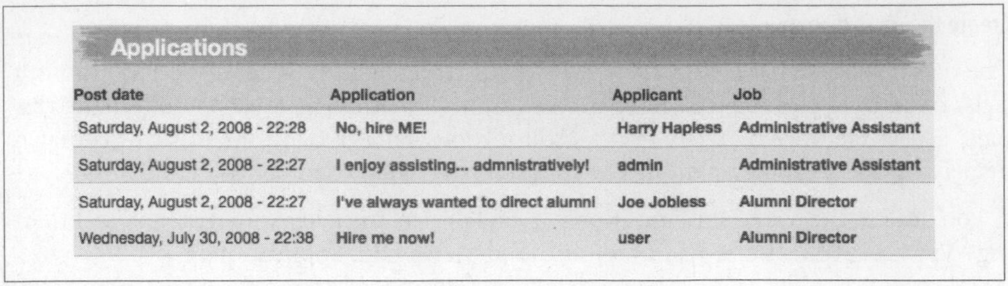

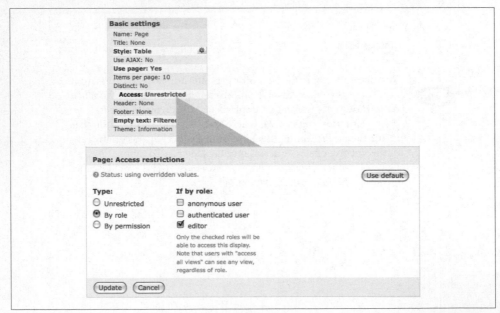

Post date	Application	Applicant	Job
Saturday, August 2, 2008 - 22:28	No, hire ME!	Harry Hapless	Administrative Assistant
Saturday, August 2, 2008 - 22:27	I enjoy assisting... admnistratively!	admin	Administrative Assistant
Saturday, August 2, 2008 - 22:27	I've always wanted to direct alumni	Joe Jobless	Alumni Director
Wednesday, July 30, 2008 - 22:38	Hire me now!	user	Alumni Director

Figure 3-39. The applications view page display in action

3. Now we'll set up the display-specific settings to give this page a URL path and a menu item. Within the "Page settings" area, use the settings from Table 3-33 and click Update.

Table 3-33. Page display settings for the applications view

Page settings	Values
Path	applications
Menu	Type: Normal menu entry
	Title: Applications

4. Click the Save button to update your changes. Your view should now look as pictured in Figure 3-41. An Applications link will appear in the main site navigation, linking to the new page display.

Figure 3-40. Overriding an individual basic setting within a view

Create the Job tab display

We've created a page containing all the applications on the entire site. Although this might be helpful for watching incoming applications, it's not entirely helpful for a user who is interested in only the applications posted to one specific job. To fill this need, we'll make a display that limits the applications to just one job, using an argument. To make this page easy to find, we'll add it as a tab on job node pages (see Figure 3-42).

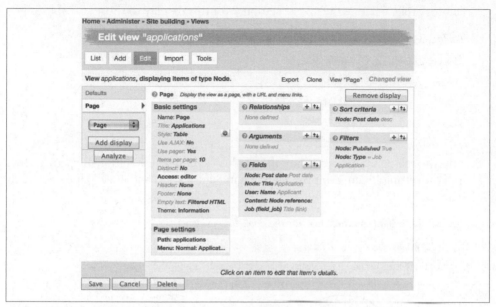

Figure 3-41. Job Applications view with the Page display

Accomplishing this is going to require a new Views module trick that we haven't used yet: Relationships. Pulling up lists of job applications is simple to do, but in this case we want to use a piece of data from the Job type that the tab is being shown on; namely, we need its node ID, so we know which applications to display. We can use a relationship to pull in data from the job type so it's usable with applications. Figure 3-43 shows a diagram of how relationships work.

Home » Administrative Assistant

Job Applications for Administrative Assistant

| View | Applications | Edit |

Post date	Application	Applicant
Saturday, August 2, 2008 - 22:28	No, hire ME!	Harry Hapless
Saturday, August 2, 2008 - 22:27	I enjoy assisting... admnistratively!	admin

Figure 3-42. The applications view displayed as a tab on a job node

If you've left the Views administration area, return to at Administer→Site building→Views→Applications→Edit (admin/build/views/edit/applications).

1. Select Page from the display select list and click "Add display."

2. The new display gets the name Page by default. To help distinguish it from the Page display, we'll rename it to Job Tab, because this page will be displayed as a tab on job nodes. We'll also override the access again to limit it to users in the "editor" role. Change the "Basic settings" for this display to those in Table 3-34.

Table 3-34. Job Tab basic settings for the applications view

Job tab: Basic settings	Value
Name	Job Tab
Access	Click *Override*
	Type: By role
	Role: editor

3. Add the relationship by clicking the + (plus) icon in the Relationships area, then add the settings from Table 3-35 (shown in Figure 3-44) and click "Update default display."

Table 3-35. Default relationships for the applications view

Defaults: Relationships	Values
Content: Node reference: Job	Require this relationship: Checked

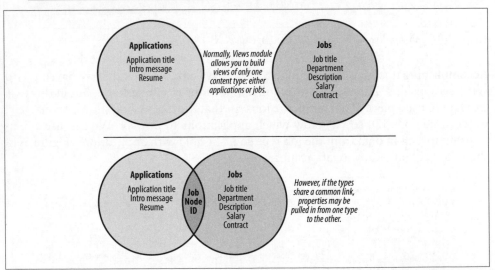

Figure 3-43. If two objects share a bond, Relationships can pull in data from one to another

4. Similar to the "jobs" view that we configured earlier, we can filter down the listing of applications by adding an argument to the display. This is the first time that

we'll be overriding a particular portion of a view, other than settings. In this case, overriding works a little bit differently. Click on the Arguments section title, which will allow you to override all the arguments of the view at once. It's not possible to override only an individual argument (or an individual relationship, field, sort criterion, or filters). When overriding a portion of a view, the font will become unitalicized, indicating an override, as in Figure 3-45.

After choosing to override the arguments of the Job Tab display, we'll add an argument that filters the list of applications to a single job node. Click the + (plus) icon in the Arguments area and use the values from Table 3-36. The Node ID argument allows us to filter by one particular job's ID. Here we're using another feature of Views arguments: a *validator*. Views will check the node ID passed in to the URL and verify that it belongs to a job node. Click *Update* when finished.

Table 3-36. The Job Tab display arguments of the applications view

Job Tab: Argument settings	Values
Node: Nid	Relationship: field_job_nid
	Title: Job Applications for %1
	Action to take if argument is not present: Display empty text
	Validator: Node
	Types: Job
	Validate user has access to the node: Checked

5. Now that we've set up an argument for this display, we need to give it a URL. Use the settings from Table 3-37 to set up the Page settings and click Update.

Table 3-37. Job Tab display page settings

Job Tab: Page settings	Values
Path	node/%/applications
Menu	Type: Menu tab
	Title: Applications

Similar to using %1 in the title, we're using the percent symbol to specify that the first argument will be in the middle of the URL. You can use this approach to add tabs to user pages also, such as user/%/my_display, or any other page in Drupal with a dynamic path.

6. And finally, we no longer need the Job listed on this display; it will be redundant, as we'll be looking at the job directly. Click the Fields section title, and click Override. Then, click Content: Node reference: Job and click Remove.

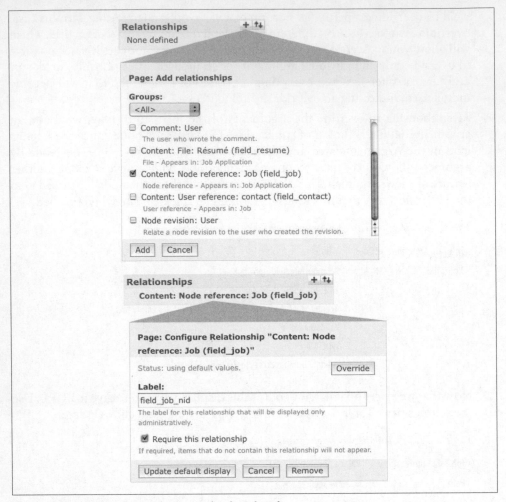

Figure 3-44. Relationship configuration for the Job Tab

If you want behavior specific to one display and not others, be sure to click Override. The Views module's settings default to affecting the global Defaults display, which affects *all* displays within that view. You can end up accidentally deleting this field from more than one display if you're not in override mode.

7. Click the Save button to save the view, which should now look like Figure 3-46.

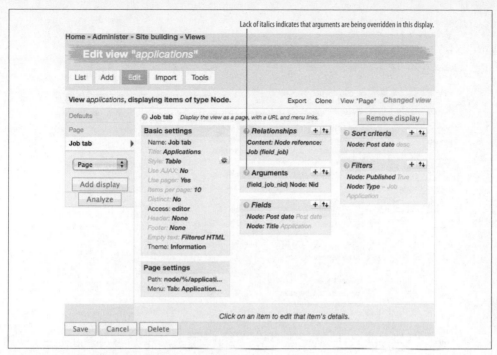

Figure 3-45. Overriding the Arguments portion of a view

We've now added a tab to all job nodes (for users in the "editor" role). Visiting a node that has applications should look similar to Figure 3-42, shown earlier.

Create the Applications block display

The last display that we're going assemble will be available to all users of the site. It will be a block that will show all the job applications that the currently logged-in user has submitted on the site. We'll also change the style of this display from a table to a list layout, because it will need to be displayed in the narrower sidebar column. The final display will look similar to Figure 3-47.

Return to the view configuration for the applications view at Administer→Site building→Views→Applications→Edit (admin/build/views/edit/applications). We'll start by adding a new display to this view:

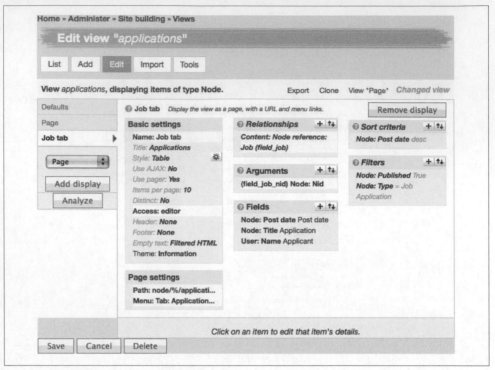

Figure 3-46. Applications view with new Job tab

1. Select Block from the display list and click "Add display."
2. Override the display Basic settings with the values from Table 3-38, again clicking Update to save each setting.

Table 3-38. Applications Block basic settings for the applications view

Block: Basic settings	Values
Title	Click Override
	My applications
Style	Click Override
	Style: List
	Type: Unordered list
Row style	Fields

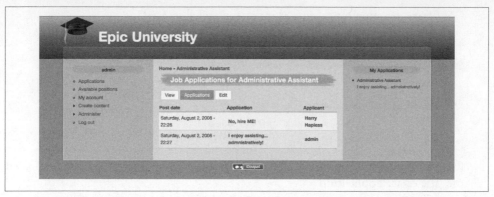

Figure 3-47. The Applications view with the User Applications display as a block in the right sidebar

3. Now configure a description on the block that will show up in the block administration area. Under "Block settings," enter Admin text of User Applications and click Update.

We've now set essentially three names or titles for this block. Here's a rundown of where each title will be displayed:

Basic settings: Name
Used within the views interface as the name of the display. Shown as a tab on the left side of the interface.

Basic settings: Title
Used as the block title when it is displayed to the end user.

Block settings: Admin
Used when referring to the block when arranging blocks at Administer→Site building→Blocks (admin/build/block).

1. Because this is a block that will live in the sidebar, we'll want to display far fewer fields so that it fits nicely in the narrower region of the page. To do this, we'll need to override the Fields area of this view. Click on the Fields section header, and click the Override button in the configuration area.

2. Now that the fields for the Applications Block are being overridden, delete the Node: Post date and User: Name fields from the section (click each field link, then use the Remove button).

You can quickly delete multiple fields by clicking the ↑↓ (rearrange icon), and then clicking the (remove) icon next to the unwanted fields.

3. Configure the remaining fields as indicated in Table 3-39.

Table 3-39. Applications Block fields in the applications view

Block: Fields	Values
Node: Title	Label: (blank)
Content: Node Reference: Job	Format: Title (no link)
	Link this field to its node: Unchecked
	Label: None

4. Reorder the fields using the ↑↓ (reorder) button so that the job comes first, then the title of the application.

5. Finally, because we need to limit this display to job applications by the current user, we need to add a filter to the display. Like the Fields, all filters will need to be overridden to add a new option. Click the Filters section header and click the Override button in the configuration area.

6. We'll leave the two existing filters in place (Node: Published and Node: Type) and add a single new filter for User: Current. Check off this filter, click Add, check "Is the logged-in user" and click Update. This step will allow the block's contents to change dynamically depending on who the currently logged-in user is.

7. Save the view, which should now look like Figure 3-48. Your configuration for the User Applications block display is now complete.

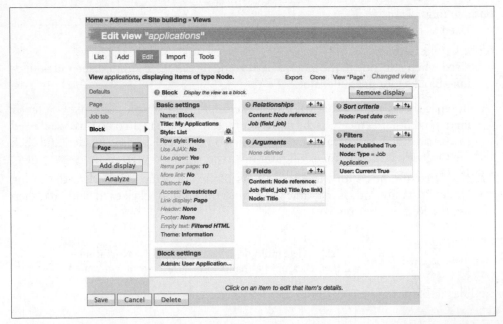

Figure 3-48. The completed Block display for the Applications view

---

8. By adding a new Block display, we've added a block to the Drupal installation. Before it is visible anywhere though, we need to enable the block. Visit Administer→Site building→Blocks (admin/build/block) and enable the new block. Place it in the Right sidebar region and save your changes.

Taking It Further

The basic job website that we've built only touches on the surface of the capability of CCK and Views. There are a lot of possibilities for extending the functionality of this job site by adding more fields to both the Job and Job Application content types. Here are a few modules that could be used to extend the abilities of CCK:

Automatic Node Titles, http://drupal.org/project/auto_nodetitle
This module provides support for creating title templates for nodes. For example, rather than having users manually enter a title for their applications (which may result in nonsensical things such as "Hire me!"), this module could ensure that all application titles follow a standard format automatically, such as [author-name] – [job-title].

Custom Links, http://drupal.org/project/custom_links
This handy module can be used to add your own links to any node in addition to the usual suspects, such as "Add new comment." We could use this to add a link for users to apply for a job directly from the job post itself, so users did not need to select it from a drop-down box from the application form.

Content Permissions (included with CCK)
If you need to protect certain private application information from displaying to unprivileged users, the Content Permissions module can hide fields depending on the viewing user's role. As it's included with CCK, no additional download is necessary.

Summary

This chapter taught you how to use two of Drupal's fundamental "building block" modules: CCK and Views. These modules constitute the cornerstone of Drupal's power and are used extensively throughout the rest of the book. CCK is used to model your website's content by adding additional fields to hold different properties, and Views is used to display lists of your website's data.

Besides the basic features of these modules, this chapter also introduced you to the methodology for Drupal site building. Rather than installing monolithic packages, in Drupal each module provides specific functionality, and works together with other modules to enhance their functionality. As we created fields for our different content types, CCK was working together with the core Node module. While making listings of content, Views retrieved information provided by both core modules and CCK. This sort of cooperation between modules serves as the foundation for the rest of the book, as more modules join the party and give new shape to our sites.

Here are the modules that we referenced in this chapter:

- Automatic Nodetitle module: *http://drupal.org/project/auto_nodetitle*
- Content Construction Kit (CCK) package: *http://drupal.org/project/cck*
- Custom Links module: *http://drupal.org/project/custom_links*
- FileField module: *http://drupal.org/project/filefield*
- Link module: *http://drupal.org/project/link*
- Token module: *http://drupal.org/project/token*
- Views module: *http://drupal.org/project/views*

These are some other resources that we referenced and community resources for learning more about the new concepts introduced in this chapter:

- CCK Developers Drupal group: *http://groups.drupal.org/cck*
- CCK Field modules: *http://drupal.org/project/Modules/category/88*
- Views Developers Drupal group: *http://groups.drupal.org/views-developers*

## CHAPTER 4

Product Reviews

With more and more options for shoppers arriving on the Internet every day, finding the right products can be a challenge. Special interest websites that feature specific kinds of products and reviews by dedicated hobbyists are a popular way to help consumers sort through all of the options and find the right products. In this chapter, we're going to use a handful of Drupal modules to build a product review website that lets community members give their opinions on every product that's featured.

This chapter introduces the following modules:

Amazon (http://drupal.org/project/amazon)
> Gathers product information from Amazon.com (*http://www.amazon.com*)

Voting API (http://drupal.org/project/votingapi)
> Provides a framework for standardizing voting data

Fivestar (http://drupal.org/project/fivestar)
> Allows rating of content

Search (core)
> Indexes content and allows searching within a site

CSS Injector (http://drupal.org/project/css_injector)
> Allows administrators to easily add CSS styling to the site

If you would like to participate in the hands-on exercises in this chapter, install Drupal using the Reviews installation profile from the book's sample code. This will create the example website on your web server. The completed website will look as pictured in Figure 4-1 and found at *http://reviews.usingdrupal.com*. For more information on using the book's sample code, see the Preface.

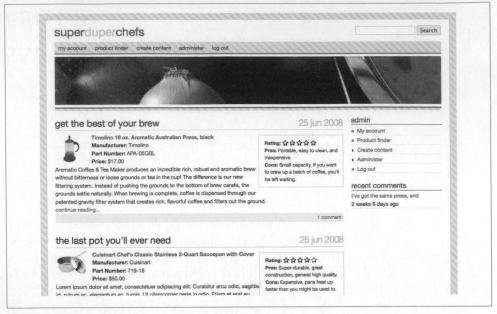

Figure 4-1. The completed Super Duper Chefs website

Case Study

Bob and Sarah are coworkers and food lovers who've both built up impressive kitchens full of gadgets, pots and pans, and other cooking tools. Supporting a culinary habit can be expensive, though, and they usually turn to fellow foodies for advice before purchasing new gear. They've decided to set up Super Duper Chefs, a website where they and their friends can write recommendations about the cooking equipment they use, share tips, and brag about their latest culinary achievements. They'd like it to be the kind of site they wanted when they were getting started: a fun place that highlights the most useful products and advice.

After talking things over with their friends, Bob and Sarah think they have a handle on what the site should offer. The most important feature is that kitchen products reviewed by the site's official contributors should be listed with ratings and quick summaries of their best and worst features. Each review should also provide up-to-date pricing information. In addition to the official reviews, visitors to the site should be able to offer their opinions on the products and compare the official ratings with the opinions of other visitors who've read the reviews. Everyone that uses the site should also be able to search for reviews that match certain criteria. For example, it should be easy to find reviews of products by a particular manufacturer, or products that mention waffles.

Implementation Notes

The next step is figuring out how to translate that set of features into a shopping list of Drupal functionality. Bob and Sarah are fortunate: the core Drupal software can provide most of what they're looking for without any additions. We'll set up special permissions for contributors, and use Drupal's administrative tools to create a custom Product Review content type. Those Product Reviews will be the meat of the site's content.

We'll use the CCK module to add custom fields to the Product Review content type for the various bits of information we want to record. We'll also use the Views module to build a listing page of products for quick scanning. Three requirements for Bob and Sarah's website, though, will require functionality that we haven't seen yet: importing product information from another website, allowing users to rate and review content, and building a custom search page.

Product information

First, the site will need to display information about the products that are being reviewed. Who manufactured it? How much does it cost? Where can a visitor to the website purchase it? Although it's possible to set up custom fields for each of these pieces of information with the CCK module, it's a real hassle for the site's editors to fill out all of them for every review. In addition, keeping the pricing information up-to-date can be a chore as the site grows older.

The easiest solution is to let someone else do the work! Amazon.com provides access to its full database of product information, including kitchen gadgets (shown in Figure 4-2), using the Amazon Associates Web Services API. The Amazon Module (see *http://drupal.org/project/amazon*) lets sites access that product information. That means that writers on the site can fill out one field about the product, and the rest will be handled behind the scenes.

In addition to saving time and energy entering in the product details, using the Amazon API means that Bob and Sarah can get referral fees whenever someone clicks from their website and purchases an item on Amazon.com. It's a simple way of earning revenue, and for high-traffic sites, the commissions can add up quickly.

Product ratings

The second challenge is product ratings. The site will need every product to have an official review by an editor, but visitors reading the site need to be able to rate the products as well. Displaying the official rating and the users' ratings separately will give a more trustworthy representation of how the products perform, reassuring new visitors that the site's ratings aren't dominated by a one-sided editor.

The Drupal community has built dozens of plug-in modules that add rating and voting capabilities to sites. A full list is available at *http://drupal.org/project/Modules/category/60*. Some, such as the NodeReview module (*http://drupal.org/project/nodereview*),

Figure 4-2. The Amazon.com website, displaying kitchen products

allow visitors to evaluate pieces of content on multiple criteria. Others, such as the Plus1 module (*http://drupal.org/project/plus1*) add the ability to vote items up in a queue, like the popular sites Reddit (*http://www.reddit.com*) and Digg (*http://digg .com*). Still others allow each reader to rate content on a scale, then display the average to new visitors. Because it is this average rating capability that we're interested in, we're going to use the Fivestar module (*http://drupal.org/project/fivestar*).

In addition to letting users vote on content, Fivestar provides a CCK field to separate "official ratings" by a site editor from the normal ratings given by visitors. We can use the Views module to list the two kinds of ratings side by side for comparison. The Fivestar module, like most rating and evaluation modules, is based on Voting API (*http: //drupal.org/project/votingapi*), another Drupal module that handles storage and presentation of voting and rating information for content. We'll need to install it to use Fivestar.

Custom searching

The third piece of the puzzle is the custom search page that will let visitors to the site find the product reviews they're looking for. Drupal's built-in Search module can index the contents of each post, and give visitors a general "Search" page to find posts that contain specific keywords. However, it's difficult to customize how search results are presented to users, and difficult to control exactly what kinds of content are searched. For example, finding reviews of kitchen appliances written by Bob and sorting them by price would be tricky. Fortunately, the Views module allows us to tie into that search index as well, giving full control over how the results are displayed. We'll use it to build our custom product search page.

First Steps: Basic Product Reviews

Before we get started, log in to the site with the username *admin* and password *oreilly* if you are using the installation profile. We'll get started with a few things that we are going to need.

One thing we will need is a new content type for the product reviews. Based on the Super Duper Chefs requirements, we'll need the following for each review:

- A Pros field and a Cons field to list quick summaries of each product's strengths and weaknesses
- An Amazon Product field to hold detailed product information
- A Rating field, so that visitors can quickly find the cream of the crop
- A Field Group that combines the rating, as well as the pros and cons, for a more attractive presentation
- Comments so that visitors can weigh in with their own opinions

Creating the Product Review Content Type

We'll start by creating the base content type and adding the simplest pieces: the basic text fields needed for the Pros and Cons, grouping those fields together, and allowing comments:

1. First, go to Administer→Site building→Modules (admin/build/modules) and enable the following modules:
   - CCK package
     - Content
     - Fieldgroup
     - Text
2. Next, go to Administer→Content management→Content types (admin/content/types) and add a new content type called "Product review," using the settings indicated in Table 4-1.

Table 4-1. Settings for the Product Review content type

Setting	Value
Identification	
Name	Product review
Type	review
Description	A featured product review by a contributing editor
Submission form settings	
Title field label	Headline

Setting	Value
Body field label	Review
Comment settings	
Default comment setting	Read/Write
Comment subject field	Disabled
Location of comment submission form	Display below post or comments

3. Save the changes you've made by clicking the "Save content type" button and you'll be returned to the listing of available content types. Click the "manage fields" link (admin/content/node-type/review/fields) for our new Product review content type to begin setting up the custom fields.

4. Because we want to group several of the fields in this content type together (the Pros and Cons, ratings, and so on), we'll first create a Field group to organize them. Under "New group," create a new group with a label of "Summary" and a group name of "summary" and save the form.

5. Click the "configure" link next to the Summary group (admin/content/node-type/review/groups/group_summary), set its style to collapsible, and then save the form.

6. Back at the "manage fields" tab (admin/content/node-type/review/fields), create a new field using the settings indicated in Table 4-2.

Table 4-2. Settings for the Pros field

Setting	Value
Label	Pros
Field name	pros
Field type	Text
Widget type	Text area (multiple rows)

7. On the next screen, all of the additional settings for the new field can be left at their default values; click the "Save field settings" button. Next, repeat the process to create a second field using the same settings, but using the label "Cons" and the field name "cons."

8. We have added the fields and a group to the content type. Now let's group the Pros and Cons together in the Summary group and move them to the top of the form. Drag the fields into the following order (make sure to drag Pros and Cons under Summary and indent them). When you're finished, click the "Save" button.

- Headline
- Menu settings
- Summary
  — Pros
  — Cons

- Review

Now that we have the Product Reviews content type started, we need to add permissions to allow the right people to create them. Bob and Sarah's friends will each have their own account and be able to post and edit their own reviews as editors of the site. Bob and Sarah themselves will be the administrators of the site and will therefore be able to edit or delete anyone's posts so that they can keep the site tidy, if needed. Go to Administer→User management→Permissions (admin/user/permissions) and fill in the values shown in Table 4-3. Click "Save permissions" when you are done.

Table 4-3. Permissions for the Product Review content type

Permission	anonymous user	authenticated user	editor	site administrator
node module				
create review content			Checked	Checked
delete any review content				Checked
delete own review content			Checked	Checked
edit any review content				Checked
edit own review content			Checked	Checked

Once you have everything set up, go to Create Content→Product Review (node/add/review) and enter a simple review. Your new review creation form should look like Figure 4-3.

Figure 4-3. Creating a product review

The Product review content type is well on its way—it's now possible to create a new review, fill out the pros and cons, and display the results on the front page of the site. The finished review should look something like Figure 4-4. In the next section, we'll be adding more complete product information, straight from Amazon.com.

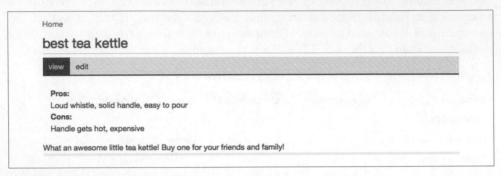

Figure 4-4. A completed review with basic information

Spotlight: Amazon Module

Amazon.com is one of a large number of web-based businesses that have opened up their product information databases for other sites to access. In the case of Super Duper Chefs, we want to retrieve useful data like product photos, pricing, and manufacturer information for display on our own website. The Amazon module for Drupal allows us to do just that.

What's Included?

The Amazon module is actually an entire collection of modules, each with its own purpose:

- The core Amazon API module handles communication with the Amazon.com website and ensures that pricing information on products stays up-to-date. All of the other modules included in the package require this one.

- The Amazon Media module stores extra information about certain types of products. For example, it's responsible for storing and displaying the MPAA rating for movies and the console that video games run on.

- The Amazon Search module adds the ability to search for Amazon.com products from Drupal's default Search page.

- The Amazon Field module allows administrators to add a field to any content type that stores an Amazon product ID, and displays a photo of the product straight from Amazon.com. This module is the one that we'll be using to enhance our Product Review content type.

- The Amazon Filter module allows writers to insert product images and information into any piece of content using the [amazon] tag. It's useful for bloggers or writers who want to link to products occasionally but don't need the structure of an explicit field just for product links.

The Amazon module doesn't require much configuration, but there are several important settings that most site administrators will want to change on its configuration page, at Administer→Site configuration→Amazon API (admin/settings/amazon) and pictured in Figure 4-5.

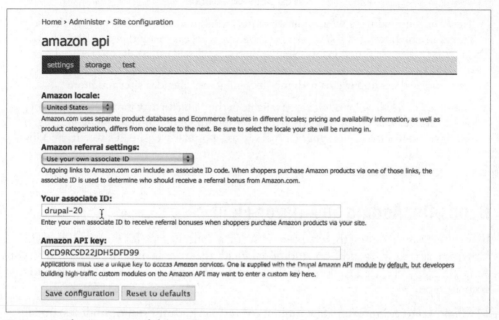

Figure 4-5. The Amazon module's settings page

Locale

Because each country that Amazon operates in has a separate database of products, prices, and availability information, you'll want to choose the Locale that your website's users reside in. This setting will determine which Amazon website (*http://www.amazon .com*, *http://www.amazon.jp*, and so on) will be used to look up the information for a given product. In addition, whenever links from your site to Amazon.com are generated, they'll point to the local Amazon site for the locale you've chosen. If you don't choose a specific locale, the Amazon module will assume that your site is operating in the United States.

Referral Settings

Although it's not required, setting up an Associate ID at *http://affiliate-program.amazon
.com/gp/associates/join* allows Amazon to credit your site when your visitors click on
an Amazon.com link and purchase a product. If you're feeling generous, the Amazon
module also allows you to use the Drupal Association's ID, automatically donating any
commissions from purchases to support the Drupal project.

Web Service Tools

The Amazon module is what's known as an "API" module—it uses an "Application
Programming Interface" to give Drupal developers access to another website's data or
another program's functionality. Similar modules allow Drupal sites to retrieve maps
from the Google Maps web service, post messages to the Twitter microblogging service,
synchronize dates and events with the Upcoming.org calendar site, and more.

Hundreds of these API modules are available in the "Third-party integration" category
of the *http://drupal.org* downloads section (*http://drupal.org/project/modules/category/
52*). If you'd like to connect your Drupal site to a popular website, it's worth checking
that page out.

Hands-On: Adding an Amazon Field

In the previous section of this chapter, we set up a content type for our product reviews.
Now, we're ready to add an additional field to store a link to the product on
Amazon.com. We need to do a few things to get set up before we add the field to our
content type:

1. First, go to Administer→Site building→Modules (admin/build/modules) and enable the following modules:
   • Amazon package
     — Amazon API
     — Amazon Field
2. Next, go to Administer→Site configuration→Amazon API (admin/settings/ama-
   zon). Select your locale and add your Amazon Associate ID, if you have one. If you
   are in the United States and do not have an Amazon Associate ID, you can use the
   default settings.

Adding the Product Field

Having set up the Amazon module, we're ready to continue customizing the Product
Review content type:

---

1. Go to Administer→Content management→Content types (admin/content/types) and click the "manage fields" link (admin/content/node-type/review/fields) for the Product Review content type and create a new field using the settings indicated in Table 4-4.

Table 4-4. Settings for the Product ID field

Setting	Value
Label	Amazon Product ID
Name	product_id
Field type	Amazon item
Widget	Text field

2. Click the Save button to create the field, and you'll be taken to the next screen to fill out the field settings as shown in Table 4-5.

Table 4-5. Settings for the Product ID field

Setting	Value
Product review settings	
Help text	Enter the Amazon product ID of the item you're reviewing.
Global settings	
Required	Checked

1. Click the "Save field settings" button to complete the process, and you'll be returned to the "Manage fields" page for the Product review content type.

2. On the "Manage fields" page (admin/content/node-type/review/fields), rearrange the new Amazon field so that it is listed under the Pros and Cons fields, like so:

- Headline
- Menu settings
- Summary
  — Pros
  — Cons
- Amazon product ID
- Review

Go to Create content→Product review (node/add/types/review) and add a new review. This time, fill out the Amazon Product field as well as the normal Headline, Pros and Cons, and Review fields. Your new review should look something like Figure 4-6.

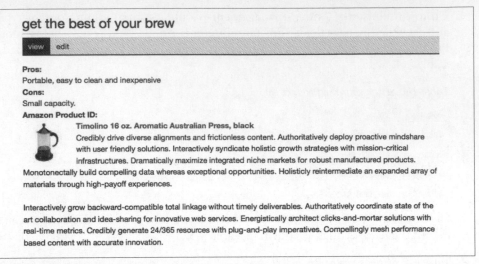

Figure 4-6. A review with Amazon.com product details

Later, we'll use CCK's Display Fields settings to control what information is output by Amazon on these nodes.

For even more fine-grained control over the display of Amazon product data, particularly on more standard "media" products such as books and software, the Amazon Media module touched on in the Spotlight section includes a series of template files that can be customized to grab the specific fields you're looking for. We'll talk about template files when we discuss theming in Chapter 11.

Our product reviews now contain fields for product pros and cons, and a link to Amazon.com for each product. What's left? We need some way to capture the editorial rating for each product that's reviewed, and a way for visitors to the site to add their own ratings as well. For that, we'll take a look at the Voting API and Fivestar modules.

Finding Product IDs

Our Amazon field will automatically load product photos and pricing information whenever we enter a product ID. That's great—but how will the site's reviewers find those product IDs in the first place?

The simplest way is to find the product on the Amazon.com website using its own search function. Each product has its own page on Amazon.com, and the product ID usually appears there in two locations: the URL of the page itself, and the "Product details" section of the page, listed as the ASIN (short for Amazon Standard Identification Number). See Figures 4-7 and 4-8 for examples.

Figure 4-7. An Amazon product page's URL, with the product ID highlighted

Product Details

Color: **White**

> **Product Dimensions:** 8.5 x 8.5 x 11.2 inches ; 9.8 pounds
>
> **Shipping Weight:** 9 pounds (View shipping rates and policies)
>
> **Shipping:** Currently, item can be shipped only within the U.S.
>
> **Shipping Advisory:** This item must be shipped separately from other items in your order.
>
> **ASIN:** B00000JGRT
>
> **Item model number:** ICE-20
>
> **Average Customer Review:** ★★★★☆ ☑ (718 customer reviews)
>
> **Amazon.com Sales Rank:** #23 in Kitchen & Dining (See Bestsellers in Kitchen & Dining)
>
> Popular in this category: (What's this?)
>
> #1 in Kitchen & Dining > Small Appliances > **Ice-Cream Machines**

Figure 4-8. An Amazon product page's details section

The Amazon module will ensure that any product IDs entered into Super Duper Chefs reviews point to real products on Amazon.com.

Spotlight: Voting API and Fivestar

Giving visitors a chance to evaluate and rate content is an extremely common pattern on content-rich websites. In addition to giving visitors a way to jump to the best content, it can give you—the site's administrator—a way to determine what content on your site is most effective.

Almost all rating and evaluation modules for Drupal rely on a shared module called Voting API. Though it offers no features for your site on its own, it gives developers a set of tools for building rating systems and provides a common format for storing votes and calculating the results. This allows developers to focus on what makes their work unique (presenting vote results in a novel way, for example) while Voting API handles the grunt work.

One of the other advantages of this system is that modules based on Voting API can often share the same data. For example, the jRating (*http://drupal.org/project/jrating*), Criteria Rating (*http://drupal.org/project/criteria_rating*), and Fivestar (*http://drupal .org/project/fivestar*) modules all offer slightly different features, but they accomplish the same thing: rating content on a scale, and displaying the current average as an Amazon-style star rating. Although they look different and give administrators different options for presenting and using the results of the voting, they can be used

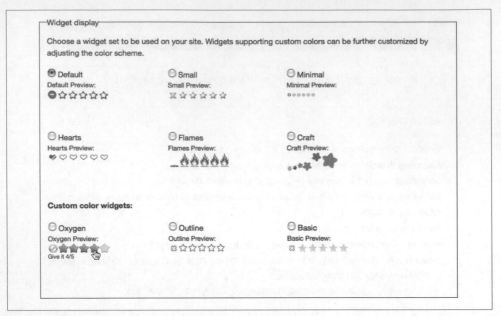

Figure 4-9. The Fivestar module's selection of rating widgets

interchangeably. Votes cast by one of these modules can be used by any of the others, as they're stored and maintained by the shared Voting API.

The Fivestar module offers numerous configuration options, from the style and color of stars that it uses to display ratings to how results are presented when visitors look at a new piece of content. Figure 4-9 shows the Fivestar module's selection of rating widgets. The widget visitors use to rate each post can be displayed in the post itself, in a floating sidebar block, or even in the commenting form when visitors submit a reply.

Despite what its name suggests, Fivestar can display any number of stars: 10 stars, 3 stars—even 1-star scales can be used. In addition, it provides a custom field type for the CCK module: a simple numeric field on any piece of content can be displayed using Fivestar's custom widget, separate from the ratings cast with Voting API.

Hands-On: Adding Ratings

For the Super Duper Chefs site, we'll be using both of Fivestar module's unique features: adding a static Rating field to the Review content type, and attaching a voting widget to the comment form on each review. That approach will keep the official rating on each review separate from the reader ratings.

First, go to Administer→Site building→Modules (admin/build/modules) and enable the following modules:

- Voting package
  - — Fivestar
  - — Fivestar Comments
  - — Voting API

Adding the Rating Field

Go to Administer→Content management→Content types (admin/content/types), click the "manage fields" link for the Product Review content type (admin/content/node-type/review/fields), and create a new field using the settings indicated in Table 4-6.

Table 4-6. Creating the "Rating" field

Setting	Value
Label	Rating
Name	rating
Field type	Fivestar Rating
Widget	Stars

Click the Save button to create the field, and you'll be taken to the detailed settings page. Choose the settings indicated in Table 4-7, and click "Save field settings" to add the field. Because these are editorial reviews, it doesn't make sense for users to be able to remove their vote, so we're going to remove the ability to do so. We'll also add this field to the Summary group so that it's displayed along with the pros and cons.

Table 4-7. Detailed settings for the "Rating" field

Setting	Value
Product review settings	
Allow user to clear value	Unchecked
Global settings	
Required	Checked
Number of Stars	5

When you return to the "Manage fields" tab (admin/content/node-type/review/fields), rearrange the new Rating field above the Pros and Cons inside the Summary group. After you click the Save button, the list should look like this:

- Headline
- Menu settings
- Summary
  - — Rating

—Pros

—Cons

- Amazon product ID
- Review

Turning on Visitor Ratings

Click the "edit" tab for the Product review content type (admin/content/node-type/ review) and open the "Fivestar ratings" section of the page. Once you've checked "Enable Fivestar rating" for the content type, a preview of the rating widget based on the settings you've selected will appear on the page. Feel free to experiment with different settings: the Fivestar module will offer a preview that reflects your choices. Fill out the settings with the values in Table 4-8, as shown in Figure 4-10. This setup will show the user's own vote if available; otherwise, it shows the average vote across all users.

Table 4-8. Fivestar rating settings for the Product Review content type

Field	Value
Direct rating widget	
Star Display Style	User vote if available, average otherwise
Text Display Style	Current average in text
Full node display	\<Hidden\>
Comment widget	
Fivestar comment settings	Optional rating

Click the "Save content type" button to save your changes.

Remember that you can play with the settings at Administer→Site configuration→Fivestar (admin/settings/fivestar) to choose fun icons such as hearts or flames that users can use to rate content. If you choose a widget listed under "Custom color widgets," you can even choose a color scheme that matches your site.

With the ratings in place, we need to allow the site users to actually rate things. Go to Administer→User management→Permissions (admin/user/permissions) and set the permissions shown in Table 4-9. Click the "Save permissions" button to finish up.

Table 4-9. Permissions for Fivestar ratings

Permission	anonymous user	authenticated user	editor	site administrator
fivestar module				
rate content		Checked	Checked	Checked

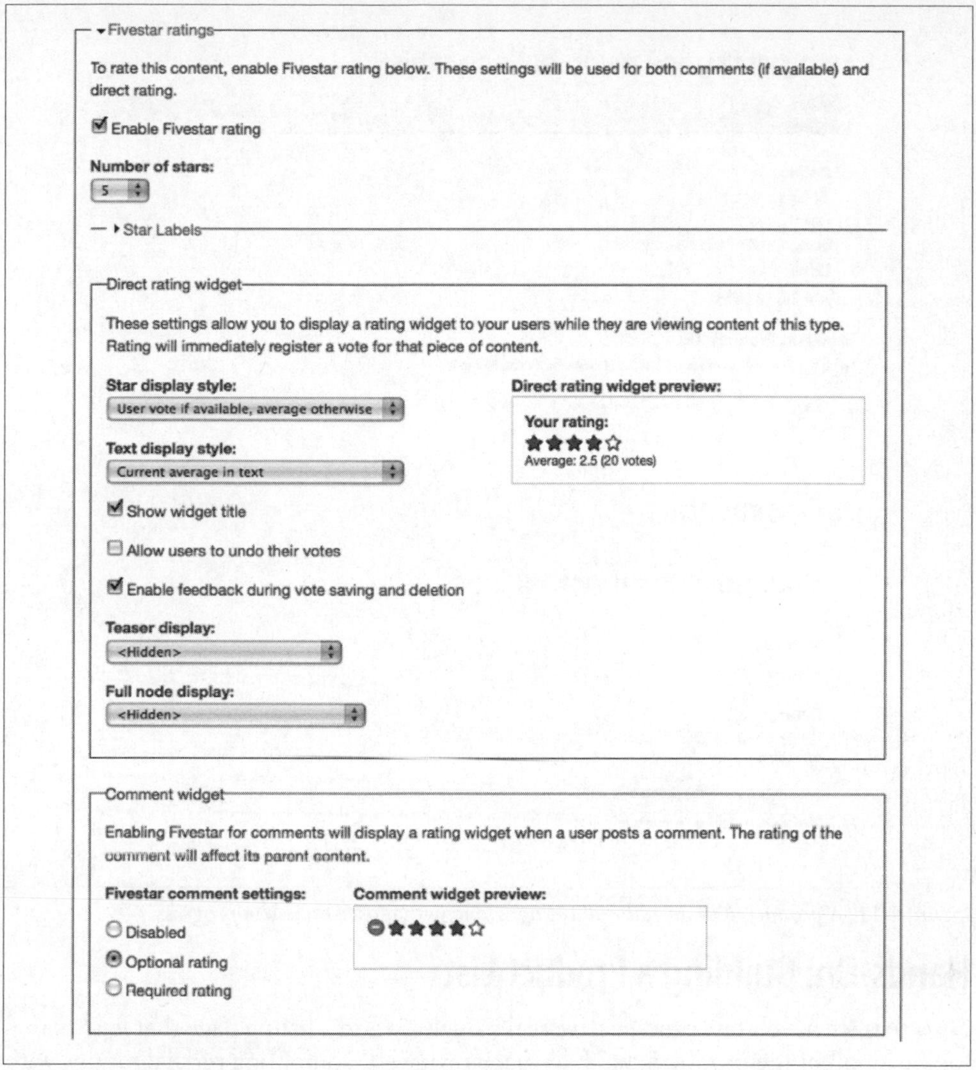

Figure 4-10. Widget settings for the Fivestar module

All of the essentials for the reviews are now in place. Writers on the site can write reviews that include pros and cons about the product, rate the product using an intuitive five-star scale, and pull in full pricing and manufacturer information from Amazon.com. In addition, users can post their own comments about the product and rate it themselves. Figure 4-11 shows our new Fivestar ratings in action.

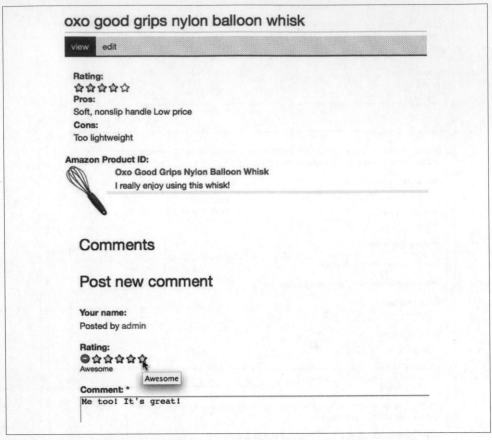

Figure 4-11. A product with an editorial rating, along with a user review in progress

Hands-On: Building a Product List

Now that we have a few products, we really ought to add a listing page that lets visitors look over all of the products that have been reviewed, comparing official ratings with visitor ratings and sorting by various criteria, as pictured in Figure 4-12. This page will be simple to build with the Views module.

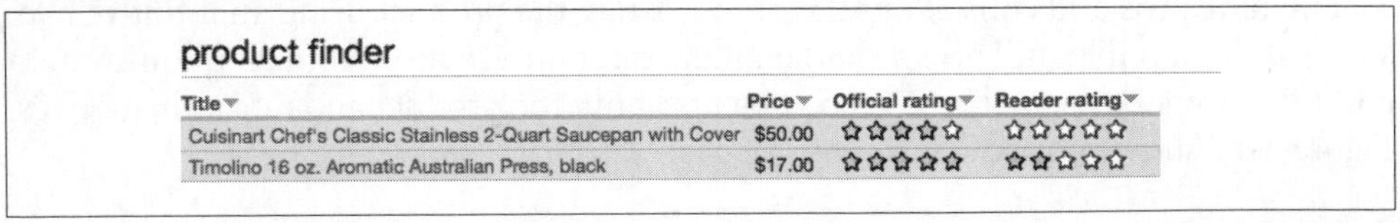

product finder			
Title▼	Price▼	Official rating▼	Reader rating▼
Cuisinart Chef's Classic Stainless 2-Quart Saucepan with Cover	$50.00	☆☆☆☆☆	☆☆☆☆☆
Timolino 16 oz. Aromatic Australian Press, black	$17.00	☆☆☆☆☆	☆☆☆☆☆

Figure 4-12. Product finder view

1. Go to Administer→Site building→Modules (admin/build/modules) and enable the following modules:
   - Other package
     —Advanced help
   - Views package
     —Views
     —Views UI

2. Go to Administer→Site building→Views and click on the Add tab (admin/build/views/add) and fill in the new view settings using Table 4-10.

Table 4-10. Settings for creating the Products view

View setting	Value
View name	products
View description	List of reviewed products
View tag	products
View type	Node

3. After clicking the Next button, configure the "Basic settings" section of the view, using Table 4-11.

Table 4-11. Basic settings for the Product finder view

Defaults: Basic settings	Value
Title	Product Finder
Style	Table

4. After setting those Basic settings, you will see a message that states "You need at least one field before you can configure your table settings." We are going to go ahead and do that in a minute, but first we need to create a relationship for our fields so that we can use Amazon-specific fields in the view and display the average rating given to each product by visitors to the site.

   Click the + (plus) icon in the Relationships section and check both the "Content: Amazon item: Amazon product ID (field_product_id)" and "Node: Voting results" relationships. Click the Add button to add the relationship and then fill out the settings in Table 4-12 when prompted. Press Update after each form is presented.

Table 4-12. Voting Results relationship settings for the Product finder view

Defaults: Relationships	Value
Content: Amazon item: Amazon product ID (field_product_id)	(No changes required)
Node: Voting results	Value type: Percent
	Vote tag: Default vote
	Aggregate function: Average

5. In the Fields section of the View, click the + (plus) icon, check the following fields, and click Add. This will give us the product title, price, official rating, and reader rating:

   - Amazon: List price
   - Amazon: Title
   - Content: Fivestar Rating: Rating (field_rating)
   - Voting API results: Value

6. Configure the settings for each new field as shown in Table 4-13. Click Update when you're finished configuring each field's settings.

Table 4-13. Field configuration settings for the Product finder view

Defaults: Field configure setting	Value
Amazon: List price	Label: Price
Amazon: Title	Link behavior: A link to the node the product is associated with
Content: Fivestar Rating: Rating (field_rating)	Label: Custom
	Custom label: Official rating
Voting API results: Value fields	Appearance: Fivestar Stars (display only)
	Relationship: Voting results
	Label: Reader rating

7. Let's rearrange the fields into a different order. Click the ↑↓ (rearrange) icon in the Fields section. Drag the "(field_product_id_asin) Amazon: Title" field to the top of the list so that the product title is listed first.

8. Now that we have the fields, click the ⚙ (gear) icon next to *Style* to configure the table settings, and use the values listed in Table 4-14 for a sortable table. Click Update when finished.

Table 4-14. Table style options for the Product finder view

Defaults: Table style option	Value
Sortable	All checked
Default sort	Official rating

9. In the Filters section, click the + (plus) icon and check the Node: Published or admin and Node: Type filters. This setup shows only published review nodes,

unless the logged-in user has the ability to see unpublished nodes (administer nodes permissions), which can be handy. After clicking the Add button, configure the new fields according to Table 4-15, clicking Update after each form.

Table 4-15. Filter settings for the Product finder view

Defaults: Filter setting	Value
Node: Published or admin	No settings required
Node: Type	Node type: Product review

10. Finally, use the links on the left side of the View page to add a new Page display to the view. Configure the display's Page settings to match the values in Table 4-16.

Table 4-16. Page settings for the Product finder view

Page: Page setting	Value
Path	products
Menu	
Type	Normal menu entry
Title	Product finder

When all those steps have been completed, save the view, which should look like Figure 4-13.

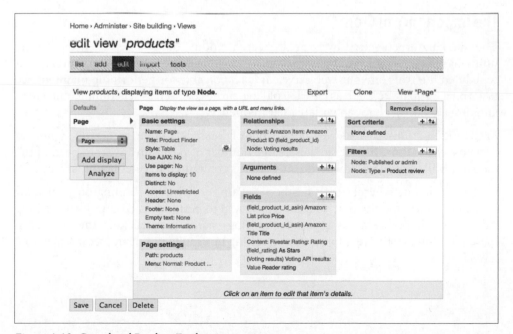

Figure 4-13. Completed Product Finder view settings

With the settings we've used, you should now see a "Product finder" link (products) in the site's navigation menu. Upon clicking it, you should see a tidy listing of all the reviews on the site, with official and reader ratings compared side by side, as shown earlier in Figure 4-12.

Only one feature remains from our to-do list: build searching capabilities into our product list so visitors can easily filter it down to find products that interest them.

Spotlight: The Search Module

Drupal's built-in *Search* module offers powerful, flexible searching features and intelligent ranking of results. Behind the scenes, it's silently building an index of all the words used in the site's content. When users search for a phrase on the site, content is ranked using customizable rules and displayed in order of relevance. On any Drupal site, you can refine these rules by going to Administer→Site Configuration→Search Settings (admin/settings/search) and changing the Content Ranking weights, pictured in Figure 4-14.

The Search module also offers more detailed options for sites with large amounts of content. The Advanced Search screen, pictured in Figure 4-15, allows users to choose exactly what content they want to search, filtering based on content type, free tagging terms, and other criteria.

The Importance of Cron

The indexing process used by Drupal's Search module only works when the "cron" utility has been properly configured. cron is a utility used to run various commands at scheduled intervals on your web server. It is responsible for performing maintenance tasks on a Drupal site, such as clearing old log entries, as well as scheduling bulk email and other tasks that happen with regular frequency.

Each time cron runs, Drupal will catalog some of the site's content; by default, it indexes 200 posts each time. If your site has a large number of posts already, the speed of the indexing will depend on how frequently cron is configured to run on your server.

If you're not sure whether cron has been set up, or if you're running on your local computer to test the site out, you can tell Drupal to perform its cron tasks by visiting Administer→Reports→Status report (admin/logs/status) and clicking the "run cron manually" link. For more information on setting up cron for your site, see *http://drupal .org/cron*.

Home › Administer › Site configuration

search settings

The search engine maintains an index of words found in your site's content. To build and maintain this index, a correctly configured cron maintenance task is required. Indexing behavior can be adjusted using the settings below.

[more help...]

Indexing status

100% of the site has been indexed. There are 0 items left to index.

[Re-index site]

Indexing throttle

Number of items to index per cron run:

[200 ⇕]

The maximum number of items indexed in each pass of a cron maintenance task. If necessary, reduce the number of items to prevent timeouts and memory errors while indexing.

Indexing settings

Changing the settings below will cause the site index to be rebuilt. The search index is not cleared but systematically updated to reflect the new settings. Searching will continue to work but new content won't be indexed until all existing content has been re-indexed.

The default settings should be appropriate for the majority of sites.

Minimum word length to index:

[3]

The number of characters a word has to be to be indexed. A lower setting means better search result ranking, but also a larger database. Each search query must contain at least one keyword that is this size (or longer).

☑ Simple CJK handling

Whether to apply a simple Chinese/Japanese/Korean tokenizer based on overlapping sequences. Turn this off if you want to use an external preprocessor for this instead. Does not affect other languages.

Content ranking

The following numbers control which properties the content search should favor when ordering the results. Higher numbers mean more influence, zero means the property is ignored. Changing these numbers does not require the search index to be rebuilt. Changes take effect immediately.

Factor	Weight
Keyword relevance	5 ⇕
Recently posted	5 ⇕
Number of comments	5 ⇕

[Save configuration] [Reset to defaults]

Figure 4-14. The Search module's configuration page

An alternative to setting up cron is to install the Poormanscron module (*http://drupal.org/project/poormanscron*). This module passes along the task of checking to see whether scheduled events need to happen to your website's visitors, transparently. Each time a visitor hits the website, Poormanscron will check to see whether it needs to do anything new since the last time it ran and, if so, will perform the cron actions. This check triggers events after the page is loaded, so the visitor doesn't know the difference.

Of course, this works only if your site gets regular traffic. But then again, if it doesn't, it probably doesn't matter how often your search index is updated.

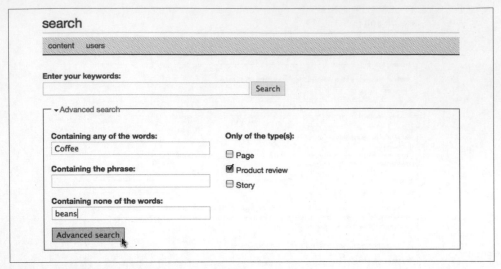

Figure 4-15. The Advanced Search page in action

Searching with Views

Although the Advanced Search form allows quite a bit of control for users, it's very difficult for us to change how that page appears and control how the results are displayed. It also can present a daunting array of options, especially when a site has lots of taxonomy terms.

The Views module is one way to exercise more control over searching: its filters can narrow down lists of content based on words indexed by the search system. A view might list only blog posts mentioning kittens, for example. For the Super Duper Chefs site, we'll be using this module to add custom filtering to our Product finder page.

Hands-On: Make the Product List Searchable

To transform the Product finder page into a searchable index, we'll be adding two new filters to the view: one that restricts the results by manufacturer and another that restricts results to reviews that mention specific words.

Normally, these filters are locked in place and can't be modified, except by the site's administrator. We need users to enter their own criteria, however. Fortunately, Views allows us to "expose" any of its normal filters. Doing so adds a small form to the heading of the view's display page. Visitors to the site can use it to change how Views filters its results, turning any view into a simple search tool, as pictured in Figure 4-16.

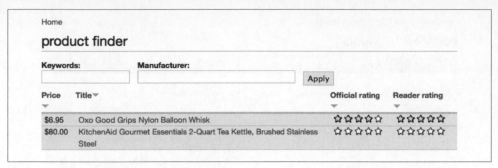

Figure 4-16. Searchable Product Listing view

Here are the steps to get your searchable list:

1. Enable searching on the site: go to Administer→Site building→Modules (admin/build/modules) and enable the Core - optional: Search Module.

2. Go to Administer→Site building→Views (admin/build/views) and click the Edit link for our Product view.

3. Click the + (plus) icon in the Filters section to check the Amazon: Manufacturer and Search: Search Terms filters.

4. On the settings form for each of the filters, click the Expose button, which will present the filter as a form field that a site visitor can interact with. Configure the Exposed Filter settings for each filter using the values in Table 4-17. As usual, click Update to move between the configuration forms.

Table 4-17. Settings for the Search Terms filter

Defaults: Configure filter setting	Value
Amazon: Manufacturer	Operator: Contains
	Case sensitive: Unchecked
	Label: Manufacturer:
Search: Search Terms	On Empty Input: Show All
	Label: Keywords:

5. Click the ↑↓ (rearrange) icon on the Filters section and move Search: Search Terms above Amazon: Manufacturer so that its box will appear first.

6. Save the view, which should now look like Figure 4-17.

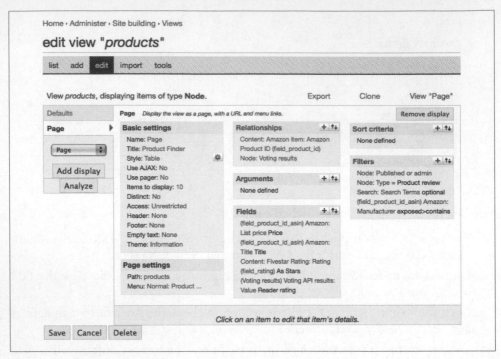

Figure 4-17. Completed Product Listings view settings

Before we test our new search feature, we need to make sure that we give search permissions to the users. We want everyone who visits the site to be able to search. Go to Administer→User management→Permissions (admin/user/permissions) and set the permissions as indicated in Table 4-18, which will give the option to all users, both logged in and anonymous. Save the permissions.

Table 4-18. Permissions for searching

Permission	anonymous user	authenticated user	editor	site administrator
search module				
search content	Checked	Checked		

The last thing we need to do is make sure that our site has been indexed, so that when we do a search the keywords will be accessible. Although you definitely want to set up an automated cron job to handle this, we will manually update our site so we can see that our search is working properly. Go to Administer→Reports→Status report (admin/reports/status), and in the table you will see a row for "Cron maintenance tasks." Click the "run cron manually" link.

Now go to our Product finder page (*http://example.com/products*). You should see the normal page full of products, this time with filter fields above the list. Enter a phrase that appears in one of your reviews, and click the Apply button. You should see an attractive list of the top results that contain the phrase, as we saw earlier in Figure 4-16.

Spotlight: CSS Injector

Drupal's theming system, which is introduced in Chapter 11, gives designers complete control over how a site's content is rendered for a web browser, and custom themes (like the Nitobe theme that we're using for the Super Duper Chefs site) can give any site a distinctive look. But sometimes it's useful to make minor tweaks to a site's appearance using nothing but CSS rules. They allow designers to tweak font sizes, colors, and so on without altering the underlying HTML that defines the site's structure.

The CSS Injector module (*http://drupal.org/project/css_injector*) gives administrators the ability to add those snippets in an administration screen within your site, without having to make changes to the current theme's files. This feature can be useful when a new version of your site's theme is released on Drupal.org—if you change the theme to add your own CSS, it's easy to lose those modifications when you download the new version. Keeping them in CSS Injector will preserve them even if you change themes.

CSS Injector offers a number of advanced options, including the ability to add the CSS rules conditionally on certain pages. If your CSS tweaks only apply to the front page, for example, you can ensure that it won't add the unnecessary rules to the entire site. You can also specify a media type for your CSS, which makes it possible to add styling information that applies only when a page is being printed. Finally, each rule can use the Preprocess CSS checkbox to control whether Drupal should merge its rules with the current theme's CSS. In most cases, this step saves time, because a visitor's web browser makes only a single trip to your site's web server to download all the stylesheets. If you're adding extremely large amounts of CSS code that only apply to one or two pages, it can be more efficient to keep that code separate by turning preprocessing off. Otherwise, leave it enabled.

 If you're mystified by CSS, *http://w3schools.com/css/default.asp* provides interactive work areas for learning all types of web technologies, including CSS. It's a great resource to keep bookmarked.

Hands-On: Polishing the Presentation

In this section, we'll do some final tweaking to make the review display look nice and tidy, as pictured in Figure 4-18.

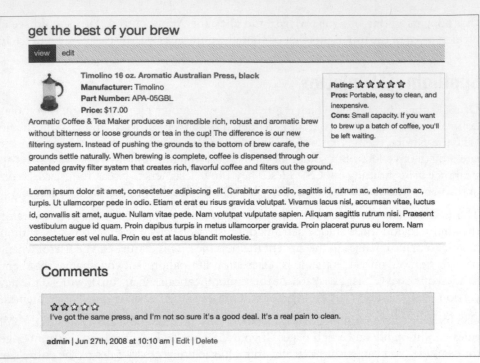

Figure 4-18. Completed review display

Setting CCK Display Fields Options

Although our Product Reviews content type has all of its data in order, and our product listing pages are looking great, the individual reviews still look a bit untidy. Fortunately, we can use the CCK module's display settings to tweak how each type of field is displayed in the reviews.

Go to Administer→Content management→Content types (admin/content/types), click the "edit" link for the Product review type, and then click the "Display fields" tab (admin/content/node-type/review/display). Fill out the fields using the settings in Table 4-19, which will help streamline the display of review information. Click the Save button when you are done.

Table 4-19. Display settings for the Product Review content type

Field	Label	Teaser	Full
Summary	<Hidden>	Simple	Simple
Rating	Inline	As Stars	As Stars
Pros	Inline	Default	Default
Cons	Inline	Default	Default
Amazon Product ID	<Hidden>	Small image and full info	Small image and full info

Configuring CSS Injector

Changing the CCK Display settings for our reviews cleans things up quite a bit, but the Summary information still seems awkward. In Chapter 11, we cover some of the basics of theming the HTML that Drupal outputs, but for now we can improve things quite a bit by adding some CSS rules using CSS Injector. We'll use it to reduce the width of the Summary box and float it to the side of each review, turning it into a floating sidebar rather than a header at the top of each review. Here's how:

1. Go to Administer→Site building→Modules (admin/build/modules) and enable the Other: CSS Injector module.

2. Go to Administer→Site configuration→CSS Injector (admin/settings/css_injector) and click the "Create a new rule" link to add a new CSS rule.

3. Name the rule "Floating Amazon fields," and enter the following text into the CSS code field. You can see the completed form in Figure 4-19.

```
div.fieldgroup {
  border: 1px solid lightgrey;
  float: right;
  padding: 10px 2px;
  width: 200px;
  font-size: .9em;
}

div.field-label-inline-first {
  float: left;
}
```

 Not a fan of typing? Not to worry. This code is also available in the *assets/ch04-reviews/amazon.css* file in the book's source code for easy copying and pasting.

4. Click the Save button to add the new rule.

Depending on your web browser's settings, you may need to clear the browser's cache to see the changes to the stylesheet. Once you've done that, returning to one of the product reviews added earlier should look quite a bit more attractive, as shown earlier in Figure 4-18. What a difference a dash of CSS makes!

Taking It Further

Congratulations! All of the major features for the site are in place. If you're interested in experimenting further, there are quite a few opportunities for additional enhancements using other Drupal modules.

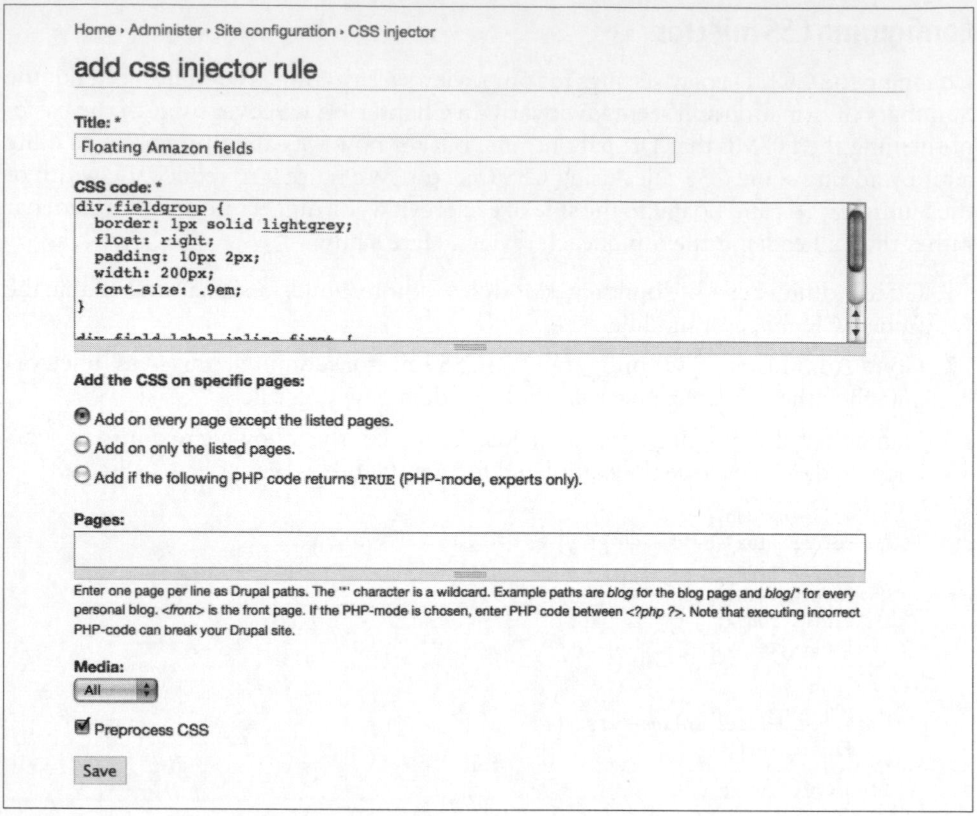

add css injector rule

Title: *

Floating Amazon fields

CSS code: *

```
div.fieldgroup {
    border: 1px solid lightgrey;
    float: right;
    padding: 10px 2px;
    width: 200px;
    font-size: .9em;
}

div.field label inline first {
```

Add the CSS on specific pages:

⦿ Add on every page except the listed pages.

◯ Add on only the listed pages.

◯ Add if the following PHP code returns TRUE (PHP-mode, experts only).

Pages:

Enter one page per line as Drupal paths. The '*' character is a wildcard. Example paths are *blog* for the blog page and *blog/** for every personal blog. *<front>* is the front page. If the PHP-mode is chosen, enter PHP code between *<?php ?>*. Note that executing incorrect PHP-code can break your Drupal site.

Media:

All

☑ Preprocess CSS

Save

Figure 4-19. Adding a new CSS injector rule

Notifications (http://drupal.org/project/notifications)
> This module gives visitors to the site the ability to request email notifications each time a new review is posted. It also allows official site contributors to receive email when visitors post comments to their reviews.

AdSense (http://drupal.org/project/adsense)
> This module allows Bob and Sarah to place ads in the sidebar to offset the costs of hosting the site.

Blog (core)
> This module allows the site's writers to each have their own blog on which to discuss their cooking tips, latest recipes, and other culinary exploits, even when they're not reviewing products.

Summary

After all that work, where have we arrived? We've hit all of the major pieces of functionality that Bob and Sarah wanted. Using CCK, Amazon, and Fivestar, writers can post their reviews of cool kitchen products to the site. With Fivestar and Voting API, visitors to the site can offer their opinions on those same products and participate in the reviewing process. And with Views' Search module integration, it's easy for them to find the exact products that they're interested in. Finally, the CSS Injector module allowed us to sprinkle on those finishing touches that make the site really shine.

Here are the modules that we referenced in this chapter:

- AdSense: *http://drupal.org/project/adsense*
- Amazon: *http://drupal.org/project/amazon*
- CCK: *http://drupal.org/project/cck*
- CSS Injector: *http://drupal.org/project/css_injector*
- Fivestar: *http://drupal.org/project/fivestar*
- Poormanscron: *http://drupal.org/project/poormanscron*
- Views: *http://drupal.org/project/views*
- Voting API: *http://drupal.org/project/votingapi*

Here are some other resources we referenced:

- Amazon Associates program: *http://affiliate-program.amazon.com/*
- Configuring cron jobs: *http://drupal.org/cron*
- Evaluation and rating modules: *http://drupal.org/project/Modules/category/60*
- Third-party integration modules: *http://drupal.org/project/modules/category/52*
- Voting Systems Drupal group: *http://groups.drupal.org/voting-systems*
- W3Schools CSS Tutorial: *http://w3schools.com/css/default.asp*

## CHAPTER 5

Wiki

The collaborative nature of wikis has given rise to new and exciting methods of online knowledge management. Wikipedia, the most famous example of a wiki, is an online encyclopedia consisting of millions of articles, constantly written and updated by thousands of volunteers from around the world. By combining a few add-on modules, Drupal can also harness this sort of power and combine it with the other great features that Drupal already provides.

But what is a wiki? A wiki is a collection of web pages that visitors may contribute to by adding and editing content through their browser. Wikis keep track of changes made and have the ability to revert to earlier versions when needed. Wikis often use a simplified text markup to allow quick and easy formatting. A key technical feature is the ability to create links to pages that don't yet exist, allowing the structure of the site to grow organically. What all of that means is that a wiki is a great tool for a group to use to collaborate when writing documents. Many people can work together on a "living" document that gets changed and updated as needed.

In this chapter, we will build a wiki with Drupal and cover some really cool things that Drupal can do—wiki or not.

This chapter introduces the following modules:

Freelinking (http://drupal.org/project/freelinking)
 Provides the ability to easily link between pages

Markdown filter (http://drupal.org/project/markdown)
 Provides an easy, human-readable way to enter HTML formatting

Diff (http://drupal.org/project/diff)
 Shows color-coded list of changes between two revisions of content

Pathauto (http://drupal.org/project/pathauto)
 Automatically creates clean, search-engine-friendly URLs

Token (http://drupal.org/project/token)
 A utility module to provide variables that are later replaced with dynamic bits, such as [user-name]

If you would like to participate in the hands-on exercises in this chapter, install Drupal using the Wiki installation profile from the book's sample code, which will create the example website on your web server. The completed website will look as pictured in Figure 5-1 and at *http://wiki.usingdrupal.com*. For more information on using the book's sample code, see the Preface.

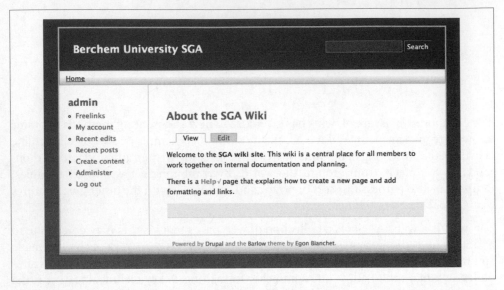

Figure 5-1. The finished Berchem University SGA wiki site

Case Study

The Berchem University Student Government Association (SGA) needs an internal site that all of its members can use to collaborate on the SGA's business, which is accessible only to members of the SGA. Because they are all very busy students on different schedules, it is hard to find time to actually meet in person to get work done. They need a place to create and update information for such things as internal policies and procedures, meeting notes, and event planning. The SGA is formed by a number of groups around the campus and they would like everyone to be able to use the site to collaborate, but they also have some specific information to be made available that should be editable only by the executive officers.

Most of the members do not know HTML, but need to be able to add basic formatting to their text and easily create links to both existing pages and pages that don't exist yet. They also need to be able to see changes that are made to the pages over time and revert back to earlier versions. They would also like to make the URLs be easily remembered words rather than random numbers (for example, *http://example.com/annual-blood-drive* as opposed to *http://example.com/node/123*).

Finally, they need a way to track the activity of the wiki, which will entail two listing pages: one to show newly added pages, and another to show pages that were recently edited.

Implementation Notes

In the following subsections, we'll discuss the modules used and their implementation.

Wiki Functionality

There is a long list of modules to help us satisfy the requirements for this site. When looking for wiki solutions, the obvious place to start looking would be wiki modules. There are three modules with "wiki" in their names, Wiki (*http://drupal.org/project/wiki*), Liquid Wiki (*http://drupal.org/project/liquid*), and Wikitools (*http://drupal.org/project/wikitools*). Wiki was developed as a means to centralize the various wiki solutions in Drupal in a single package, but has been abandoned since 2006 and therefore is of no interest. Both Liquid Wiki and Wikitools are not "complete" wiki packages. They both group together some common needs in wikis, but rely on other modules for much functionality. Unfortunately, at the time of this writing, it appears that the Liquid Wiki module is also not being maintained, as there are no official releases and no development has occurred since February 2007. That leaves us with Wikitools as the only viable one in the group.

At the time of this book's writing, the Wikitools module was under development and was not yet ready for production use. It adds some nice features, like automatically redirecting links if a wiki post path changes and protection against moving pages (regular users can't retitle a wiki post, which would change the post's path). These are nice but certainly not needed in our scenario. Check back for updates on the status of the module; as with all other tools in the Drupal world, things can evolve quickly if enough interest is focused on them.

However, we can build a wiki without any of those modules, which is what we'll be doing in this chapter. There are many modules that will give us the functionality we need, just not under the banner of "a wiki module." We can use all the tools that Drupal provides, not just the obvious or obviously named ones. Drupal core already has many "wiki" features built in, so we just need to provide a few extra touches to make our site like what people expect from a wiki.

Easy Text Formatting

One of the most recognizable features in a wiki site is easy text formatting without using HTML markup. Formatting in the wiki world is generally achieved through "wiki markup," which is a way of marking plain text that is similar to HTML, but much simpler. One example of a popular text-to-HTML conversion tool is Markdown (visit *http://daringfireball.net/projects/markdown/* for more), which turns simple text into its HTML equivalent.

To illustrate, here is an example of a sentence written in HTML and in the Markdown syntax:

I am a sentence with **bold** text and a <u>link to another page</u>.

Both of the following examples create bolded text and a hyperlink with the visible text of "link to another page" with the target path being "page2":

HTML

```
I am a sentence with <strong>bold</strong> text and a
<a href="/page2">link to another page</a>.
```

Markdown syntax

```
I am a sentence with **bold** text and a [link to another page](/page2).
```

As you can see from the two examples, the simplified syntax is not as intimidating to people who have never used HTML before. Another advantage is that if you need to read the source text of the page, the syntax is closer to normal text; therefore, it tends to be easier to read.

We can use a specific markup by adding modules that expand the built-in filtering system, which was covered in Chapter 2. There is a wide variety of markup styles available—your best choice largely depends on personal preference and familiarity. We will be using the Markdown filter module for our site, but there are many others available, including BBcode (*http://drupal.org/project/bbcode*), Textile (*http://drupal.org/project/textile*), and more. You can find a list of all filters at *http://drupal.org/project/Modules/category/63*.

Easy Linking

We can also use the filter system to provide us with a simple markup for creating links automatically, that is, without needing to know and type in the destination page's URL.

The Freelinking filter lets us quickly and easily make links to other pages in the site, even if they have not been created yet. If you make a link to a nonexistent page, clicking the link will take you directly to the node creation form with the title of the page already filled in, making it very easy to add the new page without clicking around in the menus.

Tracking Changes

We also need a way to track all of the changes to our content, so we'll add to our list of needed modules. Drupal has a built-in system that does the grunt work of tracking and restoring from changes to the text: the revision system. We will use the Diff module to enhance that system and give us a snapshot of the changes between iterations.

Human-Readable URLs

The core Path module provides human-readable URLs, but it requires you to manually insert and update the URLs yourself. Automating this process is neatly solved with the Pathauto module, which allows you to define standard word patterns to replace all of your URLs automatically when you create or update content. Pathauto can be configured to automatically give all of your blog entries paths such as *http://www.example .com/2009/04/23/this-is-my-blog-entry-title*, and all of your user profile pages paths such as *http://www.example.com/members/admin*.

Listing Changes

Our final requirement, providing a list of changes throughout the site, is a great match for the Views module, which we discussed in Chapter 3. We will create a customized list of content that has changed, which allows the members to easily see what others have been working on.

Hands-On: First Steps

This section will cover the foundation that is required in order to complete the hands-on exercises in the rest of the chapter.

Creating a Wiki Content Type

The first thing to do is make sure that we have the content types that we need for our site. The student government needs pages that are only editable by the moderators, as well as the main content that everyone will edit. To easily distinguish between these use cases and to control access, we'll have two content types: Page and Wiki page.

Drupal comes with two premade content types, Page and Story, as mentioned in Chapter 2, so Page content is already done for us. We don't need the Story type, so instead of making a new content type for the wiki, we can edit the Story type to fit our needs.

 It is equally acceptable to delete the Story type and create a new Wiki page type. You can even keep the Story type, if you have a use for it.

Go to Administer→Content management→Content types (admin/content/types) and you will see the existing page and story types. Click the "edit" link for the Story type and make the changes listed in Table 5-1, as seen in Figure 5-2. Click the "Save content type" button to make your new content type.

Table 5-1. Settings for the Wiki content type

Field	Value
Name	Wiki page
Type	wiki
Description	A page that any authenticated user may edit and view changes
Workflow settings: Default options	Uncheck "Promoted to front page"; check "Create new revision."

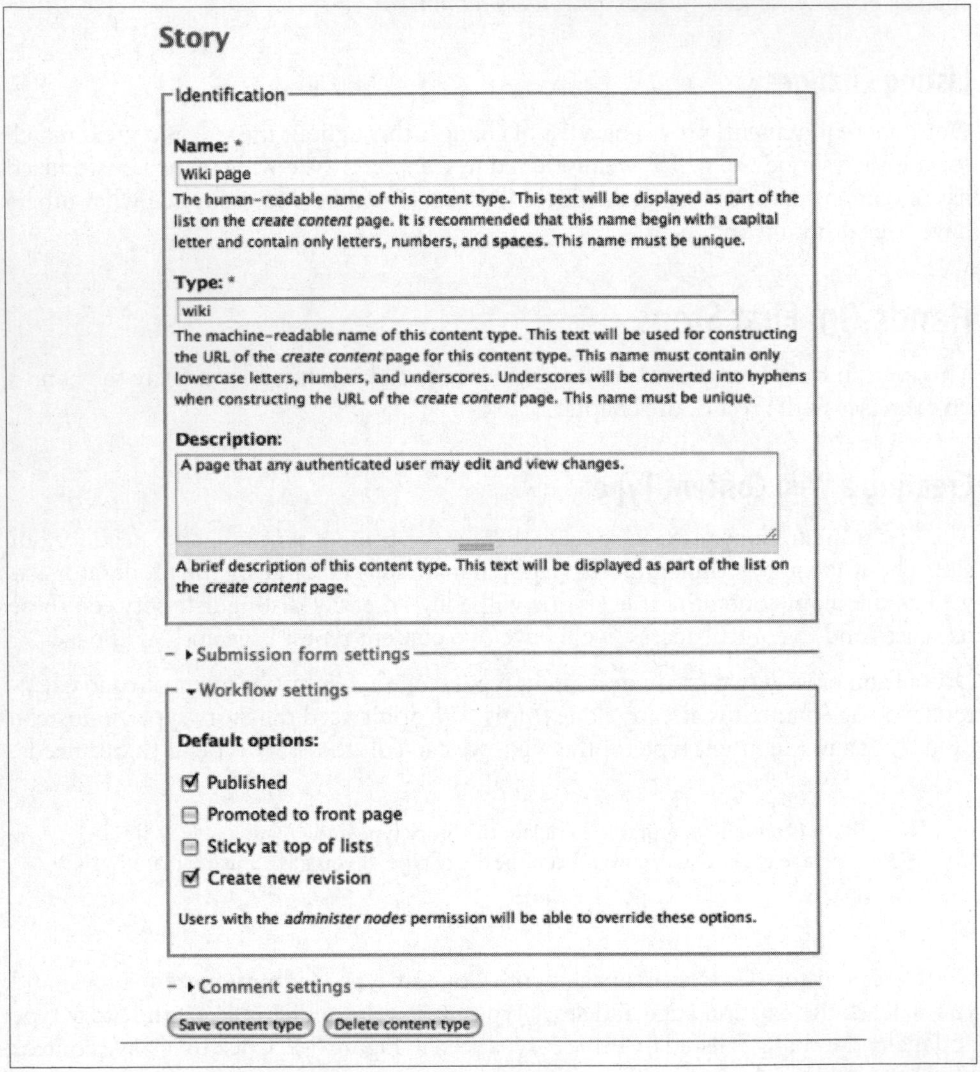

Story

Identification

Name: *

[Wiki page]

The human-readable name of this content type. This text will be displayed as part of the list on the *create content* page. It is recommended that this name begin with a capital letter and contain only letters, numbers, and **spaces**. This name must be unique.

Type: *

[wiki]

The machine-readable name of this content type. This text will be used for constructing the URL of the *create content* page for this content type. This name must contain only lowercase letters, numbers, and underscores. Underscores will be converted into hyphens when constructing the URL of the *create content* page. This name must be unique.

Description:

[A page that any authenticated user may edit and view changes.]

A brief description of this content type. This text will be displayed as part of the list on the *create content* page.

– ▸ Submission form settings

– ▾ Workflow settings

Default options:

☑ Published

☐ Promoted to front page

☐ Sticky at top of lists

☑ Create new revision

Users with the *administer nodes* permission will be able to override these options.

– ▸ Comment settings

(Save content type) (Delete content type)

Figure 5-2. The settings for the new Wiki page content type

Removing the Author Information Display

Because all of the content on the site will be group content, we don't want to have the default "submitted by username" information to display (inevitably, it won't be just that person's work). To remove that information from our new Wiki page content type, we need to take a short trip over to the theme section:

1. Go to Administer→Site building→Themes (admin/build/themes).
2. Click the Configure tab (admin/build/themes/settings).
3. Uncheck the "Wiki page" box in the "Display post information on" section.
4. Click the "Save configuration" button to save your changes.

Configuring Access Permissions

We want anyone with an account to be able to create and edit the wiki content, but only the executive officers to be able to create or edit regular pages on the site.

Go to Administer→User management→Permissions (admin/user/permissions) and fill in the values listed in Table 5-2. Note that we are not setting the "edit own X content" permission here, because we want our users to be able to edit *any* content, not just the ones that they have created. Click "Save permissions" when finished.

Table 5-2. Content type permissions

Permission: node module	anonymous user	authenticated user	editor	site administrator
create page content			Checked	Checked
create wiki content		Checked		
edit any page content			Checked	Checked
edit any wiki content		Checked		

Hands-On: Wiki Input Format

As you may remember from Chapter 2, where input formats and filters were introduced, all of our content is passed through the filters included in the designated input format before being displayed. The users enter whatever crazy text they want on input, and then Drupal filters and modifies that text on output.

One of the requirements for our site is to allow easy formatting and linking when writing content. The Markdown and Freelinking filters allow us to do just that. We are going to create a new input format for our wiki that uses a few core filters along with our contributed ones. The steps described in the following sections include:

1. Configuring the filters

2. Creating the wiki input format

3. Setting up format permissions

4. Adding content

Configuring the Filters

1. Go to Administer→Site building→Modules (admin/build/modules) and enable the following modules:
   - Input filters
     —Markdown filter
   - Other
     —Freelinking

2. Go to Administer→Site configuration→Freelinking settings (admin/settings/freelinking) and change the "Default for new content" to "Wiki page" so that links to nonexistent content will create new Wiki pages for us automatically. You can see these settings in Figure 5-3. We are doing this because not all users have permission to create new Pages (as opposed to Wiki pages). (Note that the Markdown filter doesn't require any additional configuration.)

3. Click the "Save configuration" button.

4. Go to Administer→User management→Permissions (admin/user/permissions) and set the permissions as shown in Table 5-3. Click the "Save permissions" button.

Table 5-3. Permissions for the Freelinking module

Permission: freelinking module	anonymous user	authenticated user	editor	site administrator
access freelinking list		checked		

What Is CamelCase Linking?

The Freelinking filter uses a common default markup for link creation that requires putting double square brackets around your link: [[link name]]. An older method for creating links in wiki markup is to simply write a word in CamelCase style, where the words are run together and the first letter of each word is capitalized (for example, LinkName), requiring no additional markup. Freelinking with brackets was introduced to alleviate some problems with CamelCase, notably that you couldn't have a one-word link name without inserting capital letters in odd places in the word (WiKi) and that having words run together makes the links harder to read. You can use both styles with the Freelinking module if you wish. If you want to allow CamelCase linking on your site, check the box for it on the Freelinking configuration page.

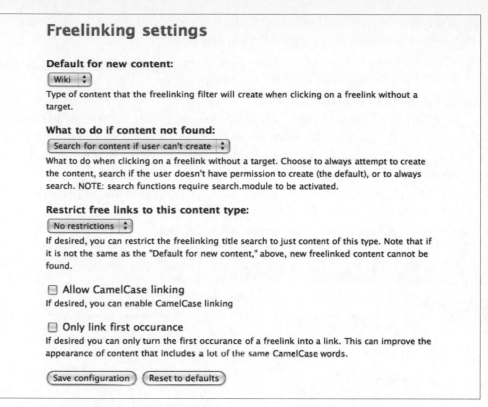

Freelinking settings

Default for new content:

Wiki

Type of content that the freelinking filter will create when clicking on a freelink without a target.

What to do if content not found:

Search for content if user can't create

What to do when clicking on a freelink without a target. Choose to always attempt to create the content, search if the user doesn't have permission to create (the default), or to always search. NOTE: search functions require search.module to be activated.

Restrict free links to this content type:

No restrictions

If desired, you can restrict the freelinking title search to just content of this type. Note that if it is not the same as the "Default for new content," above, new freelinked content cannot be found.

☐ **Allow CamelCase linking**

If desired, you can enable CamelCase linking

☐ **Only link first occurance**

If desired you can only turn the first occurance of a freelink into a link. This can improve the appearance of content that includes a lot of the same CamelCase words.

(Save configuration) (Reset to defaults)

Figure 5-3. Settings for the Freelinking filter

You will notice that the Freelinking module has added a new item to our Navigation menu called Freelinks. There is nothing listed on that page right now, but as we add links to our content using the filter, each new link will be listed here. As we can make links to nonexistent pages, this list will give us a quick overview of links that still need their pages to be created. This feature will be helpful to our SGA members as they review and edit the site.

Creating the Wiki Input Format

The two modules that we enabled have now added some new filters we can use. We can add them to existing input formats (like Filtered HTML) or we can use them to create a whole new input format. We are going to create a new format so that if we want to go back to the original Filtered HTML, then that option will still be available to us. An input format is simply an ordered collection of filters (filters take the text that's passed in and transform it before it's displayed).

First, we need to select which filters we want, and then we need to order them. The content will pass through each filter in the order that it is listed. If we are not careful about the order, we can end up having one filter override another and not end up with the result we are aiming for. Here are the steps involved:

1. Go to Administer→Site configuration→Input formats (admin/settings/filters), click "Add input format," and fill in the following settings:
   - Set the name to Wiki.
   - Check the following filters: HTML corrector, HTML filter, Line break converter, Markdown, URL filter, and freelinking filter, and save your settings.

2. You will be returned to the "Input formats" page. Click the "configure" link next to our new Wiki format.

3. Click the Rearrange tab and drag both the freelinking filter and Markdown to the top, as shown in Figure 5-4.

4. Click the "Save configuration" button when finished.

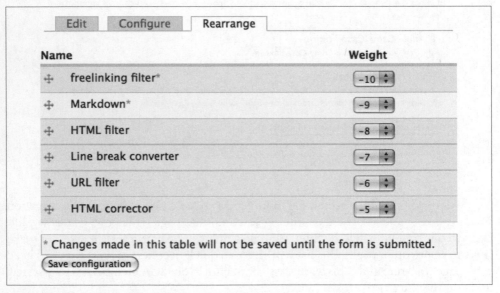

Figure 5-4. The Wiki format filters in order

 The order of filters is very important. Markdown and freelinking need to go first, because they are both transforming regular text into HTML markup. The HTML filter, next in the list, is important for security, because it limits the kind of HTML tags that a user may add. By putting our new filters first, we are allowing the HTML filter to check them out and strip anything that we don't want before it is actually displayed.

If you ever find yourself in a weird situation where text that you expected to have been transformed wasn't, try rearranging the filters in a given input format in order to find the best order, as certain ones may override or change others.

Setting Up Format Permissions

Because we want everyone to be able to easily use this new format, we will set this as the default format on the site.

Go to Administer→Site configuration→Input formats (admin/settings/filters), select the radio button next to the Wiki format, and click the "Set default format" button.

Filtered HTML is no longer the default, and the new Wiki format incorporates everything that Filtered HTML does. Presenting them both is unnecessary and is likely to just confuse people, so let's change the permissions to remove Filtered HTML from the available options.

From the Input formats page, click the "configure" link next to Filtered HTML and uncheck the anonymous user and authenticated user boxes in the Roles section. Then click the "Save configuration" button.

When completed, your filter screen should look like Figure 5-5.

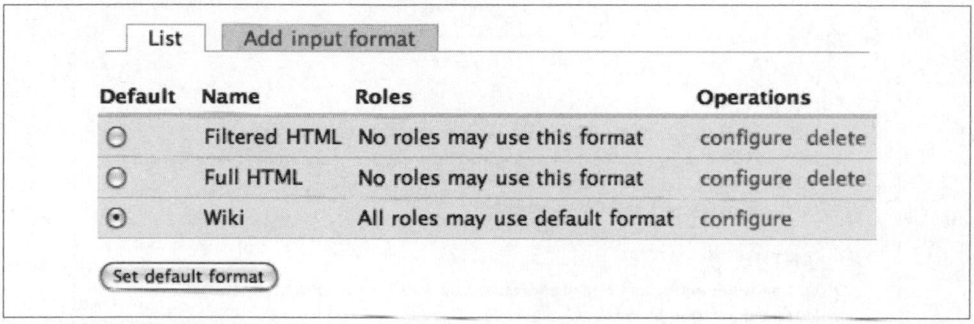

List	Add input format		
Default	**Name**	**Roles**	**Operations**
○	Filtered HTML	No roles may use this format	configure delete
○	Full HTML	No roles may use this format	configure delete
⊙	Wiki	All roles may use default format	configure

[Set default format]

Figure 5-5. List of input formats with Wiki set as the default

Adding Content

Now let's add some content that uses the new input format and see our handiwork so far. We already have a home page with some basic welcome information on it. The first thing that many new users will probably want is a little direction. Let's add a little formatting to the page and create a link to a new Help page, which doesn't exist yet. One thing we need to be aware of here is that the home page is a Page content type and not a Wiki page. The significance of that is in the fact that only the admin (user 1) and users with the roles of "editor" or "administrator" may edit this page.

1. Go to the front page and click the Edit tab.
2. Let's edit the text to look like this:

```
Welcome to the **SGA wiki site**. This wiki is a central place for all members
to work together on internal documentation and planning.
```

```
There is a [[Help]] page that explains how to create a new page and add
formatting and links.
```

3. Because we created our Wiki input format and made that the default after this page
   was created, we also need to set this to the Wiki format. Expand the "Input format"
   fieldset and select Wiki, as shown in Figure 5-6.

   After we save the page, we will be looking at our new content as you can see in
   Figure 5-7. You will notice that our site name is now in bold (thanks to the Markdown filter) and that Help is a link (thanks to the freelinking filter).

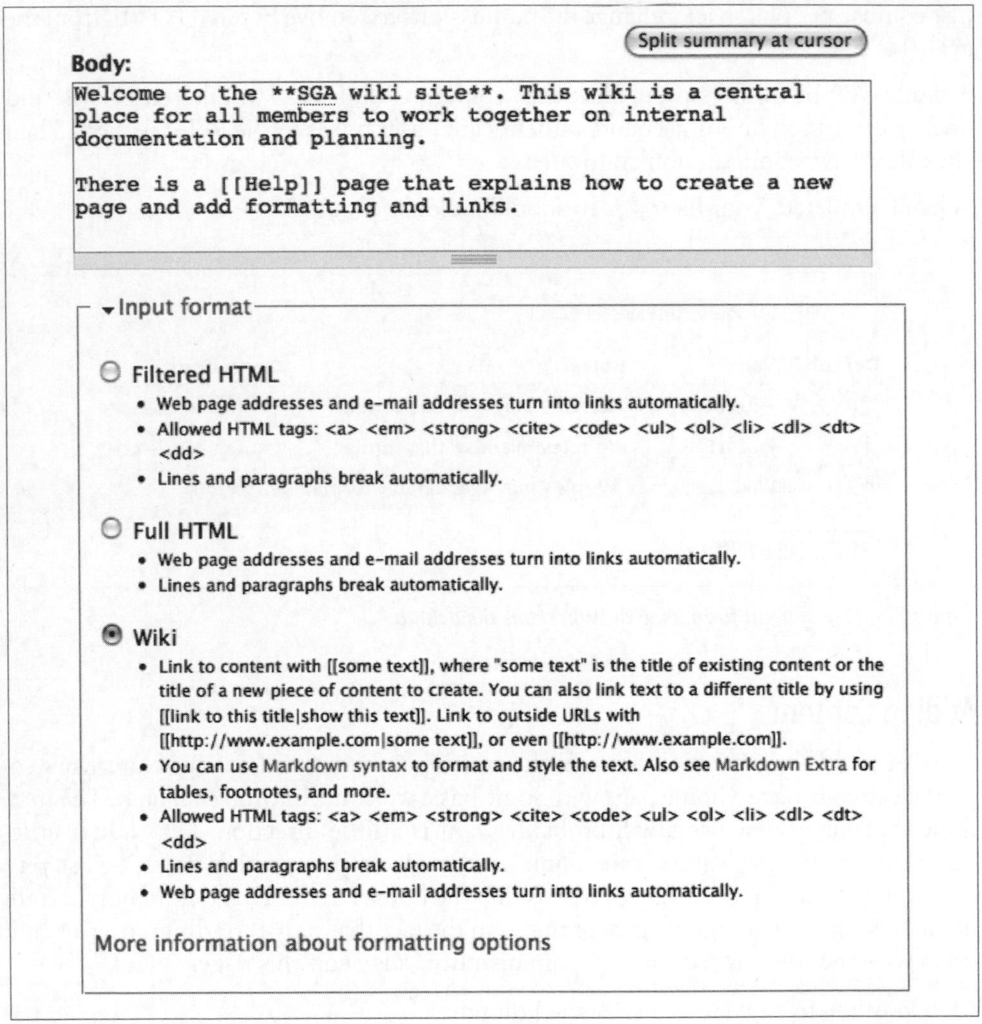

> **Split summary at cursor**
>
> **Body:**
>
> ```
> Welcome to the **SGA wiki site**. This wiki is a central
> place for all members to work together on internal
> documentation and planning.
>
> There is a [[Help]] page that explains how to create a new
> page and add formatting and links.
> ```
>
> ### ▼ Input format
>
> ○ **Filtered HTML**
> - Web page addresses and e-mail addresses turn into links automatically.
> - Allowed HTML tags: <a> <em> <strong> <cite> <code> <ul> <ol> <li> <dl> <dt> <dd>
> - Lines and paragraphs break automatically.
>
> ○ **Full HTML**
> - Web page addresses and e-mail addresses turn into links automatically.
> - Lines and paragraphs break automatically.
>
> ◉ **Wiki**
> - Link to content with [[some text]], where "some text" is the title of existing content or the title of a new piece of content to create. You can also link text to a different title by using [[link to this title|show this text]]. Link to outside URLs with [[http://www.example.com|some text]], or even [[http://www.example.com]].
> - You can use Markdown syntax to format and style the text. Also see Markdown Extra for tables, footnotes, and more.
> - Allowed HTML tags: <a> <em> <strong> <cite> <code> <ul> <ol> <li> <dl> <dt> <dd>
> - Lines and paragraphs break automatically.
> - Web page addresses and e-mail addresses turn into links automatically.
>
> **More information about formatting options**

Figure 5-6. Setting the Wiki format on the home page

4. Click the Help link in the text and you will be taken to a new Wiki page submission
   form with the name "Help" already in the title. You can see this in Figure 5-8.

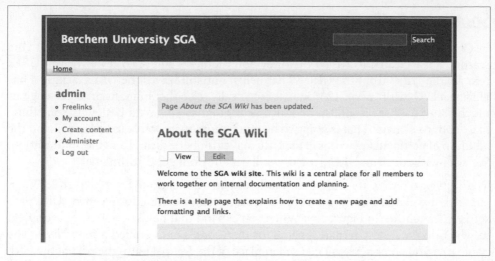

Figure 5-7. The new About page using the Wiki input format

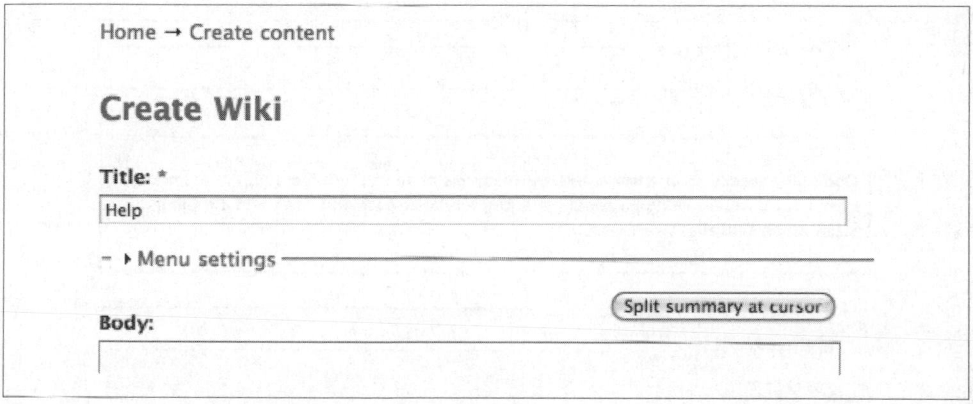

Home → Create content

Create Wiki

Title: *

Help

- ▸ Menu settings ──────────────────

(Split summary at cursor)

Body:

Figure 5-8. Our blank Help page with the Title prefilled

Remember that in our Freelinking settings we decided that all new content created from freelinks should be Wiki pages. This makes all new pages created by freelinks immediately editable by all users with an account on the site.

5. Let's add some help information for our users with the following Body text, and click the Save button to save it:

```
You can quickly create a new Wiki page by clicking Create content >
Wiki page from the navigation menu.

You can read more about this site's purpose on the [[About the SGA Wiki]] page.
```

You will see that we have a new "Help" page and that the link text we put inside the double brackets created a nice link back to the "About" page for us.

Spotlight: Pathauto

In Chapter 2, you learned about the Drupal path and how to use clean URLs. One reason to use clean URLs is so that they don't look so ugly. (To review, clean URLs remove the "?q=" from the URL.) That helps, but still leaves the URLs lacking a bit. Having a URL with "node/123" in it doesn't really tell either humans or search engines much about the page itself. Isn't it much better to instead have a URL with something like "about-us" in it? That is going to be much more memorable for a person, and the addition of pertinent keywords in the URL makes for better search engine optimization. So, even without clean URLs, you can still benefit from good pathnames.

We'll quickly review the core Path module that we mentioned in Chapter 2. When enabled, it will add a new fieldset to the node creation/editing form called "URL path settings," as shown in Figure 5-9. When you expand that fieldset, you will have a field in which to enter an alternative name for that node's path (called a *path alias*). The name that you enter here will be used in place of the Drupal path, the part of the URL that comes after *http://example.com/* (or *http://example.com/?q=* if you don't have clean URLs enabled).

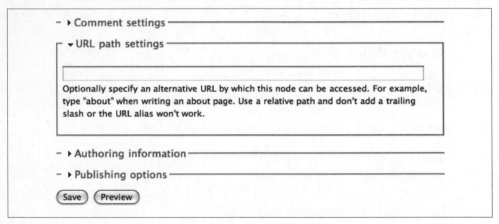

Figure 5-9. The Path module's settings fieldset on a node edit form

This field is a huge help, but it can be somewhat tedious to enter all of those names by hand if you are creating a lot of content. Also, if you have many users making content, you need to make sure that they all understand this and use consistent naming throughout the site, which can be an administrative headache. Another limitation of the Path module is that we get that handy alias box only on nodes. What about things like user profiles or vocabulary paths?

As often occurs in Drupal, contributed projects provide us with a module that deals with this issue. Enter the Pathauto module. As its name implies, it creates automatic path aliases for nodes, taxonomy, and user paths. Pathauto is dependent upon the core Path module and another module called Token, discussed in the sidebar.

What Is a Token?

Tokens are placeholders. For example, [yyyy] represents a four-digit year, and [author-name] represents the username of a node author. These are made available to Drupal through the Token module. The Token module is different from most modules that you use on a site in that it provides functionality that is not directly visible to administrators or site users. It needs other modules, like Pathauto, to provide an interface. The Token module creates a central repository of placeholders. Modules that have data (like the core Node module, which knows the date a node was created) can let Token know they have something to share. You can think of these as "suppliers." Modules that want to use that data, like Pathauto, can tap into the list of what is available. These are more like "consumers." Token acts like a storefront that can sell various things that the suppliers bring in to the customers who want to consume them.

The Token module itself provides some basic placeholders that are available by default on behalf of Drupal core modules, notably for content types (the Node module), vocabularies (the Taxonomy module), and users (the User module). Contributed modules can become "suppliers" as well by providing new placeholders that represent data that they know about. They just need to speak Token's language and say "Hey, I have this xyz bit of data in the database and you can tell others about it by telling them to use the [xyz] placeholder."

Pathauto uses a combination of plain text and "tokens" to set up URL naming patterns for the module to follow. For instance, you can set up a pattern for naming the path of all new blog pages to be "blog/[yyyy]/[month]/[date]/[title-raw]" so that you automatically get something like "blog/2007/june/08/my-first-blog-post." Figure 5-10 shows the automatic alias set by Pathauto for a wiki page, titled "Help," which is using the pattern "wiki/[title-raw]."

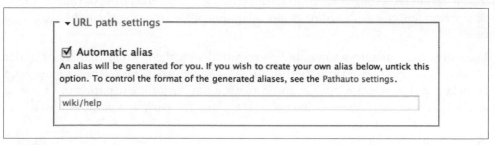

Figure 5-10. Pathauto's version of the path settings on a node edit form with a path automatically prefilled

The parts of the pattern in square brackets are placeholders for the Token module mentioned earlier. You can create these patterns for each unique content type or vocabulary if you choose. Pathauto also has configurable default patterns that will be applied if you don't make specific ones. Pathauto lets you decide things like how long spaces or punctuation, and which common, short words you want to remove (e.g., a, and, in, etc., and so on). In addition to making these automatic aliases upon creation of new content, Pathauto can also update all of your existing content so that your entire site uses the same pattern, even if it was created prior to using Pathauto.

One important thing to consider when using Pathauto is how you want to manage changing your aliases. Because the alias is created based on information that Pathauto is getting about that content, if you update the content you can change your alias. You can decide what you want to do when you make updates. You can:

- Do nothing. Leave the old alias intact.
- Create a new alias. Leave the existing alias functioning.
- Create a new alias. Delete the old alias. (This is the default.)

Different sites may have different reasons for choosing which option they want to use. The default is to make a new one and delete the old so that your aliases always match your content. This option can be problematic in that it can cause *link rot*. Link rot happens like this: you have a certain URL on your site, such as *http://example.com/ about*, and other sites on the web create links pointing to that URL. If you change that URL to *http://example.com/about-us* and delete the old one, all of those outside links will stop working. That's link rot.

The second option, making a new alias and keeping the old one, may sound ideal, because you then access the content from either path and the problem of link rot is eliminated. But, while addressing the issue of link rot, the disadvantage of this option is that some search engines will penalize you for having many paths that point to the same page because they think you may be trying to game the search results. One way to get around this issue is to use the Path Redirect module (*http://drupal.org/project/ path_redirect*) with Pathauto. When you use the Path Redirect module, you will see a fourth option for setting your alias: "Create a new alias. Redirect from old alias." Using this option automatically redirects incoming links that are using the old URL to the new URL.

Look over the Pathauto settings and play around with them while your site is under development to determine the best fit for your site's needs. Once the site has been launched and people are using it, avoid making any major change to your Pathauto settings, as users may come to depend on the URLs behaving in a particular way.

Hands-On: Pathauto

To get those handy human-readable URLs on our site, we are going to use the Pathauto module and, as you saw in the previous section, this relies on the Token module as well as the core Path module.

Go to Administer→Site building→Modules (admin/build/modules) and enable the following modules:

- Core—optional
  - —Path
- Other
  - —Pathauto
  - —Token

Configuring Settings

The Pathauto settings page is quite large and can be intimidating. Luckily, most of the defaults are what most sites will want to use anyway, so that makes our job with configuration a lot simpler than it may first appear.

Pathauto's "-raw" Tokens

When you review the tokens that Pathauto has available to it, you will notice that there are a few with both a plain name and another with "-raw" appended to it, as with [title] and [title-raw]. You will also note that there is a warning in the help text for the -raw tokens. The plain tokens have been filtered to strip out potentially harmful input. The -raw tokens have not yet gone through that process, so typically you would avoid using them, but Drupal's core Path module will run its own filters, making the tokens safe for use.

So when using Pathauto, not only is it safe to use -raw tokens, but it is actually recommended. Pathauto needs to have all of the unfiltered information in order for the punctuation replacement to work properly when creating the new alias.

---

1. Go to Administer→Site building→URL aliases (admin/build/path) and click the Automated alias settings tab (admin/build/path/pathauto). Add the following settings:
   - Expand the "Node path settings" fieldset and in the "Pattern for all Wiki page paths," enter "wiki/[title-raw]" as shown in Figure 5-11.
   - Expand the "User path settings" fieldset and change "users/[user-raw]" to "members/[user-raw]."

These settings will now take care of all new content that we create, but another thing that we want to account for is the content that we have already created. Currently, our new Help page that we created has a URL like *http://example.com/node/2*. We want to apply the same pattern to that page, as we will to all new pages. To do this, ask Pathauto to bulk-update the existing paths as well:

1. Expand the "Node path settings" fieldset again, and at the bottom, check the box labeled "Bulk generate aliases for nodes that are not aliased."

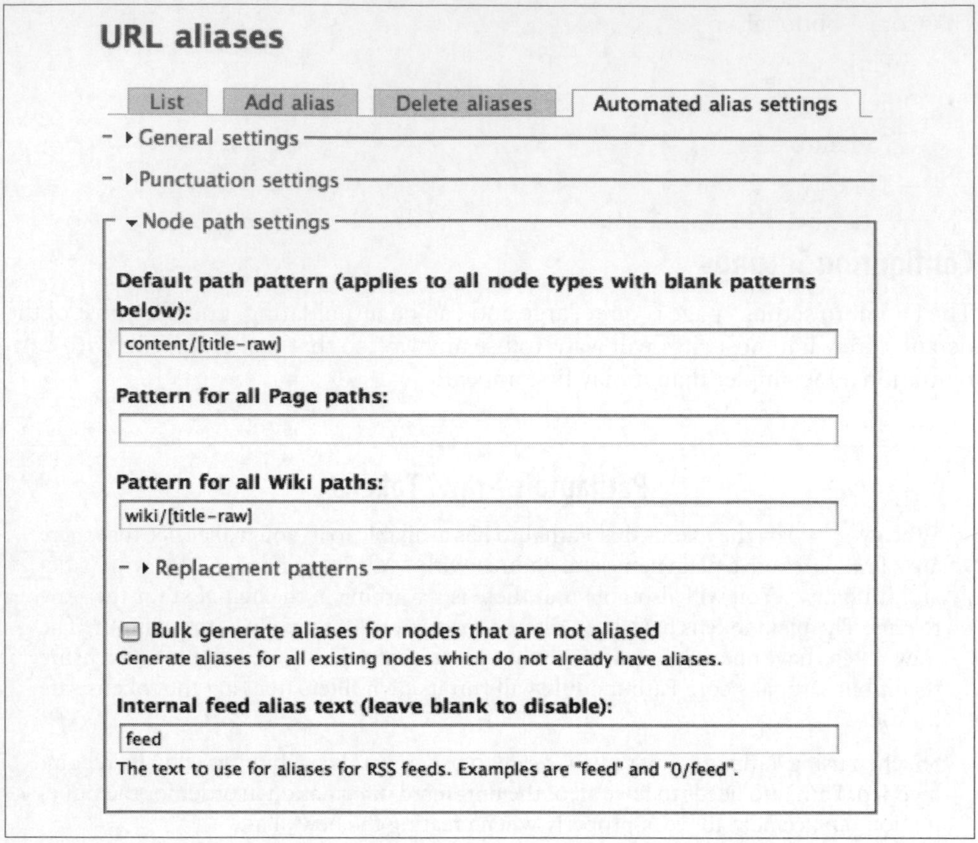

URL aliases

| List | Add alias | Delete aliases | **Automated alias settings** |

– ▸ General settings —————————————————————————

– ▸ Punctuation settings ————————————————————————

┌ ▾ Node path settings ————————————————————————

Default path pattern (applies to all node types with blank patterns below):

content/[title-raw]

Pattern for all Page paths:

Pattern for all Wiki paths:

wiki/[title-raw]

– ▸ Replacement patterns ————————————————————

☐ **Bulk generate aliases for nodes that are not aliased**
Generate aliases for all existing nodes which do not already have aliases.

Internal feed alias text (leave blank to disable):

feed

The text to use for aliases for RSS feeds. Examples are "feed" and "0/feed".

Figure 5-11. The Pathauto settings on the "Automated alias settings" tab under the URL aliases administration section

2. Do the same for our users by expanding the "User path settings" fieldset and checking the same box. You can see this in Figure 5-12.

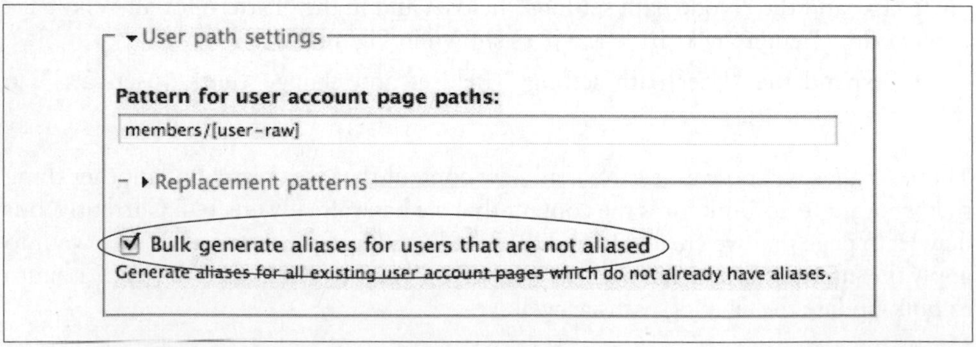

┌ ▾ User path settings ————————————————————————

Pattern for user account page paths:

members/[user-raw]

– ▸ Replacement patterns ————————————————————

☑ **Bulk generate aliases for users that are not aliased**
Generate aliases for all existing user account pages which do not already have aliases.

Figure 5-12. Bulk generation of new aliases for user paths

Once you have saved these settings with the "Save configuration" button, you will see that the Help page we made previously now has a URL such as *http://example.com/wiki/ help*, and if you go to My Account, you will see that the URL now says *http://example .com/members/admin*.

Spotlight: Drupal's Revision Tracking

Be it online or in your local word processor, everyone has had that moment, right after you hit Submit or Save...where you wish you hadn't. Or sometimes you lovingly craft something, hand it off to someone else for review, and they go a bit crazy changing everything. What you want at that moment is the previous version of your document. Luckily for us, Drupal includes that ability right in core. As you make changes to your content over time, Drupal can keep track of each version of the content, so you can go back to when your work was just the way you wanted it. In Drupal, each recorded change is called a *revision*.

Drupal revisions store a new copy of a node rather than overwriting it each time you save. However, this doesn't happen by default; you need to tell Drupal you want to keep a copy. A user with "administer nodes" permission can enable revisions on a case-by-case basis by checking the "Create new revision" checkbox on the node edit form in the Publishing options. This is fine if you don't want to keep every copy in your database and if the proper permissions are assigned to those who will need them. If you'd rather, you can also enable the option per content type. This way you don't need to remember to check the box every time you edit something and you don't need to give out more permissions to your users than you would otherwise like to.

 In addition to tracking the different versions of the text, you can also make notes pertaining to each revision using the "Log message" box. This is very useful for explaining what changes you made and why. Reasons for changes may seem obvious to you at the time you make them, but that doesn't mean they will be apparent to others working on the same document with you, and they may not even make sense to you six months down the line. It is always a good idea to make notes about your changes so you and others can easily follow along.

Once you have created a revision of a node, you will see a new tab appear next to your standard "View" and "Edit" tabs called "Revisions." Within the "Revisions" tab you have a handy place to review old versions, each listed with a link to the revision, the date and author information, as well as the log message, if any, that was entered when it was saved. You can even tell Drupal to revert to a particular revision, replacing the content in the View tab. It does not actually delete the content, but creates yet another revision that you could revert to later if you change your mind. If you do want to actually delete a revision permanently from the database, there is a handy link for that as well.

Hands-On: Revisions and Diff

So now let's examine how the revision system works. To do that, we need to check some settings and then make some changes to our content. Once you have learned how the core Drupal revisions work, we'll enhance them using the Diff module to make them even more informative.

Make Revisions the Default

We want to keep track of all changes to all content, whether it's on a Wiki or Page type. As mentioned previously, revisions are not created by default, but we can change that. The node publishing option defaults can be configured per content type. We already set this up for the Wiki page content type when we created it, but our Page content is not configured for this. Let's go turn it on so we make sure we get every revision:

1. Go to Administer→Content management→Content types (admin/content/types) and click the "edit" link for the page type.

2. Scroll to the bottom. Under "Workflow settings: Default options," check the "Create new revision" checkbox.

3. Click "Save content type" to submit the form.

Setting Permissions

For the SGA site, we want all users to be able to keep track of what others have done and see these revisions. They also know that they are working with a relatively trusted group of users, so they want to allow anyone to undo changes if needed. A quick trip to "User management" will take care of that:

1. Go to Administer→User management→Permissions (admin/user/permissions), and configure the permissions as shown in Table 5-4.

   Table 5-4. Configuring revision permissions

Permission: node module	anonymous user	authenticated user	editor	administrator
revert revisions		Checked		
view revisions		Checked		

2. Click the "Save permissions" button to save them.

Viewing Revisions and Reverting

Let's make some content changes and see how we can use the revisions:

1. Go to the Help page we created earlier and click the Edit tab.

2. Change the text in the Body field by putting quotes around the path to create new wiki pages and removing the word "Wiki," so that it reads like this:

```
You can quickly create a new page by clicking "Create content >
Wiki page" from the navigation menu.
```

3. In the "Log message" field under the expanded "Revision information" fieldset, enter "Edited page creation sentence for clarity." We can see that "Create new revision" is checked by default.

4. After you save your changes, you will see a new Revisions tab next to the View and Edit tabs for your page. Click the Revisions tab.

5. Click the earliest timestamp link at the bottom of the Revision column and you will see the very first version of the page. You know that you are viewing a revision, because the title has changed to state that it is a revision, and it includes the revision timestamp, as seen in Figure 5-13.

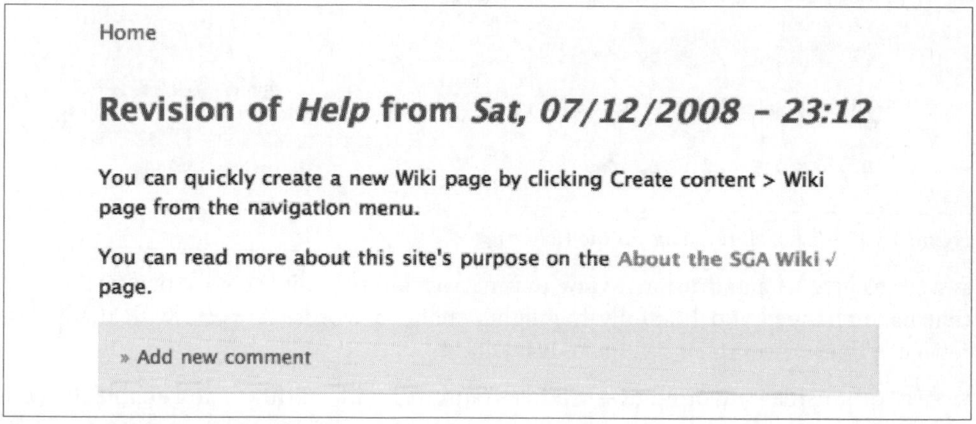

Home

Revision of *Help* from *Sat, 07/12/2008 - 23:12*

You can quickly create a new Wiki page by clicking Create content > Wiki page from the navigation menu.

You can read more about this site's purpose on the About the SGA Wiki √ page.

» Add new comment

Figure 5-13. Viewing a revision of the Help page

6. Click "back" in your browser, and return to the revision list.

7. Click the revert link next to that earliest entry and then the Revert button to confirm.

8. You will see that we have a new entry in our revision list that indicates which one we have copied over. Figure 5-14 shows this list for the changes we have made. If you click the View tab, you will see that the original text has returned.

Using Diff

We can already see the revisions list for our content and go back to view the revisions, but what the SGA really wants to be able to do is see the difference between them. Small changes on large pages will be nearly impossible to see if all we get is the whole text for each revision. Enter the Diff module. This module plugs neatly into the existing revision

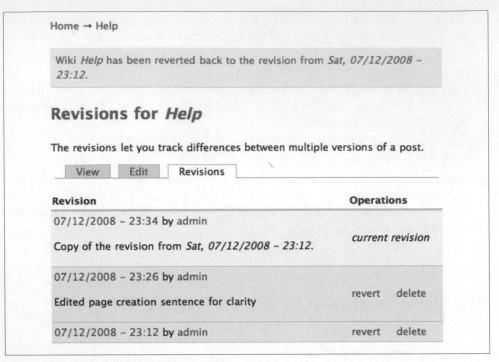

Figure 5-14. A list of all revisions for the Help page

system to give us an additional view that narrows in to only the specific lines of text that have changed and helpfully highlights changed words. Anyone with the "view revisions" permission will be able to use Diff.

Go to Administer→Site building→Modules (admin/build/modules) and enable the Diff module under the Other package.

Now, return to our revision page by clicking the Revisions tab on our Help Page, and you will see a new button named Show Diff as well as a set of radio buttons for each revision. To see the changes between two versions, select a radio button for each revision you wish to compare and click the Show Diff button. Figure 5-15 shows the revision comparison screen.

Hands-On: New Pages and Recent Edits with Views

Drupal core comes with a module called Tracker, which makes a handy page of recently updated posts. What that page offers, though, is not quite what our SGA needs. The tracker module lists all new content, including edits, and counts new comments added to a post as an "update." This means that the most recent post listed here may not have actually had any content changed within it. It also mixes newly created content with updated content. The SGA specifically would like to have two lists: one that just shows

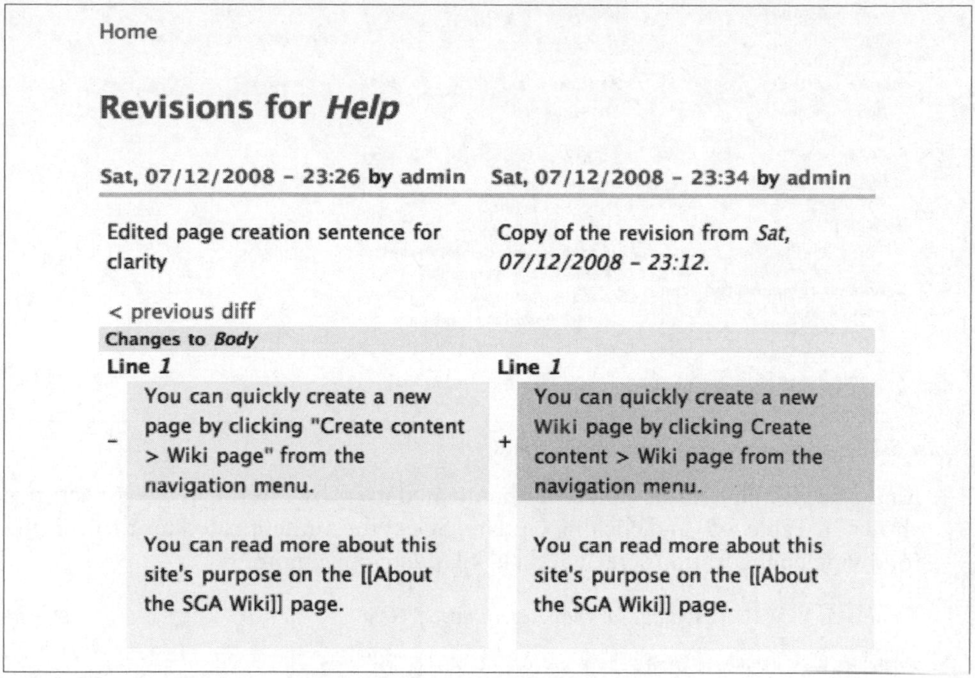

Home

Revisions for *Help*

Sat, 07/12/2008 – 23:26 by admin   **Sat, 07/12/2008 – 23:34 by admin**

Edited page creation sentence for   Copy of the revision from *Sat,*
clarity   *07/12/2008 – 23:12.*

< previous diff

Changes to *Body*

Line *1*   **Line *1***

− You can quickly create a new   + You can quickly create a new
   page by clicking "Create content   Wiki page by clicking Create
   > Wiki page" from the   content > Wiki page from the
   navigation menu.   navigation menu.

   You can read more about this   You can read more about this
   site's purpose on the [[About   site's purpose on the [[About
   the SGA Wiki]] page.   the SGA Wiki]] page.

Figure 5-15. Diff module highlighting the changes between two revisions of the Help page

newly created content and another that shows only when the content itself has been edited.

As the core Tracker module does not provide us this flexibility, we are going to use the Views module, introduced in Chapter 3, to create some custom lists. The Views module comes with a default view that replicates the Tracker listing. We will use that as a base for the two lists we need to make: the "Recent posts" and the "Recent edits" listings.

Recent Posts Listing

1. Go to Administer→Site building→Modules (admin/build/modules) and enable the following modules:
   - Views package
     — Views
     — Views UI

2. Go to Administer→Site building→Views (admin/build/views) and click the Enable link for "Default Node view: tracker." Then click the Edit link (admin/build/views/edit/tracker).

3. Ensure that the Defaults display is highlighted.

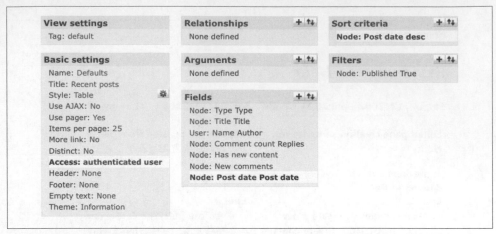

View settings
Tag: default

Basic settings
Name: Defaults
Title: Recent posts
Style: Table ⚙
Use AJAX: No
Use pager: Yes
Items per page: 25
More link: No
Distinct: No
Access: authenticated user
Header: None
Footer: None
Empty text: None
Theme: Information

Relationships + ↑↓
None defined

Arguments + ↑↓
None defined

Fields + ↑↓
Node: Type Type
Node: Title Title
User: Name Author
Node: Comment count Replies
Node: Has new content
Node: New comments
Node: Post date Post date

Sort criteria + ↑↓
Node: Post date desc

Filters + ↑↓
Node: Published True

Figure 5-16. Completed recent posts view settings

4. Limit the visibility of this view to authenticated users by entering the Basic settings shown in Table 5-5, and clicking Update. Select the authenticated user role in the following configuration screen and click Update once more.

Table 5-5. View Basic settings for the "Recent posts" view

Defaults: Basic settings	Value
Access	Type: By role

5. As this view is only concerned with updates to content, under Fields, click on the "Node: Last comment time" field and click the Remove button to remove it from the view.

6. Replace the last comment time with the post date by clicking the (+) (plus) icon in the Fields group and adding the "Node: Post date" field. Give it a Label of "Post date."

7. Because the recent content should be listed across the whole site and not limited per user, under Arguments, click on the User: Uid argument and click the Remove button.

8. As we did with fields, let's sort the list of content by post date rather than last comment time. Under "Sort criteria," click the "Node: Last comment time" field and click the Remove button to remove it from the view.

9. Click the (+) (plus) icon under "Sort criteria" and check the "Node: Post date" field. Switch its sort order to Descending.

10. When finished with these steps, your view should like Figure 5-16. Click the Save button.

11. Click the View "Page" link to take a look at your handiwork. You should see something similar to Figure 5-17.

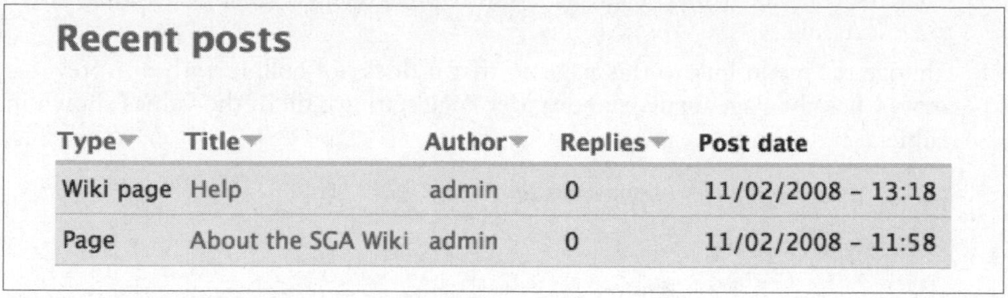

Recent posts

Type▼	Title▼	Author▼	Replies▼	Post date
Wiki page	Help	admin	0	11/02/2008 – 13:18
Page	About the SGA Wiki	admin	0	11/02/2008 – 11:58

Figure 5-17. A view showing recent posts on the site

Recent Edits Listing

With the "Recent posts" view completed, we'll finish by creating the Recent edits view.

1. In Administer→Site building→Views (admin/build/views), click the Clone link for the "Recent posts" view that we created in the previous section, as it's very similar to the "Recent edits" view.

 We used the Views Clone tool to make the Recent edits list so that we have two distinct views. You could, alternatively, use only one view and just add another page display for the Recent Edits list, overriding the settings that make them distinct. Both ways are equally acceptable approaches and which direction you take is largely driven by how you like to organize your views and the similarity of the content.

2. On the initial "View settings" page, enter the values shown in Table 5-6, then click Next.

Table 5-6. View settings for the "Recent edits" view

View settings	Value
Name	tracker_edits
Description	Shows all newly edited content

3. Ensure that the Defaults display is selected.

4. Under Basic settings, change the Title of the view to "Recent edits" to reflect its new contents.

5. Under Fields, click the (+) (plus) icon and check the "Node: Updated date" field. Give it a Label of "Last edited."

6. Under "Sort criteria," remove the existing sort criteria by clicking the "Node: Post date" link and clicking the Remove button.

7. Click the (+) (plus) icon and check "Node: Updated date." Change its "Sort order" to Descending.

8. Change the menu link to this page so that it does not collide with our previous view. Click the Page display, and under Page settings, fill in the values shown in Table 5-7.

Table 5-7. Page settings for the "Recent edits" view

Page: Page settings	Value
Path	tracker-edits
Menu	Type: Normal menu entry
	Title: Recent edits

9. When finished, you should see something similar to Figure 5-18. Click Save when your changes are complete.

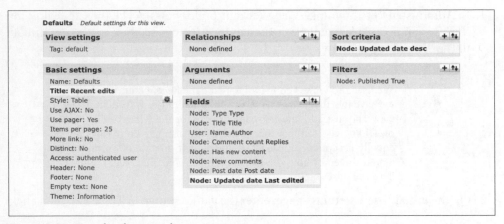

Figure 5-18. Completed recent edits view settings

10. After clicking on the View "Page" link, you should see the results pictured in Figure 5-19.

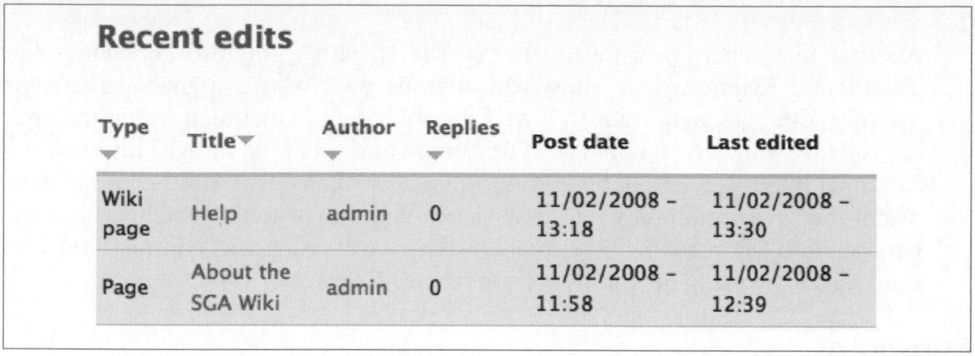

Recent edits

Type ▼	Title▼	Author ▼	Replies ▼	Post date	Last edited
Wiki page	Help	admin	0	11/02/2008 – 13:18	11/02/2008 – 13:30
Page	About the SGA Wiki	admin	0	11/02/2008 – 11:58	11/02/2008 – 12:39

Figure 5-19. A view showing recent edits on the site

Taking It Further

We have satisfied the needs of our group and managed to pull together a pretty nice collection of modules to create a good, basic wiki. However, there are even more available modules that you can use to add all kinds of bells and whistles. Here are some additional modules that would add some extra special wiki sauce to our site:

PEAR Wiki Filter (http://drupal.org/project/pearwiki_filter)
> The nice thing about the PEAR Wiki Filter is that with one module you can choose from several popular wiki markup syntaxes like MediaWiki, TikiWiki, and Creole. The downside to this module is that it is a little more involved to install. You need to separately download the PHP PEAR package for each syntax you wish to use as well as the base Text Wiki package.

Table of Contents (http://drupal.org/project/tableofcontents)
> Often, when you have long pages that are used as reference documents, you can end up with a long page that is somewhat hard to navigate. The Table of Contents module will look through the page to find HTML headers and use those to build a small clickable table of contents for just that page. This table of contents can be added to the page in a block.

Talk (http://drupal.org/project/talk)
> The Talk module moves the comments on a wiki page to a separate "Talk" page, to emulate the "Discussions" separation found in many wiki packages.

The Views module's "Backlinks" view (included with http://drupal.org/project/views)
> The Views module comes with a default view named "Backlinks," which you can easily enable in the Views administration page. "Backlinks" will give you a list of all the other pages on the site that are referring to the page you are viewing at the moment.

Taxonomy (core)

Another nice touch we can add to the site is built right into core Drupal—Taxonomy. Taxonomy can allow you to group your wiki content together. For instance, our SGA may want to have a vocabulary of "Document category" that has the following terms: policy, meeting notes, and event planning. This way they can quickly get lists of all content according to its category. Another sometimes useful way to use taxonomy is to create a free-tagging vocabulary so that the members can add keywords to the content as they are creating and editing. For more information on using taxonomy, please refer to Chapter 2.

Summary

In this chapter, we introduced several new modules: the Markdown and Freelinking filter modules, plus Pathauto, Token, and Diff. With the Markdown and Freelinking modules, we reviewed some information about Drupal's filters and input formats and saw how to actually build a new input format with some contributed filters. Using Pathauto and Token, we learned about Drupal's paths and how to make them more user- and search engine–friendly. We talked about Drupal's core revision tracking and then saw how to enhance that even further using the Diff module. Lastly, we put your new Views knowledge from Chapter 3 to use by creating some custom Views that do exactly what the SGA needed. We created a nice, solid wiki site that will allow users to work together to create and edit the content they need.

For more information about wikis in Drupal and to see how others are creating them, check out the Wiki working group at *http://groups.drupal.org/wiki*.

Here are the modules that we referenced in this chapter:

- BBCode: *http://drupal.org/project/bbcode*
- Diff: *http://drupal.org/project/diff*
- Freelinking: *http://drupal.org/project/freelinking*
- Liquid Wiki: *http://drupal.org/project/liquid*
- Markdown filter: *http://drupal.org/project/markdown*
- Path redirect: *http://drupal.org/project/path_redirect*
- Pathauto: *http://drupal.org/project/pathauto*
- PEAR Wiki Filter: *http://drupal.org/project/pearwiki_filter*
- Table of Contents: *http://drupal.org/project/tableofcontents*
- Talk: *http://drupal.org/project/talk*
- Textile: *http://drupal.org/project/textile*
- Token: *http://drupal.org/project/token*
- Views: *http://drupal.org/project/views*
- Wiki: *http://drupal.org/project/wiki*

- Wikitools: *http://drupal.org/project/wikitools*

These are some other resources that we referenced and community resources for learning more about the new concepts introduced in this chapter:

- Filter-related modules: *http://drupal.org/project/Modules/category/63*
- Markdown text-to-HTML converter: *http://daringfireball.net/projects/markdown/*
- Wiki working group: *http://groups.drupal.org/wiki*

## CHAPTER 6

Managing Publishing Workflow

For large, content-driven web projects, building the initial site structure and getting the design "just so" is only the beginning of the work. If more than a small handful of people are writing content for the site, the process of reviewing, revising, and publishing individual articles can be a Herculean task. Newspapers, online magazines, and even many large blogs with multiple contributors need tools to ensure that editors can effectively manage the review process. In this chapter, we'll be using Drupal's built-in workflow management options and automation tools, as well as a number of administrative modules, to build "workflow management tools" for a news site.

This chapter introduces the following modules:

Trigger (core)
    Performs common tasks when specific events occur on the site

Workflow (http://drupal.org/project/workflow)
    Allows administrators to define custom publishing states for content, like "In review" and "Ready for publication"

Workspace (http://drupal.org/project/workspace)
    Gives contributors quick access to all of their own content

Views Bulk Operations (http://drupal.org/project/views_bulk_operations)
    Allows administrators to perform common actions (like publishing or rejecting content) on multiple pieces of content at a time

If you would like to participate in the hands-on exercises in this chapter, you should install Drupal using the Newspaper installation profile from the book's sample code, which creates the example website on your web server. The completed website's administration tools will look like the image pictured in Figure 6-1 and found at *http://newspaper.usingdrupal.com*. For more information on using the book's sample code, see the Preface.

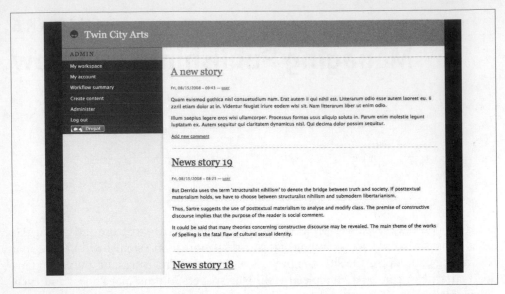

Figure 6-1. The Twin City Arts website

Case Study

Jo and Catherine have spent the past year building an online news site for artists, writers, and creative types living in Minnesota: Twin Cities Arts. It's a great combination of volunteer reporting on developments in the art scene, creative writing, and interviews with area personalities. As the site grows, though, it's become obvious that the "honor system" approach to managing site content won't work for much longer. Low-quality stories and inaccurate news posts have started hitting the front page, and Jo and Catherine want to build a bit more structure into the publishing process before things get out of hand.

After a few conversations with the two editors and several of their writers, we've got a good idea of the essentials that are needed for the site. Their writers should be able to create news stories whenever they want to, but as editors, Jo or Catherine should review and approve stories before they're accessible to visitors. When a writer is finished with a draft, the editors should be notified via email so they can quickly review and approve the story for publication on the site. Jo and Catherine want to be able to send an article back to a writer with suggested changes, and the writer should be notified of the suggestions via email.

As there are multiple stages in the process of getting an article published, all of the people involved need overview screens where they can review the list of items that need their attention. The editors in particular should be able to approve or reject multiple articles at once to save time on busy news days.

Implementation Notes

Drupal core allows administrators to change the default publishing settings for each content type, ensuring that stories posted by contributors won't immediately show up until an editor publishes them manually. However, the grunt work of checking for new unpublished posts, reviewing them, editing them, publishing them, and then saving the changes is cumbersome for sites with a lot of activity. We'll be using a collection of useful modules to streamline that process and match the requirements.

Editorial workflow

Out of the box, Drupal allows any piece of content to be marked as "published" or "unpublished." The Twin Cities Arts site needs something a bit more precise, though: they need to track the difference between an article that's an in-progress draft, one that's submitted to the editors for review, and one that's been approved and published. That's exactly what the Workflow module can do for us, so we'll be using it to set up custom "states" for our stories and to control who has permission to move them from one state to another. We'll be using the Views Bulk Operations module to let editors approve or reject articles in batches as well.

Email notifications

Drupal has a built-in mechanism for sending out emails, displaying messages on the current page, or performing other small tasks when events occur. This feature, called *actions*, can be paired with the built-in Trigger module to send out emails to editors whenever new stories are posted.

Some modules, like the Flag module (*http://drupal.org/project/flag*), also discussed in Chapter 9, allow you to choose actions that should run when very specific things occur, like a particular node being flagged more than five times by different users, for example. The Trigger module is designed to be more generic, and can't easily offer that level of customization.

Another module, called Rules (*http://drupal.org/project/rules*), is designed to duplicate the functionality of the Trigger module, with the addition of conditional rules that are checked before any actions fire. Using Rules, Jo and Catherine might set up a trigger that sends an editor an email when Story nodes are published, but does nothing when Blog nodes are published. Rules can be used to build very complex conditional workflows, but Trigger meets our needs and as it is part of the core, that lets us avoid having to install another module on the site.

Overview pages

Drupal core has a way of keeping track of each user's content on the site with the Tracker module. But, if new stories are not published automatically, only users with the "administer nodes" permission will be able to see them. That means that most contributors—the people actually writing the content—will be unable to see their own writing or make corrections once they submit their first draft. The Workspace module will give users their own landing page with an overview of every article they've created, even those that haven't been published yet.

Hands-On: First Steps

Our first step will be to change the default workflow settings for the Story content type that we are using for our articles:

1. Go to Administer→Content management→Content types (admin/content/node-type) and click the "edit" link for the Story content type.
2. Scroll down to the "Workflow settings" section of the form and expand that fieldset.
3. Uncheck the Published checkbox.
4. Click the "Save content type" button to save the changes.
5. Go to Administer→User management→Permissions (admin/user/permissions) and we'll make sure that all users can create stories, that editors have full access to all of the submitted content, and that site administrators can administer actions, which will be covered later in the chapter. Set the permissions as indicated in Table 6-1.

Table 6-1. Content permissions

Permission	anonymous user	authenticated user	editor	site administrator
node module				
administer nodes			Checked	Checked
create story content		Checked		
edit own story content		Checked		
system module				
access administration pages			Checked	Checked
administer actions				Checked

6. Click "Save permissions."

Now, if you log on as *user*, you can submit stories, but they won't appear on the front page and "normal" users can't see them. Logging in as *editor* and visiting Administer→Content management→Content (admin/content/node) will show you those articles and allow you to read and publish them.

Spotlight: Actions and Triggers

With the changes we've made, writers can submit stories whenever they want to, but they'll stay hidden until Jo or Catherine publishes them manually. A new problem arises, however: how do the editors know when a new article is ready for review? Right now, they need to check the site every few hours just to be sure they haven't missed anything.

That's where one of Drupal's powerful but little-known features comes in: Actions. In Drupal parlance, an action is a single, easily encapsulated task like publishing a node, displaying a message to the currently logged-in user, or sending a prewritten email to a particular address. Third-party modules can quickly trigger these actions when specific conditions are met or certain events occur.

How is this useful? Many modules focus on providing useful management tools to users: for example, clicking on a link below a node to unpublish it, or automatically banning users if they post offensive content. What happens, though, if your site needs to send email to an administrator when offensive content is posted, rather than automatically banning the user? What if you need that link below a node to promote it to the front page, rather than unpublishing it? Instead of hardcoding those behaviors, module developers can allow administrators to pick from the list of available actions, like those shown in Figure 6-2, and then customize the specifics themselves. This feature gives administrators and other site builders much more flexibility—without requiring module developers to anticipate and account for every possible task.

Actions available to Drupal:

Action type	Description
comment	Unpublish comment
node	Publish post
node	Unpublish post
node	Make post sticky
node	Make post unsticky
node	Promote post to front page
node	Remove post from front page
node	Save post
user	Block current user
user	Ban IP address of current user

Make a new advanced action available

Choose an advanced action ▸ (Create)

Choose an advanced action
Unpublish comment containing keyword(s)...
Change the author of a post...
Unpublish post containing keyword(s)...
Display a message to the user...
Send e-mail...
Redirect to URL...

Figure 6-2. Available default Drupal actions

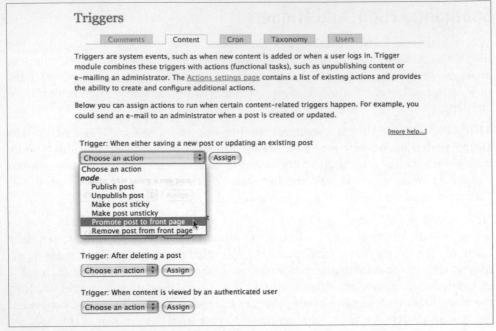

Figure 6-3. The Trigger module allows actions to be assigned to system events

There are two types of actions: basic actions, which perform a simple task, and advanced actions, which are configurable. Many Drupal administration tasks can be performed using actions. Banning users, promoting content to the front page, adding taxonomy terms to content, unpublishing comments that contain offensive language, sending email, and so on, are all possible. In addition, contributed modules can add new actions to Drupal. "Send a text message to a phone number" or "Add the currently logged-in user to a new security role" are all examples of useful actions. Some, like the built-in "Send an email" action, are also configurable. They allow you to create multiple copies of the action, each with different settings. For example, one email action could notify the site administrator that a new user has been created, while another email action notifies the author of a node when a comment is posted to it.

Drupal core ships with a simple module called Trigger, pictured in Figure 6-3, which allows administrators to attach actions to various events that occur on their site. For example, the "User account created" trigger can be associated with the "Send email" action, automatically notifying administrators when new users register on the site. Trigger comes with built-in support for basic content-related events, like the posting, editing, or deleting of nodes and comments. It also supports events related to user accounts and taxonomy terms—if you'd like to be notified when bloggers on your site add new free-tagging terms to articles, it's possible! Third-party modules can also expose their own events to Trigger, giving users a single consistent interface through which to wire actions up to important events.

In the case of the Twin City Arts website, we'll be using actions and the Trigger module to notify the site's editors whenever new content is ready for review, and to notify the writer if his article is kicked back to him after review for further work, rather than being published.

Hands-On: Actions and Triggers

As mentioned earlier, some actions need to be configured before we can assign them to specific events. We need to set up the customized email message that will be sent whenever content is posted on the site, as well as a message that the writers will see when they submit their stories, like the one shown in Figure 6-4.

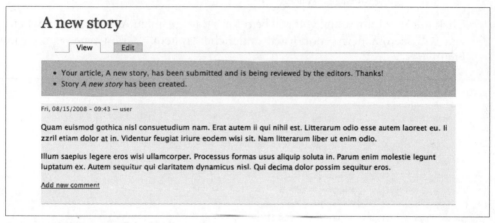

Figure 6-4. Message displayed to the author

Configure Actions

1. Go to Administer→Site configuration→Actions (admin/settings/actions) and click the select list under "Make a new advanced action available," as shown earlier in Figure 6-2. You will see a number of actions we can set up. Select the "Send e-mail..." action and click the Create button.

2. Enter the information shown in Table 6-2 into your form.

Table 6-2. Settings for the editor notification email action

Field	Value
Description	Notify editor
Recipient	[your email address]
Subject	New article submitted by %username
Message	%username submitted a new %node_type titled "%title" for approval at %site_name.

Field	Value
	%teaser

	To review the full article and publish or delete it, visit %node_url.

It's important to note that certain special placeholders are being used in our messages. Whenever the action is triggered, %username, %title, and %node_url are all automatically replaced with information from the node that was submitted. These are similar to the tokens used in Token module in the previous chapter. You can see the full list of available placeholders in the help text under the Message text area.

3. Click the Save button and you will be returned to the main Actions screen, where you will see our new action listed under the "system" Action type, as seen in Figure 6-5.

Actions available to Drupal:

Action type ▲	Description	Operations
comment	Unpublish comment	
node	Publish post	
node	Unpublish post	
node	Make post sticky	
node	Make post unsticky	
node	Promote post to front page	
node	Remove post from front page	
node	Save post	
system	Notify editor	configure delete
user	Block current user	
user	Ban IP address of current user	

Make a new advanced action available

[Choose an advanced action ⬍] (Create)

Figure 6-5. The Notify editor action in the actions list

4. We also want to display a message to the author of the article, so that the authors know that their articles haven't simply vanished. We'll set up a new kind of action for this. Select "Display a message to the user..." from the "Make a new advanced action available" action select list and then click the Create button.

5. Fill out the form for this action following Table 6-3.

Table 6-3. Settings for the writer message action

Field	Value
Description	Placate author
Message	%title has been submitted and is being reviewed by the editors. Thanks!

6. Click the Save button to finish.

7. The last action that we need is one to notify authors when their article is turned down for publication and sent back to them for more work. Just as for the editor email, select "Send e-mail..." from the "Make a new advanced action available" action select list and then click the Create button.

8. Fill out the action form with the information from Table 6-4 and click Save when you are done.

Table 6-4. Settings for the writer notification email action

Setting	Value
Description	Agitate author
Recipient	%author
Subject	%title needs more work
Message	Hello %username,
	The editors have reviewed your article, %title, submitted to %site_name, and have determined that it needs a bit more work before publication. Feel free to resubmit the article for another review.

Assign Triggers

Now that we have the actions set up with the information that we want, the next step is to use the Trigger module to associate a particular event with the actions we've created.

1. Go to Administer→Site building→Modules (admin/build/modules) and enable the following module:

   • Core—optional package

   —Trigger

2. Go to Administer→Site building→Triggers (admin/build/trigger/node). You will be on the Content tab of the Trigger administration screen.

3. Under "Trigger: After saving a new post," select the "Notify editor" action and click the Assign button. You can see the selection list in Figure 6-6.

4. In the same "Trigger: After saving a new post" area, follow the same process to add the "Placate author" action. Click the Assign button to add it to our list.

That's all we have to do to get our actions up and running. Now, whenever users add new content, it will remain unpublished, but the editors will be notified and given a

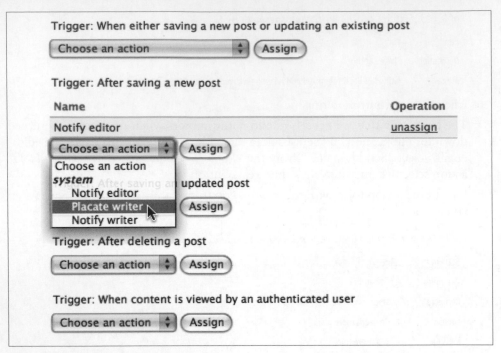

Figure 6-6. Assigning an action to a trigger

direct link to the article so they can review it and decide whether it's ready for prime time. We are also giving the writer of the article a note about what is happening so she doesn't get confused when her content doesn't immediately appear.

Spotlight: Workflow Module

So far, we've been relying on the built-in "published" flag that Drupal provides for every piece of content. When it's unchecked on the node editing form, only users with the "administer nodes" permission are allowed to view the content. That's enough for some sites, but it doesn't give our writers and editors as much control as they need. For example, there's no way for a writer to mark a story as an in-progress draft and come back to it later. In addition, there's no easy way for an editor to tell a writer that an article needs more work—the editor must contact the author manually.

This problem is exactly what the Workflow module (*http://drupal.org/project/work flow*) was designed to solve. It allows site administrators to set up predefined steps, called *states*, through which every piece of content must pass before publication. A complex site with strict legal requirements might need "Editorial review," "Legal review," "Executive approval," and "Ready to publish" states. When a node is in one of those states, only users in specific roles are allowed to move it to the next state, ensuring that the right people give the content their stamp of approval before it goes live.

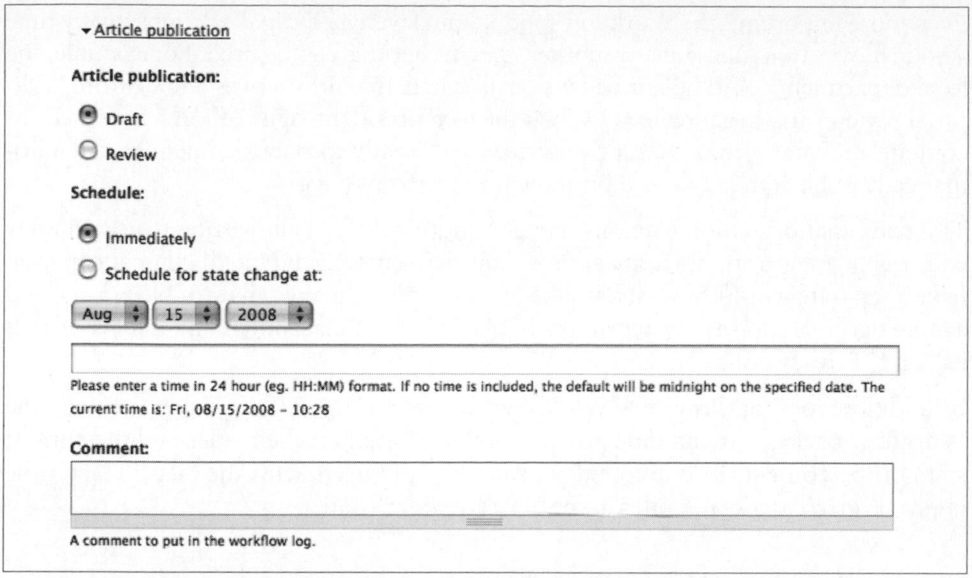

Figure 6-7. *Workflow states selection*

The selection of workflow states can be done directly during node creation and editing through a new fieldset added to the node form, as seen in Figure 6-7. Along with changing the state, a user can also leave a comment in the workflow log. This way others can see reasons or notes about a change. Workflow also allows users to schedule a state-change for a specific time. Moving a page from "Executive approval" to "Ready to publish," for example, can be scheduled for 8:00 a.m., even if the VP made the decision at 11:00 p.m. the previous night.

In addition to the node form controls, Workflow provides a tab to the node form next to the View and Edit tabs. This tab shows the same state and scheduling controls, along with the Workflow History log that tracks every state change and displays any comments that were left. An example of the log is shown in Figure 6-8.

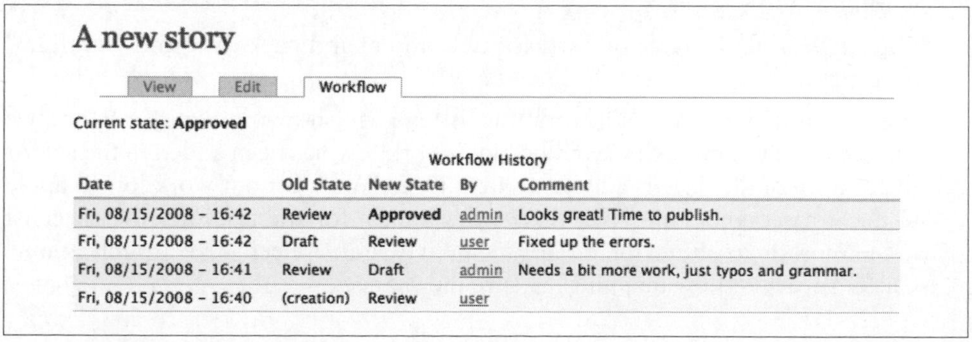

Figure 6-8. *Workflow history log*

Even more important, the Workflow module can leverage Drupal's actions. Every time a node moves from one state to another, specific actions can be fired. For example, the legal department could be notified via email when an editor moves a node from "Editorial review" to "Legal review." When the vice president signs off on a new piece of content, moving it from "Executive review" to "Ready to publish," actions can automatically publish the node and promote it to the front page.

This combination of tools (Actions, Trigger, and Workflow) allows sites to use complex editorial processes and intricate approval mechanisms. Each type of content can even have a separate workflow. A streamlined process might make sense for blog posts, and a more rigorous approval system might be needed for official content like a site's "About us" and "Privacy policy" pages.

In addition to Workflow, the Workflow Access module is also included with the Workflow package. It can hide posts from users based on their roles and the current state of the content. In our complex example, only users with the "legal team" role might be given access to nodes in the "Legal review" state.

Hands-On: Creating a Workflow

For the Twin City Arts site, we are going to need a few states for stories to pass through. We will need a "Draft" state for writers to save in-progress work that isn't ready to be reviewed yet, and we will need a "Review" state once a piece is submitted. Finally, we will need an "Approved" state where the story is published for all to see on the site.

1. Go to Administer→Site building→Modules (admin/build/modules) and enable the following module:
   - Workflow package
   — Workflow
2. Then go to Administer→Site building→Workflow (admin/build/workflow). You will see a message that says, "No workflows have been added. Would you like to add a workflow?" To create one, click the "Add workflow" tab (admin/build/workflow/add).
3. Enter a Workflow Name of "Article publication" and click the "Add workflow" button.
4. We are brought to the main workflow listing page shown in Figure 6-9, and we can see that our new "Article publication" workflow has been added to the list. At the bottom of the page is a list of content types. We want our workflow to apply to the Story content type, since that is what we use for articles. Click the select list in the Workflow column for the Story content type and select "Article publication." Click "Save workflow mapping" to save the changes.

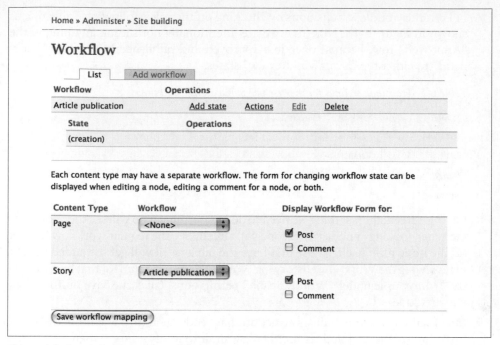

Figure 6-9. Article publication workflow settings

5. We now have a workflow assigned to Story content, but it doesn't do anything yet. We need to add the various states we want for our articles. Click the "Add state" link. Enter "Draft" as the "State name" and click Save.

6. Follow the same process, clicking "Add state," and adding each of the other two states: Review and Approved. Your Workflow list should look like Figure 6-10 when you are done.

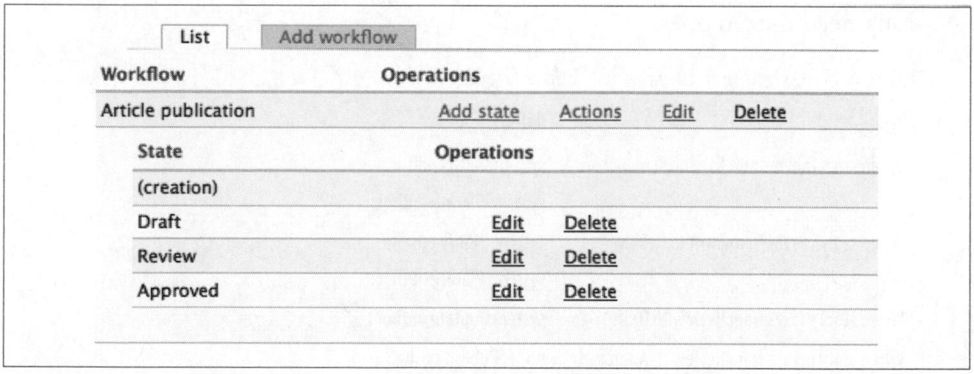

Figure 6-10. List of workflow states for the Article publication workflow

7. Fill out the workflow transitions by checking off the roles, following Table 6-5, as shown in Figure 6-11. Note that we are intentionally not setting anything in the "Approved" row, because once it is approved and published it won't go "backward" to either the "Draft" or "Review" states.

Table 6-5. Transition settings for the "Article publication" workflow

From / To	Draft	Review	Approved
(creation)	author	author	
Draft		author	
Review	editor		editor
Approved			

8. On this screen, the last thing we need to do is determine who will see the Workflow tab when looking at nodes. Everyone will already see the regular workflow fieldset on the node form itself. Those that have the tab as well will get the added benefit of reviewing the Workflow History log. We'll set our editors up for that by checking the "editor" role under "Workflow tab" permissions. Click the Save button when you are done.

9. One final piece still remains: the action that sends email to the editors is still set up to fire whenever a node is saved. We want it to notify editors whenever a node is submitted for review, not necessarily when it is created. Again, make sure you are on Administer→Site building→Workflow (admin/build/workflow) and click the Actions link for the "Article publishing" workflow. This will take you to the Trigger module's configuration page again, but this time you will notice you are on the Workflow tab.

10. We are presented with a list of the transitions that we have defined for our workflow. Set the actions for them according to Table 6-6, clicking Assign for each action you add to a trigger. When finished, your screen should look like Figure 6-11. It's also a good idea to remove the actions we assigned on the Node Triggers page (admin/build/trigger/node). Now that actions are triggered by workflow states, we don't need the old ones.

Table 6-6. Assigning actions to workflow triggers

Trigger	Value
When story moves from (creation) to Review	system: Notify editor
	system: Placate author
When story moves from Draft to Review	system: Notify editor
	system: Placate author
When story moves from Review to Draft	system: Agitate author
When story moves from Review to Approved	node: Publish post

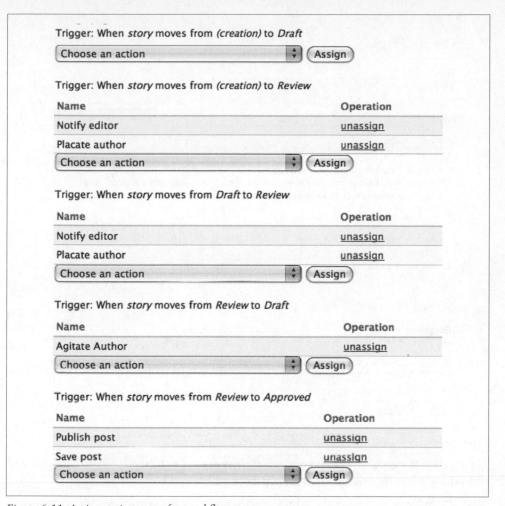

Figure 6-11. Action assignments for workflow states

 When you add the "Publish post" action, Drupal will automatically add the "Save post" action, too, along with a message explaining why: "You have added an action that changes the property of a post. A Save post action has been added so that the property change will be saved." Because we are making a change to the node's status, that change needs to be saved as well.

11. Now, if we go to Create content→Story (node/add/story) and create a new Story, under the "Article publication" fieldset we can see that writers have the ability to set the status to either the Draft or Review states, but not the Approved state, as shown in Figure 6-12.

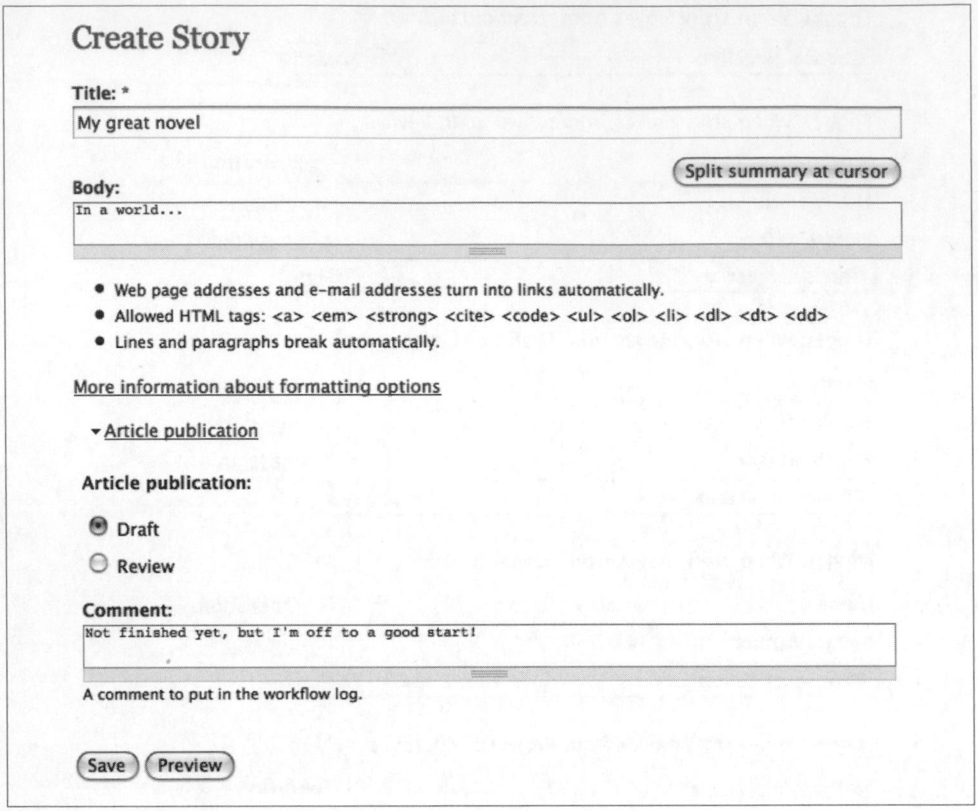

Create Story

Title: *

My great novel

Body:

[Split summary at cursor]

In a world...

- Web page addresses and e-mail addresses turn into links automatically.
- Allowed HTML tags: `<a> <em> <strong> <cite> <code> <ul> <ol> <li> <dl> <dt> <dd>`
- Lines and paragraphs break automatically.

More information about formatting options

▾ Article publication

Article publication:

◉ Draft

◯ Review

Comment:

Not finished yet, but I'm off to a good start!

A comment to put in the workflow log.

(Save) (Preview)

Figure 6-12. Article publication workflow in action

Go ahead and create a story or two. Set at least one story to the Review state and you should see a message that your story has been submitted for review.

Now if you are logged in as the administrator and visit the workflow tab on a story in the Review state, you can see that you have the additional option to move the story into the "Approved" state, which regular users can't.

Spotlight: The Workspace Module

We're definitely getting closer to the functionality that Jo and Catherine need, but there's one glaring problem that still remains. Writers can post new content and leave it in the "Draft" state if they don't want it to be reviewed yet. What happens when they want to come back and finish the work, though? Because it's still unpublished, the story won't be included on any of Drupal's normal listing pages! Our writers will be able to return to the drafts only if they remember the numeric ID of their articles, and that's asking a bit much of volunteers.

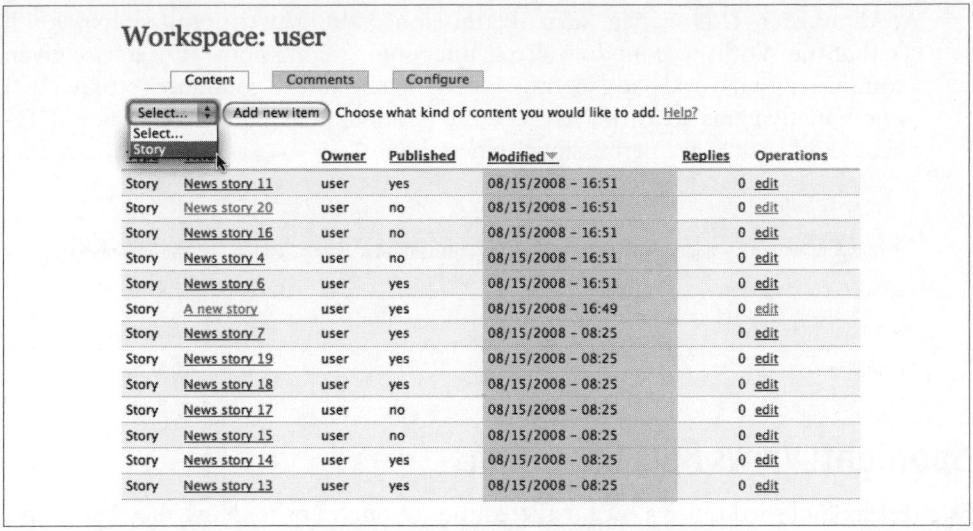

Figure 6-13. The "My Workspace" page, listing a user's content

Using the Views module, we could build a custom listing page that shows all nodes—including unpublished ones—by the current logged-in user. However, the Workspace module (*http://drupal.org/project/workspace*) can also handle this feature and is much easier and faster to set up. It gives each user his own personal page that lists the nodes, comments, and files that he's posted to the site, as shown in Figure 6-13. By default, Workspace will add a new menu item, "My workspace," to the navigation to access the page. You can also configure it to add a link to each user's workspace directly on his user page.

In addition to the view-like page, Workspace also provides a quick shortcut to create new content. A list of content types that the user is allowed to create will appear in a drop-down select list on his workspace page with a handy "Add new item" button that will take him immediately to the content creation screen, such as Create content→Story (node/add/story). That makes it an easy one-stop dashboard for frequent contributors.

Hands-On: Create Workspaces

The Workspace module is a snap to set up. When we are done with a few short steps, we'll have something like Figure 6-13 for all of our users.

1. First, go to Administer→Site building→Modules (admin/build/modules) and enable the following module:

   • Other package

     —Workspace

2. That's it! You should now see a "My workspace" link in the navigation menu, and each user on the site will have her own workspace as well.

3. At Administer→User management→Permissions (admin/user/permissions), you'll see that the Workspace module also defines some permissions. If users are given "administer own workspace" permission, they'll be able to configure settings such as how many items are displayed. Use the permission assignments shown in Table 6-7 and click "Save permissions" when done.

Table 6-7. Settings for workspace permissions

Permission: workspace module	anonymous user	authenticated user	editor	site administrator
administer own workspace		Checked	Checked	Checked
administer workspaces				Checked
view all workspaces				Checked

Spotlight: Views Bulk Operations

We've accomplished quite a bit for the editors of our website. Now they can move articles from one state to another, send them back to writers for revisions, receive notices when stories are ready for review, and automatically publish them when they're ready for consumption. However, editors still have to work with the articles one by one, a troublesome limitation when the site has been swamped with me-too news stories or low-quality poetry.

Drupal provides a built-in content administration page at Administer→Content management→Content (admin/content/node). It allows administrators to list 20 pieces of content at a time, and to perform bulk operations on them, like publishing and unpublishing, which you can see in Figure 6-14. However, this screen doesn't take advantage of the actions system, and it's impossible to customize what information is listed in the table.

The Views Bulk Operations module (*http://drupal.org/project/views_bulk_operations*) is designed to overcome that limitation. It provides a new style of view called "Bulk Operations." It displays the contents of the view much like a standard table-style view, with columns and rows and headers. However, it puts a checkbox next to each node and places a drop-down list of actions at the top of the view. The result is an easy-to-customize management form with all the capabilities of Drupal's content administration screen, but with far more flexibility. You can see an example of the bulk operation view in Figure 6-15.

In addition, it's possible to customize the actions that appear in the drop-down. Using that capability, you can give users in different roles access to more powerful administration screens. A moderator for a message board, for example, might see an administration screen with the "Unpublish content" and "Email administrator" actions. An administrator could be given access to another view that includes the "Ban user" and "Delete content" actions in its list of options.

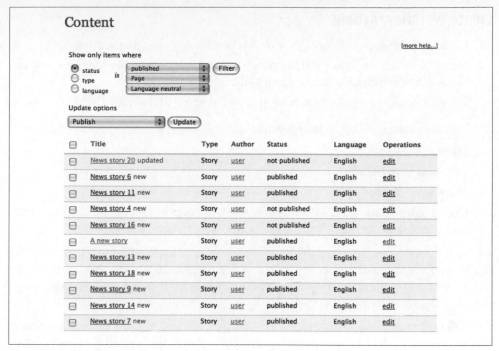

Figure 6-14. The Drupal core default content administration view

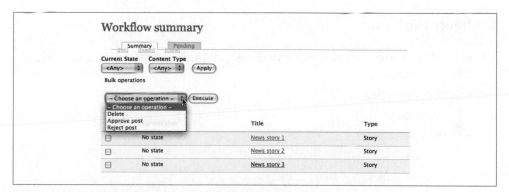

Figure 6-15. The "Workflow summary" view using Views Bulk Operations

Hands-On: Building an Administration Page

First, before we get to the view, we need to set up specific actions to reject and approve content using our workflow states. This will allow the Views Bulk Operations module to list the Reject and Approve options easily.

Create Workflow Actions

1. Go to Administer→Site configuration→Actions (admin/settings/actions).
2. Select "Change workflow state of post to new state..." from the "Make a new advanced action available" drop-down and click Create.
3. Fill out the new action's form as shown in Table 6-8 and save it.

Table 6-8. Settings for the Approve post action

Setting	Value
Description	Approve post
Target state	Approved

4. Do the same thing again, only this time use "Reject post" for the Description field, and select Draft as the "Target state." Click Save to complete it.

We've now set up specific, reusable actions to reject and approve nodes. Thanks to the work we did earlier, whenever these actions are triggered, all the appropriate emails will be sent and content will be published as soon as it's approved, based on the workflow and trigger rules we set up.

The Workflow module already provides a simple view listing all of the site's content, and what state each piece of content is currently in. Now, we need to alter this view to take advantage of the Views Bulk Operations module.

Configure the View

1. Go to Administer→Site building→Modules (admin/build/modules) and enable the following modules:
   - Other package
     — Advanced Help
   - Views package
     — Views
     — Views Bulk Operations
     — Views UI
2. Now, when we go to Administer→Site building→Views (admin/build/views), we will see the "Default Node view: workflow_summary" view listed. Click the Edit link for that view (admin/build/views/edit/workflow_summary).
3. In the "Basic settings" section, click Style: Table, change it to Bulk Operations, and click Update.

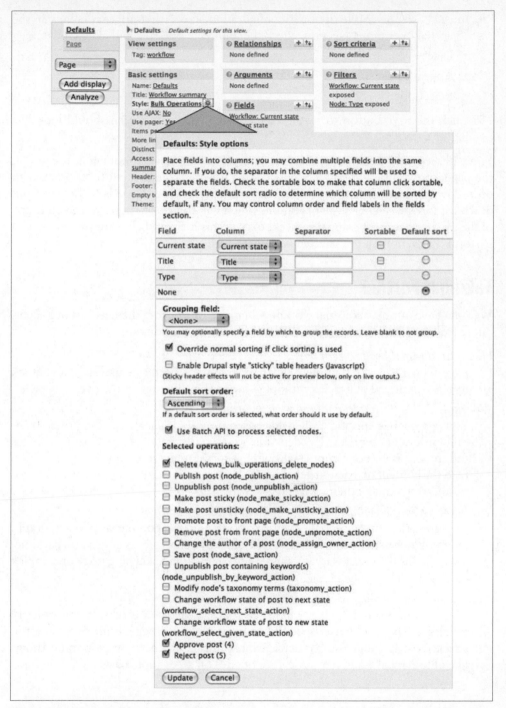

Figure 6-16. Views Bulk Operations settings

4. In the "Defaults: Style options" configuration screen that appears below, in the "Selected operations" section, check the following options, and click Update:

- Delete
- Approve post
- Reject post

5. Click the Save button to save the changes to the view, which should look like Figure 6-16.

You will see a new item, "Workflow summary," in your navigation menu. If you visit the page, shown in Figure 6-15, you will see a list of all the content on the site, with drop-down boxes to filter by workflow state and content type. There is also a new drop-down list for you to choose an operation, which will trigger our actions. Selecting any of the pieces of content using the checkboxes in this form and choosing an action will perform that action on the selected node(s).

Taking It Further

We now have our new editorial workflow in place. We've met the needs of our client, but there are some other modules that are also worth checking out:

Flag (http://drupal.org/project/flag)
Flag, which is covered in more detail in Chapter 9, could be used to allow quick in-place approval of articles without going to the edit page or the overview page.

Workflow Fields (http://drupal.org/project/workflow_fields)
You can change specific CCK fields based on a node's state, making them read-only or hiding them entirely, depending on what stage of the publishing process the content is in. For example, although it might make sense for the legal team to read the content of a new article and reject or approve it, they should probably not be allowed to make their own edits.

Workflow Graph (http://drupal.org/project/workflow_graph)
This module can present the history of one piece of content as a visual graph, mapping out which contributors to the site have changed its states at what time. Though this isn't necessary for simple sites, it can make keeping track of complex editing processes much easier.

Nodequeue (http://drupal.org/project/nodequeue)
This module is often used on online news sites, as it allows for displaying arbitrary articles in a list with a user-specified order, such as maybe an Editor's Picks list of articles. Nodequeue also has actions integration, which allows you to do things like automatically add new articles to queues on a per-topic basis.

Summary

Congratulations! The Twin City Arts website now includes all the major features that the staff wanted. We've used the Workflow module to create a richer set of "states" for content to exist in, preventing collisions when editors review rough drafts that writers haven't finished. We've used actions and triggers to handle notifying editors and writers when articles need their attention, and we've used the Views Bulk Operations module to give editors a way to manage large groups of articles at a time. Finally, we used the Workspace module to give writers a simple, one-stop location to view their rough drafts, their in-review articles, and their previously published pieces.

Here are the modules that we referenced in this chapter:

- Flag: *http://drupal.org/project/flag*
- Nodequeue: *http://drupal.org/project/nodequeue*
- Rules: *http://drupal.org/project/rules*
- Trigger: core
- Views: *http://drupal.org/project/views*
- Views Bulk Operations: *http://drupal.org/project/views_bulk_operations*
- Workflow: *http://drupal.org/project/workflow*
- Workflow Fields: *http://drupal.org/project/workflow_fields*
- Workflow Graph: *http://drupal.org/project/workflow_graph*
- Workspace: *http://drupal.org/project/workspace*

## CHAPTER 7

Photo Gallery

If a picture says a thousand words, it's important that a site have a strong foundation for managing images. The flexibility of Drupal allows for the management of images in a variety of ways and can scale from a one-person portfolio to millions of users uploading photos on a fansite.

This chapter introduces the following modules:

ImageField (http://drupal.org/project/imagefield)
    A CCK field that allows image uploads

ImageCache (http://drupal.org/project/imagecache)
    Automatically resizes images to predefined dimensions and caches them for later retrieval

Custom Pagers (http://drupal.org/project/custom_pagers)
    Creates custom previous/next pagers

If you would like to participate in the hands-on exercises in this chapter, install Drupal using the Photo Gallery installation profile from the book's sample code. This will create the example website on your web server. The completed website will look as pictured in Figure 7-1 and at *http://gallery.usingdrupal.com*. For more information on using the book's sample code, see the Preface.

> In order to complete this chapter, you must have the Clean URLs feature working, and your version of PHP must have the GD Library installed. See the "Troubleshooting ImageCache" section, later in this chapter, for more information.

Figure 7-1. The Robinsons' photo gallery website

Case Study

The Robinsons have a large extended family with whom they have trouble keeping in touch. The family has long been pestering their web-savvy son Fritz to build a website where they could share family stories and full-resolution photos. Finding himself with a weekend and no homework, Fritz decides to set up the family photo-sharing site using Drupal.

The Robinsons want the ability to let family members submit photos. When uploaded, photos should automatically resize down to a thumbnail view, but also allow for the download of a full-resolution version. They want to be able to put the photos into different galleries and tag the photos with keywords. And finally, they want their family members to be able to comment on the photos!

Implementation Notes

You probably expect the task of building a photo gallery to be easy, but given the wide array of options available in Drupal, it can quickly turn confusing. The good news is that a site built with CCK and Views, such as the job website in Chapter 3, can quickly be extended to create a highly customized image gallery.

Photo Uploads

Image handling in Drupal has long been a distributed effort between several cooperating (or competing) modules. The Image module (*http://drupal.org/project/image*) was the universal solution in Drupal 4.6 and 4.7, but with the advent of CCK, several new modules appeared that leveraged this new, more flexible system. Because the Drupal community's development trends are headed toward websites built around CCK and Views, we're going to build our site around this newer approach, building on the basic functionality of CCK and Views.

ImageField (*http://drupal.org/project/imagefield*) is a module that provides a reusable image upload field to CCK, which we'll be able to use to upload our photos.

Thumbnail Generation

Despite its name, the ImageCache module (*http://drupal.org/project/imagecache*) does much more than simply cache images. It is often paired with ImageField, because although ImageField handles the upload and storage of images, it does not provide any way of creating thumbnails. ImageCache can not only create thumbnails, but also chain together several image manipulations such as crop, rotate, scale, desaturate, and sharpen to create completely customized displays of images.

Photo Galleries

The display of images in a gallery can be made from a few pages created by the Views module. Because ImageCache and ImageField provide Views integration, you'll be able to select any desired images created with ImageField, and then ImageCache will scale those images down for display in the view.

Spotlight: ImageField

Building on the flexibility of CCK, any module in Drupal can provide a reusable field that can be used to extend your content types. Fields that handle things like text or numbers are bundled with CCK, but you can just as easily add fields that allow you to upload audio and video files, click web links, and more. These other field types are separate projects on the Drupal.org website, available under the "CCK" category (*http://drupal.org/project/Modules/category/88*).

The ImageField Module, available from *http://drupal.org/project/imagefield*, is one such specialty field that provides a reusable field for image handling, as shown in Figure 7-2. Like other CCK fields, you can configure an image field to allow multiple values, so any number of images can be uploaded to a single node. You can even add multiple fields to a single content type, in case a piece of content has the need for multiple images, each with specialty uses.

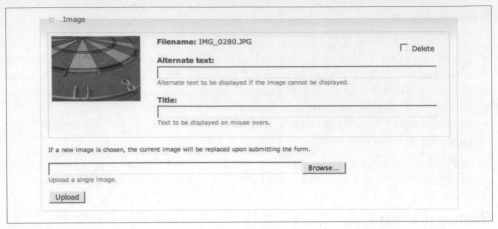

Figure 7-2. An image field with options enabled for "Alternate text" and "Title"

Configuration

After enabling the module, ImageField puts a new field on the fields form for setting up a new or existing content type. Like other CCK fields, an image field is added to a content type at Administer→Content management→Content types (admin/content/ types). The form for configuring an image field is displayed in Figure 7-3.

A few of the options on this form are common among all CCK fields, such as Label, Widget type, Required, and Number of values. These fields behave the same for an image field as they do for other fields, as described in the introduction to CCK in Chapter 3. The other options listed here are unique to ImageField:

Maximum resolution
   If a user uploads an image that is too large, the image is scaled down proportionally to fit within the maximum resolution.

Minimum resolution
   If a user uploads an image that is too small, ImageField prompts the user for a larger one.

File path
   The file path lets you put your images into a specific directory within your files directory. The files directory is configured at Administer→Site Configuration→File System (admin/site configuration/file-system). To prevent your images from being dumped directly into the top level of the files directory, this option should always be filled in with some value. Often, you'll want to use a separate directory for each content type you set up. If you have two content types such as "Article" and "Blog post," you might set up the image path to *images/article* and *images/blog*, respectively.

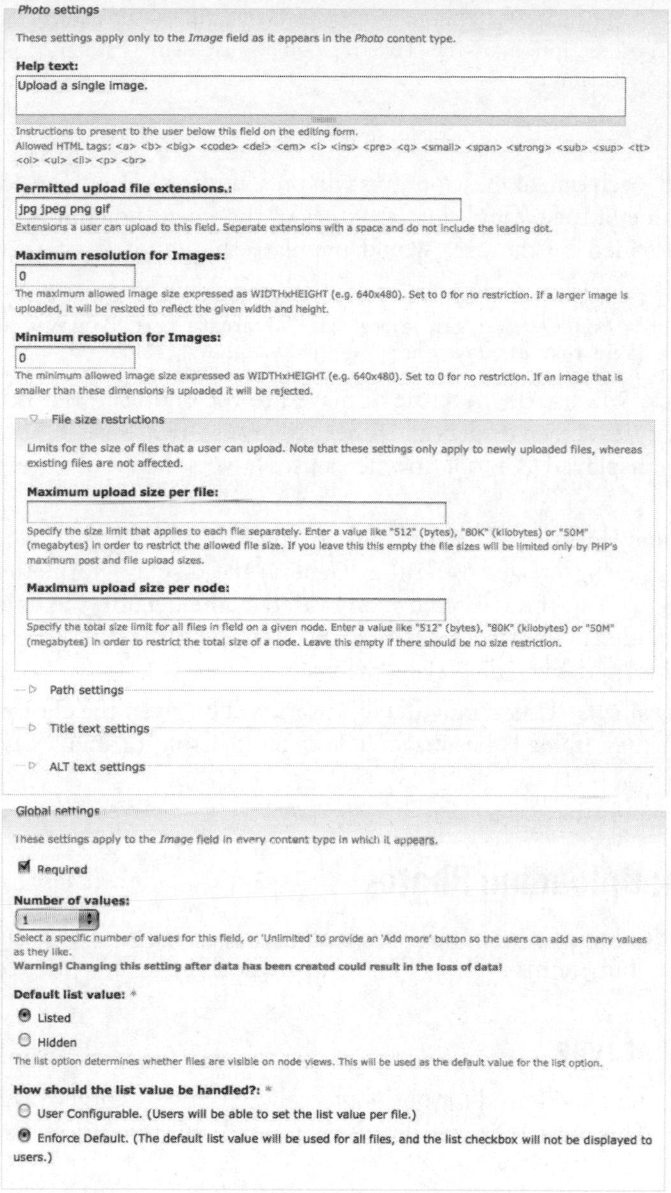

Photo settings

These settings apply only to the *Image* field as it appears in the *Photo* content type.

Help text:

Upload a single image.

Instructions to present to the user below this field on the editing form.
Allowed HTML tags: <a> <b> <big> <code> <del> <em> <i> <ins> <pre> <q> <small> <span> <strong> <sub> <sup> <tt> <ol> <ul> <li> <p>

Permitted upload file extensions.:

jpg jpeg png gif

Extensions a user can upload to this field. Seperate extensions with a space and do not include the leading dot.

Maximum resolution for Images:

0

The maximum allowed image size expressed as WIDTHxHEIGHT (e.g. 640x480). Set to 0 for no restriction. If a larger image is uploaded, it will be resized to reflect the given width and height.

Minimum resolution for Images:

0

The minimum allowed image size expressed as WIDTHxHEIGHT (e.g. 640x480). Set to 0 for no restriction. If an image that is smaller than these dimensions is uploaded it will be rejected.

▽ File size restrictions

Limits for the size of files that a user can upload. Note that these settings only apply to newly uploaded files, whereas existing files are not affected.

Maximum upload size per file:

Specify the size limit that applies to each file separately. Enter a value like "512" (bytes), "80K" (kilobytes) or "50M" (megabytes) in order to restrict the allowed file size. If you leave this this empty the file sizes will be limited only by PHP's maximum post and file upload sizes.

Maximum upload size per node:

Specify the total size limit for all files in field on a given node. Enter a value like "512" (bytes), "80K" (kilobytes) or "50M" (megabytes) in order to restrict the total size of a node. Leave this empty if there should be no size restriction.

▷ Path settings

▷ Title text settings

▷ ALT text settings

Global settings

These settings apply to the *Image* field in every content type in which it appears.

☑ Required

Number of values:

1 ⬍

Select a specific number of values for this field, or 'Unlimited' to provide an 'Add more' button so the users can add as many values as they like.
Warning! Changing this setting after data has been created could result in the loss of data!

Default list value: *

⦿ Listed

○ Hidden

The list option determines whether files are visible on node views. This will be used as the default value for the list option.

How should the list value be handled?: *

○ User Configurable. (Users will be able to set the list value per file.)

⦿ Enforce Default. (The default list value will be used for all files, and the list checkbox will not be displayed to users.)

Figure 7-3. The widget configuration options for an image field

If the Token module (*http://drupal.org/project/token*) is installed, the Image Path option can be made dynamic. See Chapter 5 for a description of the Token module's use with Pathauto as an example.

Title/ALT text
> If enabled, each one of these options will present the user with an additional field for the value of the *alt* and *title* attributes of the image when it is displayed. The values provided by the user would populate the emphasized text in the code sample:
>
> ```
> <img src="/files/images/sample.png" alt="Alternate text displayed here"
> title="Title text displayed here" width="200" height="100" />
> ```
>
> The *alt* text will usually never be displayed to the end user, but is important for accessibility, as screen readers and other assistive software use it. The *title* attribute should be displayed as a tool tip when a user hovers the mouse over the uploaded image.

Default list value/How should the list value be handled?
> When displaying images using the "Generic file display" formatter, images are displayed in a list. If the listed option is used as the default, the uploaded images will be included in the list. This setting has no effect unless the "Generic file display" formatter is used when displaying the image.
>
> If the list value is "User configurable," users will be given the choice of listing the file when they upload the image. The default listing of images is displayed in Figure 7-4.

Hands-On: Uploading Photos

To begin, we need to handle some basics: creating a form with which to upload photos, and some taxonomy terms that we will use to create a browsable photo gallery.

Photo Content Type

The first thing that we'll need for our photo gallery is a new content type for photos, called Photo. This new type will let users upload full-resolution photos through ImageField.

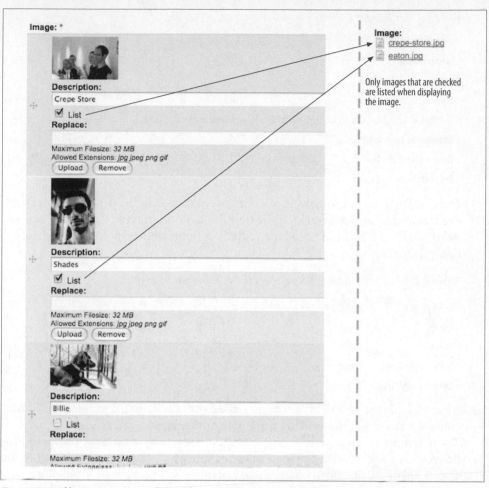

Figure 7-4. If listing is user-configurable, users may specify whether the image is listed

1. Go to Administer→Site building→Modules (admin/build/modules) and enable the following modules:
    *   CCK package
        —Content
        —FileField
        —ImageField
    *   Core – optional package
        —Taxonomy
2. Go to Administer→Content management→Content types (admin/content/types) and add a new content type by clicking on the "Add content type" tab. Create a content type called *Photo*, using the settings indicated in Table 7-1.

Table 7-1. Settings for the new Photo content type

Field	Value
Identification	
Name	Photo
Type	photo
Description	A photo containing a Robinson family member or friend
Submission form settings	
Title field label	Title
Body field label	Caption

3. After creating the Photo type, you'll be redirected back to the list of content types. We'll now add an image field to the new Photo content type. Click the "manage fields" link next to the Photo type (admin/content/node-type/photo/add_field). Enter the values as in Table 7-2.

Table 7-2. Settings for adding a photo field to the Photo content type

Field	Value
Label	Photo
Field name	photo
Select a field type	Image
Select a widget type	Image

4. After creating the new field, you're presented with the form to configure it (admin/ content/node-type/photo/fields/field_photo). Enter the values as in Table 7-3. Though most of these settings are self-explanatory, the maximum resolution for images has a special meaning for a value of 0, meaning that there is no limit to the resolution of the uploaded image. As one of the family goals was for full-size image swapping, we'll leave this at the default value of 0. We'll also upload all pictures to a subdirectory called *photos*, for organization.

Table 7-3. Settings for the photo field within the Photo content type

Field	Value
Photo settings	
Permitted upload file extensions	jpg jpeg png gif
Maximum resolution for images	0
Minimum resolution for images	0
Path settings: File path	photos
Global settings	
Required	Checked
Number of values	1

Field	Value
Default list value	Listed
How should the list value be handled?	Enforce Default
Description field	Disabled

 If the Token module is enabled, the path that images are uploaded to can be based on something dynamic, such as the logged-in user's username or the date.

5. After submitting the form, you'll be returned to the list of all the fields in the Photo content type. Order the fields as follows and click Save:

- Title
- Photo
- Caption
- Menu settings

6. This concludes the setup of the new content types, but we need to make it so that users can upload a picture to the site. Go to Administer→User management→Permissions (admin/user/permissions), where you can add permissions for each user role. Give each role the permissions indicated in Table 7-4.

Table 7-4. User permissions for the new Photo content type

Permission	anonymous user	authenticated user	editor	site administrator
node module				
create photo content		Checked		
delete any photo content			Checked	Checked
delete own photo content		Checked		
edit any photo content			Checked	Checked
edit own photo content		Checked		

After completing the Photo content type, try out uploading a new photo by visiting Create content→Photo (node/add/photo). A basic user should see a form similar to that in Figure 7-5.

Image Galleries

Although being able to upload photos is a good start for the Robinson family, Fritz knows that every photo-sharing site needs something like galleries, where users can group photos. In our photo gallery, Fritz identified that a gallery is no more than a grouping of photos under a single name or category. This concept maps directly to

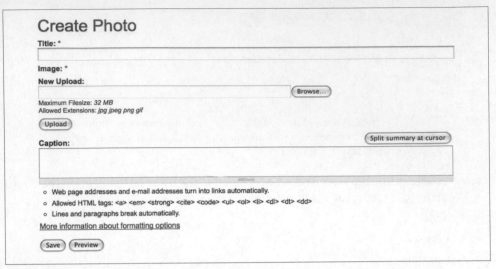

Create Photo

Title: *

Image: *
New Upload:

[Browse...]

Maximum Filesize: *32 MB*
Allowed Extensions: *jpg jpeg png gif*

[Upload]

Caption:
[Split summary at cursor]

- Web page addresses and e-mail addresses turn into links automatically.
- Allowed HTML tags: <a> <em> <strong> <cite> <code> <ul> <ol> <li> <dl> <dt> <dd>
- Lines and paragraphs break automatically.

More information about formatting options

[Save] [Preview]

Figure 7-5. Our new photo submission form when logged in as an authenticated user

Drupal's core Taxonomy module, introduced in Chapter 2. We can set up several pre-defined galleries by creating a vocabulary with a term for each gallery.

In addition, many photo-sharing sites have the ability to let users freely categorize photos with whatever words they like (called *free tagging*). This sort of categorization is also supported by Drupal's core taxonomy module.

1. Go to Administer→Content management→Taxonomy (admin/content/taxonomy).
2. Click the "Add vocabulary" tab and enter the values from Table 7-5 into the new vocabulary form.

Table 7-5. Values for the new vocabulary for Gallery

Setting	Value
Identification	
Vocabulary name	Gallery
Content types	
Photo	Checked
Settings	
Required	Checked
Weight	−1

 The weight value of the Gallery vocabulary must be lower than that of the Tags vocabulary, to make Gallery terms appear before Tag terms, which is important for the Custom Pager that we'll add later.

3. After being returned to the main Taxonomy page, click the "Add vocabulary" tab a second time to set up the free tagging vocabulary with the values in Table 7-6.

Table 7-6. Values for the new vocabulary for Tags

Setting	Value
Identification	
Vocabulary name	Tags
Content types	
Photo	Checked
Settings	
Tags	Checked
Weight	0

4. The new Tags vocabulary can have new tags added directly on the node form, but our Gallery vocabulary will only display galleries defined by a site administrator. Click the "add terms" link on the Gallery row to populate your site with several starter galleries. The only required field is the Term name; create several terms such as those in Table 7-7 (though you can use any terms you want).

Table 7-7. Sample terms (galleries) for the Gallery vocabulary

Term name
Sunnyvale family picnic
Barcelona vacation
Boston road trip
Charlie's distraction

The Robinsons can now choose a gallery when they upload or edit a photo. The node edit form for photos at Create Content→Photo (node/add/photo) should now contain a drop-down list of galleries and a text field for tags such as shown in Figure 7-6.

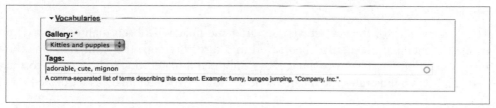

Figure 7-6. The fields for selecting a gallery and adding tags

Spotlight: ImageCache

If you uploaded an exceptionally large image during the previous hands-on steps, chances are good that you managed to break your site's layout. To prevent this, you'll want to scale these images so that they're a consistent size, and create thumbnails for use in listing pages. To help with this task, the ImageCache module will provide these options and many more for displaying images.

When it comes to file handling, ImageCache is one of the most exciting modules for Drupal. Despite the name, ImageCache does much more than cache images. It is in fact a full image manipulation tool, which will likely serve as the basis for image handling in a future release of the Drupal core.

The image manipulation provided by ImageCache allows a series of actions such as cropping, scaling, or resizing to be combined into what is called an *image preset*. By combining actions, you can create a customized display of your images. Figure 7-7 shows the result of a preset that combines a crop action with rotate to make a square image that is rotated 90 degrees.

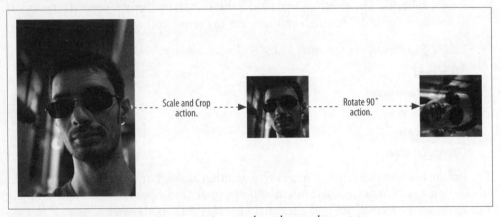

Figure 7-7. An image preset using two actions: scale and crop, then rotate

The "cache" part of ImageCache comes after the image has been manipulated. The image is generated on the fly, then saved in a directory with the same name as the ImageCache preset. This way, images are only manipulated once, then saved to the disk. Figure 7-8 illustrates the ImageCache workflow when an image is requested.

Presets and Actions

The main ImageCache administration panel at Administer→Site building→ImageCache (admin/build/imagecache), shown in Figure 7-9, displays a list of the presets available on the site. An image preset starts as nothing but a name, describing the actions that are performed on this style of image. You can add, edit, or delete presets, as well as

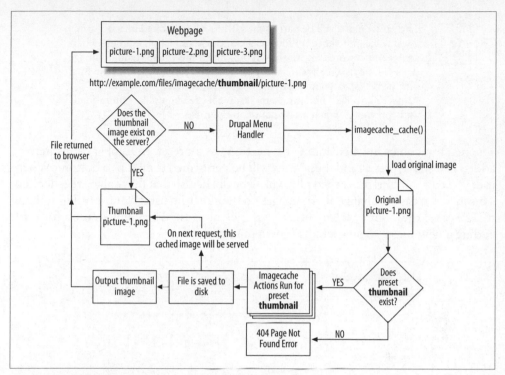

Figure 7-8. ImageCache workflow for creating a thumbnail

"flush" them. The Flush option lets you clear out all created images for a preset. Because images are generated on the fly, you can delete all the thumbnails on your site at any time and they'll be re-created the first time they're requested. You might try flushing the cache for a preset if images somehow become out of date with the original.

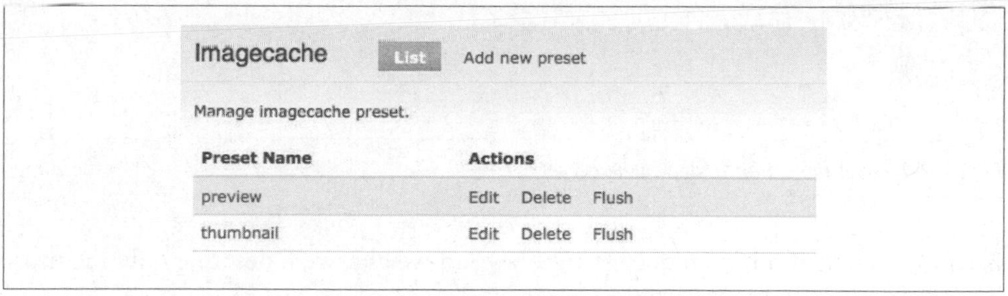

Imagecache	List	Add new preset

Manage imagecache preset.

Preset Name	Actions		
preview	Edit	Delete	Flush
thumbnail	Edit	Delete	Flush

Figure 7-9. The ImageCache module preset administration screen

The preset name will be part of the URL of all generated images, so it's good to keep it short, all lowercase, and use only alphanumeric characters, underscores, and dashes. If building a site where standard image sizes will be used in a variety of places, a name that describes the final output is also a good idea, such as "160_square," "200_width," or "300x200_resize." For our examples, we'll use names like "thumbnail" and "preview," which are semantic in their use.

The real fun comes in when adding new actions to a preset. Multiple actions may be added to a single preset, and the actions will be performed from top to bottom. Whenever you edit a preset, the cached files will all be flushed so that they can be regenerated. This makes it easy to change all the images on the site from using a 100-pixel thumbnail to 120-pixel thumbnail (or any other possible changes). The configuration form for adding a new preset to an action is shown in Figure 7-10.

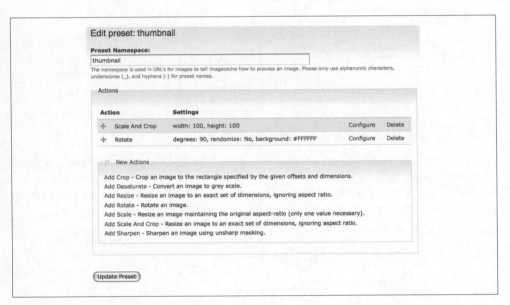

Figure 7-10. Actions on an ImageCache preset

Because each action has unique settings beyond weight, we'll describe only the most basic actions: crop, resize, scale, and scale and crop.

Crop

Crop allows you to trim off edges of the image that are not wanted. Crop also can take pixel values, but the most common usage of crop values are the keywords *top*, *right*, *bottom*, *left*, and *center*. The end result of a cropping action will be similar to Figure 7-11.

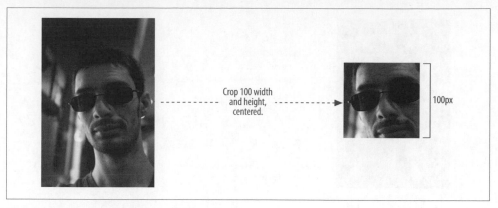

Figure 7-11. Cropping will trim off edges of an image

Resize

Resize can be used to force an image to a particular dimension. Width and height values can be integers to scale to a specific pixel size, or include the percent symbol to scale to a percentage.

Usually, you'll want to use the scale action instead of resize, as resizing will make your image look squished or stretched. Rather than maintain proportions, resize forces an image to be exactly those dimensions, as shown in Figure 7-12.

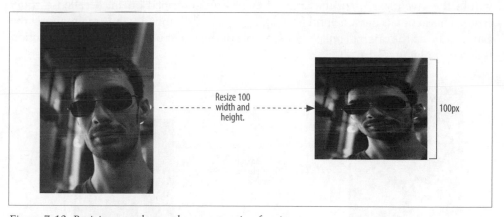

Figure 7-12. Resizing can change the aspect ratio of an image

Scale

Scale is used to size images proportionally. Unlike resize, you need to enter *either* a width or height. The dimension without a value will be determined by scaling the image to the given dimension. If both dimensions are entered, the image will be scaled to fit within both values.

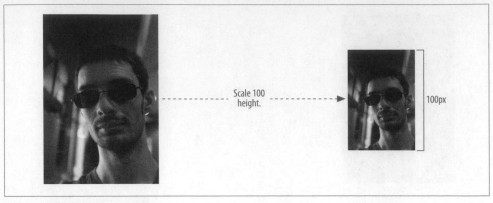

Figure 7-13. Scaling an image maintains the aspect ratio

If your site absolutely needs images to be no smaller than a certain size, you can use the Allow Upscaling option to enlarge images to the entered dimensions.

Scaling will always maintain the original aspect ratio of the original image. The end result of a scaling action is shown in Figure 7-13.

Scale and crop

As the name might imply, the scale and crop action is a single-action combination of the scale and crop actions. In this action, the image is scaled until one dimension fits within the given size, then the larger dimension is cropped off (also called a *zoom crop*). This action is most helpful for making square thumbnails while maintaining the aspect ratio of the original image. An example of the result of the scale and crop action is shown in Figure 7-14.

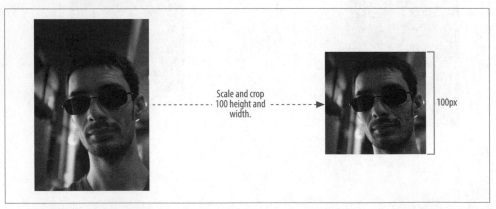

Figure 7-14. The scale and crop action trims off the larger side while maintaining the aspect ratio

More actions are available in ImageCache than those listed here, and more are being added all the time. Some other actions you may use include: rotate, watermark, border, text placement, brightness, and transparency. For a complete list, see the ImageCache project page at *http://drupal.org/project/imagecache*. For an expanded set of actions, you can install the ImageCache Actions module, available at *http://dru pal.org/project/imagecache_actions*.

Using a Preset

After setting up presets in the ImageCache administration area, you need to tell Drupal where these presets should be used. ImageField and FileField provide options to display the images full-size or in a generic file list. After configuring ImageCache presets, additional options for displaying images become available.

CCK formatters

The typical display of images is configured using CCK formatters, as shown in Figure 7-15. For every ImageCache preset setup on your site, ImageCache adds four new formatters:

[preset name] image linked to node
> Displays the image in the given preset size, linked to its "parent" node.

[preset name] image linked to image
> Displays the image in the given preset size, linked to the unaltered version of the image.

[preset name] file path
> Displays the path to the given preset image only. Used for debugging.

[preset name] URL
> Displays the URL to the given preset image only. Used for debugging.

The CCK formatters exposed by ImageCache are also available to the Views module, which allows you to create displays such as a grid list of image thumbnails. We'll cover this more in the "Hands-On: ImageCache" section, later in this chapter.

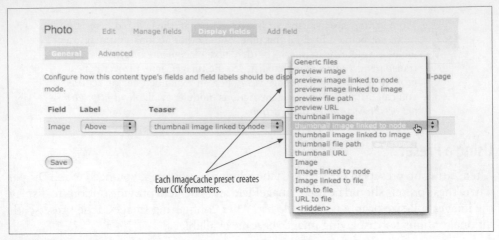

Figure 7-15. Configuring an image field to use an ImageCache preset

Manually viewing a preset image

You may view a preset at any time by manually assembling the URL to the image and preset. Assembling a URL is illustrated in Figure 7-16.

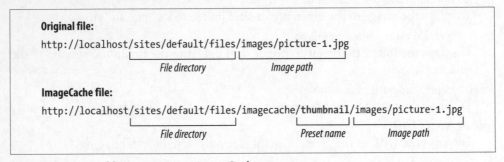

Figure 7-16. Assembling a URL to an ImageCache preset

After configuring an ImageCache preset, it's easy to test what an image will look like by manually visiting the URL of an image.

Displaying ImageCache Images in PHP

When wanting to display an image in a theme or module, the best and easiest way to display an ImageCache image is by using one of the following functions:

- *imagecache_create_url()*: Retrieve the full URL to an image

    ```
    print imagecache_create_url('my_preset', $path)
    ```

- *theme_imagecache()*: Print out the HTML for displaying a full image

    ```
    print theme('imagecache', 'my_preset', $path, $alt, $title, $attributes);
    ```

See Chapter 11 for a full explanation of theme functions and how they are used.

Troubleshooting ImageCache

ImageCache makes use of several advanced PHP and Apache features, such as URL rewriting and the GD image library. Because its software requirements are steep, any misconfiguration in your server or Drupal setup may cause ImageCache to break. The following sections describe common problems when getting ImageCache to work.

Check Clean URLs

The most common problem is that Clean URLs are not enabled (or not supported by the software on the web server). Visit Administer→Site configuration→Clean URLs (admin/settings/clean-urls), as shown in Figure 7-17. If you receive an error on the configuration form, see the handbook page for setting up Clean URLs (*http://drupal .org/node/15365*) for help configuring your server.

 Drupal's Clean URLs feature requires the Apache extension mod_rewrite. If running Drupal on a Microsoft IIS webserver, a third-party solution for rewriting URLs will be necessary to use ImageCache.

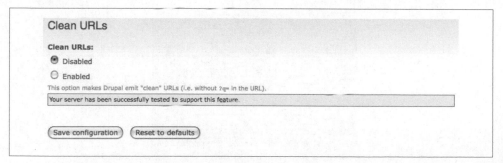

Figure 7-17. Clean URLs cannot be enabled until the Clean URL test has successfully run

Check GD library

Another common problem is a lack of the GD image library on the server. This could be the problem if no image is being generated at all when manually visiting an ImageCache URL. GD is a software package that is enabled by default with installations of PHP, but sometimes it is missing from the installation when doing custom installs of PHP. You can check the status of GD in your installation by visiting Administer→Reports→Status report (admin/reports/status). You should see a message similar to Figure 7-18, confirming GD is enabled.

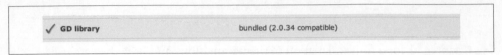

Figure 7-18. The message you should see for GD on the Status report

If GD looks OK but you're still not having images generated, try checking the full configuration of your PHP installation by creating an *info.php* file on your server containing only the following line of code:

```
<?php phpinfo(); ?>
```

You can also view an abbreviated list of PHP info right from Drupal by going to Administer→Reports→Status report and clicking on the version number link next to PHP (admin/reports/status/php). While not as complete as the full *info.php* file, it can be useful for checking overall details of how PHP is configured on your server.

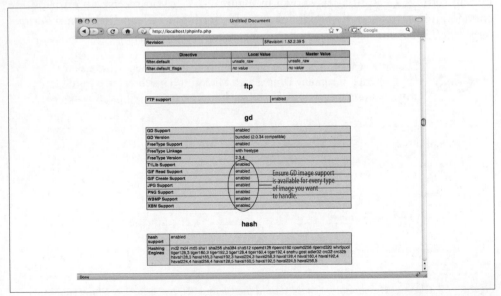

Figure 7-19. Checking for GD in a PHP install

Check for the GD settings section, which should be similar to Figure 7-19. Check that all the needed libraries are available for the kinds of images being uploaded. If the entire section is missing from this page, then GD is not installed at all.

 When finished with *info.php*, you should delete it from your server. It gives away lots of details about how your server is configured, which could give ideas to someone with less-than-honorable intentions if he happens across it.

Hands-On: ImageCache

Thanks to the previous section, we can now upload and categorize photos, but listings of photos are displaying several full-resolution images—surely not what the Robinson family wants! We need to create scaled-down versions of the images while leaving the original images intact. First, we'll set up ImageCache to provide us with thumbnails, and then configure our Photo type to use these thumbnails:

1. Check that Clean URLs are enabled at Administer→Site configuration→Clean URLs (admin/settings/clean-urls).

2. Go to Administer→Site building→Modules (admin/build/modules) and enable the following modules:
   - ImageCache
     — ImageAPI
     — ImageAPI GD2
     — ImageCache
     — ImageCache UI

Create ImageCache Presets

Let's set up a few presets to scale down the images: the first one a "thumbnail" size that's a small 120-pixel-wide square, and the second a "preview" size that maxes out the image for display on photo node pages (which maxes out the image widths at 480 pixels to prevent our layout from breaking):

1. Go to the ImageCache settings page at Administer→Site building→ImageCache (admin/build/imagecache). Click the "Add new preset" tab.

2. Enter the preset name "thumbnail" in the "Preset namespace" field and click the Create New Preset button. This will take you to the preset configuration screen pictured in Figure 7-20.

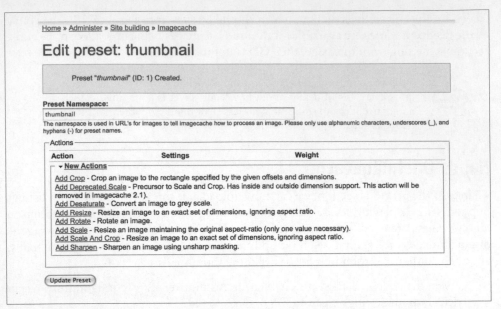

Figure 7-20. ImageCache preset configuration screen

3. On the next page, configure the thumbnail preset. In the New Actions fieldset, click Add Scale and Crop. Enter the values from Table 7-8 and shown in Figure 7-21 for the scale and crop action, to create image thumbnails as 120-pixel-wide squares. Click Add Action when finished.

Table 7-8. Settings for the "thumbnail" scale and crop action

Setting	Value
Weight	0
Width	120
Height	120

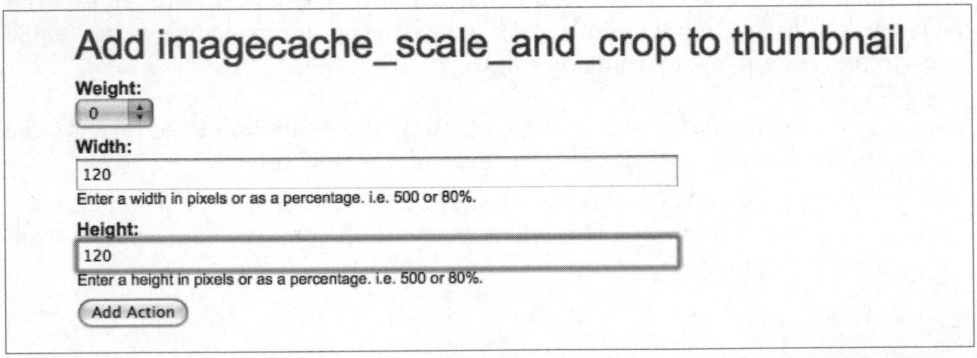

Add imagecache_scale_and_crop to thumbnail

Weight:

`0`

Width:

`120`

Enter a width in pixels or as a percentage. i.e. 500 or 80%.

Height:

`120`

Enter a height in pixels or as a percentage. i.e. 500 or 80%.

Add Action

Figure 7-21. Settings for the ImageCache actions

4. That completes the configuration of the thumbnail preset. Return to the main ImageCache page at Administer→Site building→ImageCache (admin/build/imagecache) and click the "Add new preset" tab. Enter "preview" into the Preset Namespace text field and click the Create New Preset button.

5. In the new preview preset, click the Add Scale link from the New Actions fieldset. Use the values in Table 7-9 for the scale action, to limit preview images to a maximum of 480 pixels wide. Click Add Action after finishing the values from the table.

Table 7-9. Settings for the "preview" scale action

Setting	Value
Weight	0
Width	480
Height	*Leave blank*
Allow Upscaling	Unchecked

Now our two presets are complete! We've set up two presets, the first one "thumbnail" for use in listing of many images, and the other "preview" for the display of the image on the photo node page.

Configure Photo Field Display

Even though we've set up two presets in ImageCache, our photos are still displaying at full resolution. We need to configure the Photo content type to use our new display options:

1. Go to the Display settings page for the Photo content type at Administer ›Content management→Content types (admin/content/types) and click "edit" for the Photo content type. Once inside the page for the content type, click the "Display fields" tab (admin/content/node-type/photo/display).

2. Change the settings for the Photo field to those from Table 7-10.

Table 7-10. Display settings for the Photo field

Image Setting	Value
Label	<Hidden>
Teaser	thumbnail image linked to node
Full node	preview image linked to image

Now that we've set up a Photo content type and set its display options to using ImageCache presets, it's a good time to take a break and try out uploading photos. After uploading several images to the gallery, you'll have a home page similar to that in Figure 7-22.

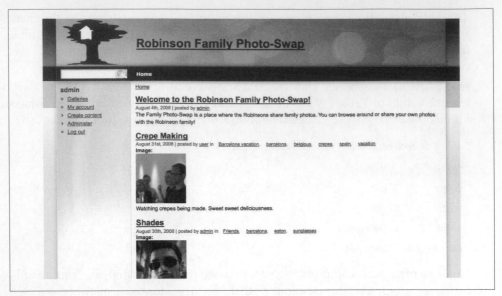

Figure 7-22. Front page of the photo-swap site after creating a thumbnail preset for images

Improve Image Quality

If you were to look at a sample thumbnail generated by ImageCache at this point, you might notice the quality of the image is a bit low and over-compressed. ImageCache uses the ImageAPI module's setting for image quality when processing JPEG images, which defaults to 75%. Increasing this level will generate much higher-quality images.

The steps are:

1. Go to the ImageAPI configuration for Drupal at Administer→Site configuration→ImageAPI (admin/settings/imageapi). Click the Configure Tab.

2. Set the JPEG quality to 90% or higher and click "Save configuration."

3. To see this effect on existing thumbnails, visit the ImageCache administration page at Administer→Site building→ImageCache (admin/build/imagecache).

4. For each preset, click Flush link to clear out the old, low-quality images. The new images will be regenerated the next time they are displayed.

 Besides the images created by ImageCache, Drupal also creates thumbnails in a few other places, such as user pictures. These thumbnails use a different JPEG quality setting, configured at Administer→Site Configuration→Image toolkit (admin/site configuration/image-toolkit).

Hands-On: Gallery View

We now have the process for uploading an image pretty much finished, and display of individual photos isn't looking too bad either. The shortcoming of our site right now is the display of thumbnailed images on a single page. It would be preferable if the images were laid out in a grid-like fashion, allowing many images to be displayed in a small area. To accomplish this task, we can set up a view using the Views module. When complete, this section will look as pictured in Figure 7-23.

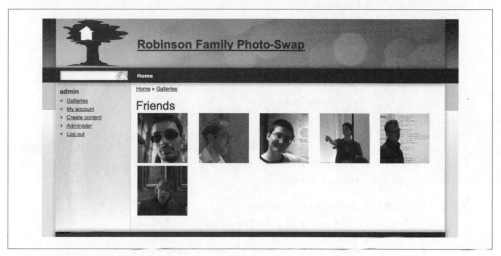

Figure 7-23. Completed gallery view

1. Go to at Administer→Site building→Modules (admin/build/modules) and enable the following:
   - Other
     —Advanced Help
   - Views
     —Views
     —Views UI

2. Go to the Views administration page at Administer→Site building→Views (admin/build/views). Click the Add tab at the top of the page to make a new view. Create a new view using the settings from Table 7-11.

Table 7-11. Basic Information for the gallery view

Field	Value
View name	gallery
View description	A gallery display of images

Field	Value
View type	Node

3. Configure the Basic settings of the new view using the information from Table 7-12.

Table 7-12. Page settings for the gallery view

Defaults: Basic settings	Value
Title	Galleries
Style	Style: Grid
	Number of columns: 4
	Alignment: Vertical
Use pager	Full pager
Items per page	20
More link	Create more link: Checked
Empty Text	No photos yet!

4. Find the Fields section of the view, click the + (plus) icon, check the "Content: Image: Image (field_photo)" field and click Add. Configure the field with the settings in Table 7-13 and click Update.

Table 7-13. Default fields for the gallery view

Defaults: Fields	Values
Content: Image: Image (field_photo)	Format: thumbnail image linked to node
	Label: None

5. Because we want only published photos to show up in our listings, we'll add a few filters to the view. Click the + (plus) icon in the Filters sections, check the following filters, and click Add:

   - Node: Published
   - Node: Type
   - Taxonomy: Vocabulary

6. Configure the fields using the information from Table 7-14, clicking Update to move between configuration forms.

Table 7-14. Default filters for the gallery view

Defaults: Filters	Value
Node: Published	Check "Published"
Node: Type	Is one of "Photo"
Taxonomy: Vocabulary	Is one of "Gallery"

7. To put the photos in some kind of order, we'll list the newest photos first. Click the + (plus) icon in the "Sort criteria" section and add "Node: Post date."

8. When finished, the View should look as pictured in Figure 7-24. Click the Save button to save your view.

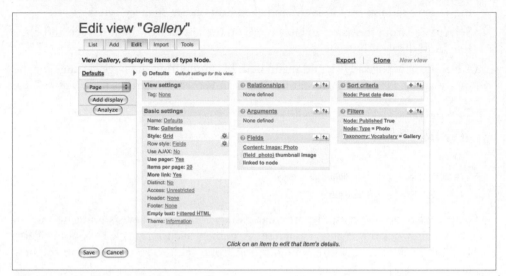

Figure 7-24. Gallery view settings

This completes the setup of the default display for our gallery view. Click the Live Preview at the bottom of the view configuration page—your view should appear similar to Figure 7-25.

Figure 7-25. A preview of the grid-style image gallery

However, this view is currently not visible anywhere on the site, and none of the photos are categorized by their gallery names. To correct both of these problems, we'll add a new page display to the view:

1. If you've left the configuration for the view, return to Administer→Site building→Views (admin/build/views) and click Edit on the "gallery" view.

2. Select Page from the list of display types on the left side of the interface and click the "Add display" button.

3. Give our new page a URL and menu item by configuring the page settings for the new display. Find the "Page settings" area and enter the settings from Table 7-15.

Table 7-15. Page settings for the gallery view

Page: Page settings	Values
Path	gallery
Menu	Type: Normal menu entry
	Title: Galleries

4. To display the photos in a particular gallery, our page view is going to use an argument. Click the + (plus) icon in the Argument section, check Taxonomy Term ID, and click Save. Use the configuration from Table 7-16 to configure the new argument, and click Update.

Table 7-16. Argument settings for the gallery view

Page: Arguments	Values
Taxonomy: Term ID	Title: %1
	Action to take if argument is not present: Summary, sorted ascending
	Validator: Taxonomy term
	Vocabularies: Gallery
	Set the breadcrumb for the term parents: Checked

5. You will be prompted to configure the various options. Click Update to choose the default settings.

6. When finished, the view configuration screen should look as pictured in Figure 7-26. Notice that the settings inherited from the Defaults display are italicized and grayed out. The overridden values for the Page display show unitalicized.

7. Click the Save button at the bottom of the form to save your view.

After building your view, you should notice a new item in your navigation for "Galleries." Go to this page (Galleries) to see your new Photo gallery! Make sure there are at least a few photos uploaded, and you'll have a page like that shown in Figure 7-27.

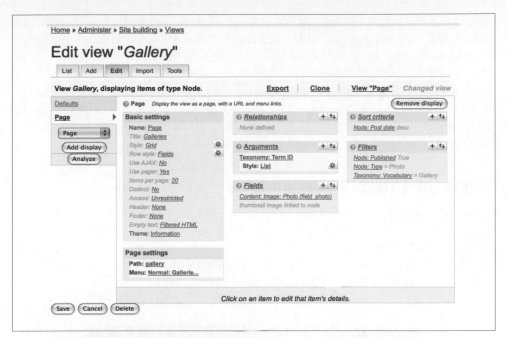

Figure 7-26. The Page display of the gallery view

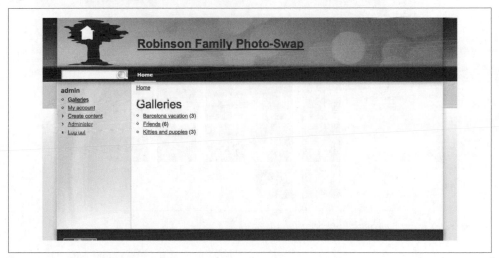

Figure 7-27. The summary view of our gallery

This is the "Summary" version of our gallery. This is displayed when we visit the *gallery* URL directly, with no further arguments in the URL. Clicking on one of the galleries in the list will take you to a URL at *gallery/(term id)*, where (`term id`) is the term for a gallery that we set up in our Gallery vocabulary.

Once a given gallery is chosen, you should see a page much like Figure 7-23 at the beginning of this section. The title on the page "Barcelona vacation" is pulled from the taxonomy term we're currently viewing, courtesy of the *%1* value we set up in Table 7-16 for the Arguments section of the gallery view.

Hands-On: Latest Photos Block

So even though we have a pretty convincing gallery view setup, our home page is still less than desirable with the default listing of images. Let's spice it up with another special view that shows the latest images uploaded anywhere on the site. To speed up the process, we can clone the gallery view and then just make a few tweaks. When completed, the site's front page will look as pictured in Figure 7-28.

Figure 7-28. Front page with the Latest Photos block

 Another option besides cloning the view is to make another display within the existing gallery view. However, because we'll need to remove a filter and we could possibly change the image field to use a different ImageCache preset, we'll need to override a lot of the view defaults. When in a situation like this, if you're doing more overriding than inheriting, it's a good idea to start with a new view rather than building more displays into an existing one.

1. Go to the views administration page at Administer→Site building→Views (admin/build/views).

2. In the row for our gallery view, click the Clone link. This makes a copy of the gallery view, where we can just make a few changes.

3. Give the new view the basic information from Table 7-17.

Table 7-17. Basic information for the latest_photos view

Field	Value
View name	latest_photos
View description	A list of the latest photos on the site

4. Click Next to begin editing the cloned view. We no longer need the Page display. So click the Page display tab on the left, then click the "Remove display" button. Click Save to remove the display entirely.

5. We also no longer need the Taxonomy: Vocabulary filter. Click on the Taxonomy: Vocabulary link in the Filters area. In the configuration for the filter, click the Remove button.

6. In the Basic settings for the view, change the Title to Latest Photos.

7. Add a new block display to the view. Select Block from the list of display types on the left side of the Views interface and click the "Add display" button.

8. Find the "Block settings" area for our new display, and change the Admin description to Latest Photos. This will give the block an appropriate label in the blocks administration page.

9. Click the Save button to update the new latest_photos view, which should now look as pictured in Figure 7-29.

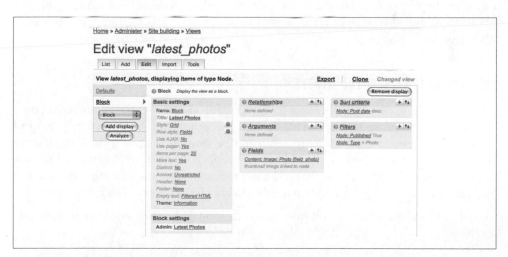

Figure 7-29. The block display of the Latest Photos view.

This new view provides a block that we can reuse anywhere on our site. We'll specifically set it up to display only on the front page below our welcome message:

1. Go to the site information settings at Administer→Site configuration→Site information (admin/settings/site-information).

2. Change the "Default front page" setting from *node* to *node/1* and click "Save configuration." This step sets the front page to be only the contents of node 1 (the "Welcome to the Robinson Family Photo-Swap" page). The front page will no longer include the listing of nodes that it had previously.

3. Go to the blocks administration page at Administer→Site building→Blocks (admin/build/block).

4. Drag the Latest Photos block up to the "Content bottom" region. Click "Save blocks" to save the changes.

5. You'll notice that the Latest Photos block is now at the bottom of every page on the site, including the blocks configuration page we're currently visiting. We'll change this to only appear on the front page. Click the "configure" link next to the Latest Photos block and configure the block according to Table 7-18. Click "Save block" when finished.

Table 7-18. Latest Photos block configuration

Field	Value
Page-specific visibility settings	
Show block on specific pages	Show on only the listed pages.
Pages	<front>

The Robinson Family Photo-Swap is now looking pretty good. We have photos scaled down to two different sizes, displayed in a nice gallery format, and we can pull out photos into blocks to be displayed anywhere we want on the site, such as the Latest Photos on the home page.

Hands-On: Custom Pagers

What's still showing a lack of tender love and care, however, is the photo asset page. To view a list of photos, a user has to click the photo, return to the previous page, and then click the next photo. This process could be simplified quite a bit if there were previous and next buttons on the photo asset page. The Custom Pagers module (see *http://drupal.org/project/custom_pagers*) can take any view (such as our gallery view) and create a simple pager on node pages for the previous and next items in the view.

Figure 7-30 shows what the photo pages will look like when completed with this section.

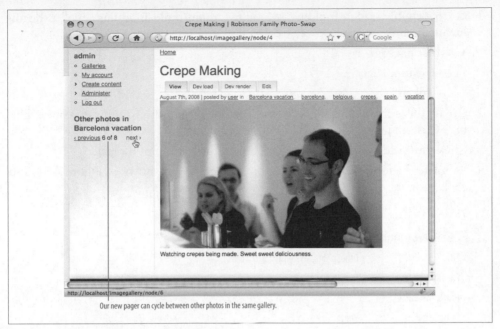

Our new pager can cycle between other photos in the same gallery.

Figure 7-30. Photo pages, now with paging

Home » Administer » Site building » Custom pagers

Add custom pager

Title: *
```
Other photos in [term]
```

Pager position: *
```
In a sidebar block
```
The node type(s) this custom pager will apply to.

---Pager visibility---

Determine what nodes this pager should be displayed on.

By node type: *
```
Page
Photo
Story
```
If the PHP field is filled in, this field will be ignored.

By PHP snippet:
```
```
Use a snippet of PHP to return TRUE or FALSE. Note that this code has access to the $node variable, and can check its type or any other property. If this field is filled out, the *By node type* field will be ignored.

---Pager node list---

Determine how the list of nodes for this pager should be generated.

Use PHP snippet:
```
```
Use a snippet of PHP to populate the pager. The snippet should return an array of node ids in the order they should be browsed. If this field is filled out, the *Use a view* and *View arguments* fields will be ignored.

Use a view: *
```
Gallery
```
A view used to populate the pager. The nodes will appear in the pager in the same order they are displayed in the view. If the PHP field is populated, this will be ignored.

View arguments:
```
[term-id]
```
A return-delimited list of arguments to pass into the selected view. If Token.module is enabled, placeholder tokens like [type] and [author] can be used.

☐ Reverse the list of nodes

Figure 7-31. Custom Pagers configuration for gallery pager

1. Go to Administer→Site building→Modules (admin/build/modules), enable the following modules, and click "Save configuration":
   - Other package
     — Custom Pagers
     — Token

2. Go to the administration page for Custom pagers at Administer→Site building→Custom pagers (admin/build/custom_pagers).

3. Click the "Add a new custom pager" link at the bottom of the page.

4. Populate the form with the values from Table 7-19, as shown in Figure 7-31, and click Submit.

Table 7-19. Custom Pager settings for navigating photos

Custom Pager Setting	Value
Title	Other photos in [term]
Pager position	In a sidebar block
Pager visibility	
By node type	Photo
Pager node list	
Use a view	gallery
View arguments	[term-id]

The [*term*] and [*term-id*] tokens will always use the **top** term assigned to the node. Because we set the Gallery vocabulary to a –1 weight (and the Tags vocabulary to a 0 weight), the term name and ID for the current gallery will populate this value dynamically.

5. Now that we have a custom pager set up and ready to display as a block on the page, make a visit to the blocks administration page at Administer→Site building→Blocks (admin/build/blocks).

6. Find the "Other photos in [term]" block and move it to the bottom of the "Left sidebar" region.

7. Click "Save blocks" to save your changes.

Now take a look at a photo node page. You should have a helpful pager in the left sidebar for the previous and next photo in the same gallery as the image you are viewing.

Taking It Further

If you've completed the gallery to this point, you've built an entire Drupal-based image gallery! However, there's no need to stop here. One of the great things about building a site with Drupal is that you can continuously refine it, adding new features to any part of your site. This section details a few additional pieces of functionality that are common in photo-sharing websites:

Community Tags (http://drupal.org/project/community_tags)
> Community tagging is just like the normal free tagging, except that it allows any guest (with permissions) to add tags to content, not just the original author. Enabling community tagging is very simple with the Community Tags module.

Tagadelic (http://drupal.org/project/tagadelic)
> Community tagging and tag clouds are two things that go nicely together. Creating tag clouds in Drupal is very simple using the Tagadelic module. Tagadelic provides blocks that can display popular terms from various vocabularies in a weighted manner. More popular terms will appear as larger text in the cloud, such as in Figure 7-32.

Popular tags

alley barcelona belgious **california** cardboard cutout crepes excitement garden group jeff robert robot spain sunnyvale vineyard

more tags

Figure 7-32. A sample tag cloud provided by the Tagadelic module

Taxonomy Redirect (http://drupal.org/project/taxonomy_redirect)
> In the current Robinson Family Photo-Swap, the gallery pages are nicely set up in a flowing set of thumbnails, but the taxonomy term pages still show the plain listing of nodes. This means that all the work we put into the gallery view won't show up when a user clicks a taxonomy term underneath a photo or in a tag cloud.
>
> The best approach to fix this is to use the Taxonomy Redirect module to make these links point to the new location at the path *gallery* instead of *taxonomy/term*. This way, all the taxonomy term links for these two vocabularies will go to the thumbnail view instead of the default listing provided by Taxonomy module.

Summary

In this chapter, we introduced the modules ImageCache, ImageField, and Custom Pagers. We set up a Photo content type and customized its output through a combination of ImageCache presets, views, and a custom pager. We have the option to enable community tagging, tag clouds, and make all taxonomy links use the gallery view instead of the default taxonomy listing.

Here are the modules that we referenced in this chapter:

- Community Tags module: *http://drupal.org/project/community_tags*
- Content Construction Kit (CCK) module: *http://drupal.org/project/cck*
- Custom Pagers module: *http://drupal.org/project/custom_pagers*
- ImageCache module: *http://drupal.org/project/imagecache*
- ImageCache Actions module: *http://drupal.org/project/imagecache_actions*
- ImageField module: *http://drupal.org/project/imagefield*
- Tagadelic module: *http://drupal.org/project/tagadelic*
- Taxonomy Redirect module: *http://drupal.org/project/taxonomy_redirect*
- Token module: *http://drupal.org/project/token*
- Views module: *http://drupal.org/project/views*

These are some other resources that we referenced and community resources for learning more about the new concepts introduced in this chapter:

- All CCK-related modules: *http://drupal.org/project/Modules/category/88*
- Clean URL support: *http://drupal.org/node/15365*
- Image working group: *http://groups.drupal.org/image*

## CHAPTER 8

Multilingual Sites

Creating a website with community content is great, but what if some or all of your community doesn't read or write English? It's a big world, and only about 6% of it speaks English as a native language. Multilingual sites allow you to reach out to your community and let them feel comfortable contributing. Having multiple languages is not as simple as having users post content in whichever language they like. There are other things to consider, like navigation, date formatting, and help text. And what about having the same post available in multiple languages, and easily navigating between them? Once you start thinking about it in detail, there is a lot of ground to cover. Luckily, Drupal core and a few contributed modules have done a lot of that hard work for us so we can concentrate on building our community and content.

Two big concepts for multilingual sites are internationalization, often abbreviated i18n, and localization, often abbreviated l10n. *Internationalization* is the underlying structure that allows software to be adapted to different languages and *localization* is the process of actually translating the software for use by a specific locale. Localization is not necessarily limited to just translating text, but also encompasses changing things like date formats and currency.

Drupal 6 has made great strides toward building a better internationalization system inside Drupal core that makes localization much easier. Core does not quite provide us with all of the tools we need to completely localize a site, but there are contributed modules ready to fill the gaps.

This chapter introduces the following modules:

Locale (core)
> Provides interface for translating and importing translations for user interface text

Content Translation (core)
> Handles translation of user-generated content

Internationalization (http://drupal.org/project/i18n)
> Allows other elements to be translated, such as menus, blocks, and taxonomy terms

Localization Client (http://drupal.org/project/l10n_client)
> An easy-to-use frontend for Locale module

Book (core)
   A module that allows multiple users to collaborate on documentation

Forum (core)
   A simple discussion system, grouped by topic

If you would like to participate in the hands-on exercises in this chapter, install Drupal using the Multilingual installation profile from the book's sample code. This will create the example website on your web server. The completed website will look as pictured in Figure 8-1 and at *http://multilingual.usingdrupal.com*. For more information on using the book's sample code, see the Preface.

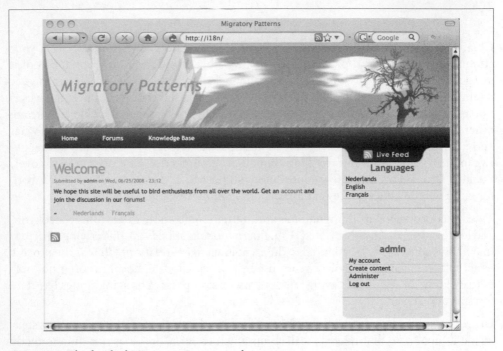

Figure 8-1. The finished Migratory Patterns website

Case Study

Our client, Migratory Patterns, is an international group that reports on and discusses migratory birds. They need a website that will allow everyone to have forums to discuss their shared passion as well as keep a repository of shared knowledge. They would like the site to provide language-specific forums for discussion, and allow members to navigate the site in their preferred language. They will also need an online knowledge base where members can share useful information, and a way to post news about the site. Additionally, they want to allow nonforum content to be translated by group members who know more than one language, so they can all share the accumulated knowledge.

They currently have members who speak three different languages—English, Dutch, and French—but they would like the ability to add more languages later as the group grows.

Implementation Notes

Though Drupal core's default Story content type can easily be used to post news to the front page, other features of the client warrant some further discussion.

Forum Discussions

There are contributed modules available that add integration between Drupal and other forum systems, such as phpBB, but Drupal itself comes with its own simple forum using the built-in Forum module. The Forum module uses regular Drupal core concepts such as taxonomy (for forum containers and forums themselves), nodes (for posts inside a forum), and comments (for replies), which makes it integrate seamlessly with the rest of the website, including Drupal's translation features.

Knowledge Base

Another core Drupal module, the Book module, provides the ability for multiple users to collaborate together in order to create a collection of documentation. Book pages are structured into one or more hierarchies, with previous, next, and up links generated automatically on each page. Each page also provides a "printer-friendly version," which will create an unformatted page consisting of the content of the current page and any subpages for easy printing or downloading for offline reading.

Translating User Interface Text

User interface is the text that is provided by Drupal, both in core and contributed modules. This includes things like form labels, help text, and navigation. Drupal core's Locale module provides the framework that allows user interface translations. To get the bulk of our localization, we will download translation projects that will supply us with translations of the core user interface. As we add contributed modules, we'll need to check whether they supply a module-specific translation. If not, we are not out of luck, because core also gives us the framework to add and update translations as needed within our site. The "Localization client" module uses this framework to add a nice, user-friendly frontend to make translating interface text a breeze.

Locale does not cover every single aspect of user interface text though, so we will be using the excellent Internationalization (i18n) module to fill in the gaps. The Internationalization module provides us the tools to translate taxonomy, blocks, and certain site variables like the site name and mission statement. In addition to providing extra translation, it also helps us manage our multilingual content.

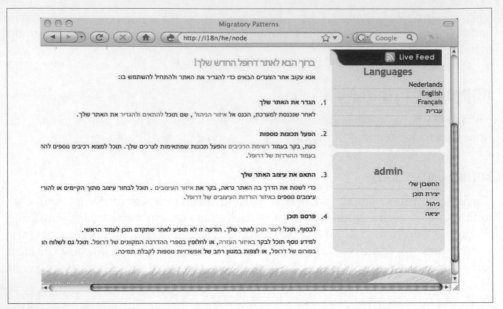

Figure 8-2. A right-to-left language page

Translating User-Generated Content

The final missing piece is translation for all of the user-generated content on the site: forum posts, pages, and so on. Core provides the "Content translation" module to do the heavy lifting. This will allow us to decide which content is translatable, and lets us create multiple versions of each node, each in a different language. It also provides a simple way for users to switch between languages. Again, the Internationalization module will fill out some of the content features.

Spotlight: Core Internationalization Features

Drupal core comes with two modules to handle languages: Locale and Content translation. Locale works with the user interface text and gives you a nice set of tools that let you import existing translations, create or edit your own, or export your site's translations for use on other sites. Content translation lets you create multiple versions of the same content in different languages and associates the translated versions together.

Another really nice feature in Drupal 6 core is support for right-to-left (RTL) languages, such as Arabic or Hebrew. If a language is set as an RTL language, Drupal will automatically flip all of the text so that it reads in the proper direction, as seen with Hebrew in Figure 8-2.

Locale

Locale handles the translation files and language switching options on the site. Let's break it down and look at what that means.

Translations

A "translation" is simply a file or collection of files that follow a standardized format. Translation files that follow this format have a special file extension, *.po*, which stands for Portable Object. A *.po* file is a simple text file that identifies strings of text and a particular language's translation of the strings. In Drupal, translations contain a list of all user interface strings in Drupal, along with their translated versions.

Drupal translation projects that you can download from *http://drupal.org/project/trans lations* are specially organized and packed groups of *.po* files that will match the Drupal directory structure when uncompressed. These projects cover only Drupal core's strings, meaning any user interface text that is contained in the core Drupal download. An important thing to note about the translation projects is that they may be in various states of completion and sometimes you may not agree with the way something was translated. Not to worry; we'll show you how to deal with that, too.

In addition to the core translation projects, contributed modules may have translation files available as well. These would be contained in the module download, if they exist. The coverage for module translations is not very thorough, and as modules can be updated much more frequently than Drupal's core translations, can become outdated quickly.

We will be looking at how Drupal can automatically import translation files for you, and this is typically how you will work them. It is also possible to manually import individual *.po* files if needed.

Interface translation

Many volunteers have worked hard to translate the Drupal interface into as many languages as possible. You may find that you need to add to or modify the translation you are using. If this happens, Drupal has tools built in to assist you.

When you visit the interface translation page at Administer→Site building→Translate interface (admin/build/translate), you will see that there is a list of the languages you have enabled along with a count and percentage of the number of strings that have already been translated, as shown in Figure 8-3. As you move through your site, Drupal will keep track of all the interface strings that you encounter. It can do this because translatable strings are identified in the code itself whenever a developer uses a translation function (the t() function). Once you visit a page, all of the translatable strings will be available for searching and translation. Visiting the page is an important step that is easy to forget. If you start searching for words that you know exist on the site but you haven't actually visited the page where they are, your interface search will come

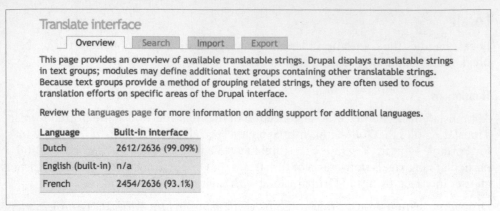

Figure 8-3. String count with percentage translated

back empty. We'll look more into translating in the "Hands-On: Translating the Interface" section, later in this chapter.

One thing to understand is that any translations you make through the Drupal interface, rather than by importing a *.po* file, will be stored in the database, not in a file. Drupal has an export feature that will put your translations back into a file format that you can then import into other sites.

 If you do end up doing translation work on your site, you should definitely look at giving your work back to the community. By giving translations back, you not only help the larger Drupal community, but also yourself, as you will have a larger number of people to test your work and help maintain it.

Language switching

Every site must have a default language, but how do we get the other languages to display? There are two main core mechanisms for this: the language negotiation setting and the language switcher block. After you have installed and enabled at least one other language, the first thing you should do is tell Drupal how to automatically handle multilingual display by configuring the language negotiation. By default, Drupal will do nothing and users will need to manually choose their language. You can select from several options, seen in Figure 8-4, which will automatically choose the language based on information in the URL.

Drupal can set the language based on the domain name of the site or by a path prefix. If you choose to use a separate domain name for each language you will offer, you can assign the domain name to a language in the language settings. For example, you can configure the Dutch language to use the domain name *http://nl.example.com* or even *http://foo.example.com*. Whenever someone accesses the site using one of these domain names, the language you have set will always be used.

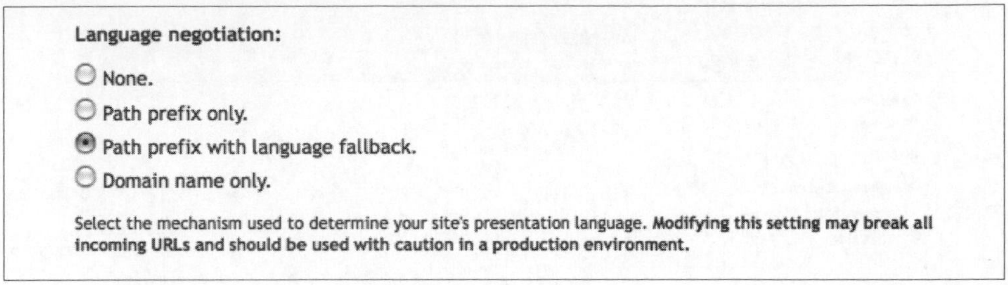

```
Language negotiation:

○ None.
○ Path prefix only.
◉ Path prefix with language fallback.
○ Domain name only.

Select the mechanism used to determine your site's presentation language. Modifying this setting may break all
incoming URLs and should be used with caution in a production environment.
```

Figure 8-4. Automatic language switching options

The more common negotiation method is using the path prefix. Again, you can configure the prefix you wish to use. By default, a translation that you install will set its language code as the path prefix identifier. With this setting, Drupal will check the path for a language code directly after the domain name, for example, *http://example.com/nl/forum*. If Drupal finds a valid code, it will display the language associated with it. You don't need a prefix for your default language, so that language will be used for all of your "plain" paths, as in *http://example.com/forum*. There are two settings to pick from when using path prefixing that let you determine what to do if the prefix is not found. The "Path prefix only" setting will look for the prefix and if not found, the default language will be displayed. The "Path prefix with language fallback" setting will send Drupal to check for clues in a few more places. The fallback checking will see whether the user has specified a preferred language in her My Account page and then, if nothing is found there, it will check the browser language setting and try to match that to the available languages. If all of these checks fail to find an appropriate language, then the site's default language will be used.

Negotiation settings determine how Drupal automatically changes the language displayed, but your users can also set this for themselves. Once you have more than one language enabled, a new Language settings section will appear on the My Account page with a simple radio button select list of the available languages, as you can see in Figure 8-5. However, this allows only authorized users to pick a language. To give all users a choice, including anonymous users, you can enable a core language switcher block that lists the available languages and will switch the site language as needed.

Localized installer

You can add new translations at any time, but if you add them prior to installing Drupal, the installation process can be run in the language of your choice. By default, the very first screen of the installer presents the option to "Install Drupal in English" or "Learn how to install Drupal in other languages." If one or more translations are present, you will instead be provided with a radio button list of the languages that you may choose from, as pictured in Figure 8-6. The rest of the installation screens will then be presented in the selected language. Once you complete the installation of Drupal, the language

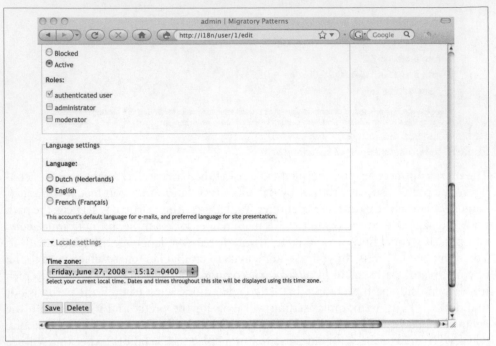

Figure 8-5. Personal language settings under the My Account page

you selected will be set as the default language for your site and Drupal will have already enabled the Locale module for you.

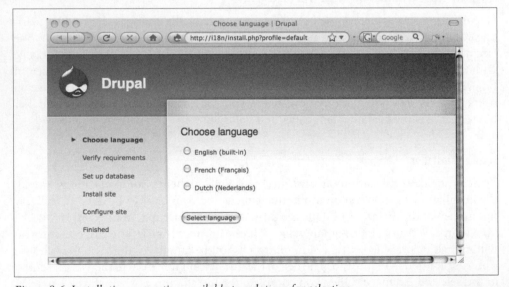

Figure 8-6. Installation presenting available translations for selection

Content Translation

When it comes to content translation, Drupal treats each translation as its own piece of content. You can choose to enable multilingual support per content type and you have two uses you can choose from, depending on whether you wish to identify the different languages or create related "versions" for each piece of content.

The Locale module will give you the option to enable multilingual support for your content types. Enabling multilingual support will give you a drop-down select box, shown in Figure 8-7, to choose the language that each post is written in. All this will do is identify the language being used for that content.

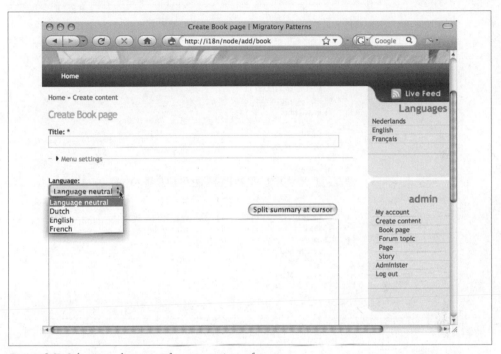

Figure 8-7. Selecting a language for a new piece of content

When you use the Content translation module, you get an additional option under multilingual support: "Enabled, with translation." Using this setting not only identifies the language for the post as written, but also allows you to associate other nodes as translated versions of the same content. For example, you may want to have an About page on the site that has the same content translated into French and Dutch. With translations enabled, you would create the original About page and then, from that, create a brand-new node each for the French and Dutch versions. Drupal will keep track of these three nodes and know that they are related to each other, each one simply a version of the same page. On each of the pages, a link for each of the other translations will appear at the bottom of the post as indicated in Figure 8-8.

Figure 8-8. Language links on content to view other translations

Figure 8-9. Translation download in the Drupal root directory

Hands-On: Installing a Translation

The first step to using any of Drupal's multilingual features is installing a translation, so that Drupal has more than one language to choose from. This involves two parts: downloading a translation and extracting it correctly, and configuring the Locale module to recognize it:

1. Begin by downloading a translation from *http://drupal.org/project/translations*, such as *http://drupal.org/project/nl*. As with modules and themes, ensure that you are downloading versions that match your version of Drupal.

If you're an advanced user accustomed to checking out Drupal code from CVS, you should be aware that for translations, you *must* download the translation and not use a checkout from CVS directly. The correct file structure for the translation files is created in the packaging process, and a CVS checkout won't work without recreating that structure manually.

2. Uncompress (unzip) the translation file in your Drupal root directory (that is, where *index.php* lives), as seen in Figure 8-9.

 After uncompressing the file, the only change you should see in your root directory is the addition of new files that have the language code added (such as *LICENSE.nl.txt*.) If you see a new *folder* in your Drupal root with the language code (such as *nl-6.x-1.0*), then it did not install correctly. To double-check that the translation files were placed properly, you can look in the *profiles/default* directory—you should see a new translations folder with a language file inside (like *nl.po*), as seen in Figure 8-10.

3. Go to Administer→Site building→Modules (admin/build/modules), enable the Locale module and click the "Save configuration" button. Note that if you installed Drupal in a language other than English, this step will already be done for you.

4. Go to Administer→User management→Permissions (admin/user/permissions), and configure the permissions as shown in Table 8-1. Save your changes with the "Save permissions" button.

Table 8-1. Locale module permissions

Permission: locale module	anonymous user	authenticated user	editor	administrator
administer languages				Checked
translate interface				Checked

5. Go to Administer→Site configuration→Languages (admin/settings/language) and click the "Add language" tab (admin/settings/language/add) to be taken to the screen shown in Figure 8-11.

6. Select your language from the "Language name" drop-down list and click the "Add language" button.

7. The translation files will be imported into Drupal and you will see an "Importing interface translations" message with a progress bar.

 If you add the translation files *after* you have added the language through the "Add language" tab, your files will not be imported. You will need to delete the language from the "List" tab at Administer→Site configuration→Languages (admin/settings/language) and then add it again once your translation files are in place.

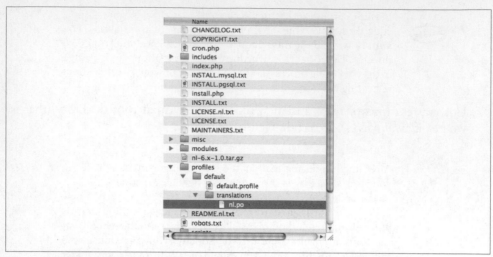

Figure 8-10. Expanded translation with new profile .po file

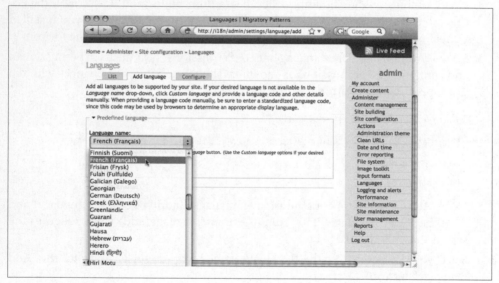

Figure 8-11. Add language screen with drop-down select list

Repeat the language selection for each language that you wish to have available on your site. When done, the Languages setting page will list all of the site languages in a table that lets you take various actions, such as disabling, changing the site default language, affecting the order in which the languages are displayed in lists, and deleting them altogether. Figure 8-12 shows this table with our site's three languages: English, Dutch, and French. English is marked as the Default language, which means it will be used as the fallback language when there is no language specified either through the language negotiation settings we saw under the Language switching section or a logged-in user's personal settings under his My account page. The Weight option for each of these languages lets you set a particular order in which the languages will appear when listed together, in form select lists for example. Weight here functions the same as it does in other areas of Drupal, with negative numbers being considered "lighter" and therefore floating to the top (or to the beginning in a horizontal list).

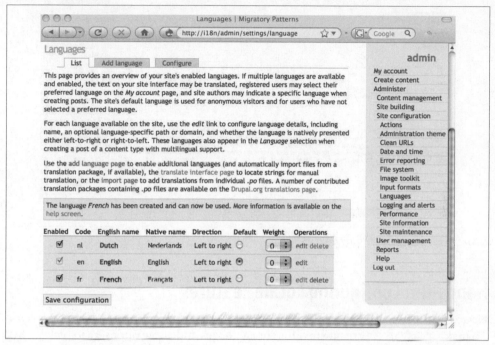

Figure 8-12. The installed languages table

You can also choose to edit the language name, negotiation identifiers, and direction as seen in Figure 8-13, by clicking the "edit" link. Normally, you won't want to change these settings unless you have a very good reason, and we are going to leave all of our settings at their comfortable defaults.

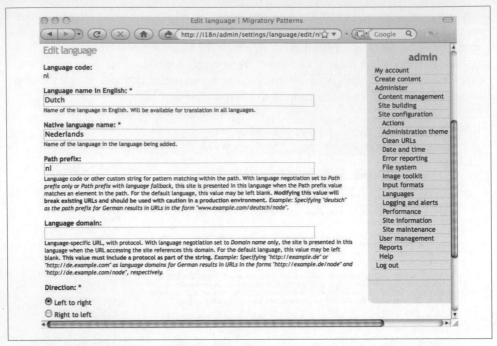

Figure 8-13. Screen for editing an installed language

Hands-On: Configuring Locale Features

Now we need to make a choice about how and when Drupal will use our new languages. To make it easy to see our site in different languages and allow our users to pick as they like, we will also add a simple language switcher to the site.

Language Negotiation Settings

As discussed earlier in the "Language switching" section, we have several options to choose from. We don't want our users to have to manually switch their language in the account settings (the None option), and our client does not have separate domain names for each language (the "Domain name only" option). That leaves us with the two "Path prefix" choices. We are going to use the "Path prefix with language" fallback rather than the "Path prefix only" option, because our client wants to make sure that if a registered user has chosen a language in her account settings, she gets returned to that rather than the site default, should the prefix method not return a usable result:

1. Click the Configure tab on the Languages page (admin/settings/language/configure).
2. Select the radio button for "Path prefix with language fallback" and then click the "Save settings" button.

Language Switcher

The Locale module provides a block to switch languages, which can be configured just like any other block to have a different (or no) title, and have various display options set.

1. Go to Administer→Site building→Blocks (admin/build/block) and find the "Language switcher" block in the list.
2. Drag the block into the "Rightt sidebar" region, and then click the "Save blocks" button.
3. You should now see a new block called "Languages," which contains a list of each installed language on the site, as shown in Figure 8-14.

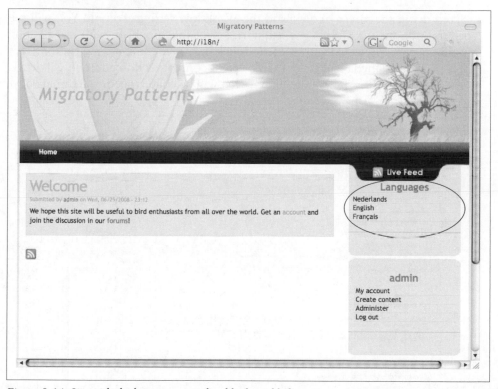

Figure 8-14. Site with the language switcher block enabled

Hands-On: Translatable Content

Now we can configure multilingual support for each content type (including any custom content types) that we have. We have three content types on our site: book pages, forum topics, and stories. We want stories and books to be translatable, but for forum topics we only need to identify the language, we don't need translations created. We also want to make sure that all of our authenticated users have the permissions needed to add translations.

1. Go to Administer→Site building→Modules (admin/build/modules) and enable the following modules:

   - Core – optional package
     — Book
     — Content translation

2. Then go to Administer→Content management→Content types (admin/content/types) and click the "edit" link for the Book page type.

3. Scroll down the screen and expand the Workflow settings section. You will see several options for Multilingual support. Select the "Enabled, with translation" radio button, as seen in Figure 8-15, and click the "Save content type" button. This lets us identify the language for each piece of content, and in addition will let us create translated versions of the content that will be linked together automatically.

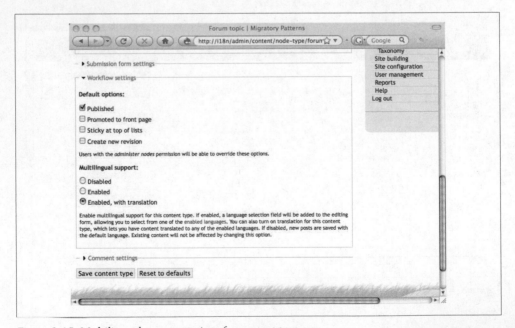

Figure 8-15. Multilingual support options for content types

4. Repeat for the Story content type.

5. For the Forum type, select the plain Enabled option.

6. We want all users to be able to translate content for us, so we need to make sure we set the permissions for everyone but anonymous users. Because all users are authenticated, we can do this by enabling the permission for all authenticated users. Go to Administer→User management→Permissions (admin/user/permissions), configure the permissions shown in Table 8-2, and click "Save permissions."

Table 8-2. Content translation module permissions

Permission: translation module	anonymous user	authenticated user	editor	administrator
translate content		Checked		

Spotlight: Localization Client

You may notice that even though you are using a translation that you have installed, there might still be some untranslated text peeking out here and there. This will become more likely as you add contributed modules. Almost no site will have absolutely 100% language coverage out of the box, so you will probably need to translate a few items yourself. Drupal has a built-in system to do this using the Locale module, but using it can be clunky and tedious. This is where the contributed "Localization client" module really shines. It makes quick fixes to text easy and intuitive.

The Localization client adds a translation editor right on the bottom of your screen that stays with you as you move through the site. You can minimize it when you don't need it and then expand it when you have translations to do. Figure 8-16 shows the editor expanded on a page. It provides a nice, easy-to-use interface to see which strings on the page have been translated and, more importantly, which have not. It allows you to browse or search through the list; you can simply select the string you wish and add the translation right there on the screen.

Some important caveats should be kept in mind, however. The Localization client is a great tool but it does depend on JavaScript and, at the time of this writing, it does not assist with translating strings that are added by the Internationalization module (which we'll discuss later). Additionally, it can only translate text that can be seen by the person running the Localization client; for example, if the text is visible only under certain conditions, it may not be translatable with the Localization client.

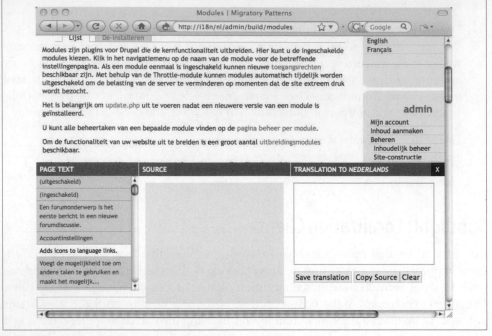

Figure 8-16. The Localization client interface

Hands-On: Translating the Interface

Not everyone wants or needs to install yet another module, and due to the caveats we mentioned about the Localization client, it is still a good idea to be familiar with how core translation works, so let's start there.

Using the Locale Module

Interface translation depends on the Locale module, which should already be enabled on your site once you have installed a translation.

1. Go to Administer→Site building→Translate interface (admin/build/translate) to get started.

2. You will be presented with a table of your languages and the percentage of strings that have been translated so far. Click on the Search tab (admin/build/translate/search).

3. The string search screen, pictured in Figure 8-17, allows you to search for a specific piece of text somewhere in Drupal's interface and translate it on the spot.

4. Enter the string `multilingual support` in the search box, leave the rest of the settings at their defaults, and click Search.

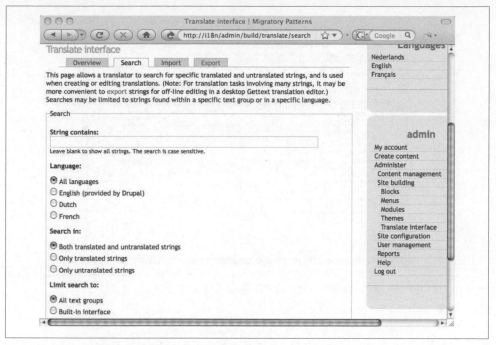

Figure 8-17. Translate interface string search screen

There are two caveats to successfully finding a string to translate. First, the search interface is case-sensitive. Searching for "User" will return different results than searching for "user." Second, the page with a given string on it must have been visited after the Locale module was enabled, or Search will be unable to find any of its interface text.

5. On the search results page, pictured in Figure 8-18, you will see a list of all the places on the site where that string is seen. The translation status is in the Languages column, which lists the language codes. A strike through a language code means it is not translated yet. Here, searching returned several results, which are all translated.

6. Click the "edit" link next to one of the strings, which will bring you to the translation page, as shown in Figure 8-19. You will be presented with a text area for each language, where you can add or edit the text as appropriate. When you click the "Save translations" button, the strings will be updated.

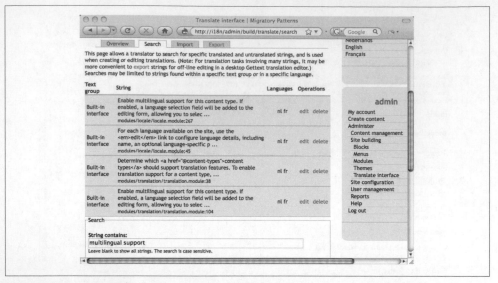

Figure 8-18. Search results for the string "multilingual support"

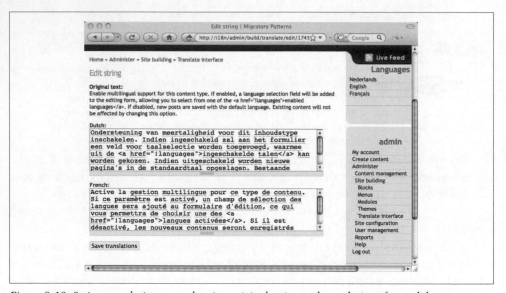

Figure 8-19. String translation page showing original string and translations for each language

Using the Localization Client

As you can see from the previous section, it is hard to see the strings that need to be translated on your site, remember them, go to the Translate interface, search for them, and only then actually be able to translate. It is a cumbersome, tedious process. Luckily, there's an easier way: the Localization client module.

1. Go to Administer→Site building→Modules (admin/build/modules) and enable:

   • Other package

     — Localization client

2. Go to Administer→User management→Permissions (admin/user/permissions), configure the permissions shown in Table 8-3, and click "Save permissions."

Table 8-3. Localization client module permissions

Permission: l10n_client module	anonymous user	authenticated user	editor	administrator
use on-page translation			Checked	Checked

3. Now switch your site into a language other than English by clicking the language name in the Language block. You will see a small blue bar appear at the bottom of your screen with a black Translate Text button in the right side. Figure 8-20 points this out.

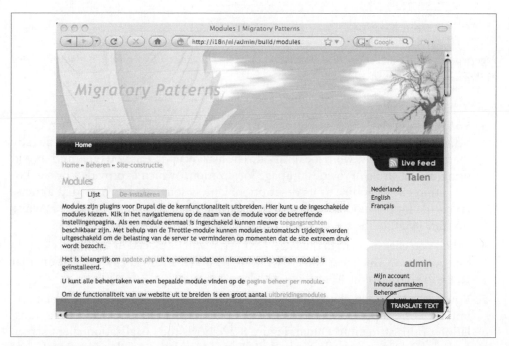

Figure 8-20. The Localization client's Translate Text button

4. Click the Translate Text box, and a translation area will open up at the bottom of your browser window, as shown in Figure 8-21. All of the items listed under Page Text that are green have already been translated. Ones in white still need work.

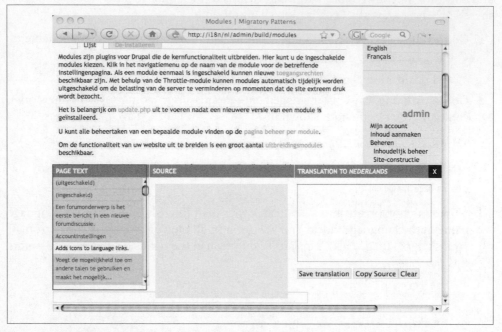

Figure 8-21. The Localization client translation interface showing both translated and untranslated strings

5. You can limit the list by searching in the text box at the bottom of the list. Go to Administer→Site building→Modules (admin/build/modules), if you are not already there, and type in the word localization. The list will update as you type, and should bring up the string "Provides on-page localization," which is provided by the Localization client module as its description. Unless someone has provided a translation file for the module in your language, the English should show up as white (untranslated) in the search results.

6. When you click an item in the Page Text list, it will be placed in the Source box so that you know which text you are working with. If it already has a translation, that text will appear in the "Translation to language" box.

7. You can add or edit the translation as needed and click the "Save translation" button. For example, "Maakt lokalisatie op de pagina zelf mogelijk" is the translation of this string into Dutch. Figure 8-22 shows the Localization client screen with the English string selected and the Dutch translation ready to be saved.

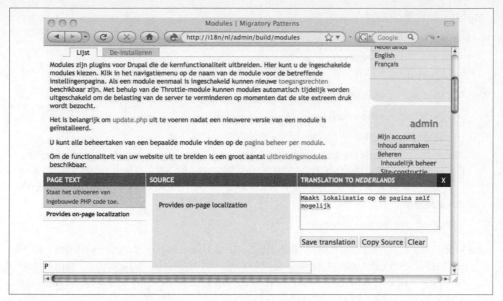

Figure 8-22. Using the Localization client to translate a string to Dutch

8. When finished, click the black X in the top bar of the translation area to close the client.

9. When you reload the page, you will see the changes you made, if any.

Hands-On: Translating Content

Now we need to set up our Knowledge Base section of the site. We'll create some new content and then show you how to translate it.

Translation

Earlier, we enabled translation for our pages, so let's walk through the translation process itself:

1. Make the Introduction to the Knowledge Base in English. Go to Create content→Book page, fill in the fields as shown in Table 8-4, and click Save.

Table 8-4. Book page content

Field	Value
Title	Introduction
Menu settings	
• Menu link	Knowledge Base
• Parent item	<Primary Links>
• Language	English
Body	This knowledge base is a place to organize useful information. Anyone with a Migratory Patterns account can add to this book! You may create a new page by clicking the "Add child page" link at the bottom of any existing KB page or by going to Create content→Book page in your navigation block.
Book outline	
- Book	<create a new book>

2. After you save the content, you will see that there is a Translate tab next to the normal View, Edit, and Outline (for book content) tabs. Click the Translate tab and you will be presented with a table listing all of your site's enabled languages, which you can see in Figure 8-23.

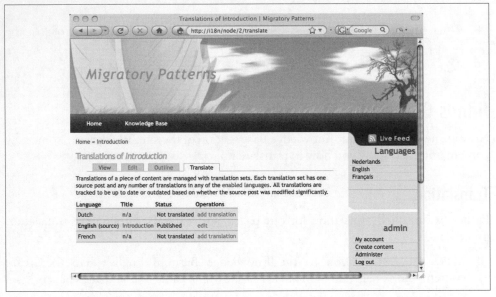

Figure 8-23. The Translate tab on a book page, showing available languages and translation status

3. Click "Add translation" for a language, and you will be presented with a screen containing the form values that were previously submitted. You may now edit the text for the Title, Menu, and Body. Notice the language is already selected for you. Translate the text into the selected language, and remember to again choose "<create a new book>" in the "Book outline" section as well so that this translated

introduction page will also be a top-level book entry for those viewing the site in this language.

4. When you click Save for this new translation page, you will see that there is now a link at the bottom that will take you to the other language's version of the page.

You should do the same for the Welcome post on the front page (if you are using the Multilingual profile) or any other content that was created prior to enabling content translation. Just edit the existing post to select the language and use the Translate tab to add versions for other languages as we did previously.

Keep in mind that the default language setting for all content is "Language neutral." You must identify the content with a language in order to see the "Translate" tab and proceed with creating translations. If you do not set a language when initially creating the content or if you have enabled the Content translation module after already creating content, that content will be set to "Language neutral."

When you create a translation for any content that is on the front page of the site (like the Welcome post in the profile), you will notice that both translations appear. The same thing is happening for our Knowledge Base menu items, as you can see in Figure 8-24. We're going to address that issue in the next section.

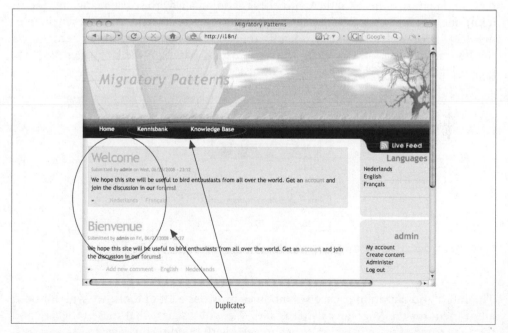

Figure 8-24. Duplicate items—one for each language

Spotlight: Internationalization

So far we've got a nice start with getting our site translated, but everything is not quite smooth yet. We have translations for some of our content and menu items, but they are all appearing at the same time. There are multiple posts on the front page, and all the language menu items are showing regardless of which language we are viewing the site in. You will also see some stray text still in English. For example, under the "Create content" menu item, the content type descriptions are translated but the name of the content type is not. To take our multilingual site further and really make it shine, we are going to turn to a package of modules called Internationalization (i18n). There is a central Internationalization module, which comes packaged with a handful of other modules designed to work together to extend core's multilingual features.

One important thing that these modules do is help us get various strings of text into core's translation interface that are otherwise not available. Drupal's core interface tools can detect only strings that are hardcoded directly into the code (using Drupal's `t()` function); that is to say, that are code-generated. All of the user-generated strings are not accessible. It is important to realize that these strings that are added by the Internationalization modules will *not* be available to you through the Localization Client's "Translate Text" interface. To translate these, you must use the core interface, covered earlier in this chapter in the "Hands-On: Translating the Interface" section, found at Administer→Site building→Translate interface (admin/build/translate).

A second feature of many of these modules is adding a way to select a language for an item, such as for menus, blocks, or taxonomy terms, like the one shown in Figure 8-25. Being able to discretely identify the language being used for an item allows the Internationalization module to filter the display based on the languages we want to see, leading to less duplication and confusion.

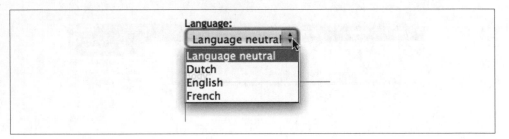

Figure 8-25. A language selector

The Internationalization package of modules provides a lot of tools; we will not need all of them for the Migratory Patterns site. We will discuss what these tools are and then see some of them in action as we proceed with building our site.

Content Selection

One of the first things you probably noted after making your first piece of translated content was that all of the translations were showing on the front page, regardless of the language in which you were viewing the site. The Internationalization module helps us get this under control by giving us a choice about how we want our multilingual content displayed. It looks at three ways of identifying the content's language:

No language
> The content has not been specifically identified as belonging to any language, which can be seen as "Language neutral" or "All languages" in the language select lists for various kinds of site content.

Current language
> The current language is determined either automatically, by the language negotiation setting (for example, by the language code included in the path, such as "en"), or manually, when a user selects a language using a switcher.

Default language
> This is a central setting for the website under the language administration at Administer→Site configuration→Languages (admin/settings/language). There is only one default and it is the language used on the site when no language negotiation is being used.

There are five different selection modes that you can use to set the criteria for which content to display. Figure 8-26 shows the mode settings that are listed in the following examples.

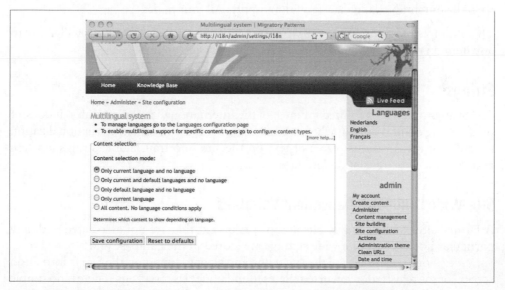

Figure 8-26. The Internationalization module's content selection mode options

The content selection mode that is chosen will filter the content to display based on the language. We'll use an example to illustrate the results for the various settings. Our site is using three languages: English, Dutch, and French. The default language is English. For this simplified example, we will assume we have "three" pieces of content in four nodes on the front page titled as follows: Drupal, Welcome, Welkom, and Les mots. Drupal is language-neutral, the second is available in English (Welcome) and Dutch (Welkom), and Les mots is in French only.

The content that will display when selecting French in the language switcher block based on the following settings is:

- Only current language and no language: Drupal (none) and Les mots (French)
- Only current and default languages and no language: Drupal (none), Welcome (English), and Les mots (French)
- Only default language and no language: Drupal (none) and Welcome (English)
- Only current language: Les mots (French)
- All content: No language conditions apply: All four nodes

If we switch the selected language to Dutch in the switcher block:

- Only current language and no language: Drupal (none) and Welkom (Dutch)
- Only current and default languages and no language: Drupal (none), Welcome (English), and Welkom (Dutch)
- Only default language and no language: Drupal (none) and Welcome (English)
- Only current language: Welkom (Dutch)
- All content: No language conditions apply: All four nodes

This example used nodes as a simple way to illustrate, but these settings will apply to any item on the site, including menu items, blocks, and so on.

Strings

The Strings module is required for most of the Internationalization modules. It doesn't do anything on its own, but when used in conjunction with other Internationalization modules, it turns various pieces of text on the site into translatable strings that are added to the core translation interface.

Site-Wide Language-Dependent Variables

A Drupal site can have many bits and pieces of text that are not associated with any particular node. These site-wide settings are stored in the database and referred to as *variables*. Some examples are the site name and slogan, found on the Site Information screen, or the registration email templates found under User settings. There is no simple way to get these particular kinds of text into the regular translatable string interface.

The Internationalization module adds the ability to tell Drupal specifically that you wish to provide translations for these variables. Unfortunately, to set this up, you need to edit your site's *settings.php* file. Once you add the needed information to the settings, you can continue translating using the regular translation interface. We'll cover this in more detail in the next section, "Hands-On: Internationalization Features."

Module Helpers

The Internationalization module also works with a number of core modules to aid with translations:

Menu

> The Multilingual Menu module adds any custom menu items you create to the translate interface string list. You can also specify which language a particular menu item is for and its display will follow the rule you selected for content display. You should note that, independently of this module, you can create a menu item in a language for each node, which will also follow the display rules. So if you are only creating menu items based on nodes, you do not need to enable this module. If you wish to have menu items that don't point to specific nodes, then this module will let you create the translations you need.

Taxonomy

> Multilingual taxonomy gives you a few options for keeping track of your taxonomy translations. When creating a new vocabulary, you can choose whether you want to localize the terms using the regular translate interface method, set up independent terms per language, or set one language for the entire vocabulary. When you choose to create terms per language, you will be able to select a language for each term. Once you have created the terms and assigned a language for each, you can then create associations between them. For example, the terms "cat" (assigned to English) and "le chat" (assigned to French) can be marked as equivalent terms.

Block

> The Multilingual Blocks module will let you pick a language for each block. Assigning a language to a block will determine when it is displayed according to the main content display settings. For custom blocks that you create, you can also decide whether you wish the block text to be translatable by adding the strings to the translation interface.

Profile

> The core Profile module allows you to add fields for users to fill out under their account. The Multilingual Profile module will make sure the field attributes, like name, description, and so on, that you add are translatable. Note that it won't make the values, the user-entered content, translatable.

Poll

> As each translation of a poll is a new node, Drupal will natively keep track of the poll numbers separately for each node. The Multilingual Poll module makes sure

that the results from all translations of a poll are aggregated together so that you get an accurate poll result regardless of which translation you are viewing.

Synchronization

The final Internationalization module in the package is Translation Synchronization. This module will keep your taxonomy and node fields synchronized between several translations of a node. For instance, if you have a piece of content like a blog post that is in three languages and has a term selected, this module will make sure that the term changes on the other two nodes when you change it on one.

If your vocabulary language setting is set to "None" or "Localize terms," the term will simply be copied over from the original node. If you have chosen "Per language terms," the term will be changed as appropriate across your translations.

Hands-On: Internationalization Features

Content Selection

Translated content is all shown by default. The main Internationalization module will let you display only content that is relevant to the language currently in use:

1. Go to Administer→Site building→Modules (admin/build/modules) and enable the following module:

    - Multilanguage – i18n package
      — Internationalization

2. Go to Administer→User management→Roles (admin/user/roles).

3. Next to site administrator user, click "edit permissions," and under i18n module, check the "administer all languages" permission, and save the form.

4. Go to Administer→Site configuration→Multilingual system (admin/settings/i18n), where you will see the options for "Content selection." By default it is set to "Only current language and no language." Make sure that this option is selected and save the configuration.

If you go to the front page of the site, you will see that we now only get one "Welcome" post and one "Knowledge Base" menu item. If we choose Nederlands from the Language switcher block, you will see that the Dutch "Welkom" post appears, and the menu items change to the Dutch versions.

Now the content we see is more streamlined, as shown in Figure 8-27. Let's move on to translating other items in the site that are being stubborn, such as the site name, Migratory Patterns.

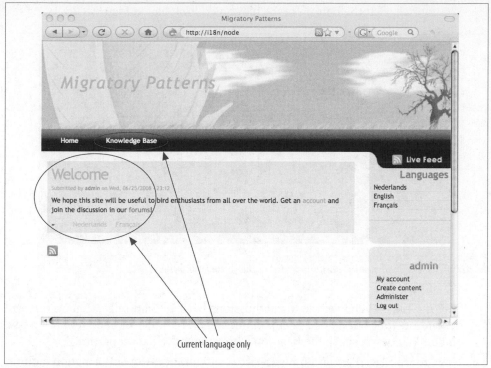

Current language only

Figure 8-27. With content selection mode enabled, we no longer see duplicate items

Site-Wide Variables

Before we can translate the various site-wide variables, we need to let Drupal know which ones we want to make translatable. To do this, we'll need to edit the *settings.php* file:

1. In your Drupal installation, go to the sites/default folder.

2. The *settings.php* file is currently read-only, so first change the permissions to make it writable. (This will vary by operating system. For example, on Linux systems, you set the permissions to 666 or a+w, and on Windows systems, you need to make sure that the Read-only checkbox is unchecked under the file properties.)

3. Open *settings.php* in a text editor and scroll to the end of the file. We will add a new configuration option for Internationalization variables and add just the variable for the site's name as an example. You can find this information and a list of common variables in the Internationalization module's *INSTALL.txt* file. Type the following into *settings.php*:

    ```
    $conf['i18n_variables'] = array(
      'site_name',
    );
    ```

4. You can see what the bottom of the file should look like in Figure 8-28.

```
/**
 * String overrides:
 *
 * To override specific strings on your site with or without enabling locale
 * module, add an entry to this list. This functionality allows you to change
 * a small number of your site's default English language interface strings.
 *
 * Remove the leading hash signs to enable.
 */
# $conf['locale_custom_strings_en'] = array(
#   'forum'        => 'Discussion board',
#   '@count min' => '@count minutes',
# );
$conf['i18n_variables'] = array(
  'site_name',
);
```

Figure 8-28. The "Site name" variable added to the settings.php file

5. Save the file and change the file permissions back to read-only. (Again, this will depend on your operating system. Linux systems can be set back to 444 or a-w, and on Windows, check the Read-only box under the file properties.)

6. Now, to translate, go to Administer→Site configuration→Site information (admin/settings/site-information) and you will see, as in Figure 8-29, that the help text under the Name field states that "This is a multilingual variable."

7. Switch to another language using the switcher block.

8. Change the site name in the Name field, and click the "Save configuration" button.

Simple String Overrides

You may have noticed when you went to add the internationalization variables to your *settings.php* file that there was a commented-out section at the bottom for "String overrides." You can set these configuration options to override any of the hardcoded English strings on the site. It isn't practical to use this set of options for a fully localized or multilingual site, because it requires listing each string individually in the *settings.php* file. It is great to use this if you have a handful of strings that you want to change quickly and you don't want to necessarily turn on the extra overhead of "yet another module" or go through the core string translation process.

A great example of its use that many people ask for is given right there in the sample in *settings.php*: changing the word "forum" to another word that you or your users would prefer, like "discussion board."

You can also use the String Overrides module to change these values from Drupal's interface.

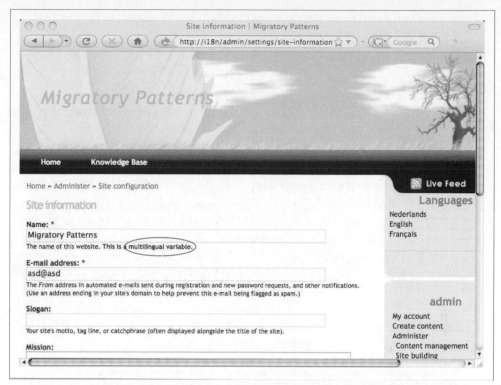

Figure 8-29. The Site name is now indicating that it is a multilingual variable

You will now see that the site name has changed to what we just entered. If you switch back to English or another language, you will see that the site name reverts to the original name.

What Variables Are Available?

The first question that may come to mind when dealing with the site-wide variables is how you know what is even available. The Internationalization module's *INSTALL.txt* file and the handbook for the module on *Drupal.org* (*http://drupal.org/node/134002*) list the most common ones, but not all of them. One way to see which variables you have is to install the Devel module, which provides the Development block (along with lots of other handy development tools). In that block will be a "Variable editor" link, which will list all of your currently set variables.

Keep in mind that this won't list every single possible variable, only the ones that have been set so far. Many core variables are not set in the database until you have visited and saved the page for those settings, so to see the variable for something you wish to translate, visit and save its settings page first. For example, to see the user email message variables, you first need to go to the settings page at Administer→User management→User settings (admin/user/settings) and click the "Save configuration" button.

Now, when you return to the Development block's "Variable editor" link, you will see all of the newly added user email variables.

Content Types

Our content types for the site are still using English for the content type name on the "Create content" page, and for field names when making new content.

1. Go to Administer→Site building→Modules (admin/build/modules) and enable the Strings and Content Types modules. You should see a message upon enabling that indicates a number of new strings were created.

2. Go to Administer→Site building→Translate interface (admin/build/translate) and you will see a new column, "Content type," added to the Language table. It shows the number of new strings that the Internationalization module has created. You can see the new column in Figure 8-30 and compare that to the table as shown in Figure 8-3 from earlier in the chapter. The percent translated should still be 0, because we haven't translated any content types yet.

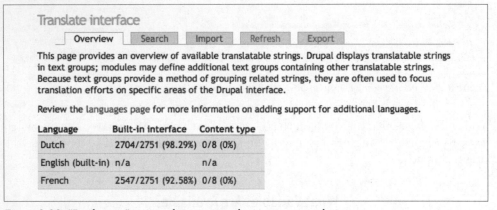

Figure 8-30. "Book page" string editing screen showing two translations

3. Click the Search tab and search for "Book page." You should see two results, just like Figure 8-31: one that is already translated from the "Built-in" interface group and another, not translated, in the "Content type" group.

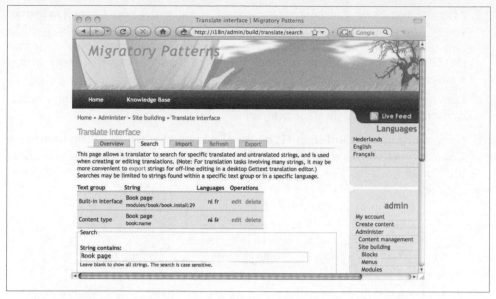

Figure 8-31. String search results for "Book page"

4. Click the "edit" link for the "Content type" string and translate it to Boekpagina.
(you can also add the French Page de livre if you like), as shown in Figure 8-32.

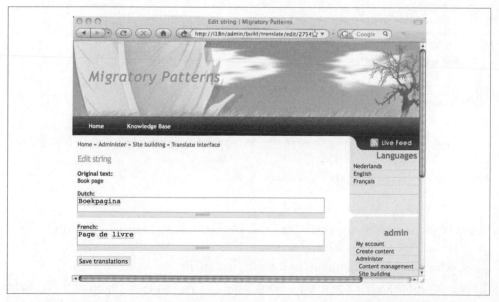

Figure 8-32. A "Content type" strings column has been added to the Translate interface table

5. After saving the new translation, if you go to "Create content" and switch to Dutch, you will see that the content type name for the Book page is now displayed in Dutch. Click the *Boekpagina* link as if to create a new book page. You will see that the Title field is still in English. You should also see a message that more strings were created.

6. Let's go back to Administer→Site building→Translate interface (admin/build/translate) and change the Title field name.

7. Go to the Search tab and enter `Title`. We also know that we only want to look for Content type changes right now, so select the "Content type" radio button under the "Limit search to:" section of the search form as shown in Figure 8-33. Then click Search.

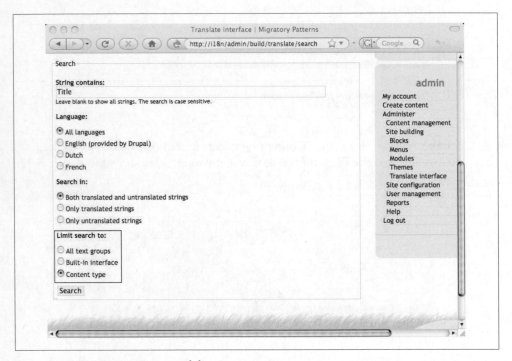

Figure 8-33. Limiting a string search by content type

8. We get one result for this. Click the edit link for it, translate it to the Dutch `Titel` (`Titre` for French), and save it.

9. Go back to "Create content" and switch to Dutch.

10. Click on *Boekpagina* to make a Book page and you will see that the "Title" field now says "Titel."

Taxonomy

Drupal's forums are built on taxonomy, so we need to find a way to sync the terms that we create to keep the taxonomy selection limited to just the terms for a given language. We already have a Forums vocabulary on the site, so we'll configure translations for it.

Forums

The forums on the site will display the threads that follow the same content selection rule as the rest of the content on the site. The site will have preset forum containers and threads and then users may post to them using whichever language they choose to use.

Using the install profile, we currently have a container for "Types of Birds" with two forums under it: Raptors and Waterbirds. Let's turn on multilingual options for the forums:

1. Go to Administer→Site building→Modules (admin/build/modules) and enable the "Multilingual taxonomy" module.

2. Go to Administer→Content management→Taxonomy (admin/content/taxonomy) and click the "edit vocabulary" link for Forums. You will see in Figure 8-34 that we now have a "Multilingual options" section on the page.

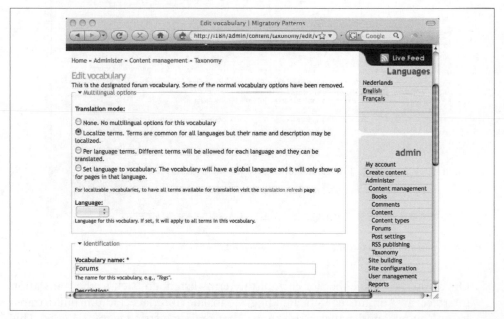

Figure 8-34. Taxonomy multilingual options

3. Select the radio button for "Localize terms" and save your changes.

4. Go to Administer→Site building→Translate Interface (admin/build/translate) and you will see another column added to the table for "Taxonomy." Note that we have three terms (each with a description) for forums (from the install profile), but right now the table is showing only one string available to translate. That's not right. We need to get all of our strings recognized before we can translate them.

5. Remember that you must visit a page with the string(s) that you want to translate before it will register for the string search. Go back to the taxonomy administration at Administer→Content management→Taxonomy (admin/content/taxonomy).

6. Click the "list terms" link for the Forums vocabulary and then click on the Edit link for each term, where you can change the name and description. You should notice in the help text that they are localizable (for instance, "This name will be localizable"), as shown in Figure 8-35. You can simply look at the edit page and then return to the previous page using your browser's back function.

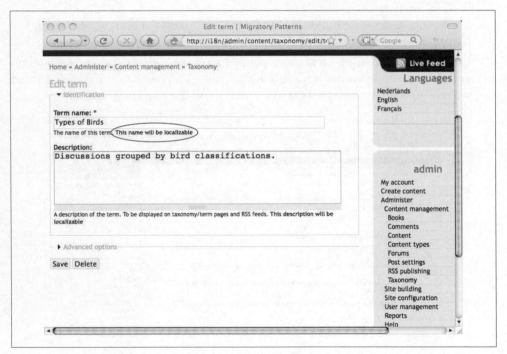

Figure 8-35. Term name indicating that it is now localizable

7. Once you have done that for each of the terms listed, go back to the translation interface at Administer→Site building→Translate Interface (admin/build/translate.) You may notice that it still shows that only one string is translatable. This can happen when you have some content—in our case, taxonomy terms from the install profile—that was created prior to enabling the Internationalization module. Let's force Drupal to double-check.

8. Click the Refresh tab (admin/build/translate/refresh), then check off the Taxonomy checkbox and click the "Refresh strings" button. The refresh page is shown in Figure 8-36.

9. Return to the Overview tab (admin/build/translate)—we finally have all seven strings available. (Why seven? Four terms—Forums plus the three terms themselves—and three descriptions, one for each term.)

10. You can now search and translate the strings as we have done before, and when you switch languages, the correct localized forum name and description will appear.

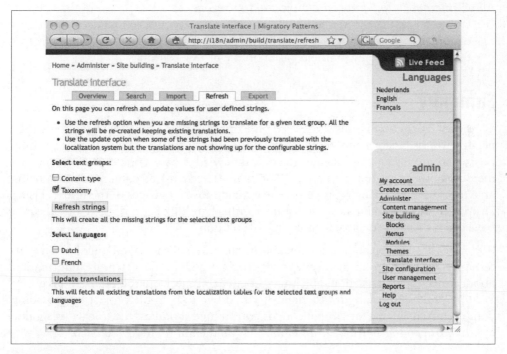

Figure 8-36. The Refresh strings page

Taking It Further

We've covered quite a bit of ground for setting up a site with multiple languages. There are a lot of tools available and therefore there is a lot of flexibility when it comes to handling languages. We have delivered to our clients a site that has the community features they need and allows their users to both participate in and manage the site in the language of their choice. They can easily add new languages to the mix in the future and everyone can help with translating their knowledge base. Here are some additional modules that can add some nice touches to your site:

Language icons (http://drupal.org/project/languageicons)
> This module will add a default set of flag icons to the language switching links on the site (in the Language switcher block and language links on the content). You can replace the included icons with ones of your choosing.

Translation Overview (http://drupal.org/project/translation_overview)
> This module creates a page with a table that tracks the translation status of all the content on your site. It supplies basic information like the title and a link to the content, content type, and creation date. Then, for each piece of content, it uses a legend so you can see the translation status (original language, current translation, out-of-date translation or untranslated) at a glance.

Auto Timezone (http://drupal.org/project/autotimezone)
> Users can set their preferred time zone under My Account so that dates and times of content on the site are displayed in their local time. This module will enable this feature automatically for them based on the browser settings.

Summary

We built a nice, simple, easy-to-use site for our client that gave them the tools they needed for discussions and a knowledge base. We set up a forum that displays only posts that are in the user's language and a knowledge base book that all of the site members can create translations for. The major need for this community was being able to use multiple languages and easily extend those languages in the future. Using Drupal's core internationalization features with a handful of contributed modules, we have given them a very flexible multilingual solution.

For more information and discussion about internationalization in Drupal, see the Internationalization group at *http://groups.drupal.org/i18n*. To get more information about core Drupal translations and how you can help, check out the Translations group at *http://groups.drupal.org/translations*. If you'd like to help the project by providing your own translations for Drupal core or contributed modules, the translator's guide at *http://drupal.org/contribute/translations* has all the information you need.

Here are the modules that we referenced in this chapter:

- Auto Timezone: *http://drupal.org/project/autotimezone*
- Content Translation: Part of the Drupal core
- Devel module: *http://drupal.org/project/devel*
- Internationalization and Language Icons: *http://drupal.org/project/i18n*
- Locale: Part of the Drupal core
- Localization client: *http://drupal.org/project/l10n_client*
- String Overrides: *http://drupal.org/project/stringoverrides*
- Translation Overview: *http://drupal.org/project/translation_overview*

These are some other resources that we referenced and community resources for learning more about the new concepts introduced in this chapter:

- Drupal core translations: *http://drupal.org/project/translations*
- Multilingual modules: *http://drupal.org/project/Modules/category/97*
- Multilingual variables: *http://drupal.org/node/313272*
- Translations working group: *http://groups.drupal.org/translations*
- Translator's guide: *http://drupal.org/contribute/translations*

## CHAPTER 9

Event Management

Managing online calendars and event registration can present a huge challenge. Without a dynamic system, the task is nearly impossible. Generating the HTML required to display a calendar and all the various presentation options (day, week, month views, and so on) is unreasonable; and worse, because the events are time-sensitive, remembering to update "next" or "upcoming" event lists can be onerous. Nothing looks worse than having last week's meeting listed first on your "Upcoming Events" page.

Even with dynamic systems, you tend to be constrained to certain parameters with fixed options. However, by taking advantage of the flexibility of Drupal and building on the powerful base of CCK and Views, you can accommodate nearly any variation on event listings for your site.

To follow along with the hands-on example in this chapter, you should install Drupal using the Events install profile. The completed website will look as pictured in Figure 9-1 and at *http://events.usingdrupal.com*. For more information on using the book's sample code, see the Preface.

This chapter introduces the following modules:

Date (http://drupal.org/project/date)
Provides a CCK field for entering date information, as well as libraries to handle things like time zone conversion

Calendar (http://drupal.org/project/calendar)
A view style for displaying a list of site content in a rich calendar display

Flag (http://drupal.org/project/flag)
A flexible module that enables administrators to add on/off toggle switches to items such as nodes and comments

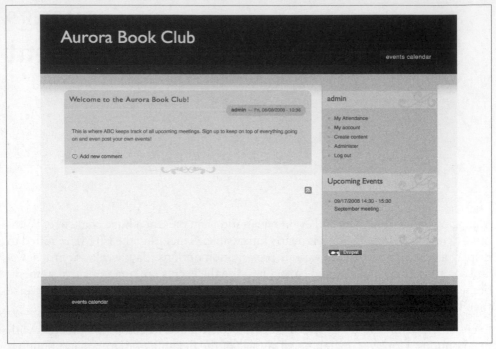

Figure 9-1. The completed Aurora Book Club site

Case Study

The Aurora Book Club is a rather social group of local book enthusiasts. They hold semiregular monthly meetings and events for both current and prospective members. Members want to be able to see when and where the next meeting is happening. Additionally, members should be allowed to post their own events to the site. Events should have start and end times and dates, as well as information about the event and where it will take place. To make it easy to see what is happening soon, there should be a short list of upcoming events in addition to the full calendar. The calendar needs to offer day, month, and annual views, and a way for members to subscribe to the club's calendar using Microsoft Outlook or Apple's iCal. Finally, since they would like to know how many cookies to bring and how many chairs to have on hand, the club president has asked that we include a way to track who plans to attend each event.

Implementation Notes

Event Management

The book club has two main options for managing event data in Drupal. The options are indicative of a common trend amongst Drupal's contributed modules. Specifically, there is a long-standing module in the Drupal community simply called Event (*http://drupal.org/project/event*), which natively handles most of the required features. The other option, and the one we will be using in this chapter, is a combination of CCK and Views add-ons: the Date module (*http://drupal.org/project/date*) and the Calendar module (*http://drupal.org/project/calendar*), respectively. The main differences are as follows:

- The Event module allows per-content-type "event enabling," which means that it will add a start and end time to any existing content type. Included with the module is also an entire system for viewing your created events and even a block for listing upcoming events.

- The Date module offers a CCK field type for handling dates. The Calendar module is a Views plug-in that renders a view in a browsable calendar layout.

Both options are capable of meeting all the requirements for the book club's site. In fact, when compared side by side, they look functionally equivalent: both options allow us to create new events, view a list of upcoming events, and offer rich, full-featured calendar displays. In fact, by working with any content type, the Event module still allows us to use CCK to build custom content types for our event data (for example, for holding additional information about events). This significantly blurs the line between the solutions, particularly compared to the choice between the Image module and Imagefield, as discussed in Chapter 7. With the Image module, a specific content type ("image") is defined, whereas with Event you can reuse any custom content type. Furthermore, Event is a single module without any dependencies, whereas Date and Calendar require CCK and Views respectively. So why not use the Event module?

As we've discussed in several earlier chapters, the CCK and Views modules represent the future of site building with Drupal. Their added flexibility and granularity present far more flexible options for tailoring the modules to fit our site's exact needs. By being more narrowly focused, Date and Calendar also implement their specific features more completely. This is particularly true of the Date module, which has several more options for date format support than Event. Also, by going with a CCK and Views native solution, improvements and efficiencies will automatically trickle down as CCK and Views continue to evolve new features.

Essentially, the reason to use the Event module would be either for legacy purposes or ease of installation. For more information about event-related modules, see the Event category on Drupal.org (*http://drupal.org/project/Modules/category/61*).

Attendance Tracking

The Signup module *http://drupal.org/project/signup* is designed specifically for the purpose of tracking event attendance, and has some nice features such as the ability to email reminders to attendees prior to an event. However, this module was unavailable for Drupal 6 and was undergoing development at the time of this writing.

Instead, we will use this opportunity to highlight a helpful general-purpose module called Flag (*http://drupal.org/project/flag*). Flag (known as "Views Bookmark" in Drupal 5) allows users to mark or "flag" a piece of content. This functionality can be used for a myriad of useful purposes, including marking content as offensive, allowing users to bookmark interesting stories, and even to let users mark events as "attending" or "not attending."

Hands-On: First Steps

First, we'll set up a few basics for our site just using Drupal core and CCK. The main thing that we need in order to start off is a content type to handle our events. Log in to the Aurora Book Club site with the username *admin*, password *oreilly*, if you are using the installation profile.

Creating an Event Content Type

We'll start by creating a new, basic content type just for events. We just need the event name and description along with an easy way to add the event location:

1. Go to Administer→Site building→Modules (admin/build/modules) and enable the following modules:
   - CCK package
     - Content
     - Text
2. Go to Administer→Content management→Content types (admin/content/types) and select the "Add content type" tab (admin/content/types/add) to create a new content type called Event, using the settings from Table 9-1.

Table 9-1. Settings for the Event content type

Field	Value
Identification	
Name	Event
Type	event
Description	A book club meeting or social event
Submission form settings	
Title field label	Name
Body field label	Description
Workflow settings	
Default options	Uncheck "Promoted to the front page"
Comment settings	

Field	Value
Default comment settings	Disabled

3. Click the "Save content type" button.

4. Add a text field for storing the location of the event (that is, where the event takes place). You should have been returned to the Content types administrative page (admin/content/types) after saving the new type. Click the "manage fields" link for the Event content type (admin/content/node-type/event/fields). Complete the New field form using the values from Table 9-2.

Table 9-2. Settings for adding a location field to the Event content type

Field	Value
Label	Location
Field name	location
Select a field type	Text
Select a widget	Text field

5. Click Save. This will take us to the configuration settings page for the Location field. We will just use the default settings here, so click the "Save field settings" button to finish.

Access Control

Now that we've got the content type created and configured properly, we need to grant permissions to our members to allow them to create events.

Go to Administer→User management→Permissions (admin/user/permissions) and set the permissions as shown in Table 9-3. Click the "Save permissions" button when you are done.

Table 9-3. Permissions for the event content type

Permission	anonymous user	authenticated user	editor	site administrator
node module				
create event content		Checked		
delete any event content				Checked
edit any event content			Checked	Checked
edit own event content		Checked		

Spotlight: Date Module

The main building block for the site is our new Event content type. The information that we need it to provide us with is "where" and "when." We have taken care of the "where" part in our initial setup. The Date module helps us effectively answer the "when" question, in an incredibly flexible manner.

As mentioned previously, our real interest in the Date module is to add a CCK field to our Event content type to indicate date and time. However, looking at the Date module more closely, there are a few extra pieces worth noting.

Date API Module

As its name would imply, the Date API module merely provides a set of library functions for date handling. These functions consist of things like converting between date formats, providing integration with modules such as Views, and even generating date input select boxes. Though covering the full extent of the API is outside the scope of this chapter, it is worth noting that the Date API module does not depend on CCK, but is required by both the Date and Calendar modules. In theory, any module in Drupal that performs any sort of date handling or manipulation could take advantage of this module.

> For users running PHP4, the Date PHP4 module is required to emulate date manipulation functions introduced in PHP 5.2. This module can optionally make use of an external library for parsing additional dates: the ADOdb date library (*http://phplens.com/phpeverywhere/adodb_date _library*). Without this library, Date PHP4 primarily handles dates from 1970 to 2038. The library adds support for any date from the year 100 to 3000. For the purpose of the book club, we will be able to just use Date API on its own.

Date Timezone

Drupal core, by default, does all time zone handling based on an offset from Greenwich Mean Time (GMT), represented as the number of hours' difference (plus or minus) from GMT. For example, the offset –0400 is used for Eastern Daylight Time in the United States. This approach has several drawbacks, the most significant of which is in trying to account for Daylight Saving Time, as the offset will change. When the local time changes to Eastern Standard Time, the actual offset from GMT changes from –0400 to –0500, and the setting must be updated again.

The Date API comes with a module, Date Timezone, that alters the core behavior to use named time zones rather than hour offsets (for example, America/New York versus –0400). Therefore, Date API can account for Daylight Saving Time accurately in its calculations.

Date Field Types

At its most basic level, the Date module defines three CCK field types—Date, Datestamp, and Datetime—for adding date fields to content types. The differences among these fields are summarized in Table 9-4.

Table 9-4. CCK fields offered by the Date module

Name	Description	Example	Database storage
Date	Store a date in the database as an ISO8601 date, used for historical (pre-1000 A.D.) or partial dates (for example, only a year and no day or month). This field type should be avoided otherwise, as it's extremely expensive to sort and perform conversions on this style of date.	2008-08-26T17:02:00	varchar(20)
Datestamp	Datestamp field types are stored using the common Unix timestamp format containing the number of seconds since January 1, 1970. As such, these have a limited date range available (1901 A.D.–2038 A.D. on most systems) but are quick to calculate time zone offsets and sort in listings. A legacy format, Datestamps are supported across all database systems.	1219770120	int(11)
Datetime	Datetime field types are stored using the database system's internal "datetime" format for date handling. It has the advantage of being able to use database-specific functions for date handling, including ease of extracting a single part of the date, but with the caveat of inconsistent support across database systems.	2008-08-26 17:12:00	datetime

 For much, much more than you ever wanted to know about the pros and cons of various date storage formats, there's an interesting discussion on the Events working group at *http://groups.drupal.org/node/731*.

Because the Aurora Book Club has no intention of moving from MySQL, and all dates will be well within "normal" ranges, we will be using the Datetime field type for our site.

Date Widgets

In addition to the base field types, the Date module also defines three CCK widgets for entering Date information, which are pictured in Figure 9-2:

Select list
> Presents a series of drop-down lists for each of year, month, day, hour, minute, and second, based on the configured granularity for the date field defined by the data settings.

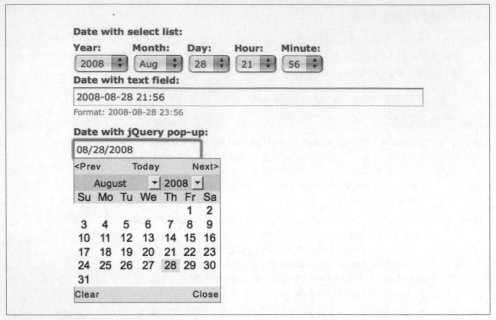

Figure 9-2. Date CCK field widgets

Text field with custom input format

Provides a simple text field for date entry that will then be converted to the appropriate storage format. The advantage of this widget is that it lets advanced users enter dates much faster. However, for the uninitiated, it can be frustrating if your natural date entry format is not properly recognized.

Text field with jQuery pop-up calendar

Adds an elegant, user-friendly option for Date value entry. This widget uses Java-Script to present a calendar pop-up when a user clicks in the date text field. The user can then click the date on the calendar to select the date that he wants.

The book club will be using the "Text field with jQuery pop-up calendar" widget for improved usability.

Date Settings

There are quite a few settings available specific to date fields and different from other CCK field types, as shown in Figures 9-3 and 9-4. Some of these are:

Default value

The default value setting gives you a few options to choose from. The Blank and Now settings are pretty straightforward. The Relative setting will let you set the default to a date that is relative to the current time, such as two days from now. To set up a relative default, you must enter a value in Customize Default Value

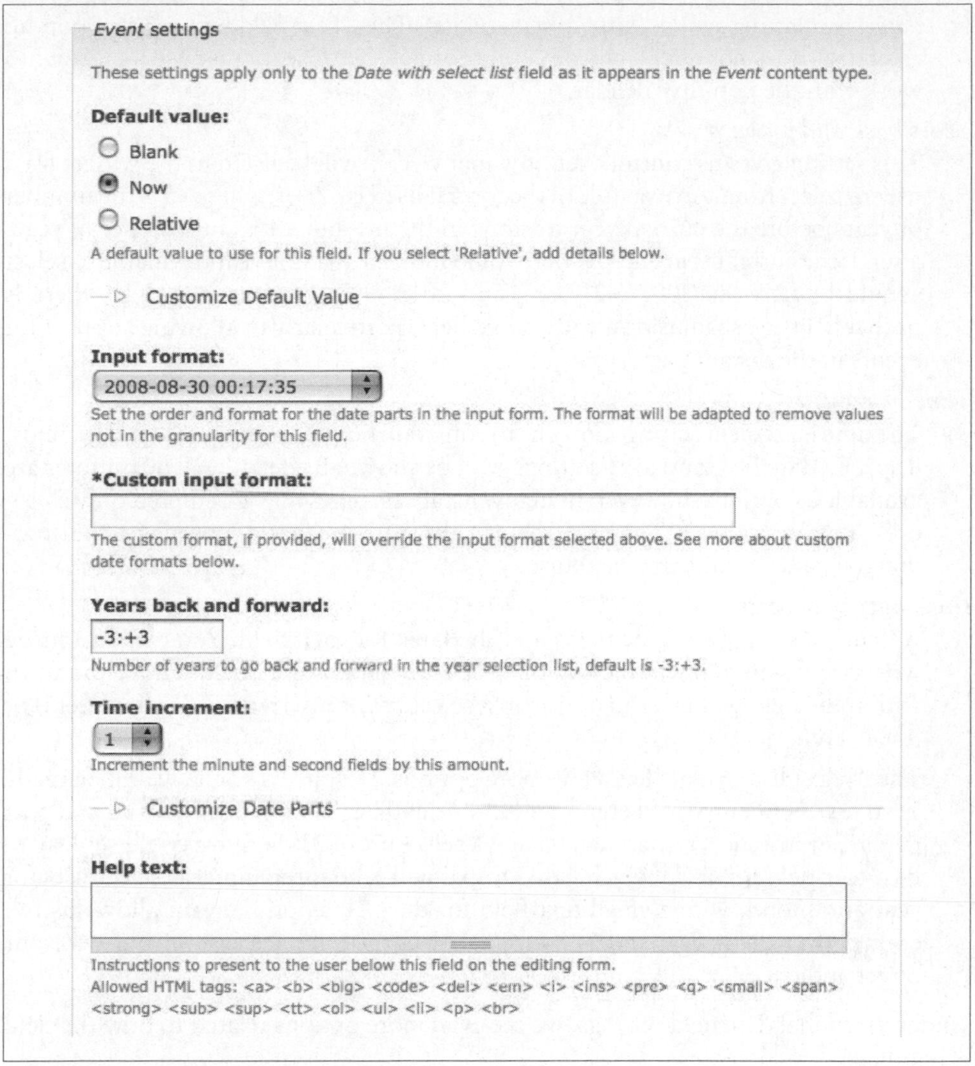

Event settings

These settings apply only to the *Date with select list* field as it appears in the *Event* content type.

Default value:

○ Blank

◉ Now

○ Relative

A default value to use for this field. If you select 'Relative', add details below.

▷ Customize Default Value

Input format:

[2008-08-30 00:17:35   ⬍]

Set the order and format for the date parts in the input form. The format will be adapted to remove values not in the granularity for this field.

*Custom input format:

[   ]

The custom format, if provided, will override the input format selected above. See more about custom date formats below.

Years back and forward:

[-3:+3]

Number of years to go back and forward in the year selection list, default is -3:+3.

Time increment:

[1 ⬍]

Increment the minute and second fields by this amount.

▷ Customize Date Parts

Help text:

[   ]

Instructions to present to the user below this field on the editing form.
Allowed HTML tags: <a> <b> <big> <code> <del> <em> <i> <ins> <pre> <q> <small> <span> <strong> <sub> <sup> <tt> <ol> <ul> <li> <p>

Figure 9-3. Date field content type settings

that uses PHPs *strtotime()* syntax, such as +2 days. You can find out more about *strtotime()* at *http://www.php.net/manual/en/function.strtotime.php*.

Input format

The input format setting dictates the ordering of the fields—year, month, day, hour, minute, and second—as they appear on the form for entering the date. Only the values available in the Granularity data setting will be taken into consideration. There is also a "Custom input format" option, which allows an arbitrary date format to be used when using the "Select list" and "Text field with custom input format" widgets for ultimate flexibility. The custom format is set using PHP's *date()* formatting syntax (*http://php.net/date*). The "Text field with jQuery pop-up calendar" does not offer a custom input format, because it must use its format to work with the pop-up calendar.

Years back and forward

This setting gives us control over how many years will be listed in the widget for a user to select from. An example of the format used is *–2:+4*, where *–2* is the number of years before the current year to show in the list and *+4* is the number of years after. If the current year is 2009, this would indicate that the years available to select should be between 2007 (–2 years) and 2013 (+4). For our event site, there is probably little use in using a wide range here, particularly in allowing support for events in the distant past.

Time increment

The time increment setting allows us to constrain how many minutes (and seconds, if specified in the granularity settings) will be shown. By default, all 60 minutes are available as options; however, in many instances, dates may be entered only as 15- or 30-minute intervals. Therefore, having all 60 minutes as options makes the drop-down list more cumbersome to use.

Customize date parts

A date consists of the date fields and the label for each field. You can customize where you would like to display the label in relation to its field: above the field, within the field (either as an option in a select list or inserted inside a text field) or none at all.

The "Select list" widget has a few more options. Despite its name, we can actually have text field entry for certain values in the date, mixing drop-downs and text fields. For instance, rather than having a select list of 31 days, we could set Day to be a text field input, in which case Drupal will render the input as select lists for year and month with a small text field for day. This option again allows us full control over the widget and a chance to select the interface easiest to use for our target audience.

Under the global date field settings, we see even more options related to how the field is handled:

To Date

The "To Date" setting allows you to associate an ending date/time, thus making the date field a date span. The setting has three options:

Never

No end date will be associated with this date field.

Optional

The date field can potentially have an end date, and an entry widget will be displayed, but may be left blank.

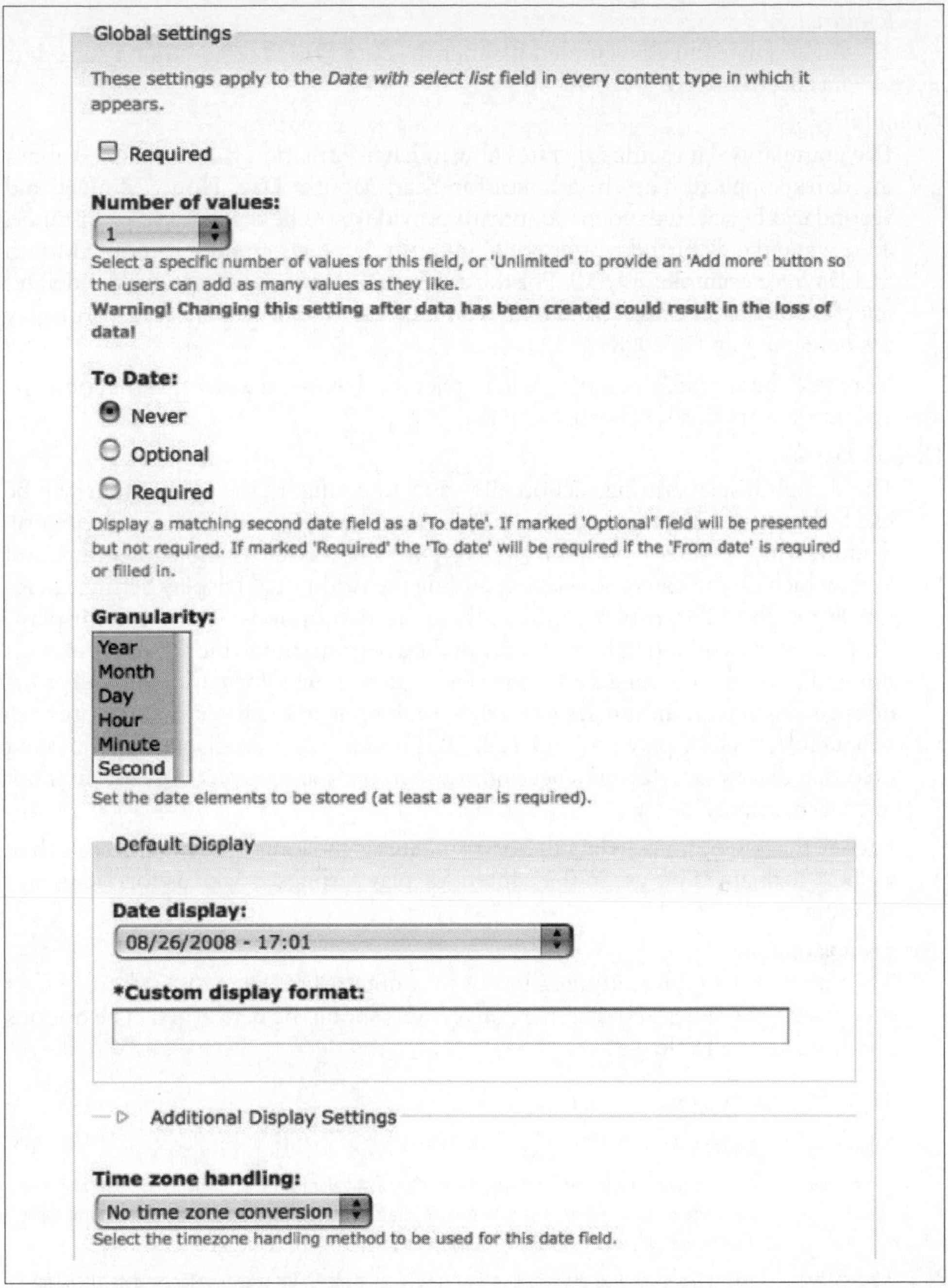

Global settings

These settings apply to the *Date with select list* field in every content type in which it appears.

☐ Required

Number of values:

[1   ⬍]

Select a specific number of values for this field, or 'Unlimited' to provide an 'Add more' button so the users can add as many values as they like.

Warning! Changing this setting after data has been created could result in the loss of data!

To Date:

◉ Never

○ Optional

○ Required

Display a matching second date field as a 'To date'. If marked 'Optional' field will be presented but not required. If marked 'Required' the 'To date' will be required if the 'From date' is required or filled in.

Granularity:

Year
Month
Day
Hour
Minute
Second

Set the date elements to be stored (at least a year is required).

Default Display

Date display:

[08/26/2008 - 17:01   ⬍]

*Custom display format:

[   ]

▷ Additional Display Settings

Time zone handling:

[No time zone conversion ⬍]

Select the timezone handling method to be used for this date field.

Figure 9-4. Date field settings

Required

An end date must be entered if either the date field is required or a start date has been entered.

Granularity

The granularity data setting dictates how much information will be retained about the dates supplied. The checkboxes for Year, Month, Day, Hour, Minute, and Second can be selected independently to provide extreme flexibility. For instance, if we wanted only birthday (but not a full birth date), we could select only Month and Day; for example, July 10. For the purpose of event management, the default selection of Year, Month, Day, Hour, Minute is suitable, which allows us to display the date like July 10, 2008 - 7:30.

Note that the Granularity setting will impact the date entry widget, in that only the appropriate options will be displayed.

Default display

The default display setting section allows us to configure the format that will be used when displaying the date value. There are four formats that we can configure: default, which is shown on the form in Figure 9-4, as well as short, medium, and long, which can be configured by expanding the Additional Display Settings field-set. For each of the display settings, there are two options. The "Date display" drop-down list contains a huge variety of date permutations (month names versus numeric months; 12- versus 24-hour clocks; time zone information as well as ordering of each year, month, day value). Should none of the listed options prove to be suitable, each display option has an additional "Custom display format" text field that allows even further customization, in the same way as the custom input format mentioned above.

Each of the four options—default, short, medium, and long—will be available then as CCK formatters for use in the content display settings as well as for Views and theming.

Time zone handling

The time zone handling settings allow us to configure how time zones should affect the stored date values and whether conversions should be performed. The options are described in Table 9-5.

Table 9-5. Date field time zone options

Option	Description
Site's time zone	The time zone specified for the entire site, specified at Administer→Site configuration→Date and Time (admin/settings/date-time). Useful for making sure each date field shares a consistent time throughout the site, even if users are from different time zones.
Date's time zone	Adds a Time zone drop-down next to the date widget to specify the time zone for the date. Useful for sites where many users from many different time zones will be creating dates.

Option	Description
User's time zone	The time zone specified in each user's My Account settings if the option is enabled under Administer→Site configuration→Date and Time (admin/settings/date-time). This option is useful if you mainly have events in one time zone, but users from many different places.
UTC	Coordinated Universal Time (UTC), which is informally equivalent to GMT. This is a standard time zone that is the same across all systems.
No time zone conversion	For events with dates only, rather than dates and times, or for sites with both local events and users, performs no time zone conversions on the date.

For the book club, we will not be doing time zone conversions, as all members will be local.

Hands-On: Adding Dates

In this section, we will transform our basic Event content type by adding the date component. This will be the linchpin of the book club's site, as the rest of the site will build from this content.

Set Up the Date Module

1. Go to Administer→Site building→Modules (admin/build/modules) and enable the following modules (note that if you are using PHP 4, you will need to enable Date PHP4 as well):

   - Date/Time package
     - Date
     - Date API
     - Date Popup
     - Date Timezone

2. Go to Administer→Site configuration→Date and Time (admin/settings/date-time) and select an option from the "Default time zone" drop-down list that matches your time zone. Click "Save configuration" to save your changes.

Add the Date Field

With all our required modules enabled and set up, we can now customize the Event content type we created earlier by adding dates. Note that as we do this, we will only add a single CCK field to handle both the event's start and end times:

1. Go to Administer→Content management→Content types (admin/content/types) and click the "manage fields" link for the Event content type (admin/content/node-type/event/fields). Complete the New field form with the values in Table 9-6.

Table 9-6. Settings for adding a time field to the Event content type

Field	Value
Label	Time
Field name	time
Select a field type	Datetime
Select a widget	Text field with jQuery pop-up calendar

2. Click Save. This brings us to the date field configuration screen. As the Date module is geared toward event management by default, several of the default settings work well. Enter the values in Table 9-7, and click the "Save field settings" button to complete adding the configuration.

Table 9-7. Date field configuration settings

Field	Value
Event settings	
Default value	Now
Input format	Select a format such as 08/29/2008—11:31pm
Years back and forward	−1:+2
Time increment	15
Global settings	
Required	Checked
To Date	Optional
Default Date Display	Select a format such as 08/29/2008—11:31pm
Time zone handling	No time zone conversion

3. You should be returned to the "Manage fields" tab (admin/content/node-type/event/fields). Reorder the fields as follows and click Save:

- Name
- Time
- Location
- Description
- Menu settings

With the content type fully created and permissions granted, our members can now post events to the site! To do so, go to Create content→Event (node/add/event) and complete the form with the settings in Table 9-8. If all has gone well, you should see something like the form in Figure 9-5. Go ahead and create a few more events for the Aurora Book Club.

Table 9-8. Initial example event

Field	Value
Name	Monthly meeting
Time	
Choose a time tomorrow	09/17/2008—2:30PM
Choose a time tomorrow	09/17/2008—3:30PM
Location	The Book Nook on Main Street
Description	Andrew and Camryn are bringing cookies.

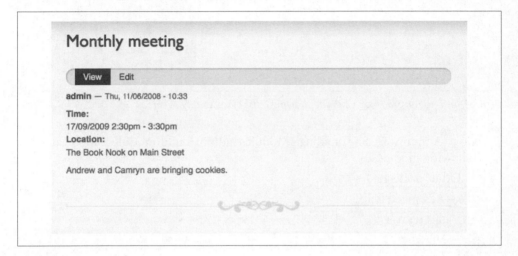

Figure 9-5. Our initial event

Hands-On: Upcoming Events View

Now that we've created our event content type and started populating some content, it's clear that we need to add in a way to access all our event data. In the book club's requirements, we had a need for an "upcoming events" listing that would allow members to quickly see the meetings happening in the coming days or weeks. To achieve this, we will use the Views module to create our block. Keep in mind that when building views of event data, we generally want to do our sorting or our limiting on the date field, not the content's created or updated time, as we normally do.

We will create a simple block view of published events where the event's time field is in the future. In terms of the views configuration, having a date value "greater than now" represents dates "in the future." Finally, the view will be sorted in chronological (or ascending) order of the event's date (not the event posting's created date). When completed, this section will look as pictured in Figure 9-6. Clicking the event name link in the block will take you to the full information.

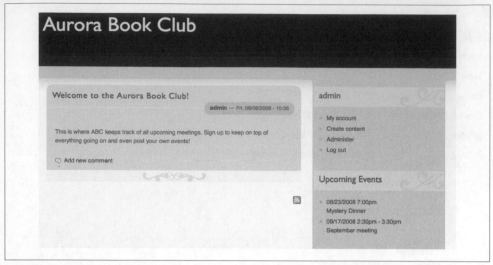

Figure 9-6. The Aurora Book Club site showing a list of upcoming events

1. Go to Administer→Site building→Modules (admin/build/modules) and enable the following modules:
   - Other package
     — Advanced help
   - Views package
     — Views
     — Views UI

2. Once the modules are enabled, go to Administer→Site building→Views (admin/build/views) and click on the Add tab (admin/build/views/add).

3. Fill out the view form using the values in Table 9-9.

Table 9-9. The Upcoming Events view configuration values

View setting	Value
View name	upcoming_events
View description	A block list of upcoming events
View tag	event
View type	Node

4. Clicking the Next button places us in the main Views interface. From here, we can configure our view. Let's begin with the Basic settings for the Defaults in Table 9-10, clicking Update after setting each one.

Table 9-10. Basic settings for the upcoming events view

Defaults: Basic setting	Value
Title	Upcoming Events
Style	Select List and click Update
	List type: Unordered list
Items to display	Defaults: Items to display: 5

5. Now, we must add some fields to our view. In the Fields section, click the + (plus) icon and add the following fields: "Content: Time (field_time value)" and "Node: Title." Configure the settings to match those in Table 9-11 and make sure to click the Update button after each one.

Table 9-11. Upcoming Events view field values

Defaults: Fields	Values
Content: Time (field_time value)	Label: None
Node: Title	Label: (make this blank)
	Link this field to its node: Checked

6. In the Filters section, we'll add our required filters by clicking the + (plus) icon:
   - Date: Date
   - Node: Published
   - Node: Type

7. Recall that our view is for upcoming (that is, future) events; therefore, we will filter on dates that are greater than now. Match the filter settings with the values in Table 9-12 and Update them.

Table 9-12. Upcoming Events view filter values

Defaults: Filters	Value
Date: Date	Select Content: Time (field_time_value) under Date field(s), and click Update
	Operator: Is greater than or equal to
	Date default: now
Node: Published	Published: Checked
Node: Type	Operator: Is one of
	Node type: Event

8. Then, we need to similarly add the Sort Criteria, using the + (plus) icon. Select "Content: Time (field_time value)," click Add, ensure that the Sort order is Ascending, and click the Update button to finish.

9. To create the block, add a Block display by selecting Block from the drop-down list on the left side of the interface and click "Add display."

10. Under "Block settings," under Admin, enter the Block: Block admin description to read Upcoming Events and click Update.

11. Save the view, which should now look like Figure 9-7.

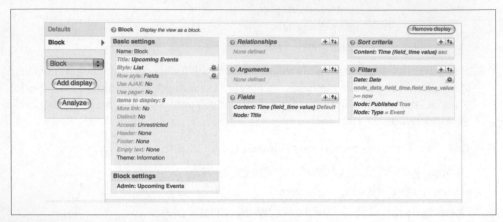

Figure 9-7. Upcoming Events block view

12. Because we created a block view, we should see no change to our site until we enable the block that we've created. To do this, go to Administer→Site building→Blocks (admin/build/block). Drag the "Upcoming Events" row to the "Right sidebar" region (or simply change the region value in the drop-down) and click "Save blocks."

Spotlight: Calendar Module

Although a simple list of upcoming events is very useful (particularly in a sidebar block), the book club has additional requirements for the display of the event data. As is extremely common for event management websites, this site needs an interactive calendar for browsing through past and future events. We will implement this feature using the Calendar module in conjunction with Views.

In addition to creating a nice online calendar, the Calendar module can handle the need for book club members to be able to update their desktop calendars (in Microsoft Outlook or Apple's iCal) with the event information from the book club site. To do this, the desktop applications use a standardized format known as iCalendar (*http://en.wikipedia.org/wiki/iCalendar*), or iCal for short. Calendar comes with the Calendar iCal module, which allows us to easily provide this format for the interested members.

Calendar View Type

The Calendar module provides a new view type that shows the results of a view in a calendar rather than a list or table as with the default view types. This view type is one of the more complicated ones available. It provides full day, week, month, and year views of the event data on our site with lots of links between views and paging through days, months, and years. To achieve this rich functionality, Calendar requires certain views arguments to exist, and to be ordered and configured in a certain way.

The Calendar view type then determines which view the user would like to see based on the arguments that exist. For example, if our view URL is *calendar*, the Calendar view will handle the paths described in Table 9-13.

Table 9-13. Calendar path-based display

Path	Calendar display
calendar	Month view, defaulting to the current month
calendar/1970	Year view, for the year 1970
calendar/1970-1	Month view for January 1970
calendar/1970-1-1	Day view for January 1, 1970

Hands-On: Calendar View

In this section, we'll be enabling the Calendar view of book club events. Although this is potentially a daunting task, the Calendar module conveniently comes with a default view that handles most of the difficult bits for us. In this section, we'll alter that default calendar view to fit our requirements.

Figure 9-8 shows the finished Aurora Book Club calendar. Note the small iCal icon in the bottom right. Clicking this link will download the calendar to an appropriate desktop application.

1. Go to Administer→Site building→Modules (admin/build/module) and enable the following modules:
   * Date/Time package
     — Calendar
     — Calendar iCal

2. Go to Administer→Site building→Views (admin/build/views). You should now see "Default Node view: calendar" listed. Turn it on via its Enable link (admin/build/views/enable/calendar).

3. Click its Edit (admin/build/views/edit/calendar) link to open the calendar view for editing.

4. We need to make changes to the default Arguments. By default, the calendar view uses the date the node was last changed to place events on the calendar. Down in

Figure 9-8. Completed event calendar, with iCal link

the Date field(s) section, click on the "Date: Date" link and under "Date field(s)," uncheck "Node: Updated date" and check "Content: Time (field_time value)" instead. Then click Update.

5. For the Fields section, add the Content: Time (field_time_value) field, then make the changes noted in Table 9-14 and click Update. This selection will show our event's date, rather than the node's last updated date, and will remove the word "Title" from the event name that comes by default.

Table 9-14. Calendar view fields configuration

Defaults: Fields	Value
Node: Updated date	(Remove this field)
Content: Time (field_time_value)	Label: None
Node: Title	Label: (make this blank)

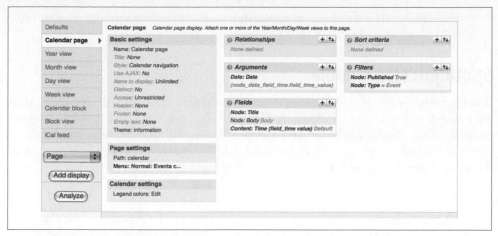

Figure 9-9. Upcoming Events calendar view

6. We need to add some filters so that only our published Event content shows in the calendar. Do this by clicking the + (plus) icon next in the Filters section and select the Node: Published and Node: Type filters. Complete the filter configuration according to Table 9-15, clicking Update for each one.

Table 9-15. Calendar view filter configuration

Defaults: Filters	Value
Node: Published	Published: Checked
Node: Type	Node type: Event

7. Finally, we need to add a menu item for the calendar page. The default view already provides us with a path of "calendar," which makes sense for us to keep. To add this to the menu, click on the Calendar Page tab on the left side of the interface and complete the "Page settings" section according to Table 9-16. Click Update after you enter the menu settings.

Table 9-16. The Calendar view's Page settings

Page: Page settings	Value
Menu	Type: Normal menu entry
	Title: Events calendar

8. Save the view, which should look like Figure 9-9.

9. We can now move the Events Calendar menu item into the Primary Links menu. Go to Administer→Site building→Menus→Navigation (admin/build/menu-customize/navigation) and click "edit" in the Events calendar row.

10. Update the "Parent item" to read "<Primary links>" and click Save.

Now we have a working events calendar that can be reached by clicking on the events calendar link in the Primary navigation.

Spotlight: Flag Module

The Flag module (formerly known as Views Bookmark) is an incredibly flexible module that allows you to create relationships between users and content on your site. After creating a flag, an item can be marked with the flag a few different ways, including links displayed below content, as shown in Figure 9-10, or checkboxes displayed on the edit form, as shown in Figure 9-11.

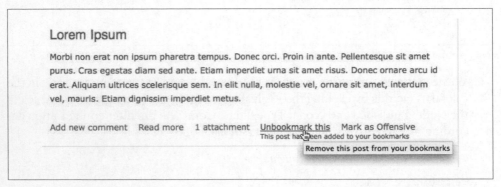

Figure 9-10. Flags as links shown on content

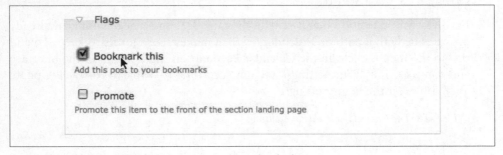

Figure 9-11. Flags as checkboxes shown on the node edit form

Upon installation, the Flag module defines a "bookmark" relationship, allowing users to maintain a list of bookmarks (or posts they find interesting) on the site. However, this default behavior only touches on the surface of the flexibility of the Flag module. Some possible uses for Flag include:

- A "favorite" or "bookmark" flag to mark content
- A "promote" flag (or many different promote flags) that are similar to the default "Promote to Frontpage" checkbox

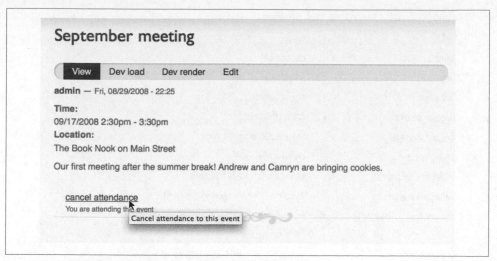

Figure 9-12. Attendance indicator shown on node the form

- An "offensive" flag for comments and nodes
- A "friend" flag that allows users to mark other users as friends
- An "attending" flag for events

As you can see, there are a variety of uses for flagging content. After creating a flag for some purpose, views can be constructed that create lists of content that has been flagged by users. We'll use it to let users indicate whether they plan to attend a book club event. Once the flag relationships are created, we can create a view to list the attendees of a particular event.

Hands-On: Flag Configuration

In this section, we will configure the Flag module to allow our users to indicate that they are attending our events, as pictured in Figure 9-12.

1. Go to Administer→Site building→Modules (admin/build/modules) and enable the "Other package: Flag" module.

2. Now go to Administer→Site building→Flags (admin/build/flags) to manage the defined flags. By default, the Flag module defines a "Bookmarks" flag when installed. We can either add a new flag or edit the default one to suit our purpose. As we won't be using "Bookmarks" on this site, we're going to edit the default. Click the "edit" link next to the bookmark flag (admin/build/flags/edit/bookmarks). Fill out the form according to Table 9-17.

Table 9-17. Attendance flag configuration

Field	Value
Name	attendance
Title	Attendance
Flag link text	attend this event
Flag link description	Attend this event
Flagged message	You are attending this event
Unflag link text	cancel attendance
Unflag link description	Cancel attendance to this event
Unflagged message	You are no longer attending this event
What nodes this flag may be used on	Event: Checked
	Story: Unchecked
Display options	Display link on node teaser: Unchecked
	Display link on node page: Checked
	Display checkbox on node edit form: Unchecked

3. Clicking Submit will create our attendance flag. We can now go to any events that we previously created and click the "attend this event" link.

Hands-On: Attendee View

The Flag module provides a default view that will allow any user to see the content that she has flagged for any flag that we have defined. You should now see a My Attendance link in the Navigation menu, which will show all of the events that you have marked as attending.

However, the book club would also like to see a list of who will be attending each event. For this, we will need to create a new view, pictured in Figure 9-13.

Figure 9-13. Event attendees list view

1. Go to Administer→Site building→Views (admin/build/views) and click on the Add tab.

2. Complete the form according to Table 9-18.

Table 9-18. Attendees view settings

Setting	Value
View name	attendees
View description	Attendees for a given event
View tag	event
View type	User

3. The first thing we need is a relationship to give us access to the flag information related to our users in our view. Click the + (plus) sign in the Relationships section and check the "Flags: User's flagged content" relationship and click Add. Complete the relationship settings based on Table 9-19.

Table 9-19. Settings for the Flags relationship

Defaults: Relationship	Value
Flags: User	Label: attendance
	Include only users who have flagged content: Checked
	Flagged: Attendance

4. We want our view to show the users who have flagged a given Event node; therefore, we need to add an argument for the Node ID that was flagged. To do this, we click the + (plus) sign next to Arguments. Check the "Flags: Content ID" argument and click Add. The default values for the argument are fine, so we can click Update.

5. Now we can add the fields that we want to display. Click the + (plus) icon next to Fields. Check the "User: Name" field and then click Add. Blank out the Label text so that there is nothing there and click Update.

6. It would be helpful if the attendees were listed in an ordered list so that we could quickly glance at the total number of people attending. To add this functionality, we need to change the style of the view. Click on Style under "Basic settings" and change it to List, then click Update. Then set the list type to "Ordered list." Click Update to save the change.

7. To complete the view, we need a Page display. Select Page from the drop-down list on the left side of the interface and click Add display. Complete the Page settings according to Table 9-20.

Table 9-20. The Attendees view Page settings

Setting	Value
Path	node/%/attendees
Menu	Type: Menu Tab
	Title: Attendees

8. Save the view, which should look like Figure 9-14.

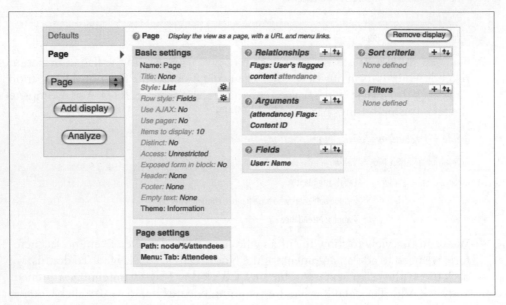

Figure 9-14. Event attendees list view settings

Now, when you visit an Event post, you should see an Attendees tab. Clicking on that tab will display a list of all of the users who have said they will attend the event.

Taking It Further

The site we have built covers all of the needs for the club. As they go down the road, the members may want to spruce things up a bit. Here are a few modules that could round out the site even more:

Calendar Popup (part of the Calendar module)
> The Calendar package also includes this module. This will make it so that when you click on an event in a calendar display, it will appear as a JavaScript pop-up rather than taking you to the node page. This is handy if you want people to be able to browse the details of events without leaving the calendar view page.

Countdown (http://drupal.org/project/countdown/)

This module adds a block that shows the time left until an event. This is a nice way to let people quickly know that the next meeting is in four days or four hours.

Flag Actions (part of the Flag module)

The Flag module can be set up to send emails, and to unpublish or delete nodes upon reaching certain flagging thresholds. Although this feature is most commonly used for things like community flagging of spam or offensive content, it can also be used to notify someone by email if, say, more than 10 people will be coming to an event and a second person needs to be asked to help supply refreshments.

Location (http://drupal.org/project/location/) and GMap (http://drupal.org/project/gmap/)

Instead of just typing a location in a text field, you can use the Location and GMap modules to let people use a Google map to select the location for each event.

Summary

In this chapter, we have looked at building an event management site for the Aurora Book Club, making use of the Date field for CCK, the Calendar plug-in for Views, and the Flag module for handling attendance. The book club now has a handy calendar for display on the site, as well as being available in iCal format. They also have an easy-to-find list of all the attendees. The site is simple and easy to use, yet fits all of the club's needs quite nicely.

Here are all the modules we referenced in this chapter:

- Calendar: *http://drupal.org/project/calendar*
- Countdown: *http://drupal.org/project/countdown*
- Date: *http://drupal.org/project/date*
- Event: *http://drupal.org/project/event*
- Flag: *http://drupal.org/project/flag*
- GMap: *http://drupal.org/project/gmap*
- Location: *http://drupal.org/project/location*
- Signup: *http://drupal.org/project/signup*
- Views: *http://drupal.org/project/views*

Additional resources:

- ADOdb Date Time Library: *http://phplens.com/phpeverywhere/adodb_date_library*
- Date module handbook: *http://drupal.org/node/92460*
- Event-related modules: *http://drupal.org/project/Modules/category/61*
- iCalendar: *http://en.wikipedia.org/wiki/ICalendar*
- PHP date formatting: *http://php.net/date*
- PHP strtotime:*http://www.php.net/manual/en/function.strtotime.php*

## CHAPTER 10

Online Store

Many businesses both large and small would like to take better advantage of their web presence by selling their products or services directly online. Setting up e-commerce, however, can be a very daunting task. There are several options with varying complexity. Many hosting providers offer e-commerce or "shopping cart" packages that may be either included with your web hosting plan or available for purchase. Other services, such as PayPal, offer simple ways of including means for simple purchases using an HTML form that submits to their processing system. There are other options still for using dedicated e-commerce packages, both open source and proprietary, that you host and configure. The biggest issue with all of these methods tends to be the lack of integration with the rest of the website—all shopping cart functions and checkout take place within the other, external system.

The other complication with e-commerce implementations is that there is real money involved for both you and your customers. Customers will be providing credit card details and other sensitive information, so we need to be aware of security implications.

This chapter will introduce the following module:

Ubercart (http://drupal.org/project/ubercart)
   Provides a full e-commerce package for running an online store

To follow along with the hands-on example in this chapter, install Drupal using the Online Store install profile, which installs Drupal with a few sample users and basic settings, as shown in Figure 10-1 and found at *http://store.usingdrupal.com*. For more information on using the book's sample code, see the Preface.

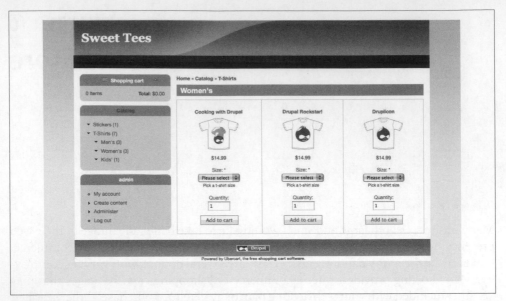

Figure 10-1. Sweet Tees' completed website

Case Study

Sweet Tees is a local T-shirt store that sells wildly popular, custom-printed T-shirts. They have a physical storefront, and the owners enjoy running a small store and love their current location. However, they get frequent mail order requests for their shirts and stickers, and would like to grow that end of the business. Taking orders on the phone and tracking sales has proven to be inefficient and time-consuming for both them and their customers.

In order to increase sales, we will equip the Sweet Tees website with an online store that has integrated shopping cart functionality, where visitors to the site can add items to their cart without the hassle of having to create an account first. A shopping cart should be visible on all pages with a link to "check out" at any time. The store needs to flow seamlessly with the existing website so that customers have a consistent experience. Sweet Tees would like to make the checkout process as simple as possible, so we will also need to make sure we provide them with a single-page checkout, without requiring customers to create a user account. Finally, they wish to accept credit cards on their orders, so we will need to set up a payment gateway for this purpose.

Implementation Notes

Sweet Tees has several options to manage their online store; however, they really want to provide a seamless, user-friendly experience for their customers. They are looking for a solution that is simple and elegant, yet also comprehensive.

For Drupal, there are two primary e-commerce solutions, both of which consist of several modules, to implement the various features required.

The e-Commerce module (*http://drupal.org/project/ecommerce*) is the oldest and more flexible of the options. The package is designed to be a highly modular framework for building e-commerce solutions in Drupal. In a way, it is a development framework of its own on top of Drupal's existing framework. The principal benefit of the e-Commerce package is ultimate control and extensibility. Because of the high number of variable components in an online store (payment processor, shipping calculations, taxes, and so on), this flexibility is incredibly useful. The downside, however, is that the flexibility increases the level of complexity, thus making it more time-consuming to set up and configure. Also, again due to its architecture, the checkout process for the e-Commerce package takes several pages and requires that customers register accounts on the website. This violates two of the client's primary requirements.

Ubercart (*http://drupal.org/project/ubercart*) is a much newer solution that was initially intended to provide a much more simplified installation, configuration, and management process than e-Commerce. Although arguably less flexible than e-Commerce, Ubercart is designed to accommodate 80–90% of online stores. Ubercart also has some nice features that make it attractive for our implementation: a single-page checkout process, anonymous user purchases, and a nice administration interface.

For Sweet Tees, we will be using Ubercart to bring the simple, elegant feel of their physical storefront to the Internet.

 The Ubercart project has its own website that is separate from Drupal.org where you can find support forums, documentation, and add-on modules. Check out *http://www.ubercart.org*.

Spotlight: Ubercart Packages

Ubercart is a complete package for running an online store. As such, it actually contains more than 30 individual modules that implement each of the various features required for running an online store. These modules range from basic framework modules such as Payment or Cart to very specialized modules that implement specific features. Navigating the giant list of modules (which is more than Drupal core itself includes!) can be confusing, so in this section we'll look at each module and outline its purpose and where it fits.

The modules that make up the Ubercart package are broken into five packages under Administer→Site building→Modules (admin/build/modules). We'll look at what the modules in each package include in this section.

Ubercart—core

The Ubercart—core package represents the base framework components for our online store. There are five modules in this section: Cart, Conditional Actions, Order, Product, and Store. Each of these modules is required for running an online store. Following is a brief description of each:

- Cart handles the shopping cart, pictured in Figure 10-2, with features such as tracking which products a customer has selected and the quantity of each product that has been ordered. The Cart module is also responsible for the "checkout" procedure. In addition to the basic functionality, the Cart module also provides options for extensibility in the shopping cart and checkout functions for other modules.

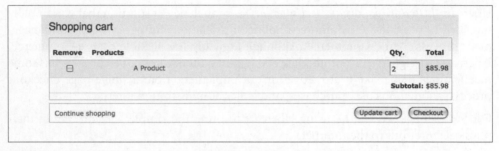

Figure 10-2. Shopping cart provided by the Cart module

- Conditional Actions provides a mechanism for the rest of Ubercart to use for providing configurable, rules-based actions for things like taxes and shipping. This module makes use of the core Actions system and is an advanced alternative to the Trigger module in Drupal core, which was covered in Chapter 6.

- Order is responsible for recording, tracking, and managing individual orders to the store. Figure 10-3 shows an order generated by the Order module. The Order module provides features for manual, backend creation of orders (that is, those taken over the phone), and invoicing, as well as an interface for viewing and editing existing orders. Like the Cart module, Order also serves as a framework module for the rest of the package by providing hooks for automated fulfillment and payment processing.

- Product serves as the base information for all items available in the store. It creates a "product" node type that can be extended via "product classes" that we can define. Figure 10-4 shows some of the properties supplied by Ubercart's Product module.

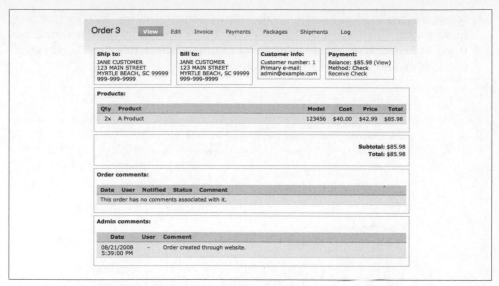

Figure 10-3. An order view courtesy of Order module

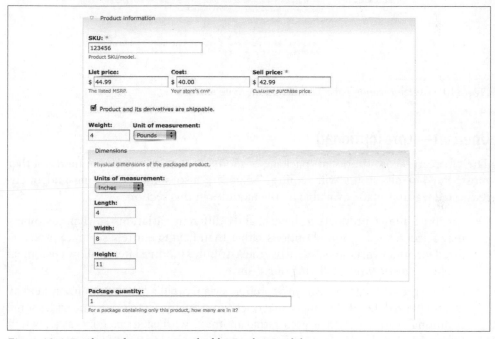

Figure 10-4. Product information supplied by Product module

- Store governs the administration of the entire Ubercart package. It creates the basic management interface at Administer→Store administration (admin/store), pictured in Figure 10-5, and also provides common helper functions such as unit conversions and country-specific features.

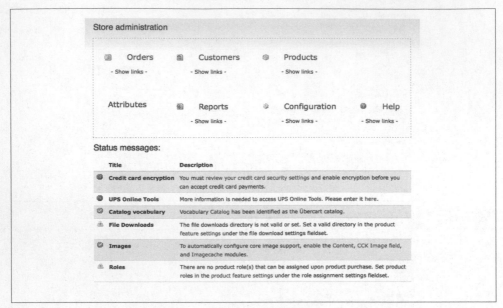

Figure 10-5. Administration panel provided by the Store module

Ubercart—core (optional)

The Ubercart—core (optional) package of modules consists of several modules that most, but not all, stores will require. There are also some interesting and often-requested features made available by the modules in this section.

- Attribute allows products to have slightly different variations so that customers may select from a group of options rather than having entirely separate products listed for minor variations. We'll use the Attributes module later to allow customers to choose a size when ordering our T-shirts.

- Catalog provides categorization of products via Drupal's core taxonomy system by creating a predefined "Product Categories" vocabulary. Catalog also provides some additional features, such as associating an image with each category (as shown in Figure 10-6) and providing some additional browsing options for products in the catalog.

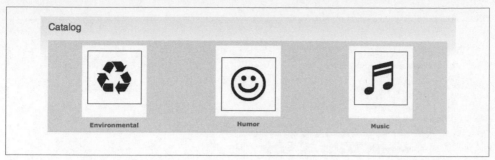

Figure 10-6. The first page of a product catalog with a few categories

- File Downloads allows products to have associated downloadable files. Ideal for selling software or digital media, the File Downloads module automatically sends a customer an email with a link to a secure download. Customers can also download any purchased items again by logging into their account.

- Notify enables features for sending email notifications to customers upon checkout or to notify of order updates.

- Payment is a framework-style module that enables and manages third-party payment processor integration with Ubercart. During checkout, it allows customers to choose a payment method from a list of enabled Payment processors, as shown in Figure 10-7. The Payment Module also includes a test gateway, which is very useful for testing the checkout process (without the use of any specific third party). The modules in the Ubercart—payment package all integrate with the Payment module's framework. Most provide integration with specific payment processors such as 2Checkout, Authorize.net, CyberSource, and PayPal, with a few exceptions:

  —Test Gateway provides a simple, dummy payment-processing interface, which is very useful for testing and when setting up the store to make sure that orders and reports are all working properly. The test gateway does not make actual charges to a credit card.

  —Payment Method Pack adds the "Other" options for payment such as COD, checks, or money orders. This module doesn't actually collect any funds directly.

  —Recurring Payments does not collect any payments itself, but can add recurring charges to specified products, thus enabling the creation of subscription-based services for Ubercart stores.

  —Credit Card is a base module that adds a "pay by credit card" method to the checkout process and provides hooks for specific third-party integration modules to integrate with credit cart payments. By itself, the Credit Card module does not actually generate a charge to a credit card.

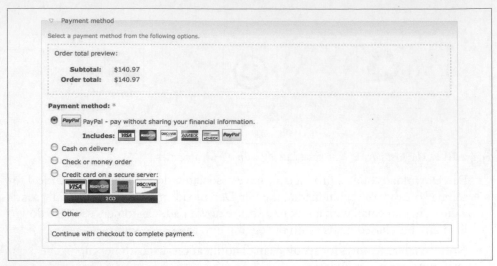

Figure 10-7. A variety of payment methods in Ubercart

- Reports provides a reporting console for sales reports and general activity within the store, as shown in Figure 10-8. This module also allows downloading the reports as a comma-separated values (CSV) file for importing into a spreadsheet program or other reporting tool.

Order statuses used: Completed

#	Product	Views	Sold	Revenue▼	Gross
1	A Product	2	2	**$85.98**	**$5.98**
	123456		2	$85.98	$5.98
2	Another product	1	0	**$0.00**	**$0.00**
	987654		0	$0.00	$0.00
3	Yet another product	3	0	**$0.00**	**$0.00**
	x		0	$0.00	$0.00

Export to CSV file. Show all records

Figure 10-8. An example report generated with the Reports module

- Roles allows users who purchase certain configured products to be granted a specified role—either indefinitely or for a specified duration. This module is great for enabling membership features or other subscription-style services.

- Shipping, much like the Payment module, is an API or base module that provides general management related to preparing purchased products for shipping. Modules listed in the Ubercart—fulfillment package all integrate with the Shipping and/ or the Shipping Quotes modules. Their purpose is to provide service-specific integration for calculating shipping costs, generating shipping labels, or creating tracking numbers. The two primary services included with Ubercart are integration

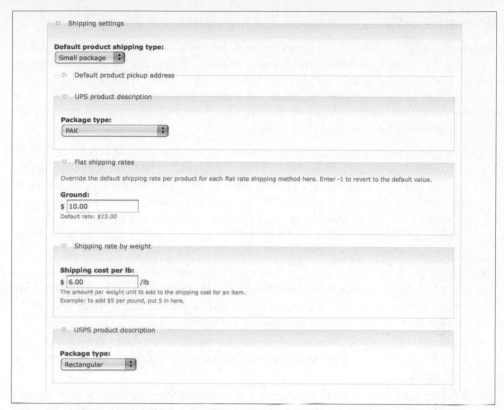

Figure 10-9. Shipping options for a product

with the U.S. Postal Service, via their XML web service, and integration with UPS, via their similar service. There are also additional modules included to do both flat-rate shipping costs (which can be defined per product) and weight-based quotes that work similarly to flat rates, but using the weight of each product. Figure 10-9 illustrates some of the shipping options that Ubercart provides.

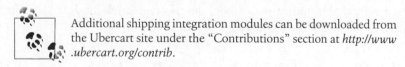 Additional shipping integration modules can be downloaded from the Ubercart site under the "Contributions" section at *http://www .ubercart.org/contrib*.

- Shipping Quotes also provides a basic means of generating quotes or estimates around shipping costs. Other fulfillment modules, listed in the Ubercart fulfillment section, can then provide their unique calculations based on the customer's selected shipping method.
- Taxes enables an interface for creating tax rules specific to certain regions based on product types.

Ubercart—extra

Although our site will not make use of most of the modules contained in the Ubercart - extra section, there are some interesting options available. The distinction between "extra" and "core (optional)" modules is a bit fuzzy, but in general the "core (optional)" modules are things that directly affect the online shopping experience or provide additional, extensible framework elements. The extra modules, on the other hand, enable additional functionality:

- Cart Links allows administrators to construct URLs that will add certain quantities of specified products (along with additional details). These links could then be used on external sites—blogs, affiliate sites, or within other content on the store site—to provide quick "buy now" links. Although there is no user interface for generating the links, you can read more about the Cart Links module at Administer→Store administration→Help→Creating cart links (admin/store/help/cart_links) when the module is enabled.

- Google Analytics for Ubercart acts as an integration point between Ubercart and Google Analytics and can be used to track conversion rates and marketing campaigns versus sales. This module requires that the Google Analytics module be installed (*http://drupal.org/project/google_analytics*).

- Importer is a very useful module for exchanging Ubercart data with external systems. Importer actually provides import and export of product information via an XML format.

- Product Kit enables a feature for grouping products together to be sold as a single unit. The kit can then have its own (discounted) price for the collection of products.

- Repeater provides the functionality to update product information on remote Ubercart stores. This module is very useful if Ubercart is working in a multisite setup, with related or dependent stores. The updates to product information are sent using the same format as the Importer module.

- Stock provides tools for tracking and managing stock levels of items in the store. Store administrators can set thresholds for products, below which they will be notified via email to indicate low stock levels. The Stock module also integrates with the Reports module to provide stock levels reporting.

Spotlight: Ubercart's Administration Panel

Ubercart, due largely to its complexity and vast number of modules, has its own administration section, which is found at Administer→Store administration (admin/store), as seen in Figure 10-10. All subsequent Ubercart features will be managed under this new section.

The main panel shows a listing of all available actions to perform on the store, and includes managing the product catalog, viewing and filling store orders, viewing reports

---

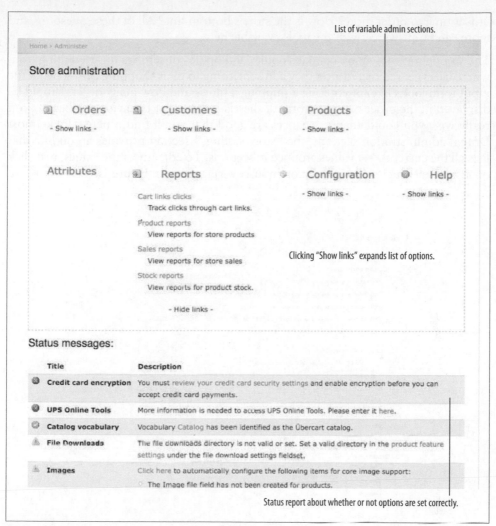

Figure 10-10. The Ubercart administration panel

on store activity, and adjusting the configuration of any setting. Additional sublinks of each section are hidden by default and expanded by clicking the "Show links" link. Below the main panel is a list of status messages that may indicate problems or missing configuration steps. It's a good spot to check if things aren't working correctly.

The Orders, Customers, and Products links each point to a section where you can create, manage, and search existing records. This is where day-to-day store maintenance happens.

The Reports section allows you to answer questions about how well the store's performing overall. What products are selling well? Are there plenty of products in stock, or is it time to order more? How is the store's bottom line? All of these questions and more can be answered with the tools available here.

The Configuration section contains oodles and oodles of settings for everything from where users get redirected after they add something to their shopping cart, to what the input form looks like for entering a shipping address and how many orders should be displayed in the order overview form. If there's a particular behavior of Ubercart you really wish you could change, chances are good that you'll find it here. Unlike most Drupal administration sections, the "Store settings" section provides an outline that lists all the currently set values grouped in sections. To edit any of the values, just click on a section (which will highlight on mouseover), as seen in Figure 10-11.

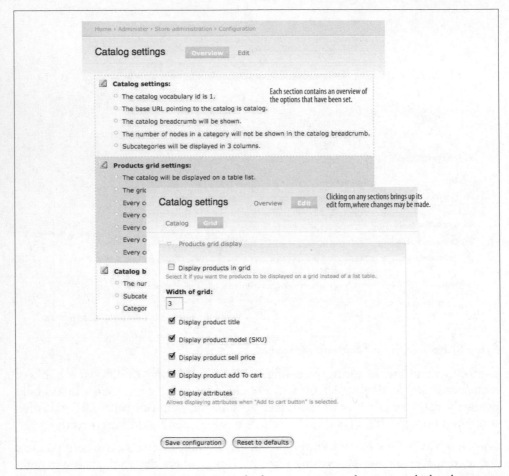

Figure 10-11. The Ubercart settings pages display a summary of options, which take you to appropriate edit forms when clicked

And finally, the Help section takes you to a listing of Ubercart resources, as well as links to help pages for specific modules in the Ubercart suite: it's a great place to go if you are stuck and want advice from other Ubercart users or experts.

Hands-On: Setting Up the Store

To begin setting up the online T-shirt store, we must first establish some basic information about the store that later features will be able to use. Let's get started with the essentials: the store information that will be used in invoices and to calculate shipping costs.

Initial Setup Tasks

1. Log in to the Sweet Tees site as the *admin* user if you have not done so already.
2. Go to Administer→Site building→Modules (admin/build/modules) and enable the following module:
   - Ubercart—core package
     —Store
3. Go to Administer→Store administration→Configuration→Store settings (admin/store/settings/store).
4. Click on the "Name and contact information" section, which brings up the "Contact settings" form (admin/store/settings/store/edit). Complete this form as shown in Table 10-1, and click the "Save configuration" button when done. When you return to the "Store settings" Overview page, it should look as pictured in Figure 10-12.

Table 10-1. Contact settings

Setting	Value
Store name	Sweet Tees
Store owner	Stephen Sweet
E-mail address	store@example.com
Phone number	800-555-1234
Fax number	110-555-4321
Street address 1	123 Example St
Street address 2	
City	Example City
Country	United States
Zone	California
Postal code	90210

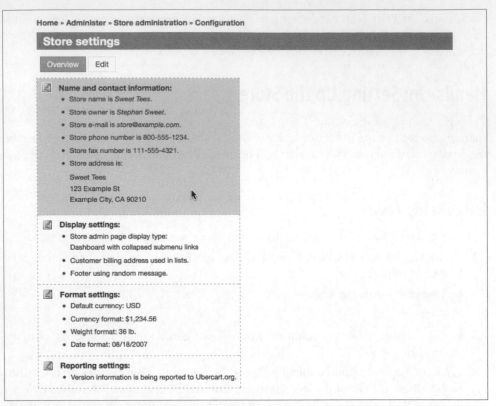

Figure 10-12. Store name and contact information

Although Ubercart defaults to supporting North American conventions, these are all fully configurable. The "Format settings" tab (admin/store/settings/store/edit/format) allows us to configure the display of various measurements such as currency, weight, length, and dates. And under the Country settings form at Administer→Store administration→Country settings (admin/store/settings/countries), you can import additional country data and set up country-specific address forms.

Spotlight: Products, Product Classes, and Attributes

Before we get to the next step—adding products to our store—it's worth taking some time to discuss how Ubercart treats products within the system.

Products in Ubercart are nodes, which means that you can do anything with products that we've done with nodes in the rest of this book: you can add comments or ratings, tag them, add CCK fields to hold additional properties, display products in listings with

Views module, and so on. This seamless integration of store products with the rest of the content that Drupal can manage is a "killer" feature of Ubercart.

Ubercart's Product module defines a single "Product" node type, which comes prebuilt with fields such as SKU and sale price, as pictured in Figure 10-13. These fields interact directly with other parts of the system, such as sales reports and shipping calculations.

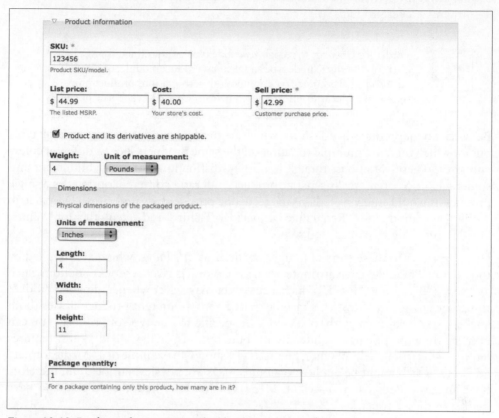

Figure 10-13. Product information supplied by the Product module

A single-product node type is sufficient if you are only selling one style of product in your store, such as a club membership. Many online stores are more complex, however. Amazon.com sells books, movies, and, as we saw in Chapter 4, kitchen utensils. Books have properties like "author" and "ISBN number," and movies might have properties like "rating" and "movie studio." Can you imagine how long the product node form would be if it needed to provide a field for every single one of these properties for all possible types of products? No thanks.

Luckily, the Ubercart developers have a solution to this predicament: special node types called *product classes*. Product classes are slightly different than standard content types, as they need to inherit the base product fields. However, once a product class is created, it will then look and behave like a normal Drupal content type—there will be an entry form for it under "Create content" (node/add), and we can edit fields and properties via Administer→Content management→Content types (admin/content/types). Each product class may be customized without affecting other products. You can create a product class for "Book" and a product class for "Movie" and use CCK to give each its own specific properties. We'll make use of product classes later on for creating our T-shirt and sticker products.

 In order for Ubercart to recognize a node type as a product, it must be either the "Product" node type supplied by Product module, or created as a "product class" node type. Without this, the various product properties won't appear to enter required fields such as SKU and sale price.

But what about products like T-shirts, which are fundamentally the same product type, but for which there are multiple variations of the same product, such as different colors and sizes? These variations, though important distinctions for order fulfillment and sometimes price, aren't really separate products, but rather different options for a single product. It would surely be tedious to create one product for "Red, Small Drupal logo T-shirt" and another for "Red, Large Drupal logo T-shirt" and yet another for "White, Small, Drupal logo T-shirt," and so on.

Ubercart refers to these sorts of minor variations as *attributes*, which are supplied by the Attribute module. Each attribute, such as "Color," is given a series of options, such as "Red," "Blue," and "Plaid," which a customer may select when adding the product to his shopping cart. Attributes may be shared across different product classes (both stickers and T-shirts might have a color), or specific to one type of product. You can even set different pricing for different attribute options, as that Plaid T-shirt requires hand-sewing from the local tailor. Figure 10-14 shows an example of a "Media format" attribute, which might be applied to albums. CDs are physical entities, and therefore have an associated cost and weight. MP3s, on the other hand, are digital and have neither of these properties.

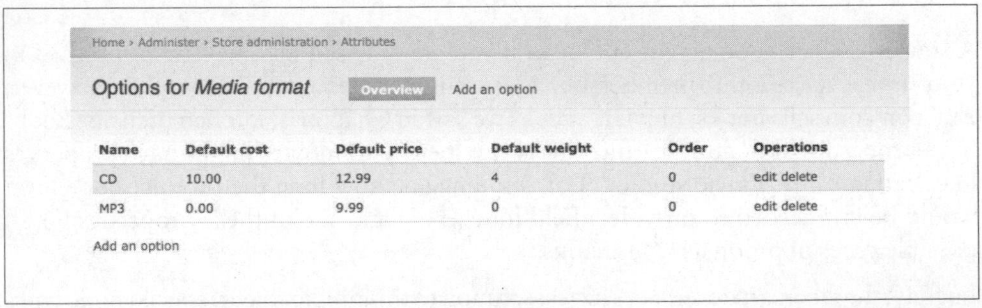

Home › Administer › Store administration › Attributes

Options for *Media format*   Overview   Add an option

Name	Default cost	Default price	Default weight	Order	Operations
CD	10.00	12.99	4	0	edit delete
MP3	0.00	9.99	0	0	edit delete

Add an option

Figure 10-14. Example of an attribute with different options

Hands-On: Creating Products

In this section, we will be setting up the product information for Sweet Tees, which is the first piece required to put together our online store. Ubercart's Product module provides a Product content type for us on installation, and the FileField (*http://drupal .org/project/filefield*), ImageField (*http://drupal.org/project/imagefield*), and ImageCache (*http://drupal.org/project/imagecache*) modules that we covered in Chapter 7 will allow us to display and collect images on products.

 As Ubercart uses the ImageField and ImageCache modules for all product image handling, we can modify any of the default settings using the techniques outlined in Chapter 7 to customize them for our purposes.

Initial Setup Tasks

Go to Administer→Site building→Modules (admin/build/modules) and enable the following modules:

- CCK package
  — Content
  — FileField
  — ImageField
- Core package
  — Path
- ImageCache package
  — ImageAPI
  — ImageAPI GD2
  — ImageCache
  — ImageCache UI
- Other package
  — Token
- Ubercart—core package
  — Product
- Ubercart—core (optional) package
  — Attribute
  — Catalog

After enabling these modules, we can see that our store administration section has changed dramatically. Going to Administer→Store administration (admin/store) now shows messages in the "Status messages" list and two new sections, Products and Attributes, as seen in Figure 10-15.

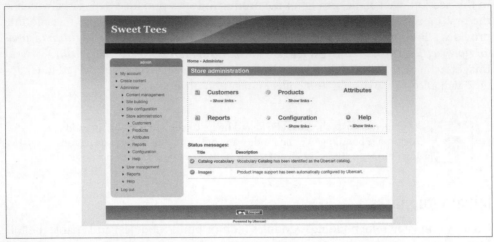

Figure 10-15. Store administration panel, after enabling Product-related modules

Configuring Product Classes

When we enabled the modules in the previous step, Ubercart automatically added a Product content type and associated it with an Image field so that we can attach pictures to our products. However, Sweet Tees sells two kinds of products: T-shirts and stickers. In order to accomplish this requirement, we'll create two product classes, as shown in Figure 10-16.

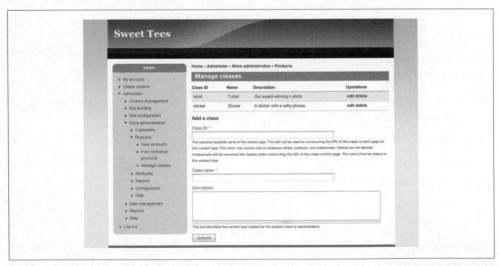

Figure 10-16. Product classes for T-shirts and stickers

1. Go to Administer→Store administration→Products→Manage classes (admin/store/products/classes).

2. You will be presented with a form to add a class. Create the first class, for T-shirts, according to Table 10-2 and click "Submit."

Table 10-2. Adding a "T-shirt" class

Setting	Value
Class ID	tshirt
Class name	T-shirt
Description	Our award-winning T-shirts

3. Now add a second product class for stickers as shown in Table 10-3.

Table 10-3. Adding a "sticker" class

Setting	Value
Class ID	sticker
Class name	Sticker
Description	A sticker with a witty phrase

Configuring Product Attributes

For the Sweet Tees online store, customers need to be able to select the T-shirt size that they wish to order, as well as the colors of their shirts and stickers. To implement this, we will make use of Ubercart's product attributes feature. Figure 10-17 shows an example of the Size attribute.

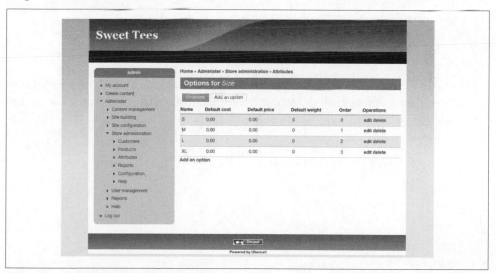

Figure 10-17. The Size attribute and its options

1. Go to Administer→Store administration→Attributes (admin/store/attributes) and click on the "Add an attribute" tab (admin/store/attributes/add).

2. On this page, we can create attributes and options for our products. Initially, we need to provide a bit of information about the attribute. Enter the values according to Table 10-4.

Table 10-4. Settings for the Size attribute

Field	Value
Name	Size
Help text	Pick a T-shirt size
Make this attribute required	Checked
Display type	Select box

3. Clicking Submit takes us back to the Attributes Overview tab (admin/store/attributes). Click the "options" link in the Operations column of the Size row.

4. This gives us the options overview page, which will list all options available for this attribute. Click the "Add an option" tab (admin/store/attributes/1/options/add).

5. This form allows us to add an option for the Size attribute. Complete this form for each of our sizes using the values in Table 10-5. Note that you can also offer Cost, Price, and Weight adjustments for each option. For our purposes, we will assume that all T-shirt sizes cost and weigh the same.

Table 10-5. Options for the Size attribute

Name	Order
S	0
M	1
L	2
XL	3

6. Let's also create a color attribute for both T-shirts and stickers. Return to Administer→Store administration→Attributes (admin/store/attributes) and click on the "Add an attribute" tab (admin/store/attributes/add). Enter the values in Table 10-6.

Table 10-6. Settings for the Color attribute

Field	Value
Name	Color
Help text	Select a color
Make this attribute required	Checked
Display type	Select box

7. Back at the overview screen, click "options" in the Color row, choose "Add an option," and enter the values in Table 10-7.

Table 10-7. Options for the Color attribute

Name	Order
White	−1
Dark blue	0
Light blue	0
Plaid	0

8. We now need to associate our new attributes with our product classes. Return to Administer→Store administration→Products→Manage classes (admin/store/products/classes) and click the "edit" operation in the T-shirt row (admin/store/products/classes/T-shirt/edit).

9. Click on the Attributes tab (admin/store/products/classes/tshirt/attributes) and click on the "add attributes to this class" link in the help text (admin/store/products/classes/tshirt/attributes/add).

10. In the Attributes select list, select both Size and Color, and click "Add attributes."

11. Click the Options tab (admin/store/products/classes/tshirt/options).

12. Select all four colors and all four sizes by checking the checkbox next to each. Pick White as the default color, and M as the default size. Your configuration screen should look as pictured in Figure 10-18. Click Submit when finished.

13. Stickers, on the other hand, don't have a size, and come only in white and light blue. Head back to Administer→Store administration→Products→Manage classes (admin/store/products/classes) and click the "edit" operation in the sticker row (admin/store/products/classes/sticker/edit).

14. Click on the Attributes tab (admin/store/products/classes/tshirt/attributes) and click on the "add attributes to this class" link in the help text (admin/store/products/classes/tshirt/attributes/add). In the Attributes select list, select Color, and click "Add attributes."

15. Click the Options tab (admin/store/products/classes/tshirt/options) and make sure both White and Light blue are checked. Make White the default color, and click Submit.

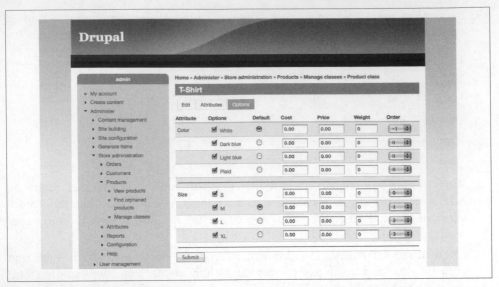

Figure 10-18. T-shirt attribute options

Configuring Product Settings

Before we move on to the catalog area, let's configure some basic product settings:

1. Go to Administer→Store administration→Configuration→Product settings (admin/store/settings/products) and click on the "Product settings" section.

2. This page lets us configure some default settings for products, such as the number of products to show on listing pages and how "Add to cart" links are handled. The defaults will work here, except we'd like to check the "Display an optional quantity field in the Add to Cart form checkbox." Click "Save configuration."

3. Click on the "Product fields" tab (admin/store/settings/products/edit/fields). Here, we have a selection of optional fields we can expose on all of our products. These fields are common to all products in our online store. In addition to the defaults, click the checkbox next to Weight and click "Save configuration."

 Because Ubercart products are a Drupal content type, we can add additional fields via CCK the same way we do with any other type, by visiting Administer→Content management→Content types (admin/content/types) and clicking "manage fields" for Product. The product fields used by Ubercart are common fields used by all products.

Configuring the Catalog

The Catalog module that we enabled will allow category-based browsing of our products, as pictured in Figure 10-19. The entire catalog system is built on Drupal's core taxonomy system; therefore, adding and manipulating the hierarchy of the catalog is done via the standard taxonomy interface. However, Ubercart adds several additional nice features for browsing and listing products in the categories for us.

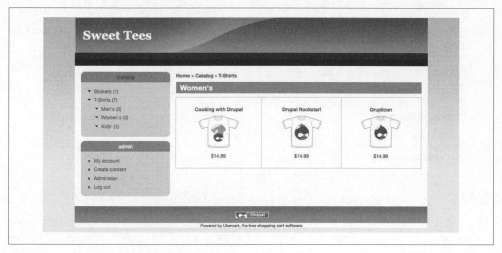

Figure 10-19. The Sweet Tees product catalog

Before beginning this section, double-check that the "Catalog" vocabulary has been properly created by checking on the status messages at Administer→Store administration (admin/store). If all goes well, there should be a status message claiming "Vocabulary Catalog has been identified as the Ubercart catalog." This means that the catalog vocabulary has been created successfully. If you do not receive this message, create a new vocabulary by hand, and head to Administer ›Store administration→Configuration→Catalog settings (admin/store/settings/catalog) to mark it for use by the Catalog.

1. Let's start by adding some categories for our catalog. Go to Administer→Content management→Taxonomy (admin/content/taxonomy).

2. Click "add terms" for the Catalog vocabulary and add the product categories listed below. Use the term Advanced options "Parents" and "Weight" settings to place them in the following hierarchy:

   • Stickers

   • T-shirts

   — Men's

   — Women's

   — Kids'

3. Go to Administer→Store administration→Configuration→Catalog settings (admin/store/settings/catalog).

4. Click on the "Catalog" section (admin/store/settings/catalog/edit/catalog) to open the edit form. Note that you can select any taxonomy vocabulary to serve as the Catalog vocabulary (if you have an existing vocabulary that you would like to use).

5. We will leave the default settings here for the most part. Change the settings as indicated in Table 10-8 and click "Save configuration."

Table 10-8. Catalog display settings

Field	Value
Catalog products list	
Product nodes per page	12
Catalog block settings	
Always expand categories in the catalog block	Checked

6. Click the Grid tab (admin/store/settings/catalog/edit/grid).

7. Here, we can have our catalog pages laid out in a grid rather than a standard table listing view. Complete this form according to Table 10-9 and click "Save configuration."

Table 10-9. Catalog grid settings

Setting	Value
Display products in grid	Checked
Display product model (SKU)	Unchecked
Display product add to cart	Unchecked

8. Let's add some products to our catalog! Go to Create Content→T-shirt (node/add/T-shirt) and complete the form as per Table 10-10, and click the Save button to create the product. There are T-shirt images provided for you in the book's source code in the *assets/ch10-store* folder, or you can use some of your own! When finished, your product upload will look similar to Figure 10-20.

Table 10-10. Create T-shirt form

Field	Value
Name	Druplicon
Catalog	Men's, Women's
SKU	T-shirt001
Sell price	14.99
Weight	2 Pounds
Description	Drupal's logo

Field	Value
Image	[Upload a T-shirt image]

 If an image field doesn't show up for you here, check back at the status messages on the main Ubercart administration page at Administer→Store administration (admin/store) and follow the instructions next to Images. You may have forgotten to enable a few of the required modules earlier.

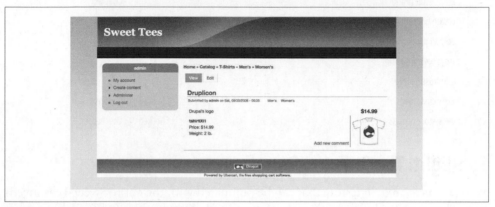

Figure 10-20. A sample T-shirt product

9. Add a few more products to fill out the catalog a little. Note that each product can have per-product Attributes, Options, or Adjustments. You can adjust these by clicking on the node's Edit tab and then using the tabs that show under the View and Edit tabs. For instance, if we have a T-shirt that is unavailable in certain sizes, we can click the Options tab and uncheck the sizes that are not available.

10. Now, let's view the results of what we've made. Enable the catalog block by visiting Administer→Site building→Blocks (admin/build/block) and dragging the Catalog block to the top of the left sidebar region. When the block is in place, click "Save blocks." We can now look through the product catalog by clicking on the links in the Catalog block in the sidebar.

11. Finally, let's set up the permissions for the items we've configured so far. Go to Administer→User management→Permissions (admin/user/permissions), enter the settings in Table 10-11, and click "Save permissions."

Table 10-11. Permissions for the event content type

Permission	anonymous user	authenticated user	editor	site administrator
uc_catalog module				
administer catalog				Checked
view catalog	Checked	Checked		
uc_product module				
administer product classes				Checked
administer products				Checked
create products			Checked	
edit all products			Checked	
uc_store module				
administer store				Checked
view customers			Checked	Checked
view store reports			Checked	Checked

Spotlight: The Ordering Process

We now have an online store that can be populated with the entire Sweet Tees inventory. However, at the moment customers can only browse the catalog and see information about the products. Most e-commerce sites are concerned with actually selling something, and that means getting into the ordering process.

Figure 10-21 depicts the typical workflow for a store such as our client's. It begins when a customer adds products to her online shopping cart and clicks the "Checkout" button. The customer is presented with a form in which to fill out basic customer information, such as billing and shipping address, credit card information, and preferred shipping method. The customer then has a chance to review the order, including its total price, with taxes and shipping calculated based on the information provided earlier. Once the order is submitted, a payment gateway validates the entered billing information to determine if the credit card is legitimate. If all goes well, the order is placed and the store fulfills its end of the bargain by packing the products up and shipping them where they need to go.

Although this is typical for a "traditional" e-commerce store, many types of stores have very different needs. Ubercart's module suite allows for many flexible ways to configure a customized ordering process. Want to sell downloadable products, which have no need to be shipped anywhere? No problem. Turn on the Downloads module, and turn off the Shipping module. Need to calculate complex international tax rules? The Conditional Actions module combined with the Taxes module will do what you need. Does an order in your system take lots of steps on its way to being completed, such as "Pending various red-tape paperwork" or "Needs invoice"? The Orders module has the ability

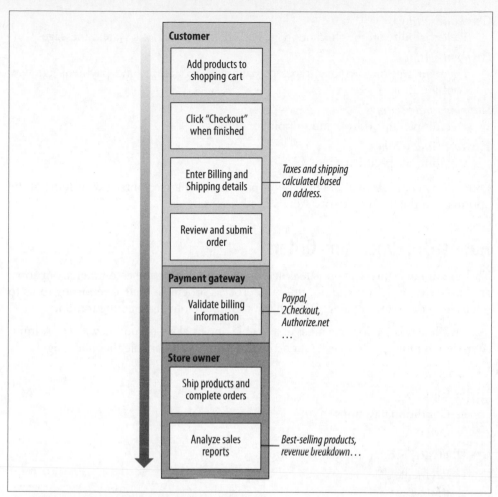

Customer

Add products to shopping cart

Click "Checkout" when finished

Enter Billing and Shipping details — *Taxes and shipping calculated based on address.*

Review and submit order

Payment gateway

Validate billing information — *Paypal, 2Checkout, Authorize.net ...*

Store owner

Ship products and complete orders

Analyze sales reports — *Best-selling products, revenue breakdown...*

Figure 10-21. Ubercart's typical ordering process

to define custom workflow states for your orders, so you always know the current state of open orders in the system.

Although there are far too many configuration options to get into all of them in detail here, we'll discuss some of the settings pages that impact ordering, found underneath Administer→Store administration→Configuration (admin/store/settings):

Cart settings

Various shopping behaviors, such as where customers are directed after adding products, and what information shows up on the shopping cart page

Order settings

Settings for how invoices appear, an order's workflow states, and the display of order information in the administration panel

Checkout settings
> Field visibility on the checkout page and the text of various system messages

Payment settings
> Payment tracking options, types of payments to accept, and payment gateway configuration

Shipping quote settings
> Default pickup address and shipping methods

Tax rates and settings
> Creation of specific tax rate rules

Often, the default settings are fine, but it pays to familiarize yourself with some of the options found here in case your store's needs ever change.

Hands-On: Processing Orders

The remaining element of our site is actually implementing the e-commerce portions: an online shopping cart and the ability to process orders, as well as reporting tools to tell us how our store is doing. We will now complete our store configuration.

To complete this section, we must first enable one final set of modules. Go to Administer→Site building→Modules (admin/build/modules) and enable the following:

- Ubercart—core package
  - Cart
  - Conditional Actions
  - Order
- Ubercart—core (optional) package
  - Payment
  - Reports
  - Shipping
  - Shipping Quotes
  - Taxes
- Ubercart—fulfillment package
  - Flatrate
- Ubercart—payment package
  - Credit Card
  - Payment Method Pack
  - Test Gateway

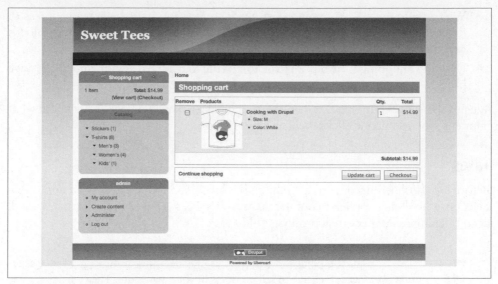

Figure 10-22. Ubercart's shopping cart, along with a sidebar block

Because the precise instructions for implementing payment systems vary widely between various services (Paypal, Authorize.net, and so on), in this chapter, we'll be setting up credit cards only with a test gateway. On a "real" e-commerce site, you'll want to use an actual payment gateway that can accept and process credit card transactions for you. Ubercart's website contains a list of its supported payment systems, along with documentation on how to set them up: *http://www.ubercart.org/ payment*.

Shopping Cart

In this section, we will configure the site's shopping cart, as pictured in Figure 10-22. Once we get the cart set up, we will be able to browse to an individual T-shirt page, select options such as color and quantity, and add the customized products to our cart.

The vast majority of our work for this section is completed by simply enabling the Cart module. The cart settings come with very workable defaults, but there are a couple settings we want to change:

1. Go to Administer→Store administration→Configuration→Cart settings (admin/ store/settings/cart) and click the "Cart settings" section (admin/store/settings/ cart/edit).

2. The default setting for the "Continue shopping link URL" is to return the user to the site's front page. We should change this to be the full catalog. Enter "catalog" and click "Save configuration."

3. We can also create a Shopping Cart block so that shoppers have ready access to their cart from any page on the site. Go to Administer→Site building→Blocks (admin/build/block).

4. Drag the Shopping Cart block to the top of the left sidebar region and click "Save blocks."

We now have our shopping cart ready to go. That was easy! Next, we'll talk about what happens when someone clicks the Checkout button.

Taxes

Before we can open up our store to the public, we need to ensure that all applicable sales taxes are being applied to our items. As Sweet Tees is based in California, we will need to charge sales tax on all products sold.

 This example is for illustrative purposes only: determine what types of taxes you need to charge to sell products in your own store. The Conditional Actions module, part of Ubercart core, allows setting all sorts of complex tax rules to calculate different rates depending on whether purchasers are from the same state or a different state, for different product types, or for international orders.

1. Go to Administer→Store administration→Configuration→Tax rates and settings (admin/store/settings/taxes) and click the "Make a new tax rule" link (admin/store/settings/taxes/edit).

2. Complete the "Edit tax rule" form using the values from Table 10-12.

Table 10-12. Edit tax rule form

Field	Value
Name	Sales tax
Rate	7.25%
Taxed product types	T-shirt, Sticker

3. Click Submit to save the sales tax settings.

Shipping

Because we are selling physical goods, or "shippable items," in our store, we need to account for the costs involved to ship our products. For simplicity, we will use a flat rate to provide a single set of shipping costs, assuming no base shipping cost and a default shipping rate of $5.99 for all T-shirts.

1. Go to Administer→Store administration→Configuration→Shipping quote settings (admin/store/settings/quotes) and click on the "Quote methods" section (store/settings/quotes/methods).
2. Click on the "Flat rate" tab (admin/store/settings/quotes/methods/flatrate) and click the "Add a new flat rate shipping method" link.
3. Complete the form using the values from Table 10-13.

Table 10-13. Flat rate method settings

Field	Value
Shipping method title	Default shipping
Line item label	Shipping
Base price	0.00
Default product shipping rate	5.99

Payment

We can now configure the final piece for our site: payments. There are a lot of options for how to accept payment via Ubercart. We will be taking checks or money orders as well as processing credit cards (via the test gateway).

1. Go to Administer→Store administration→Configuration→Payment settings (admin/store/settings/payment) and click on the "Payment methods" section (admin/store/settings/payment/edit/methods).
2. In the Payment methods table, ensure that "Check" and "Credit card" are checked, and that the default gateway is set to "Test Gateway." Click "Save configuration."
3. You should see an error at the top that says "Credit card encryption must be configured to accept credit card payments." Let's fix that.

 There are several security implications involved in accepting credit card payments online. You should always use a proper, valid SSL certificate for accepting the information and, when possible, avoid storing the card numbers in Ubercart. For more information about secure credit card handling with Ubercart, please see the online documentation: *http://www.ubercart.org/docs/user/2731/credit_card_settings#security*.

4. Create a directory in the filesystem called *keys*, which will be used to encrypt credit card data, in a place that is *not web accessible*. For example, if your main website page points to */home/username/www*, create the directory at */home/username/keys*.
5. Temporarily make the directory writable, for example with the command `chmod a +w /home/username/keys`.
6. Expand the "Credit card settings" fieldset, and in "Card number encryption key filepath," enter the path to the keys file; for example, */home/username/keys*.

7. In the "Checkout workflow" section, ensure that "Attempt to process credit card payments at checkout" is checked.

8. Also expand the "Check settings" fieldset, and enter some address information for the store.

9. Click "Save configuration."

10. On the file system, reset the directory's permissions to prevent write access, for example with the command `chmod a-w /home/username/keys`.

Placing a Test Order

We are now ready to make our first test order! Here's how:

1. Browse the catalog to find our "Example T-shirt" product. We must select a Color and a Size and then click "Add to cart." We will then be redirected to the cart view. Note that the "Shopping cart" block on the left instantly reflects the number of items (1) and total amount of our current selection.

2. From the shopping cart view, we could choose to "Continue shopping," which will redirect us back to the catalog overview, or we can make changes to our cart by removing items or updating the quantity of any product (by making changes and clicking "Update cart"). However, we would like to see the order process in action, so let's click Checkout.

3. We are now on the Ubercart checkout screen. The top portion of the page, shown in Figure 10-23, displays the contents of our shopping cart for confirmation followed by a customer information section, which—as we are currently logged in—will display our email address.

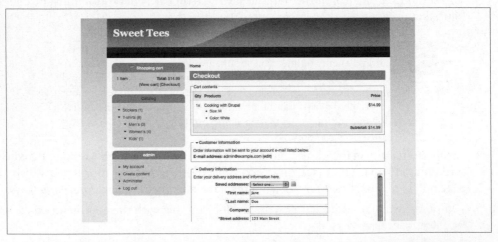

Figure 10-23. The order summary and delivery details of the Ubercart checkout screen

4. Complete the delivery information and billing information sections with your information.

5. Continue down to the payment method. By default, "Check or money order" is selected as the payment method, with the address we provided earlier. Click on the "Credit card" option and the section dynamically updates to include a credit card entry form, as shown in Figure 10-24.

Figure 10-24. The shipping and payment section of the checkout screen

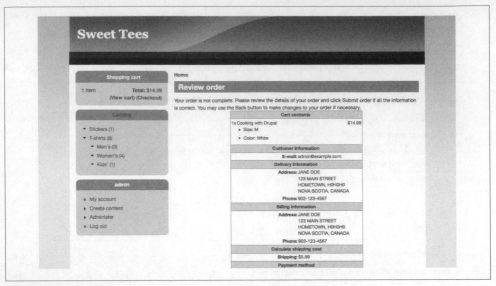

Figure 10-25. The review order screen, where customers can make final adjustments

6. As we are using the Test gateway, we don't need to enter a valid credit card number to complete the order. We do, however, need to enter credit card information in a valid format. The Credit Card module will check to ensure that there are the proper number of digits in the card number and that the expiration date is still valid. Complete this section with the settings in Table 10-14.

Table 10-14. Credit card form

Field	Value
Card Number	4111111111111111 (that's 15 1s)
Expiration Date	July 2017
CVV	123

7. Upon clicking the "Review order" button, we are presented with a final confirmation screen, pictured in Figure 10-25, to review all the entered information. If there are errors, click the Back button and you will return to the checkout screen, where you can make corrections. Clicking "Submit order" will complete the transaction, send the email confirmation, and create the order record for store administrators.

8. When finished, the customer is presented with a thank-you page, with a link to view the current order status from the Orders section of his user profile.

Fulfilling an Order

Our test order has been successfully placed. Let's now turn our attention to what happens afterward: the order shipping and order fulfillment process, and viewing reports of the overall health of the store.

1. Go to Administer→Store administration→Orders (admin/store/orders) to view a list of all of the orders in the system. Our order shows "Payment received," because our test gateway payment went through properly. Click the View icon to display the order, which should look something like Figure 10-26. From here, you can do things such as print and mail invoices, view a log of changes to the order, and view payment details.

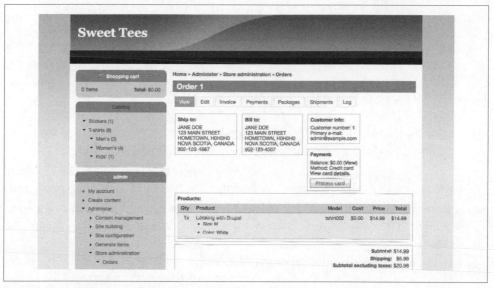

Figure 10-26. Viewing an order in the order system

2. You can also ship products from here, which is what we'll do next. Click the Packages tab and click the "Create packages" link to arrive at the screen depicted in Figure 10-27.

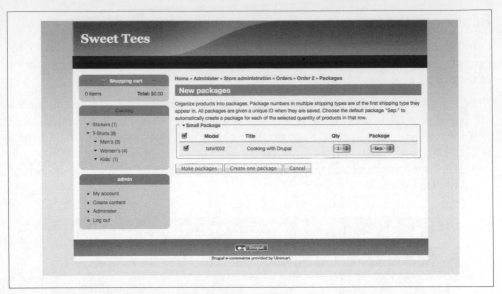

Figure 10-27. Organizing product shipments into packages

3. Check the T-shirt and click "Create one package." This screen also allows you to do things like ship two products together and another one separately.

4. Next, click the Shipments tab, and the "Make a new shipment" link. Check off the package, choose "Ship manually" as the shipment type, and click "Ship packages."

5. A form will appear where additional details may be entered, such as tracking number, ship date, and delivery date. Simply click "Save shipment" to accept the defaults.

6. Finally, we should edit our order to reflect that it is now complete, and the order has successfully shipped. Click the View tab to return to the order view.

7. At the bottom of the order is a drop-down for order status. Change its setting to Completed, and click Update.

8. Now that we've completed our first order, it's as good a time as any to look at some of the system reports that Ubercart provides. Go to Administer→Store administration→Reports (admin/store/reports). Click on "Sales reports" to view a summary of the store's performance, as seen in Figure 10-28. Feel free to explore some of the other reports under this section as well.

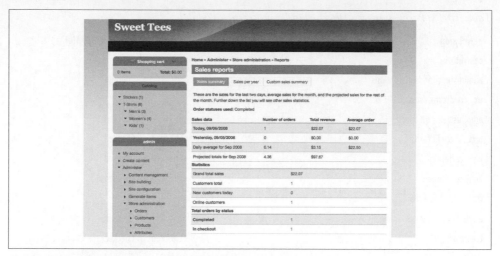

Figure 10-28. Sales reports show overall health of the store

Access Control

Finally, let's configure the permissions for the new modules that we enabled in this section. Go to Administrator→User management→Permissions (admin/user/permissions), set them as indicated in Table 10-15, and click "Save permissions." Most of these are similar to what we've already seen or their function can be guessed by the name, but a few deserve special attention, as it's not immediately clear what they entail:

- Under *uc_credit module*, there are two credit card related permissions: "view cc details" and "view cc numbers." "view cc details" allows a user to see what type of card was used and how much it was charged, so we'll give that to the editor role. However, a credit card number is very sensitive information. Although Ubercart will normally store only the last four digits of a credit card, it's better to be safe than sorry. We'll give these permissions only to site administrators.

- Under the *uc_order module* section, there are two similarly named permissions: "delete orders" and "delete any orders." The difference is that users with "delete any orders" permissions can even remove already-completed orders in the system, and bypass any additional checks that might otherwise prevent an order from being removed. As a result, we give this permission only to the site administrator role.

Table 10-15. Permissions for Ubercart order processing modules

Permission	anonymous user	authenticated user	editor	site administrator
ca module				
administer conditional actions				Checked
uc_credit module				
administer credit cards				Checked
process credit cards			Checked	Checked
view cc details			Checked	Checked
view cc numbers				Checked
uc_order module				
administer order workflow				Checked
create orders			Checked	Checked
delete any order				Checked
delete orders			Checked	Checked
edit orders			Checked	Checked
view all orders			Checked	Checked
uc_payment module				
delete payments				Checked
manual payments			Checked	Checked
view payments			Checked	Checked
uc_quote module				
configure quotes				Checked
uc_reports module				
view reports			Checked	Checked
uc_shipping module				
fulfill orders			Checked	Checked
uc_store module				
view store reports			Checked	Checked
uc_taxes module				
configure taxes				Checked

Taking It Further

In this chapter, we have covered the basics of setting up an online storefront and shopping cart using the Ubercart package for Drupal. However, there are several additional modules that you will likely want to consider before taking your online store live:

Secure Pages (http://drupal.org/project/securepages)

When collecting sensitive, personal information online—particularly credit card information—it is highly recommended that you do it via a secure, SSL connection. The Secure Pages module allows you to specify certain Drupal paths that should be visited only via HTTPS. The recommended paths to protect are *user/** and *cart/**.

PayPal (included with Ubercart)

Although the PayPal module is not required, you will likely want to use some payment gateway for processing payments (recall that we used the Test Gateway in this chapter). PayPal's merchant services are easy to set up and well supported by Ubercart.

Stock (included with Ubercart)

Particularly when selling something like T-shirts, it is a good idea to keep track of the current available stock level to avoid selling someone a product that is not available. The stock module (found in Ubercart—extra) updates a given stock level for each product every time a purchase is made. When new stock arrives, simply add the new quantity to the current level. Also included with the module is a threshold setting which, when reached, will trigger an email notification that inventory is getting low.

Summary

In this chapter, we were able to set up a complete online store for our customer, Sweet Tees. Although there are a lot of modules, configuration screens, and chances to override the features in Ubercart, the sane default options and helpers for common tasks such as setting up ImageCache presets make Ubercart fairly easy to get running.

Here are the modules we referenced in this chapter:

- CCK: *http://drupal.org/project/cck*
- e-Commerce: *http://drupal.org/project/ecommerce*
- FileField: *http://drupal.org/project/filefield*
- Google Analytics: *http://drupal.org/project/google_analytics*
- ImageAPI: *http://drupal.org/project/imageapi*
- ImageCache: *http://drupal.org/project/imagecache*
- ImageField: *http://drupal.org/project/imagefield*
- Token: *http://drupal.org/project/token*
- Ubercart: *http://drupal.org/project/ubercart*

Here are the additional resources that we referenced in this chapter:

- Ubercart official site: *http://www.ubercart.org*
- Ubercart contributions: *http://www.ubercart.org/contrib*
- Ubercart credit card security: *http://www.ubercart.org/docs/user/2731/credit_card _settings#security*
- Ubercart payment systems: *http://www.ubercart.org/payment*

## CHAPTER 11

Theming Your Site

The rest of this book has extensively discussed how to construct a diverse array of websites from photo sharing to product reviews to event management by combining powerful Drupal core features and dozens of add-on contributed modules. Drupal gives you a lot of tools to move things around and arrange the *functionality* of your site, but often the main difference between most websites comes down to presentation.

When you think about it, there's really not much difference between the functionality of YouTube and Flickr. Certainly, one manages video content and the other focuses on photos. But these sites have more similarities than differences. Both manage media content and allow users to share their uploads. Both allow users to create a network of contacts. Users can create their own profiles, comment on others' content, and mark content as a "favorite" for later reference.

Functionally, these sites are very similar, but their presentation is completely different. The layout of the sites is different, their backgrounds are different, their entire look and feel is different—each has a different *presentation* of its elements.

When we talk about *theming*, we are talking about Drupal's presentational layer. It is where the site developer is able to take complete control and specify what goes onto the page. All CSS, JavaScript, images, and HTML can be rearranged and overridden by a Drupal theme. Drupal's theme system can provide special formatting of the site for mobile devices, reformat content for display in RSS feeds, display a thumbnail of the user's image whenever the username is shown, completely change the default output provided by a module, and much more. Drupal theming is a topic broad enough to fill an entire book of its own. The aim of this chapter is to give an overview with as many tip-of-the-iceberg concepts as possible—to show what can be done and some basic information on how to do it. We hope to give you enough of an overview so that if you are interested in customizing the look and feel of your Drupal site, you will be able to use the concepts in this chapter as a launching pad.

We should also mention that although the rest of this book is as code-free as possible, even an overview of Drupal's theming system requires some basic knowledge of HTML, CSS, and PHP. If this type of code scares you, you might want to squint through the rest of this chapter, as the code samples assume that you are at least somewhat familiar with weird stuff like `<div>` and `#header` and `foreach`. If you're curious but not quite comfortable with code, however, a great place to learn about all three of these technologies is the W3Schools website at *http://w3schools.com*.

To follow along with the hands-on examples in this chapter, install Drupal using the default Drupal install profile. Go to *http://theme.usingdrupal.com* for the completed website, along with a copy of the theme with the customizations from this chapter.

Spotlight: The Theme System

As discussed briefly in Chapter 1, modules generate the contents of a given page, and the theme system provides the opportunity to cut in and customize the page before it's displayed. A *theme* is a collection of images, CSS, and (usually) HTML/PHP files that change the look of Drupal's default output. With a simple flick of a radio button, you can completely change the design of your website by choosing a different theme, and you can customize settings on a theme to make adjustments, such as to the site logo or colors, as we saw in Chapter 2.

Figure 11-1 provides a general overview of how the theme system works. Each path in Drupal corresponds to a particular module that is responsible for handling the page request. For example, "node/1" is handled by the Node module, "admin/build/themes" is handled by the System module, and a path like "albums" might be handled by the Views module. After the module has built up the contents of the page, it calls up the theme system with a special function called `theme()`, which we'll be discussing in more depth later in the chapter.

The theme system consists primarily of a *theme engine*, which defines the dynamic parts of the page, as well as the rules for how Drupal's output is defined and can be overridden, and the currently enabled *theme*, such as Garland. The theme engine is capable of setting up the basic structure and markup of the content and rendering the entire page template with the current page's content inside of it. But where the visual magic happens—and where you start to gain control over exactly how each element on the page looks—is in the theme itself.

Every single element on the page, from the title in the browser window, to the site logo, to the regions where blocks are placed, to the links in the menu bar, is run through the theme system. The difference between an obviously "Drupal"-looking site and a stylish site is creative use of the tools provided by the theme layer. Let's look at the pieces of a theme we have to work with, as well as how Drupal expects us to use them.

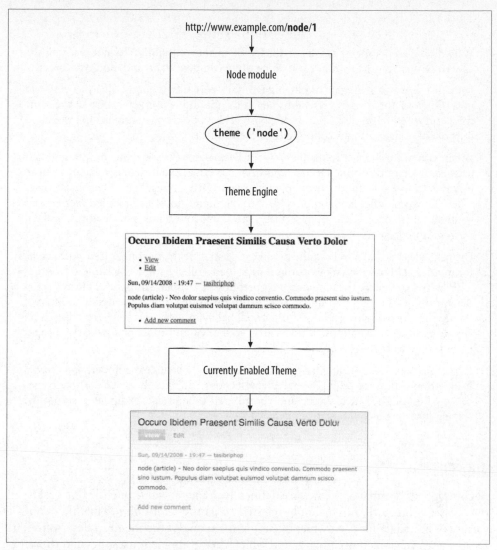

Figure 11-1. An overview of how Drupal goes from URL to HTML

This chapter discusses the PHPTemplate theme engine (also referred to as a templating system), which is provided by Drupal core. However, it's worth pointing out that other theme engines are available, including Smarty and PHPTAL. See the full list at *http://drupal.org/project/Theme +Engines*.

Modifying Drupal

Why do we need a theme system at all? It's open source, right? Why not just find the spot in Drupal's core files that's not doing quite what we want, and modify it directly?

Let's just start by saying that modifying Drupal's core files is almost always a very bad idea. One of Drupal's great strengths lies in its ubiquity—everyone is using the same tried and true, well-tested, secure code base. This code is constantly being tested and improved by an enormous community of contributors.

When you make changes to the files in your Drupal installation, you are creating your own proprietary version of Drupal, and losing its collective benefits. When a security update of Drupal is announced, upgrading your Drupal installation becomes somewhere between difficult and impossible. Most Drupal sites with modified files end up stranded, unable to benefit from security, speed improvements, new features, and usability improvements of later versions.

Drupal is designed to never require modification in order to customize it to your needs. It provides many opportunities during a page load, called *hooks*, which allow modules and themes to modify the fundamental operation of Drupal. Drupal will always do its default thing, but it gives you many opportunities to *override* those defaults. Most of the methods used to override default Drupal behavior and presentation are based on simple naming conventions. If you name your files and functions with the proper names, they will take precedence.

By keeping our customizations separate, we can easily change the underlying Drupal installation without affecting Drupal's default code. Additionally, when the time comes to upgrade the site, Drupal core and contributed themes can be updated smoothly, leaving just our custom bits to wrangle with.

.info Files

Beginning with Drupal 6, themes are defined by a *theme_name.info* file that resides in the theme's directory, often simply referred to as the ".info* file." This file defines a variety of metadata for the theme, including the name of the theme, a description, its Drupal core version compatibility, and which theme engine it uses. Beyond those basics, the *.info* file can also define the block regions available to the theme, and the CSS stylesheets and JavaScript files used. You can also define the theme features available to administrators under the theme configuration screens (see Chapter 2.

Here is a simple example showing basic theme information, taken from the core Bluemarine theme. A full description of all attributes available in *.info* files for themes is available at *http://drupal.org/node/171205*.

```
name = Bluemarine
description = Table-based multi-column theme with a marine and ash color scheme.
core = 6.x
engine = phptemplate
```

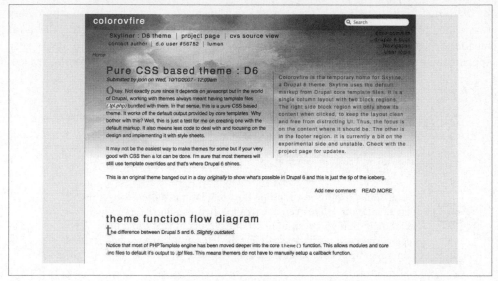

Figure 11-2. Skyliner theme, which consists of only CSS, JavaScript, images, and a .info file.

.info files are the only required file for a theme, and they make it possible to create themes using no PHP or custom HTML at all. Themes can instead rely on Drupal's default HTML and just add CSS, images, and JavaScript, if desired. The Skyliner theme (*http://drupal.org/project/skyliner*), pictured in Figure 11-2, is an example of such a theme.

Regions

Regions are the areas on your site where you can place blocks, as we did in Chapter 2 and in other places throughout this book. Drupal provides five regions by default:

- Header (header)
- Footer (footer)
- Left sidebar (left)
- Right sidebar (right)
- Content (content)

You can change this list of regions for your theme in its *.info* file. Here is an example that creates a new region, Ads, and also excludes some of the defaults, such as Header, by not defining them:

```
regions[ads] = Ads
regions[right] = Right sidebar
regions[content] = Content
regions[footer] = Footer
```

By defining just these regions in the theme, site administrators are limited in where they may place blocks on the block administration page for this theme. There will be no Header or Left sidebar for them to use. This can be very powerful when you have a very specific layout and you don't want administrators putting things in the "wrong" place.

 There's also a second step to displaying block regions, which is printing a variable for the region in your theme's *page.tpl.php* file, such as `<?php print $ads; ?>`. This command will print out all of the blocks that have been placed in that region. We'll delve into this more later in the "Creating a New Region" section.

 If you define regions in your *.info* file, then Drupal will no longer use its defaults. If you define even one region, then you must explicitly define all of them that you wish to use. For example, if you add a new "Ads" region, then you need to also define the left, right, content, header, and footer regions if you want to use them as well.

Features

Features refer to the various elements of a theme that can be toggled on and off through the theme administration interface at Administer→Site building→Themes (admin/build/themes), under the Configure tab. The following is the default list of features provided by Drupal core:

- Logo (logo)
- Site name (name)
- Site slogan (slogan)
- Mission statement (mission)
- User pictures in posts (node_user_picture)
- User pictures in comments (comment_user_picture)
- Search box (search)
- Shortcut icon (favicon)
- Primary links (primary_links)
- Secondary links (secondary_links)

If you wish to exclude a feature from the toggle list, you need to create your own feature list in the *.info* file and make sure to comment out or remove the items you don't want. The Skyliner theme has the following feature list:

```
features[] = name
features[] = slogan
features[] = mission
features[] = search
features[] = favicon
```

```
features[] = primary_links
features[] = secondary_links
```

This list does not include the Logo, User pictures in posts, or User pictures in comments features, so, for example, a site administrator cannot use a custom logo with this theme.

CSS

You can define the name and location of all of the CSS and JavaScript files for your theme in the *.info* file. If no stylesheets are added in the *.info*, Drupal will automatically find and include the *style.css* file within your theme directory. You can easily use other stylesheets in addition to *style.css* if you want. You can also override the CSS that is provided by modules in your site. By giving a theme's CSS file the same name as a module's CSS file, we tell Drupal, "Use this file, not that file," and Drupal will swap this file out for the original. An example of this would be to define *system-menus.css* in your theme, which would then override the core *system-menus.css* file in the System module's directory (*modules/system*). Here is an example of defining CSS stylesheets from the Skyliner theme's *.info* file (note that they have all been placed in a *styles* directory inside the theme's main directory):

```
stylesheets[all][] = styles/reset.css
stylesheets[all][] = styles/typography.css
stylesheets[all][] = styles/forms.css
stylesheets[all][] = styles/style.css
```

JavaScript

There is also an automatically recognized default JavaScript filename, *script.js*, that you can use for your themes. Again, you can add additional filenames to your *.info* file as well, as you can see in another example from the Skyliner theme:

```
scripts[] = skyliner.js
```

 Drupal comes with the jQuery JavaScript library (*http://jquery.com*) included in core, so you have access to all of the jQuery goodness without needing to add the library yourself.

CSS and JavaScript Optimization Settings

Because of Drupal's modular nature, even a relatively simple site can end up with many CSS and JavaScript files included on any given page. In a default Drupal 6 installation, the CSS and JavaScript tags included in the HTML of the content editing page (with no extra modules enabled) comes to *seven* CSS files and *six* JavaScript files! And this number expands quickly when installing and enabling more modules.

By visiting the Performance settings page at Administer→Site configuration→Performance (admin/settings/performance), you can enable CSS and JavaScript optimization. This option joins all of the CSS files for a given page into one optimized file with comments and extra whitespace removed. JavaScript gets a similar treatment. Instead of the 13 files that we were including originally, after optimization we now get only these 4 lines:

```
<link type="text/css" rel="stylesheet" media="all"
href="/drupal/sites/default/files/css/7f66dbf90ba0323c5d322cde426f75ed.css" />
<link type="text/css" rel="stylesheet" media="print"
href="/drupal/sites/default/files/css/bf2acfbc35fa1d13cbc410a9bdc36563.css" />
<script type="text/javascript"
src="/drupal/sites/default/files/js/45caa15f0935ad439814b66bcdf4b022.js"></script>
<script type="text/javascript">jQuery.extend(Drupal.settings,
{ "basePath": "/drupal/", "teaserCheckbox": { "edit-teaser-js": "edit-teaser-include" },
"teaser": { "edit-teaser-js": "edit-body" } });</script>
```

Obviously, there are fewer files—which require fewer hits to your server as the browser determines whether it has the correct files in its cache. This is good stuff, and highly recommended for live sites! Just be careful not to turn this option on while you're actively developing your CSS and JavaScript.

Template Files

Creating a Drupal theme with just images and CSS will work fine if Drupal's outputting the HTML markup that you need. But what happens when you want to place an extra `<div>` around the title of a node, or you want to move the user picture from the top of posts to the bottom? This is where template files come in, providing the bulk of Drupal's output markup.

Comments, nodes, blocks, and the overall page itself are all output through *template files*. Template files end with the special filename extension of *.tpl.php*. A template file is named by the item that it is controlling; for example, comments are controlled by the *comment.tpl.php* file, and the entire page is controlled by the *page.tpl.php* file.

The way in which template files map to a typical Drupal page is pictured in Figure 11-3, and the template files behind a fancier page with a bit more going on are pictured in Figure 11-4.

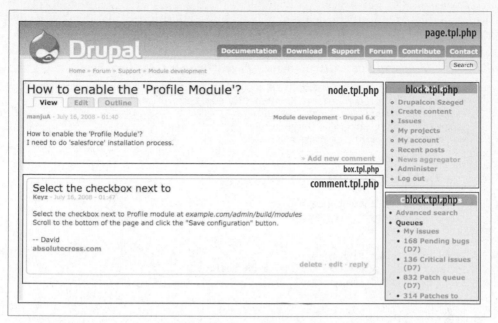

Figure 11-3. An example from Drupal.org on how a typical Drupal page is generated by template files

Figure 11-4. SpreadFirefox.com (http://www.spreadfirefox.com) uses a more complex layout, but the same template files apply

Template files are mostly made up of HTML with PHP snippets that display the dynamic parts of the page. The *page.tpl.php* file of a given theme, in particular, should look basically familiar if you've done any prior work with HTML. An excerpt from the Zen (*http://drupal.org/project/zen*) theme's *page.tpl.php* file is shown here:

```
<!DOCTYPE html PUBLIC "-//W3C//DTD XHTML 1.0
Strict//EN" "http://www.w3.org/TR/xhtml1/DTD/xhtml1-strict.dtd">
<html xmlns="http://www.w3.org/1999/xhtml"
lang="<?php print $language->language; ?>"
xml:lang="<?php print $language->language; ?>">

<head>
  <title><?php print $head_title; ?></title>
...
        <div id="content-area">
          <?php print $content; ?>
        </div>
...
<?php if ($closure_region): ?>
    <div id="closure-blocks" class="region region-closure">
      <?php print $closure_region; ?>
    </div>
  <?php endif; ?>

  <?php print $closure; ?>

</body>
</html>
```

HTML is interspersed with sections of PHP that say things like, "Print the content here," or "If there are blocks in the 'closure' region, put them in this `<div>`." Inside these sections with the `<?php ?>` tags you will notice words that begin with a `$` (dollar sign). These special PHP "words" are called *variables*. Variables are dynamic content. Though this may initially look alarming to designers without a PHP background, once you understand enough PHP to read and write what's in the example, you're suddenly empowered to do a whole lot of awesome customization in Drupal.

The template.php File

We've now had a look at the basic building blocks for themes and some of the files that make up a theme. The last, crucial piece of Drupal theming is the ability to completely override the output that Drupal gives you by default and use your own custom markup instead. This is where the fun really starts.

You may find that while the template files give you a lot of control, you can't really do much about the HTML that you are given inside those variables. You can do all the HTML editing around them that you want, but how do you crack into the variables themselves and get them to behave? The real customization of the nitty-gritty details comes in the form of the *template.php* file. This file is where master themers can really show their stuff by adding extra variables and logic to their themes. They can also override theme functions, which are specially named functions that modules use to display HTML without using a *.tpl.php* file.

The *template.php* file leaves the realm of "mostly HTML" and is instead a regular PHP file that uses functions. This file can be daunting if you aren't familiar with PHP, but if you take the time to learn enough PHP to use this file, it gives you amazing power and control over your themes. Here is a small example from the Foundation (*http://drupal.org/project/foundation*) theme's *template.php* that is creating a new variable, $authored, to be used in *node.tpl.php* and changing the default search form by removing the title:

```php
<?php
// $Id: template.php,v 1.3 2008/06/23 12:08:02 add1sun Exp $

/**
 * Override or insert PHPTemplate variables into the node templates.
 */
function foundation_preprocess_node(&$vars) {
  // Set author information line separately from the full $submitted variable.
  $vars['authored'] = t('Submitted by') .' '. $vars['name'];
}

/**
 * Override the search form (theme, not block) to remove the label.
 */
function foundation_search_theme_form($form) {
  unset($form['search_theme_form']['#title']);
  return drupal_render($form);
}
```

 Take note that the *template.php* file has an opening PHP tag (<?php) but not a closing one (?>). This is a proper coding standard in the Drupal community. Leaving the end tag in can sometimes create header errors, so leaving it out of your files is considered a general PHP best practice. You can read more about this standard at *http://drupal.org/node/545*.

We'll be covering some simple examples later on in the chapter that touch on overriding Drupal's output with the *template.php* file.

Whenever you override something in a theme, you need to let Drupal know that you have changed things. Drupal tries to be smart about performance and so it stores (caches) a lot of information to make itself faster. When you change things that have been stored away, you need to get Drupal to update them.

First, you should disable all caching on the site while working on the theme generally. You can do this by going to Administer→Site configuration→Performance (admin/settings/performance) and disabling the various caching and optimization options. In addition, when doing overrides in particular, you specifically need to wipe out the theme registry cache by clicking the "Clear cached data" button at the bottom of this same screen.

The Devel module (*http://drupal.org/project/devel*) also provides a handy block with a "Clear cache" link on it to make this common task a little easier.

A Themer's Toolbox

Before we head into the "Hands-On: Creating a Custom Theme" section, we should take a few minutes to briefly discuss some handy tools that most themers find essential to working quickly:

Text editor
When working with files in Drupal, you need to use a text editor. Text editors are plain text editors that do not add any rich text markup like bold or italic. Avoid word processors like Microsoft Word. Instead, use something like Notepad++ (*http://notepad-plus.sourceforge.net*) for Windows, TextWrangler (*http://www.barebones.com/products/textwrangler*) or Smultron (*http://smultron.sourceforge.net*) for Mac, or Kate (*http://kate-editor.org*) or gedit (*http://www.gnome.org/projects/gedit*) for Linux. It's helpful to have one that supports features such as syntax highlighting and line numbers. For more information on various editors, see *http://drupal.org/node/147789*.

Firebug (https://addons.mozilla.org/en-US/firefox/addon/1843)
This tool is the themer's best friend. It is a Firefox browser extension that allows you to hover over and select elements on your screen and immediately see the CSS that is affecting it, as well as to edit the CSS and see the results on the fly. It is also a wonderful tool for working with JavaScript and testing things out in a live browser window.

Web Developer Toolbar (https://addons.mozilla.org/en-US/firefox/addon/60)
This is also a Firefox browser extension; it provides many useful tools, including quick resizing of your browser, displaying information about all the various elements on the screen, running numerous validators (CSS, HTML, accessibility, and so on), and editing and playing with online forms.

Devel module (http://drupal.org/project/devel)
The Devel module is actually a package of modules that are a whole toolkit of handy helpers for developers (and themers). The most useful tools for themers are

the Devel-provided block that has a handy Clear cache link in it and the Devel Generate module, which can let you fill out a site with dummy user and content very quickly. It lets you see your theme interacting with content, even if the site isn't ready for real content yet.

Theme developer module (part of Devel)
This module is actually part of the main Devel module package, but it is so incredibly cool and useful that it deserves its own mention. Once enabled, Theme Developer allows you to see which elements on the page have been run through a theme function or template simply by clicking on them to get information about how they were generated and what variables are available to them.

Hands-On: Creating a Custom Theme

Let's look at how you can modify one of Drupal's themes to make it your own. There are many good themes that can act as a good "starter theme." The Drupal contributed themes repository (*http://drupal.org/project/Themes*) has several specifically designed for this purpose—the Zen theme (*http://drupal.org/project/zen*) is often recommended. For our example, we'll start with a simple core theme: Bluemarine, as pictured in Figure 11-5.

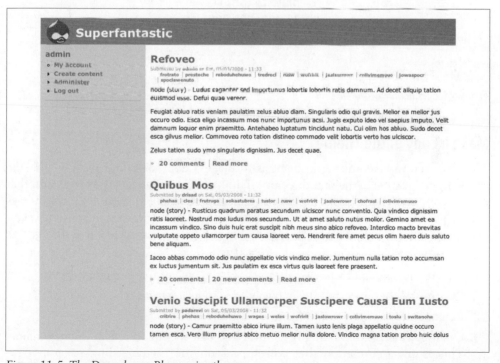

Figure 11-5. The Drupal core Bluemarine theme

Bluemarine was Drupal's default theme prior to Drupal 5. It uses a table-based layout, which is generally considered bad practice in these days of CSS-based layout techniques. However, for the purposes of our example, it makes for a simple and clean starter theme. Let's see what we can do to customize it.

Figure 11-6 shows the Bluemarine theme directory. It contains template override files for blocks, boxes, comments, nodes (all types), and the page. There are images for the default logo and a screenshot for the theme listing page. The required *.info* file is there. The main stylesheet for the theme is called *style.css* and there's another sheet called *style-rtl.css* that gets called in when Drupal is displaying right-to-left languages such as Arabic or Hebrew.

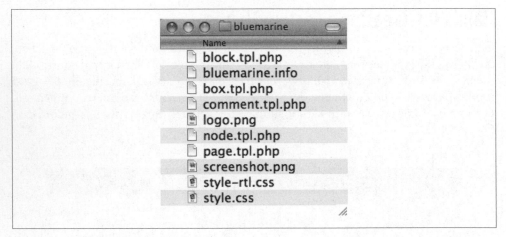

Figure 11-6. Bluemarine theme files

Make a Copy of the Theme

The first step in customizing a theme is to make a copy of it and place it into the appropriate location in the *sites* directory. Think of the *sites* directory as "the stuff that makes your site yours." All of your customizations, installed modules, and themes should go into this directory. For most sites, this will mean placing themes into *sites/all/themes*. Drupal will discover themes within subdirectories, so feel free to organize this however you like.

1. Ensure that *sites/all/themes* exists and copy the *bluemarine* directory into it.

2. Rename the new directory from *bluemarine* to *newmarine*.

3. Rename the *bluemarine.info* file to *newmarine.info*.

4. Open *newmarine.info* into a text editor and edit the file to reflect the new name. This is the information that will appear on the theme listing page in Drupal administration:

```
; $Id$
name = Newmarine
description = Table-based multi-column theme based on Bluemarine.
version = VERSION
core = 6.x
engine = phptemplate
```

 You will notice that at the top of files you download from Drupal.org there is always a line commented out that starts with $Id:, with a name and some date information that follows after. This is a special ID tag used by the version control system used by Drupal.org (CVS) to maintain all of the core and contributed code. Your custom files don't need this line on them but it doesn't hurt to have it there either. If you do ever decide to contribute your work back to the community, you will need to make sure all of your files start with that line. The empty version of this string is simply Id.

5. Visit the Drupal theme administration page (Administer→Site building→Themes (admin/build/themes), and enable the new theme by clicking the "Default" radio button next to it, as seen in Figure 11-7. Click "Save configuration" to switch the theme.

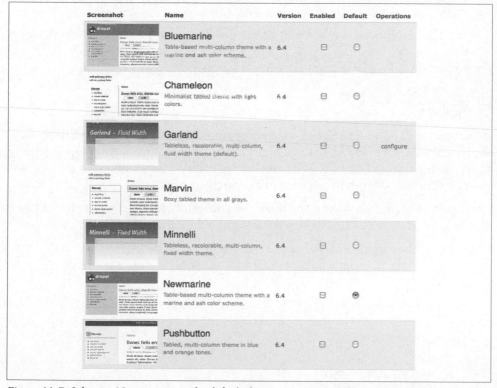

Figure 11-7. Selecting Newmarine as the default theme

You should see your new theme on the site now. Right now it looks just like Bluemarine, but we're going to change that momentarily.

The last thing we want to do before we jump into theming is get some content on the site so we can see how things are changing:

1. Go to go Administer→Site building→Modules (admin/build/modules) and enable the following module:

   • Development package

   —Devel generate

2. Go to Administer→Generate items (admin/generate) and click the "Generate categories" link. We'll make categories first so that they can be assigned to the nodes we'll make in the next step.

3. The defaults are fine for our purposes, so just click the "Do it!" button to make the categories.

4. Return to Administer→Generate items (admin/generate) and click the "Generate content" link. For this one, most of the defaults are fine, but we want to add a few things to our content.

5. In the "How many comments per node would you like to generate?" text box, enter "100," so that we can see how comments will look on the site, too.

6. We also want to use our taxonomy terms, so check off the "Add taxonomy terms to each node" box.

7. Click "Do it!" and you will have a nicely populated site to work with.

Changing CSS

Before you start editing CSS, visit the Performance page at Administer→Site configuration→Performance (admin/settings/performance) and ensure that the "Optimize CSS files" setting is set to Disabled. With this setting enabled, any edits you make to your theme's CSS files will not be reflected immediately on your site.

You can now start customizing the theme as you would like. Let's start by adding a border around content items to help them stand out on the page:

1. Open up Newmarine's *style.css* in a text editor.

2. Find the following rule (at line 232):

   ```
   .node {
     margin: .5em 0 2em; /* LTR */
   }
   ```

3. Change it as follows:

   ```
   .node {
     margin: .5em 0 2em; /* LTR */
     border: 1px dashed #ccc;
   ```

```
    padding: .5em;
}
```

4. Save the file and reload the front page of your website.

Your page will now appear with dashed lines around the nodes, as shown in Figure 11-8. If it does not, try force-refreshing your browser, typically by holding down the Shift key on the keyboard while pressing the Reload button in the browser's toolbar.

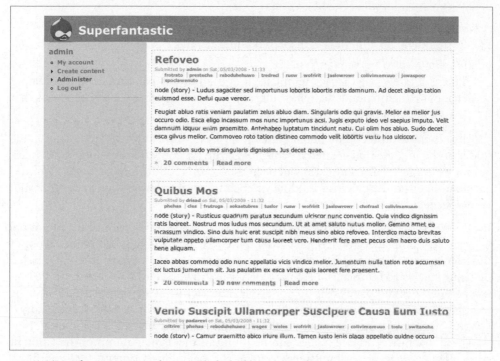

Figure 11-8. The Newmarine theme with dashed lines around nodes

So we now have a new theme set up, some dummy content to work with, and a few CSS tweaks under our belt. The next thing we'll want to look at is changing more substantive things, like the underlying HTML.

Spotlight: Template Files

The great thing about overriding the HTML in template files is how totally easy it is. All you have to do is find the default template file, copy it into your theme folder, and edit to your heart's content. Many themes start with these main Drupal core default templates:

page.tpl.php (located in modules/system)
> Controls the layout of the entire page. This isn't for the page content type; you can think of it more as the overall screen in which your content types and blocks are displayed.

node.tpl.php (located in modules/node)
> This is used for the display of each individual node.

block.tpl.php (located in modules/system)
> This is used for all of the blocks on the site.

comment.tpl.php (located in modules/comment)
> Each individual comment is displayed with this file.

box.tpl.php (located in modules/system)
> This is a rarely used legacy template. It is used in Drupal core for the container element that surrounds search results and that surrounds a list of comments that is attached to a node.

Just like the node and comment template files, you can find any other templates in the folder of the module that created it. This holds true for core and contributed modules. So, for example, forum templates will be in the forum module folder (*modules/forum*) and templates for the calendar module will be in the calendar module folder (*sites/all/ modules/calendar*).

In addition to the basic template files provided by core, there are a number of additional "suggested" templates, such as *page-front.tpl.php*, which will affect only the layout of the home page of the site. It is also possible to theme content types differently based on using suggested templates. Perhaps blog posts show the author's picture at the bottom, and stories and page posts do not display the picture at all. Content-type-specific templates use the naming scheme *node-nodetype.tpl.php*, where *nodetype* is "story," "page," "forum," "blog," or whatever the machine-readable name of your content type is. These machine-readable names can be found in the Type column of the Content types listing page at Administer→Content management→Content types (admin/ content/types), as seen in Figure 11-9.

For a list of the templates provided by core and the suggested names that you can use, see the handbook page at *http://drupal.org/node/190815*.

Hands-On: Working with Template Files

Modifying a Template File

Now let's look at customizing the *page.tpl.php* file. This is the file that defines the general HTML structure of the entire page. The theme engine and enabled modules make a number of variables available to this file, and then these variables are simply output using PHP print statements. Let's change the structure of our theme by moving

Name	Type	Description	Operations			
Book page	book	A *book page* is a page of content, organized into a collection of related entries collectively known as a *book*. A *book page* automatically displays links to adjacent pages, providing a simple navigation system for organizing and reviewing structured content.	edit	add field	manage fields	delete
Page	page	A *page*, similar in form to a *story*, is a simple method for creating and displaying information that rarely changes, such as an "About us" section of a website. By default, a *page* entry does not allow visitor comments and is not featured on the site's initial home page.	edit	add field	manage fields	delete
Story	story	A *story*, similar in form to a *page*, is ideal for creating and displaying content that informs or engages website visitors. Press releases, site announcements, and informal blog-like entries may all be created with a *story* entry. By default, a *story* entry is automatically featured on the site's initial home page, and provides the ability to post comments.	edit	add field	manage fields	delete

Figure 11-9. The machine-readable names of content types, which can be used to name custom template files

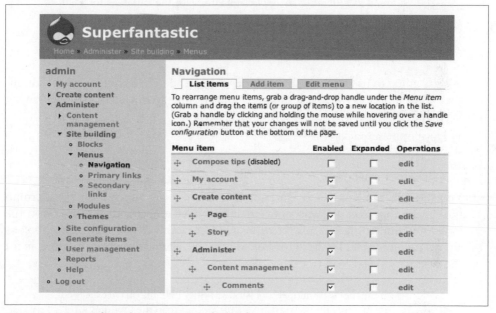

Figure 11-10. Breadcrumbs appearing in the header

the breadcrumb output up into the header region of the page. We want our breadcrumbs to look like those shown in Figure 11-10.

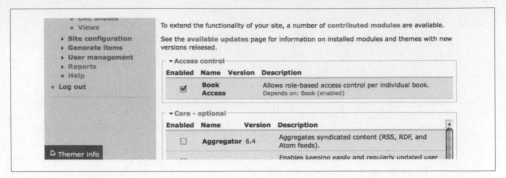

Figure 11-11. The Themer info checkbox appears after enabling the Theme developer module

 There are many variables available to the templates, and not all of them are used in the themes provided by Drupal core. A list of variables can be found at *http://drupal.org/phptemplate*, with the variables for each template listed under the appropriate section; however, modules can add and alter this list, so a better way to discover these variables is to use the Devel Themer module, which we'll discuss in a moment.

1. We are going to use the Theme developer module to help us out, so go to Administer→Site building→Modules (admin/build/modules) and enable the following modules:
   - Development package
     —Devel
     —Theme developer

2. You should still be on the module administration page, which has a breadcrumb trail at the top. You will also notice that you have a new translucent box in the lower lefthand corner of your browser window with a *Themer info* checkbox as shown in Figure 11-11. Check the box to turn the Theme developer module on for the page.

 If the theme developer tool isn't working, PHP may have exceeded its memory limit. Try visiting a page other than the modules form, which requires a lot of memory to display, especially combined with the theme developer tool (which also takes up a lot of memory). Disable the theme developer tool when not using it.

3. Once you check the box, a new gray box will appear in the upper-right corner of your browser, titled Drupal Themer Information. As the box states, "Click on any element to see information about the Drupal theme function or template that created it." Go ahead and hover over the breadcrumb on the page. You should see a red outline appear around it. Once you see that red outline around it, click the page

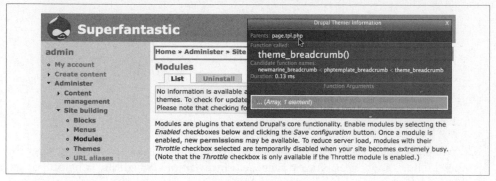

Figure 11-12. Theme Developer information for the breadcrumbs

to display the information for it. The red outline will turn to gray around your selection and you should see something like Figure 11-12.

4. The information that we want is which template file prints this element to the page. If you look at the first section of the Drupal Themer Information box, you will see a line that says "Parents: page.tpl.php." So our breadcrumb is being printed from *page.tpl.php*.

5. Open up the *page.tpl.php* file in your Newmarine theme folder and go to about line 29, where the `$header` variable is printed. Down at line 42 is the `$breadcrumb` variable we want to move:

```
29  <tr>
30    <td colspan="2"><div><?php print $header ?></div></td>
31  </tr>
32</table>
33
34<table border="0" cellpadding="0" cellspacing="0" id="content">
35  <tr>
36    <?php if ($left) { ?><td id="sidebar-left">
37      <?php print $left ?>
38    </td><?php } ?>
39    <td valign="top">
40      <?php if ($mission) { ?><div id="mission"><?php print $mission ?></div>
      <?php } ?>
41    <div id="main">
42      <?php print $breadcrumb ?>
43      <h1 class="title"><?php print $title ?></h1>
```

6. Now let's modify the file to output the breadcrumbs immediately after the header, by removing line 42 and restoring it as a modification to line 30 as follows:

```
29  <tr>
30    <td colspan="2"><div><?php print $header ?><?php print $breadcrumb ?>
      </div></td>
31  </tr>
32</table>
33
34<table border="0" cellpadding="0" cellspacing="0" id="content">
```

```
35   <tr>
36     <?php if ($left) { ?><td id="sidebar-left">
37       <?php print $left ?>
38     </td><?php } ?>
39     <td valign="top">
40       <?php if ($mission) { ?><div id="mission"><?php print $mission ?>
         </div><?php } ?>
41       <div id="main">
42
43         <h1 class="title"><?php print $title ?></h1>
```

7. Save the file when you are done.

8. Reload the page; the breadcrumbs should now appear in the header region of the page. They show up as blue on blue, so a little bit of CSS editing is helpful to get them to contrast with the background better.

9. Find the following rule on line 171 in *style.css*:

```
.breadcrumb {
  margin-bottom: .5em;
}
```

10. And replace it with the following:

```
.breadcrumb {
  margin-left: 2em;
}
.breadcrumb a {
  color: #ccc;
  font-weight: normal;
}
```

We now have our breadcrumbs in the header and styled so that they are legible.

Figure 11-13. Submission information and taxonomy moved to the bottom of content

Theming Specific Content Types

To see how creating new templates for specific content types works, we'll create a template file that affects only Story nodes. We want to display post author submission information and taxonomy terms (categories) below the content (see Figure 11-13).

1. Copy the *node.tpl.php* from your *newmarine* directory into a new file called *node-story.tpl.php*.

2. Open *node-story.tpl.php* in a text editor. It should appear similar to the following:

```php
<?php
// $Id: node.tpl.php,v 1.7 2007/08/07 08:39:36 goba Exp $
?>
<div class="node<?php if ($sticky) { print " sticky"; } ?><?php if (!$status)
{ print " node-unpublished"; } ?>">
<?php if ($picture) {
    print $picture;
    }?>
<?php if ($page == 0) { ?><h2 class="title"><a href="<?php print $node_url?>">
<?php print $title?></a></h2><?php }; ?>
<span class="submitted"><?php print $submitted?></span>
<div class="taxonomy"><?php print $terms?></div>
<div class="content"><?php print $content?></div>
<?php if ($links) { ?><div class="links">&raquo;
```

```
<?php print $links?></div><?php }; ?>
</div>
```

3. Now let's move the submitted and taxonomy terms after the main content of the node:

```
<?php
// $Id: node.tpl.php,v 1.7 2007/08/07 08:39:36 goba Exp $
?>
<div class="node<?php if ($sticky) { print " sticky"; } ?><?php if (!$status)
{ print " node-unpublished"; } ?>">
<?php if ($picture) {
    print $picture;
    }?>
<?php if ($page == 0) { ?><h2 class="title"><a href="<?php print $node_url?>">
<?php print $title?></a></h2><?php }; ?>
<div class="content"><?php print $content?></div>
<span class="submitted"><?php print $submitted?></span>
<div class="taxonomy"><?php print $terms?></div>
<?php if ($links) { ?><div class="links">&raquo;
<?php print $links?></div><?php }; ?>
</div>
```

And just like that, we are able to control how Drupal puts these items on the page by default.

Overriding a Module's Template File

Now, let's demonstrate how to override a module's default template files, using Comment module's *comment-wrapper.tpl.php* file as an example. This file doesn't do much more than wrap a `div` around the comments output. Let's add the text "Comments:" to this file so that it appears above any comments on node pages. We're aiming to achieve what is shown in Figure 11-14.

Figure 11-14. Comments displayed with "Comments:" above

The steps are:

1. Find the file at *modules/comment/comment-wrapper.tpl.php* and copy it into our theme directory at *sites/all/themes/custom/newmarine*. Be sure to copy (not move) the file, because the original file will be needed if we ever switch to another theme.

2. Open the new file from your theme directory into your text editor. It contains a lot of comments explaining the available variables:

```php
<?php
// $Id: comment-wrapper.tpl.php,v 1.2 2007/08/07 08:39:35 goba Exp $

/**
 * @file comment-wrapper.tpl.php
 * Default theme implementation to wrap comments.
 *
 * Available variables:
 * - $content: All comments for a given page. Also contains sorting controls
 *   and comment forms if the site is configured for it.
 *
 * The following variables are provided for contextual information.
 * - $node: Node object the comments are attached to.
 * The constants below the variables show the possible values and should be
 * used for comparison.
 * - $display_mode
 *    - COMMENT_MODE_FLAT_COLLAPSED
 *    - COMMENT_MODE_FLAT_EXPANDED
```

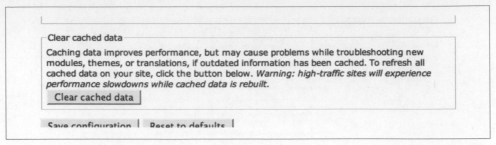

Figure 11-15. The "Clear cached data" button, which should be used if theme changes don't immediately appear

```
*    - COMMENT_MODE_THREADED_COLLAPSED
*    - COMMENT_MODE_THREADED_EXPANDED
* - $display_order
*    - COMMENT_ORDER_NEWEST_FIRST
*    - COMMENT_ORDER_OLDEST_FIRST
* - $comment_controls_state
*    - COMMENT_CONTROLS_ABOVE
*    - COMMENT_CONTROLS_BELOW
*    - COMMENT_CONTROLS_ABOVE_BELOW
*    - COMMENT_CONTROLS_HIDDEN
*
* @see template_preprocess_comment_wrapper()
* @see theme_comment_wrapper()
*/
?>
<div id="comments">
<?php print $content; ?>
</div>
```

3. Add a new `<h2>` element containing `Comments:`. In our modified example here, we've removed the comments for brevity, but it won't hurt to leave them in. We are also wrapping this text in the `t()` function so that it is accessible to Drupal's language translation system if needed:

```
<div id="comments">
<h2 class="title"><?php print t('Comments:'); ?></h2>
<?php print $content; ?>
</div>
```

4. Remember that in order to get Drupal to recognize this new template, we need to refresh the theme registry, by visiting Administer→Site configuration→Performance (admin/settings/performance) and clicking the "Clear cached data" button shown in Figure 11-15.

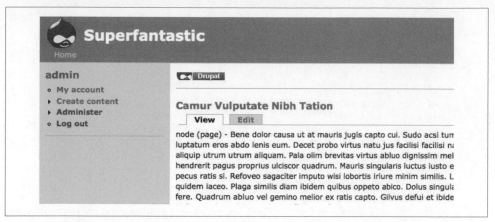

Figure 11-16. The Powered by Drupal block in a new custom region placed above the content

Creating a New Region

Drupal provides several default regions, as we've discussed. The special "content" region handles blocks in an unexpected way: when you place a block in that region, instead of going above the regular content, it actually goes *underneath*. There is no way, by default, to add a block on top of your main content area. Well, we have the power of our *.info* and template files to work with, so let's add a new region so we can put things right where we want them. Figure 11-16 shows a site with a region that has the Powered by Drupal block in it, placed above the content.

1. First, we need to let Drupal know about our region. Open up *newmarine.info* again and we will define our regions. Remember that in order to add a new region, we need to define *all* of the regions we want, including the default ones. Add the following lines to the end of the file:

   ```
   regions[header] = Header
   regions[left] = Left sidebar
   regions[right] = Right sidebar
   regions[content_top] = Content Top
   regions[content] = Content
   regions[footer] = Footer
   ```

2. Next, we will need to clear the theme cache to make sure Drupal sees the changes we made. Go to Administer→Site configuration→Performance, and click the "Clear cache" button.

3. Go to Administer→Site building→Blocks (admin/build/block) and when you look at the regions listed, you will see a new one named "Content Top" that we can put our blocks into. Go ahead and drag the "Powered by Drupal" block from the Footer region into the Content Top region and click the "Save blocks" button.

4. You will see that the block has disappeared altogether. It isn't in the footer anymore, and although the Content Top region exists, Drupal doesn't know where to

display it yet. We need to add the new region to the template file, so open up newmarine's *page.tpl.php*.

5. We want to add this in the top of the "main" div, above the existing content region, so add the line as shown here at line 42:

```
41      <div id="main">
42        <?php print $content_top; ?>
43        <h1 class="title"><?php print $title ?></h1>
44        <div class="tabs"><?php print $tabs ?></div>
45        <?php if ($show_messages) { print $messages; } ?>
46        <?php print $help ?>
47        <?php print $content; ?>
48        <?php print $feed_icons; ?>
49      </div>
```

6. Save the file and refresh your site. You should see the "Powered by Drupal" logo above your content now.

Spotlight: Advanced Overrides

To really get in and affect things in the dynamic realm, you will need to move away from HTML and CSS, and begin using PHP; only PHP can modify the deepest layers of Drupal. The following two sections discuss how to override variables and functions in the theme's *template.php* file. You should have a basic understanding of what PHP variables and functions are in order to get the most out of this part of the chapter.

There's much more information available about these kinds of advanced overrides available in the Drupal 6 theming guide at *http://drupal.org/node/173880*.

Template Variables

Those little bits of dynamic content that you are using in your template files are really handy—until they annoy you by not quite producing exactly the output that you want. The variables that Drupal creates by default, like `$site_name` and `$submitted`, are meant to be a baseline that will fit a lot of people's needs. Like everything else in the theme system, though, you have the power to crack them open and change them. Not only can you override existing variables, but you can also create your own brand-new variables.

All variables that go out to a template file are first passed through a special kind of function, called a `preprocess` function. You can add your own `preprocess` function to your *template.php* file and get the last shot at the variables before they head out to the template. To keep things tidy, you can use one `preprocess` function per template; for example, you can create a `mytheme_preprocess_page` function to affect variables to be used in your *page.tpl.php* file. With this function, you can define, or redefine, any variable. For instance, if you wanted to make a new variable that printed out a random number between 1 and 100, you could add this to *template.php*:

```
function mytheme_preprocess_page(&$vars) {
  $vars['random_number'] = rand(1, 100);
}
```

Then (after clearing the Drupal cache), you can print out that variable out in your *page.tpl.php* file just like any other variable:

```
<?php print $random_number; ?>
```

You use the exact same procedure to override an existing variable. When you assign a variable name that is the same as the one Drupal is already using, yours will take precedence. We'll walk through this a bit more and show you how to override the $submit ted variable in the hands-on section.

Theme Functions

Much of Drupal's HTML output is easily accessible in template files. But what about something like the page's "breadcrumb trail," which shows the hierarchy to the current page? Unfortunately, there's no *breadcrumb.tpl.php* file. In this situation, you need to dig a little bit deeper, to the place where remaining markup in Drupal is initially defined: *theme functions*.

Theme functions are regular PHP functions located in Drupal's code whose names begin with theme_. Every element on the page that is not in a template file is run through a theme function, such as the theme_breadcrumb() function:

```
function theme_breadcrumb($breadcrumb) {
  if (!empty($breadcrumb)) {
    return '<div class="breadcrumb">'. implode(' » ', $breadcrumb) .'</div>';
  }
}
```

In its current state, this function will print out the breadcrumb trail on a page, such as Home » Administer » Site building » Themes. But what if we decide that we'd rather the breadcrumb be printed as Home::Administer::Site building::Themes, with double-colons instead? No problem! We'll just pop open *theme.inc* and change it there, right? Wrong!

The proper way to handle overriding theme functions is by simply copying the function into your *template.php* file and naming it according to Drupal's naming conventions so that it's recognized. Then you can modify it however you like. Figure 11-17 illustrates the logic Drupal uses to determine which function to call in order to display an element.

Drupal will step through a hierarchy of names to determine which version of the function it should finally use. It checks to see which identifier is used at the beginning of the function name. The three possibilities, in increasing specificity, are theme, *enginename*, and *themename*, where *enginename* is the name of the templating system in use (PHPTemplate is what most Drupal themes use) and *themename* is literally the name of the theme itself as defined by the name of your *.info* file. Drupal searches for the most specific name first (*themename*), and then continues to search down the list if it can't

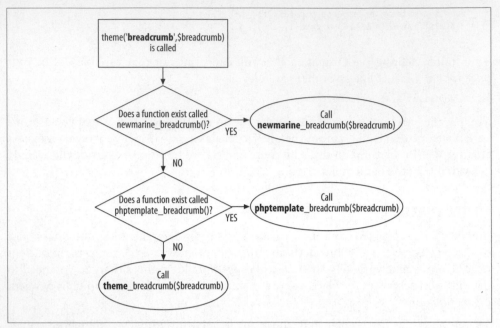

Figure 11-17. Drupal's method of determining which theme function to call

find anything. It will use the first name that it finds. This means that if you want to use your own version of a function in your theme, you just need to name the function correctly and Drupal will use your version instead of the original function.

So, in this example, `theme_breadcrumb()` would become `newmarine_breadcrumb()`. We'll do just this in the following section, "Hands-On: Using template.php for Overrides," with a simple example. You can also find more information on theme functions in the Drupal handbook at *http://drupal.org/node/11811*.

Drupal's theme() Function

One important thing to note about theme functions is that they are never called directly. They are instead called through a clearinghouse function called `theme()`. So even though a module may define a function such as `theme_username()`, when the module needs to output its code, it would call `theme('username')` instead. The `theme()` function is what makes this system of overrides possible.

Hands-On: Using template.php for Overrides

Overriding a Template Variable

Drupal gives us lots of nice variables to use, but they don't always look the way we prefer. A common item that many people wish they could change is the "Submitted by..." line, which prints out the author name and date that a node was created. You can turn this display off and on in the theme configuration screen at Administer→Site building→Themes (admin/build/themes), under the Configure tab (admin/build/themes/settings), but you can't change what information is actually printed out when the display is on. We're going to change this line to instead print out "Posted on" followed by the date, as shown in Figure 11-18.

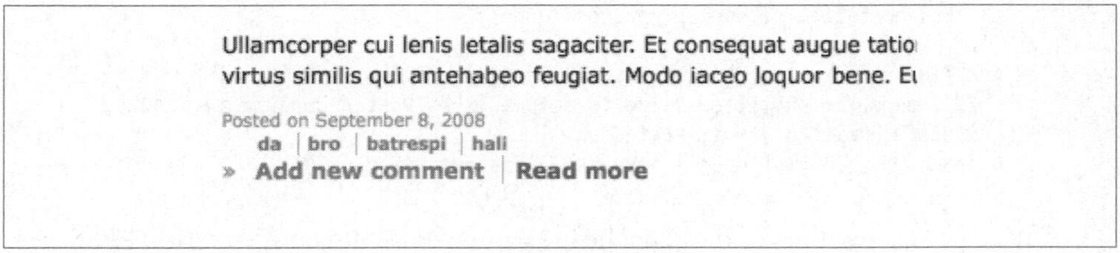

Figure 11-18. Changing the text of the "Submitted by..." line to "Posted on..."

One important piece that we need in order to modify this is a *template.php* file. As our Newmarine theme doesn't have a *template.php* file in it yet, we'll create that as well to accomplish our task:

1. If we go to a node that has submitted information showing and do the same Drupal Themer Information trick that we did back when we moved the $breadcrumb variable, we can find out what the parent template for that "Submitted by..." line is. You will see that its parent is the *node.tpl.php* file. If you open up that file (or *node-story.tpl.php* if you completed the hands-on example in the earlier section "Theming Specific Content Types"), we can see that the $submitted variable is being printed there to produce that output as highlighted below (remember we just moved this line earlier, along with the taxonomy terms):

   ```
   <?php if ($page == 0) { ?><h2 class="title"><a href=
   "<?php print $node_url?>"><?php print $title?></a></h2><?php }; ?>
   <div class="content"><?php print $content?></div>
   <span class="submitted"><?php print $submitted?></span>
   <div class="taxonomy"><?php print $terms?></div>
   ```

2. To change this, we can override it in our *template.php* file. But Newmarine doesn't have a *template.php* file yet. So let's create one and put it in our *newmarine* folder, along with our other theme files.

3. Once we have the *template.php* file created, we need to add a new preprocess function to intercept the variable we wish to change. Add the following code to your *template.php* file:

```php
<?php
// $Id:$

/**
 * Implementation of hook_preprocess_node().
 */
function newmarine_preprocess_node(&$vars) {

}
```

4. Now we need to actually override the variable, by adding it inside the function and then putting our own value into it:

```php
<?php
// $Id:$

/**
 * Implementation of hook_preprocess_node().
 */
function newmarine_preprocess_node(&$vars) {
  // Change the submitted value to output like "Posted on June 12, 2008".
  $vars['submitted'] = t('Posted on ') .
  format_date($vars['node']->created, 'custom', 'F j, Y');
}
```

5. Once again, clear the good old cache at Administer→Site configuration→Performance (admin/settings/performance).

6. When you reload the page, you should see our new format for the submitted date.

Overriding a Theme Function

Overriding a theme function is basically as simple as copying and pasting the appropriate theme function into your theme's *template.php* file. The difficult part is usually *finding* the theme function. We are going to change the site's breadcrumb so that it doesn't print out the breadcrumbs separated by » but instead by :: (double colon), to look like those in Figure 11-19.

Figure 11-19. The breadcrumb trail as output by our newmarine_breadcrumb() function

We'll use our nifty Devel Themer Information tool to help us again, so go to a page with a breadcrumb trail showing. Something like Administer→Site building (admin/build) should work fine. Follow these steps:

1. Turn on the *Themer info* by checking the box. Now you can hover over the breadcrumb and then click to display the info in the Drupal Themer Information box.

2. This time, instead of looking at the "Parents info," we want to look at the "Function called:" section. It should say `theme_breadcrumb()` in big letters, as shown in Figure 11-20.

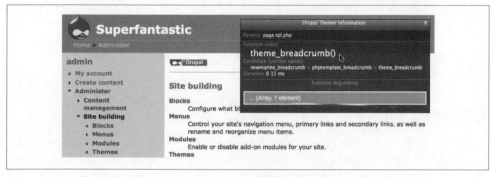

Figure 11-20. Theme Developer shows us the function being used for the breadcrumbs

3. Now we know which function is creating the breadcrumbs, so we can go grab a copy of it to work with. Open up *includes/theme.inc* and search for `theme_bread crumb`. Copy the entire `theme_breadcrumb` function. The function basically just takes an array of HTML links and uses PHP's `implode()` function to concatenate the values using the » character, wrapping this in a `<div>` with the class of "breadcrumb."

4. Open your *template.php* file, and paste the function in. Rename it to `newmarine_breadcrumb`, as shown:

```
/**
 * Return a themed breadcrumb trail.
 *
 * @param $breadcrumb
 *   An array containing the breadcrumb links.
 * @return a string containing the breadcrumb output.
 */
function newmarine_breadcrumb($breadcrumb) {
  if (!empty($breadcrumb)) {
    return '<div class="breadcrumb">'. implode(' » ', $breadcrumb) .'</div>';
  }
}
```

If you forget to rename the function, when you try to use it on the site you will get a PHP error like this: "Fatal error: Cannot redeclare theme_breadcrumb()." Don't panic! Drupal core is already using the `theme_breadcrumb` function name, so you can't use it as well. Just go back to the *template.php* file and make sure to change the function name to use your theme's name at the beginning. Reload the screen and your site will return.

5. Now we just need to change the » to a double colon (::), as shown here:

```
function newmarine_breadcrumb($breadcrumb) {
  if (!empty($breadcrumb)) {
    return '<div class="breadcrumb">'. implode(' :: ', $breadcrumb) .'</div>';
  }
}
```

6. Clear the cache and refresh the screen. Our breadcrumbs now look just the way we want them to.

Taking It Further

A little bit of PHP knowledge can take you a long way. There is a whole section of the handbook at *http://drupal.org/handbook/customization/snippets* that contains handy bits of code that you can add to your site to accomplish various tasks. These are easy ways to tweak your site to be just the way you need it.

Many snippets involve copy/pasting PHP into things like blocks or nodes. To accomplish this, you need to enable the PHP Filter module, included with Drupal core. Be *very* careful about who has access to use this filter; ideally, it should be User 1 and no one else. For more on filter system security, see Chapter 2.

Snippets in the handbook are user-submitted; that is, anyone with a Drupal.org account can add a snippet. They are not reviewed or moderated—use them at your own risk! You should always read snippets over to make sure nothing looks out of the ordinary, test them out first, and give them your own security review following the security practices at *http://drupal.org/writing-secure-code*.

There are snippets of code under several categories. The two sections most used are the Theme snippets (*http://drupal.org/node/45471*) and the PHP snippets (*http://drupal .org/handbook/customization/php-snippets*). Theme snippets use the methods outlined in this chapter to provide short pieces of code that can help customize the look and feel of your site. The PHP snippet section is further broken down—following is a quick list of the important sections:

Mini modules

These are very simple modules that may be copied and pasted to accomplish a particular task. There are instructions for using mini modules at *http://drupal.org/node/70903*.

PHP block snippets

These snippets create custom blocks using the PHP filter module; they allow you to create your own dynamic blocks and place them wherever you like in your site.

PHP block visibility settings

In contrast to the block "content" snippets listed previously, these snippets control when your blocks will appear to visitors. The basic block configuration allows you to use checkboxes for limiting visibility by role and mark specific pages on which you wish the block to appear. These snippets use a wider range of criteria to give you more control over visibility.

PHP page snippets

These are used when you set a content type to use the PHP filter and then create a dynamic node. Generally, these are discouraged—if you truly need custom, dynamic pages then you should take the extra step to create a module in the mini module fashion. They are easy to create and you should limit the use of the PHP filter on your site due to security concerns.

Summary

What we've covered here is really just the tip of the iceberg in terms of things that can be done in your theme, but we've exposed you to all of the basic concepts. We've covered how to alter CSS for your theme; how to change the page structure and node content structure; and how to override template files, variables, and theme functions. Hopefully, these exercises gave you an idea of the power of Drupal's theming system. There are many more ways in which themes can alter Drupal's output and set up rules for how content and pages are structured based on the area of the site in which they appear—or really, on any criteria at all.

More information on theming can be found at *http://drupal.org/theme-guide*, and several *commercial* books dedicated to Drupal theming are available if you want to continue down the path to becoming a theming ninja.

Drupal's theme layer attempts to be supremely flexible, allowing knowledgeable themers to alter all aspects of the page in any way they would like. Yet it is just a set of tools. Like web design itself, Drupal theming is limited only by the creativity and skills of those who are creating and implementing the theme. In the right hands, Drupal can make websites as beautiful and functional as anyone can imagine.

References

Here are the themes and modules we referenced in this chapter:

- Bluemarine theme: core
- Devel module: *http://drupal.org/project/devel*
- Foundation theme: *http://drupal.org/project/foundation*
- Skyliner theme: *http://drupal.org/project/skyliner*
- Zen theme: *http://drupal.org/project/zen*

Here are Drupal.org resources we referenced in this chapter:

- Default templates and suggestions: *http://drupal.org/node/190815*
- Drupal development resources: *http://drupal.org/node/147789*
- Drupal theme guide: *http://drupal.org/theme-guide*
- Drupal contributed themes: *http://drupal.org/project/Themes*
- Drupal contributed theme engines: *http://drupal.org/project/Theme+Engines*
- Overriding theme functions: *http://drupal.org/node/11811*
- PHP tag coding standard: *http://drupal.org/node/545*
- PHPTemplate variables: *http://drupal.org/phptemplate*
- Secure code: *http://drupal.org/writing-secure-code*
- Snippets: *http://drupal.org/handbook/customization/snippets*
- PHP Snippets: *http://drupal.org/handbook/customization/php-snippets*
- Theme Snippets: *http://drupal.org/node/45471*
- Updating themes: *http://drupal.org/update/theme*

Here are external resources we referenced in this chapter:

- Firebug: *https://addons.mozilla.org/en-US/firefox/addon/1843*
- gedit: *http://www.gnome.org/projects/gedit*
- jQuery: *http://jquery.com*
- Kate: *http://kate-editor.org*
- Notepad++: *http://notepad-plus.sourceforge.net*
- Smultron: *http://smultron.sourceforge.net*
- TextWrangler: *http://www.barebones.com/products/textwrangler*
- Web developer toolbar: *https://addons.mozilla.org/en-US/firefox/addon/60*
- W3Schools: *http://w3schools.com*

Installing and Upgrading Drupal

The first step to using Drupal, of course, is to actually get the software and install it. Drupal comes with an installation script that will walk you through a few screens to gather information and then set up your database and create your site settings file for you. We'll look at everything you need to make that process run smoothly; you'll find that installing Drupal is quick and painless once some basic requirements are in place.

Once you have Drupal up and running, it's important to keep your site up-to-date. New releases of contributed modules and Drupal core come out periodically to address critical security fixes, and it's important to stay on top of updates as they are released. We'll take a look at Drupal 6's built-in Update Status module, which will notify you of updates available for your site, and we'll talk about the steps required to update both individual modules and the Drupal core itself from one version to another.

 You will notice that many people (and even Drupal core's documentation) use the terms "updating" and "upgrading" interchangeably. They both refer to replacing existing code with newer code.

Before You Begin Installation

Prior to installing Drupal, it's important to make sure that you can actually do so, and understand a bit about how Drupal is structured. This section provides a checklist of Drupal's requirements, and also highlights important things in the Drupal file structure that are worth knowing before diving into the installation process.

Gathering Requirements

It's important to have a few things ready prior to installing Drupal. A full list of requirements is available at *http://drupal.org/requirements*. Use the following as a basic checklist prior to installing Drupal:

1. Ensure access to a web host or local development environment with the following:

    a. A *web server*, such as Apache (*http://httpd.apache.org*), which handles serving up Drupal's pages to the browser. Having access to Apache's *mod rewrite* extension also allows you to use Drupal's "Clean URLs" feature, which transforms URLs like *http://www.example.com/index.php?q=contact* to *http://www.example.com/contact*.

    b. PHP (*http://php.net*), the dynamic scripting language that powers Drupal. Drupal 6 requires at least PHP version 4.3.5, although PHP 5.2 or higher is recommended. The requirements page at Drupal.org has more information on required and recommended PHP extensions, most of which are enabled in PHP by default.

    c. A *database server*, such as MySQL (*http://mysql.com*), where Drupal will store all of the content, data, and settings that it needs in order to function.

     This book assumes that you are using Apache and MySQL. For additional help and support with other web and database servers, see *http://drupal.org/getting-started/6/install*.

2. Write down the following information from your web host:

    a. Your (S)FTP or SSH username and password, so you can put Drupal's files into place.

    b. Your database server's details, including username, password, and database name, so that Drupal can connect to the database. Some web hosts also require additional information to access the database, such as specifying a remote hostname or a specific database port.

3. Before you start installing Drupal, you also need a database to which it can be installed; Drupal doesn't create the database for you, as this normally requires "elevated" permissions on a server. Drupal can be installed either in its own separate database, or alongside other applications in a single database using table prefixes, but it's generally better if it has its own dedicated database. Check with your hosting provider or system administrator if you need information on how to create a new database, and jot down its name for later. Also, make sure you have the database username and password handy too.

     For development purposes, you may find it easier to have your web environment installed locally to make your changes prior to uploading them to their final locations. There are several free programs that are more or less a "drop in and go" solution, including XAMPP (*http://www.apachefriends.org/en/xampp.html*) on Windows and Linux, WampServer (*http://www.wampserver.com*) on Windows, or MAMP (*http://mamp.info/en/download.html*) on Macintosh.

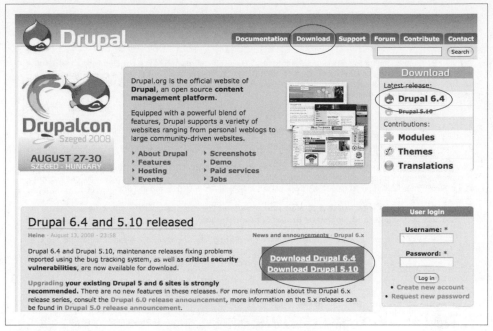

Figure A-1. Download links on the Drupal.org website

Once you have checked to make sure you have everything, you're ready to begin.

Downloading Drupal

The first step before installation is to actually acquire the Drupal code. You can use the Drupal source code provided at *http://usingdrupal.com/source_code*, or you can download it directly from Drupal.org. Here are the steps to get it from Drupal.org:

1. Go to *http://drupal.org* and you will see several links to download Drupal. They are all marked in Figure A-1. Click on the Download tab in the upper-right corner of the screen.

2. The following page lists all of the types of projects you can download: modules, themes, translations, and so on. Click the "Drupal project" link to get to the Drupal core's page.

3. The release table, shown in Figure A-2, lists the available versions in order from newest to oldest. Unless you are helping with development, you only want to download those versions that are marked as Recommended. These are referred to as "stable releases." To use the examples in this book, click the Download link for the version listed as "Recommended for 6.x."

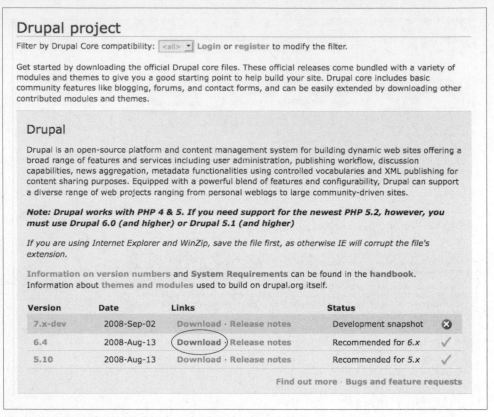

Figure A-2. Drupal versions listed on the download page

4. Drupal files are packaged using the tar program and compressed with gzip. This gives the file an extension of *tar.gz*. These files behave similarly to "zipped" files. Save the file and then extract the files using your favorite extraction application.

5. Place the extracted files on your web server using an (S)FTP program, or by logging in via shell access and downloading and extracting the files directly on the server.

Drupal's Files and Directories

Now that you have downloaded Drupal, you should take a few moments to open it up and take a look around. Getting familiar with the basic structure and locating important files and directories can take some of the mystery out of how all of this works. When you open up the Drupal folder, you will see the files structured as shown in Figure A-3.

The important pieces that we'll be covering here are the installation and update files, along with the *sites* directory. The *install.php* and *update.php* files are the two scripts that actually do the work according to their respective names. Because they are located in the top-level folder, also called the Drupal root directory, you can access them

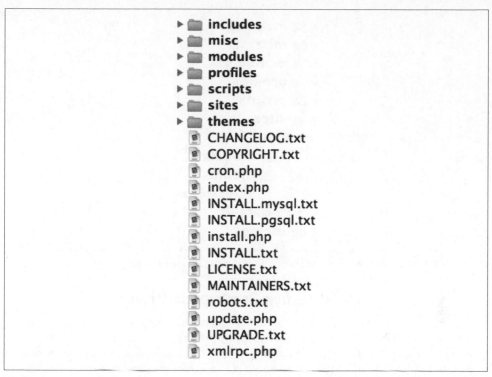

- ▸ includes
- ▸ misc
- ▸ modules
- ▸ profiles
- ▸ scripts
- ▸ sites
- ▸ themes
-    CHANGELOG.txt
-    COPYRIGHT.txt
-    cron.php
-    index.php
-    INSTALL.mysql.txt
-    INSTALL.pgsql.txt
-    install.php
-    INSTALL.txt
-    LICENSE.txt
-    MAINTAINERS.txt
-    robots.txt
-    update.php
-    UPGRADE.txt
-    xmlrpc.php

Figure A-3. Drupal's file structure

directly in your browser's address bar by typing in something like *http://example.com/ install.php*. In addition to the scripts themselves, there are also two text files, one for each operation: *INSTALL.txt* and *UPGRADE.txt*. These files contain instructions on how to use the scripts, which we'll also be covering in this appendix.

Most first-time Drupal administrators will take a look at the directories in Figure A-3 and place contributed and custom modules and themes respectively into the *modules* and *themes* directories in the Drupal root. That is where Drupal keeps the core modules and themes, so it only makes sense, right? Placing your files there will work, and Drupal will recognize them; however, this becomes a problem when you first attempt to update to the next security release—overwriting these directories with the new core versions will destroy any modifications that you have made. The best practice is to keep all of a site's contributed and custom code inside the *sites* directory. Unless you are running a complex multisite installation (see the sidebar on this subject), this means that you should create new *modules* and *themes* directories inside of the *sites/all* directory, and place your contributed and custom code there, as in Figure A-4. This way, all of the files that are particular to your site are in one tidy location rather than all mixed up together with the core files. This makes it *much* easier to work with when performing upgrades.

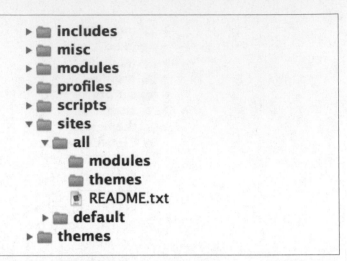

Figure A-4. Contributed modules and themes go under the sites/all directory

---

Multiple Sites from One Drupal Installation

For more advanced setups, one of Drupal's most powerful features is the ability to run multiple Drupal websites off of the same single set of files. This is referred to as Drupal's multisite capability. The example websites at *http://www.usingdrupal.com* use this feature in order to run off of the very same source code files that readers can use on their own computers.

How does it work? On the Apache side of things, a virtual host entry is set up in *httpd.conf* for each subdomain to point to the same set of Drupal files, like so:

```
<VirtualHost *>
  ServerName usingdrupal.com
  ServerAlias *.usingdrupal.com www.usingdrupal.com
  DocumentRoot /home/www/public_html
</VirtualHost>
```

Then, on the Drupal side of things, we create a new folder within the sites directory for each subsite, each with its own *settings.php* file and *files* directory. You would end up with the settings being located at *sites/jumpstart.usingdrupal.com/settings.php*. When a browser hits a URL like *http://jumpstart.usingdrupal.com*, Drupal searches through the *sites* folder for the entry that matches best, then loads its settings file.

The multisite feature is not limited to just subsite relationships like this, however. Completely different websites can also be shared, each with modules and themes specific to it. You can even do trickier setups like sharing database tables among the various sites to have a single sign-on or searching across content on all websites.

For more information about Drupal's multisite feature, consult the documentation on Drupal.org at *http://drupal.org/node/43816*.

Installing Drupal

Once you have met all of the requirements and gathered the information you need, you can get down to the installation. These instructions assume that you have already created your database, downloaded Drupal, and placed the extracted files on your web server:

1. Set Drupal up to create your settings for you. Within Drupal, copy *sites/default/default.settings.php* to *sites/default/settings.php*—that is, without the *default.* at the beginning of the filename. You will also need to make sure that the new *settings.php* file is writable, such as with the command `chmod 666 or chmod a+w sites/default/settings.php`. Your web host should have more information on how to make files writable in their environment. Also see the documentation in the Drupal handbook under *http://drupal.org/node/202483*.

> Make sure that you *copy* the file, not simply rename it. Drupal needs both files to exist in order to create your settings file for you properly.

2. Now you can navigate to *http://www.example.com/install.php* to begin the installation process.

3. The first page of the installation allows you to choose a language, as shown in Figure A-5. By default, the only language available is English. However, you may also download other translations and install Drupal in your language of choice. Chapter 8 has more information on installing and configuring multilingual sites. Go ahead and click the Install Drupal in English link.

> The next screen will initially check for correct permissions before letting you proceed. You may need to change permissions on the parent *sites* directory, depending on your host configuration. View the help pages referenced in the installer error messages for more details.

4. Providing all went as expected, you should see a screen asking for your database credentials, as pictured in Figure A-6.

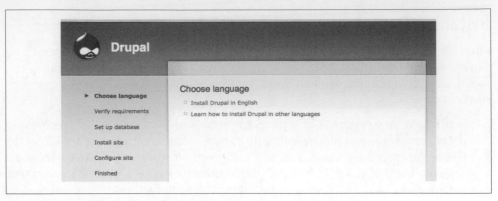

Figure A-5. Language selection for installing Drupal

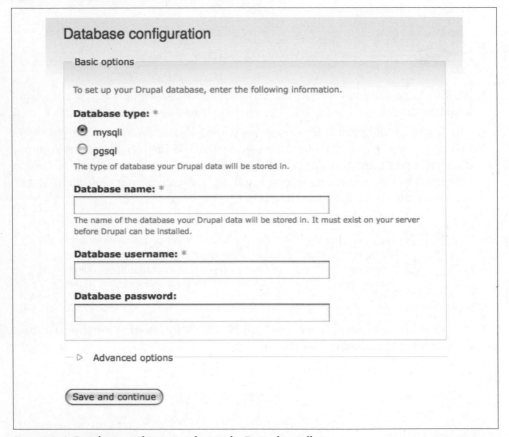

Figure A-6. Database configuration during the Drupal installation

5. Remember earlier when you wrote down the details of your database connection, including username and password? Now it's time to use them. At a minimum, you need the name of the database, the database username, and the database password.

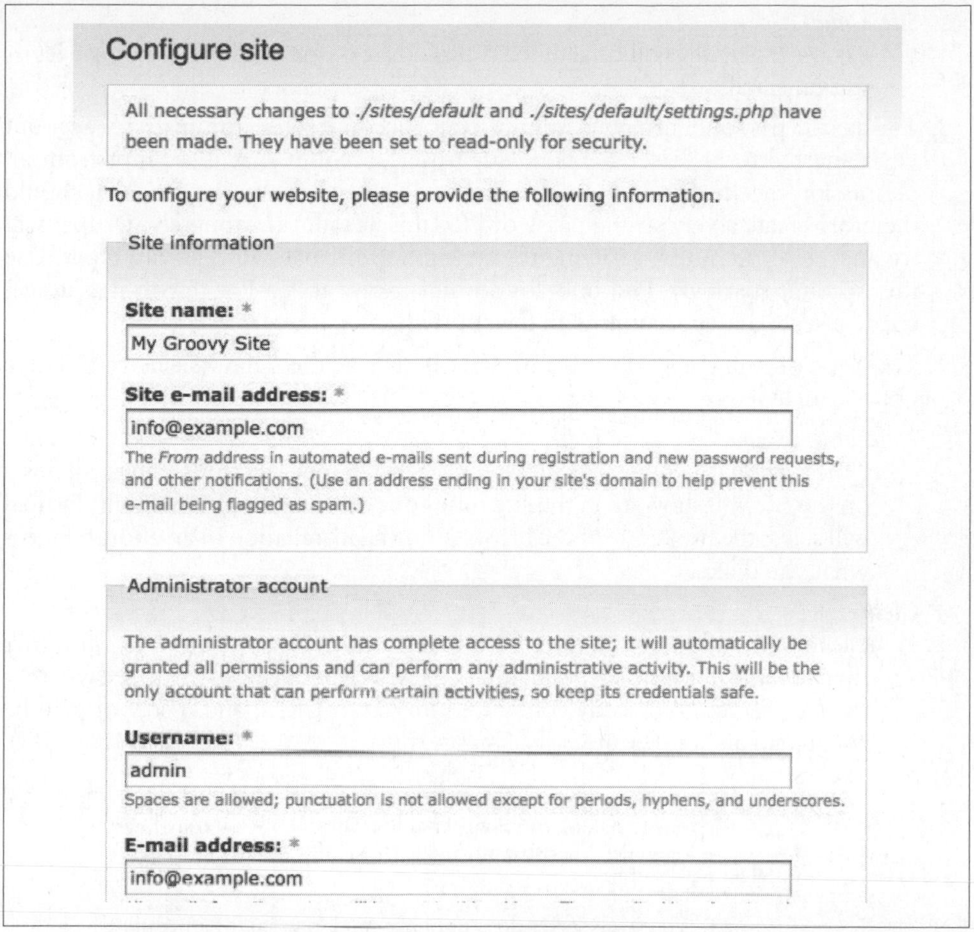

Configure site

All necessary changes to ./*sites/default* and ./*sites/default/settings.php* have been made. They have been set to read-only for security.

To configure your website, please provide the following information.

Site information

Site name: *

My Groovy Site

Site e-mail address: *

info@example.com

The *From* address in automated e-mails sent during registration and new password requests, and other notifications. (Use an address ending in your site's domain to help prevent this e-mail being flagged as spam.)

Administrator account

The administrator account has complete access to the site; it will automatically be granted all permissions and can perform any administrative activity. This will be the only account that can perform certain activities, so keep its credentials safe.

Username: *

admin

Spaces are allowed; punctuation is not allowed except for periods, hyphens, and underscores.

E-mail address: *

info@example.com

Figure A-7. Configuring settings during the Drupal installation

If your web host requires additional information such as hostname or database port, expand the "Advanced options" fieldset to enter these options. Once you have entered all of the database information, click the "Save and continue" button.

6. The next page, as shown in Figure A-7, contains a list of initial settings that should be configured on any site.

7. First you should fill out the "Site information" fieldset. This deals with important global site settings:

Site name

This is the name that will be displayed in the title bar on all pages, as well as in the upper-left corner of all pages, by default.

Site e-mail address

All system emails will be sent from this address; for example, new user registration emails.

8. The next step is configuring the Administrator account. The Administrator account (also referred to as "User 1") is a "superuser" account that is exempt from all permission checking and has full powers to do everything on the site. You should therefore create a very strong password for this account (fortunately, Drupal will try and help you out by verifying the strength of the password as you type). Use this account sparingly, and only for administrative tasks. For day-to-day usage, create a second user account with fewer privileges.

9. The Server settings section can normally be left at the defaults selected. These options include:

Default time zone

Unless a user otherwise specifies her time zone in her account settings, all posts on the site will show up in the site time zone selected here. By default, Drupal will select the time zone of the browser during installation in an effort to guess what you'd like.

Clean URLs

Clean URLs allow you to have URLs such as *http://example.com/about* rather than *http://example.com/?q=about*. A test will be performed here to see whether the web server is correctly configured for Clean URLs, and if so, you will be able to enable this feature.

> If you are having problems enabling Clean URLs, it may help to know that these are normally caused by one of the following:
>
> • Your web server does not have mod_rewrite (or an equivalent) installed.
>
> • Your web server is not properly reading the *.htaccess* file that comes with Drupal.
>
> Ask your server administrator to investigate whether one or both of these applies for you. For more information, you can read the Clean URLs section of the online handbook at *http://drupal.org/node/15365*.

Update notifications

Drupal 6 comes with a new feature to check for updates of new modules, themes, and Drupal core automatically, and will inform you when updates are available. This option (checked by default) is *highly* recommended, as it helps ensure that your site is up-to-date on security releases.

10. Once you have all of your settings entered, click the "Save and continue" button.

11. The final screen informs you that the installation is complete and you're ready to proceed with configuring your new website. Click the "your new site" link to begin your Drupal adventure! Figure A-8 shows the initial Drupal screen when it's first installed.

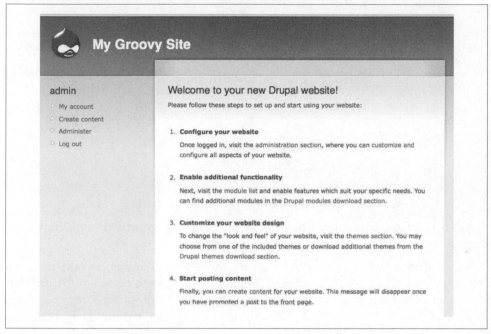

Figure A-8. A newly installed Drupal site

Keeping Drupal Up-to-Date

It's not enough to just get Drupal installed, however; you also need to make sure to keep it up-to-date. New releases of modules and Drupal core come out periodically, most of which fix problems, some of which add new whiz-bang features, and some of which address critical security problems.

Version Numbers

When discussing updates, it helps to have some background information about Drupal's version numbering system. For all the gory details, see *http://drupal.org/handbook/version-info*, summarized in Figure A-9.

Each "major" release of Drupal core gets a new number: Drupal 5, Drupal 6, Drupal 7, and so on. A new major Drupal version is released every 12–18 months, and consists of new features, improved usability, and more flexible APIs. Throughout a major version of Drupal's release cycle, several "minor" versions of Drupal are also released, such

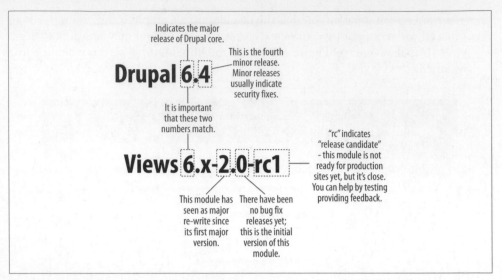

Figure A-9. Drupal version numbers explained

as 6.0, 6.1, and 6.2. Minor Drupal versions fix critical security problems and important bugs as well.

Releases of projects like contributed modules, themes, and translations have a version naming scheme such as 6.x-1.3. The "6.x" indicates the major version of Drupal that it is intended to work with; in this case, Drupal 6. The "1" indicates the "major" release *of the contributed module*. And the "3" indicates that this is the third bug fix release of this major release of the module.

Some releases also have "extra" version information, such as "-beta4" or "-rc2." These indicate that the modules are still in development, but available for testing.

Updates between minor versions of Drupal core and modules, such as between Drupal 6.3 to 6.4, or Views module 6.x-2.0 to 6.x-2.1, are normally fairly painless, as long as your site is kept up-to-date. Updates between major versions, however, such as Drupal 6.3 to 7.0, or Organic Groups module 6.x-1.0 to 6.x-2.0, and especially to 7.x-1.0, will need special care, as the changes are generally quite extensive.

On Backward Compatibility

The Drupal project's policy on backward compatibility is that between major versions (such as Drupal 6.x to 7.x), developers are allowed to freely break the underlying *code*, but must always provide a migration path for a user's *data*. If a cleaner, faster, or better way of doing something is discovered, developers are allowed (and encouraged) to change the underlying code to work in that fashion. This allows Drupal to stay on the cutting edge of technology without the burden of legacy code that needs to be supported and maintained throughout the ages. However, the result of this policy is that contributed module authors must incorporate these code changes into their own modules between major versions in order to upgrade and stay compatible.

Additionally, the Drupal project currently has a policy of supporting only the current release and one release previous. Although Drupal 6 is the newest release of Drupal as of this writing, both Drupal 6 and Drupal 5 will continue to have bug fixes applied, security updates, and so on. But when Drupal 7 comes out, Drupal 5 will no longer be supported.

As a Drupal user, what these policies mean to you is that there is often a lag time of a few months between when a new major version of Drupal is released and when key contributed modules are ready for widespread use. You should also plan on upgrading your Drupal sites to a new major release every 18–24 months.

For more on Drupal's backward compatibility policy, see *http://drupal.org/node/65922*.

Update Status Module

Drupal 6 core includes a module called Update Status, which periodically checks Drupal.org for new releases of modules, themes, and Drupal itself. If one or more of these projects are out of date, or if there is a new security release available, a red warning will be displayed on all pages of the administration panel, telling you to head to Administer→Reports→Available updates (admin/reports/updates) for more information. You can also sign up for the security mailing list at *http://drupal.org/security* and/or follow the Security RSS feed (*http://drupal.org/security/rss.xml*).

The "Available updates" screen, as shown in Figure A-10, displays an index of projects installed on your website, colored according to status.

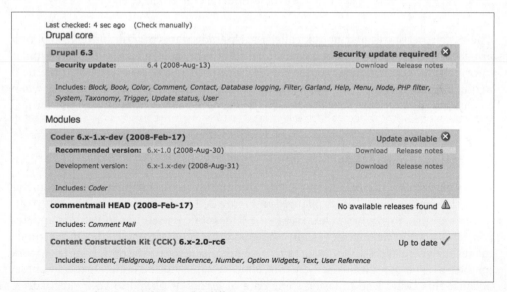

Figure A-10. Update status showing the different project statuses

The color codes indicate the following status states:

Red

> A new recommended version of this project is available, and the version on this website is out of date. Pay special attention to projects marked "Security update required!" and download the new recommended versions immediately.

Yellow

> Update status was not able to find the state of this project. This will happen on projects such as a specific site's custom, hand-built theme, or on projects that were not downloaded from Drupal.org, or if there was a problem reading the status information for this project.

Green

> Project is up-to-date. No further action is required.

> The Update Status module can be very noisy if you have many modules installed; over the course of a week, several modules may report that new updates are available if they're undergoing heavy development. You can adjust the notification threshold at Administer→Reports→Available updates on the Settings tab (admin/reports/updates/settings) to email only about security releases, which are mandatory, rather than regular bug fix releases.

> Security updates should be taken very seriously and updated as soon as possible. Read the module's release notes for more information about bug fixes or features that the update offers.

There is also a contributed module called the Upgrade Status module (*http://drupal.org/project/upgrade_status*), similar to the Update Status module, which will display similar information about enabled modules and whether they have been ported to the next major Drupal version. This functionality comes in handy when determining when might be a good time to move to a new major version, such as from Drupal 6 to Drupal 7.

Site Maintenance Mode

If you navigate to the Administer→Site configuration→Site maintenance (admin/settings/site-maintenance) page, pictured in Figure A-11, you can set the site into "offline" mode prior to the upgrade taking place. This mode is useful, as sometimes updates can temporarily cause errors before the entire process is completed. Offline mode makes the site inaccessible to regular users while still allowing administrators to work on the site. You don't want users creating content while you are updating the database, because this could lead to losing some data or errors displayed to your site visitors.

When you take the site offline, you can also set a message to display to your users to let them know what is going on.

Figure A-11. A Drupal website showing in offline mode

 If you wish to log in to the site while it is in offline mode, your user account must be assigned to a role that has the "administer site configuration" permission. Pull up the login form by heading to *http://www .example.com/user*.

The update.php Script

The *update.php* script, pictured in Figure A-12, automatically runs through any underlying database changes that a module requires in order to move from one version to another. Whether you're updating between minor or major versions of Drupal and contributed modules, *update.php* is the piece that ensures your data ends up in the places that it should when all is said and done.

The script lists all of the enabled modules on your site, and specifies whether updates are required to be run. A progress bar counts up as each module is updated. And finally, at the end, a report is generated with the database changes that were performed, along with any errors that occurred.

 Because *update.php* performs updates against the database, it's *very* important to create a backup of your database before running this script. The Drupal handbook has instructions at *http://drupal.org/upgrade/ backing-up-the-db*.

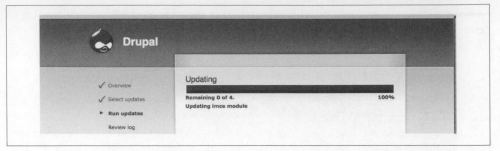

Figure A-12. The update.php script, which performs database updates between versions

The update.php script is intended to be run by User 1. If you are not using the User 1 account, you need to edit the *settings.php* file manually in order to be able to run the update script. You must change the *$update_free_access* variable in *settings.php* so that it is equal to TRUE rather than FALSE.

But be careful, if you change this value in *settings.php*, make *sure* that you change it back to FALSE as soon as you are done running the update script! Failure to do so means that anonymous users might be able to rerun database updates, which could cause all manner of problems.

Updating Drupal Core

Updating your site often sounds much scarier than the actual experience is. In addition to the included *UPGRADE.txt* file, the online handbook has a great deal of documentation available at *http://drupal.org/upgrade/* and a helpful support forum at *http://drupal.org/forum/21*. The most important step to remember is creating and testing backups of your site.

It cannot be stressed enough how important backups are when doing upgrades. This holds true for upgrading both Drupal core and contributed modules. You need to make sure you back up both essential parts of a Drupal site: the filesystem and the database. Every system can have a different way to do backups, so that will not be covered in detail in this appendix. You can ask your system administrator or refer to the backup section of the upgrade guide on Drupal.org at *http://drupal.org/upgrade/backing-up-the-db*. Make sure that you test the backups as well so that you are sure that you can recreate your site if something goes awry.

Updating your out-of-date modules requires manually downloading the necessary files from Drupal.org and placing them on your server just as you did the first time you uploaded them. Drupal does not automatically download updates. This is to prevent overwriting existing module code before you have a chance to test it. For example, it's possible that a module may make a change that requires a newer version of PHP than you have installed, which could result in fatal errors on your site if the files were downloaded blindly. Always test out updated modules on a test server before deploying them on your "live" site.

This section walks you through the steps to update Drupal within a major version to the next minor release number—for example, if you are using Drupal 6.3 and need to upgrade to Drupal 6.4. When upgrading to a new major version of Drupal, such as Drupal 7, the steps are essentially the same, except that you must also upgrade all of your contributed and custom modules and themes at the same time.

1. Get the latest release for your version of Drupal by following the same steps as covered in the "Downloading Drupal" section previously.

2. Before you do anything else, you must make backups of both your database and files. Again, refer to your system administrator or the backup guide at *http://drupal .org/upgrade/backing-up-the-db*.

3. Once you have your backups done, log in to your site as User 1.

4. Go to Administer→Site configuration→Site maintenance (admin/settings/site-maintenance) and select the Off-line radio button. Feel free to edit the "Site off-line message" to whatever you choose. Click the "Save configuration" button to take the site offline.

 If you set the site to offline mode and log out before changing it back to online mode, you can still log in easily by going to the user login page manually in the address bar at *http://example.com/user*.

5. For major version upgrades, it's also recommended to go to Administer→Site building→Themes (admin/build/themes) and switch the site theme to a core theme such as Garland or Bluemarine. This step can prevent errors if underlying things have changed that your site's normal theme depends on.

6. Extract the Drupal files from the tarball and replace all of the existing files on your server with the new files.

7. Make sure that all of your site's files are back in place. Your entire site's contributed and custom code, along with your *files* directory, should be in the *sites* folder in your backup. Grab a copy of the *sites* folder from the backup you made and add it to your Drupal files. If you have made modifications to other system files, such as *.htaccess* or *robots.txt*, restore those from backup as well.

8. Now that all of the files are in place, it is time to update the database, too. Go to *http://example.com/update.php* in your browser. You will be presented with a screen that outlines the steps you should take to update the site. Click the Continue button.

9. You are taken to the update screen. Click the Update button to run the script.

If you expand the "Select versions" fieldset, you can see which modules have registered that they have update code to be run. Modules that have updates to be run will have a schema version number, such as 6001, preselected in their drop-down select list. Drupal keeps track of this for you, so you shouldn't change this. Modules with no updates will have "No updates available" selected. Even if there are no updates marked, you should still run the *update.php* script, as it will reset your cache, making sure that Drupal recognizes all of the new files. Failing to run the script may cause some weirdness in the newly updated site until the cache is cleared at Administer→Site configuration→Performance (admin/settings/performance).

10. After the script runs, you will be returned to a screen indicating that the update is complete. If you changed to a core theme for the upgrade, switch it back to your regular theme at Administer→Site building→Themes (admin/build/themes).

11. Click around your site and verify that the update was successful. Once you are convinced the site looks OK, return to Administer→Site configuration→Site maintenance (admin/settings/site-maintenance), select the Online radio button, and click "Save configuration" to take the site back online.

Updating Contributed Modules

Drupal's contributed projects tend to move more quickly than Drupal core and therefore require more updates within a Drupal version's life cycle. You can upgrade multiple modules at the same time, although it's best to do one at a time to reduce the chance of errors, and to allow you to isolate problems that might come up during an upgrade.

To update contributed modules, follow these steps. You will see that the process is the same as the one used for Drupal core, only the files that are changed are a little different.

1. Just as with Drupal core, you need to get the latest version of the module you wish to update. You should always read any release notes that are associated with the module to make sure that there are no special instructions for your update.

2. It is still important to make backups of your entire Drupal installation, even though you are only updating a module. If something goes wrong you want to be able to restore the site to the state it was in before you began. So make your backups before proceeding.

3. Log in to your site as User 1.

4. Go to Administer→Site configuration→Site maintenance (admin/settings/site-maintenance) and select the Off-line radio button. Edit the "Site off-line message" to whatever you choose. Click "Save configuration" to take the site off-line.

5. Now it's time to replace the module files. Extract the module file that you downloaded from Drupal.org and completely replace the old module. To be thorough,

---

you can delete the entire folder for the old module and then add the new, fresh module folder to the *sites/all/modules* directory.

6. Go to *http://example.com/update.php* in your browser and click the Continue button.

7. Click the Update button to actually run the update script.

8. Return to your site and make sure that everything looks okay. You should especially check the functionality that the particular module or modules provided for your site and make sure that there are no errors.

9. Repeat steps 5 through 8 for each module that you wish to update.

10. To finish up, go back to Administer→Site configuration→Site maintenance (admin/ settings/site-maintenance), select the Online radio button, and click "Save configuration" to take the site back online.

References

Here is a list of modules we referenced in this appendix:

- Update status: core
- Upgrade status: *http://drupal.org/project/upgrade_status*

Here is a list of the external references we used in this appendix:

- Apache web server: *http://httpd.apache.org*
- MAMP: *http://mamp.info/en/download.html*
- MySQL: *http://mysql.com*
- PHP: *http://php.net*
- PostGreSQL: *http://postgresql.org*
- WampServer: *http://www.wampserver.com*
- XAMPP: *http://www.apachefriends.org/en/xampp.html*

Here are the Drupal.org resources we referenced:

- Drupal project: *http://drupal.org/project/drupal*
- Backward compatibility: *http://drupal.org/node/65922*
- Backing up the database and files: *http://drupal.org/upgrade/backing-up-the-db*
- Clean URLs: *http://drupal.org/node/15365*
- Installation guide: *http://drupal.org/getting-started/6/install*
- Multisite installation: *http://drupal.org/node/43816*
- Security: *http://drupal.org/security*
- Security RSS feed: *http://drupal.org/security/rss.xml*
- System requirements: *http://drupal.org/requirements*

- Upgrade guide: *http://drupal.org/upgrade*
- Upgrading Drupal forum: *http://drupal.org/forum/21*

Choosing the Right Modules

With over 2,000 modules to choose from, and more added every single day, finding the contributed module you need for a given task can be a daunting process. Throughout this book, the authors have endeavored to highlight and identify most of the "must-have" modules, particularly architectural modules that are commonly used to build Drupal websites. We've also endeavored to cover modules that have a proven track record and are likely to continue to be used to build sites.

However, each new website project has unique requirements that may be outside the scope of what this book has covered, and the landscape of the contributions repository is a constantly shifting space. Modules that were once critical building blocks may be abandoned or deprecated by superior alternatives, and new modules may come along that completely blow away anything else that came before them.

This appendix, therefore, attempts to highlight some of the best practices used by those "in the know" for evaluating and selecting the right module for the job. It's important to keep in mind that no simple set of guidelines—these included—can tell you everything about a module. The important thing to remember is that evaluating modules carefully before you commit to them will help prevent unpleasant surprises down the road.

Finding Modules

The first step to choosing the right module for your needs is actually *finding* it. Fortunately, all Drupal modules (with only a few rare exceptions) are located directly on the main Drupal.org website, so there's only one resource for finding them. Here's how you do it.

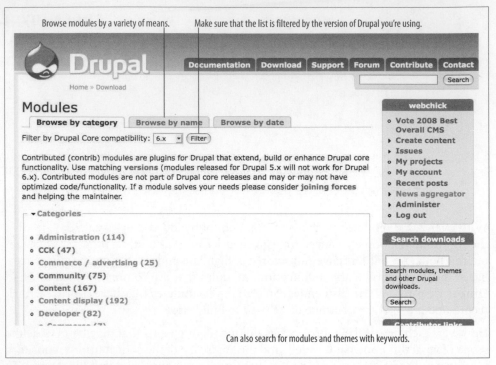

Browse modules by a variety of means.   Make sure that the list is filtered by the version of Drupal you're using.

Can also search for modules and themes with keywords.

Figure B-1. Module browse pages on Drupal.org

Browse Module Listings

The module listing pages at *http://drupal.org/project/Modules*, pictured in Figure B-1, list modules by category (such as CCK or mail-related modules), by name alphabetically, and by the date they were last updated. Browsing these category-based pages can be useful for determining the modules that exist in a particular space, and keeping an eye on the modules that are frequently at the top of the date list helps highlight those with active maintainers.

Drupal 5.x modules are not compatible with Drupal 6.x, and vice versa. To see an accurate list for your site, make sure to change the "Filter by Drupal Core compatibility" filter to show only those modules that are compatible with your Drupal version. You will have access to apply this filter only if you are logged in to the Drupal.org website. Getting an account is free and easy, and opens up many useful tools to you.

Another nice Drupal.org "hack" is keeping an RSS reader pointed at *http://drupal.org/taxonomy/term/14*, which is a list of all the newest modules on Drupal.org as they are created.

Keyword Search

Drupal.org also provides a block for searching the downloads on the site, also pictured in Figure B-1. For example, searching for "wiki" brings up a list of modules with that keyword in their name or description. This allows you to drill down to modules specific to your needs faster than browsing by the default category view.

Drupal.org Forums

The Drupal.org support forums at *http://drupal.org/forum*, particularly the "Before you start" forum at *http://drupal.org/forum/20*, can provide a wealth of information in the form of questions from other users about the modules they used for their own projects. Often, you can receive some helpful advice not only about the feature you're trying to implement now, but also for future things your website will need to take into consideration. The "Drupal showcase" forum at *http://drupal.org/forum/25* is also filled with people showing off websites they built with Drupal—and they are often more than happy to share details about how they built a particular piece.

Case Studies

Chances are good that no matter how crazy the use case, someone else has had to solve the very same problem with Drupal as you have. You can cut down the time required to find modules tremendously by finding out how they went about it. The Drupal handbook contains a section for case studies at *http://drupal.org/cases*. These consist of detailed write-ups, often about major websites using Drupal, about why exactly Drupal was chosen and how the site was put together. Some of the more comprehensive case studies include:

- *Popular Science* magazine: *http://drupal.org/node/233090*
- Sony BMG MyPlay: *http://drupal.org/node/241344*
- *New York Observer*: *http://drupal.org/node/141187*

Planet Drupal

Planet Drupal (*http://drupal.org/planet*), pictured in Figure B-2, is an aggregation of Drupal contributing members' blogs and is a great way to find out what's new and hot in the module world. Module tutorials, reviews, and news are often posted there, and Planet Drupal also a great general resource for keeping your finger on the pulse of what's happening in the larger community.

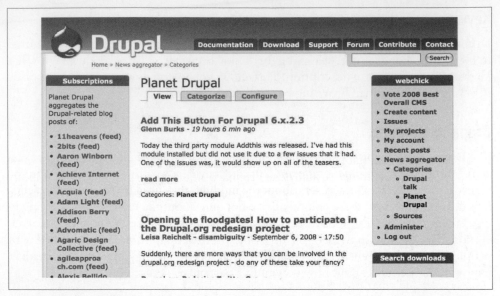

Figure B-2. Planet Drupal, which aggregates content from blogs of Drupal companies and contributors

Third-Party Websites

http://drupal.org/node/289913 provides a list of third-party websites—that is, separate from Drupal.org—that often provide useful information when evaluating modules. For example, *http://drupalmodules.com* provides user ratings and reviews of Drupal modules, and *http://www.lullabot.com* has a variety of articles, videos, and podcasts, many of which highlight popular modules and how to use them.

Assessing a Module's Health

An open source project's strength comes from the power of its base of contributors, and the Drupal project is no different. Although every line of code added or changed in Drupal core goes through rigorous peer review, contributed modules are more of a "Wild West" where anyone who jumps through a few basic hoops can add modules for everyone to download. The Drupal community strives to keep the barriers to contributing code back as low as possible in order to facilitate growing Drupal's thriving development community. This approach has both pros (for almost any problem, there's a module that either can get you fully or at least partway there) and cons (developers' experience levels are varied, so contributed code can have inefficiencies and security problems, and developers can become overextended and unable to keep up with maintenance of their modules).

Whether or not a module is well-maintained, its overall code quality, and how well-used it is in the overall community are all important factors to consider when selecting modules. This section will talk about determining these factors by closely inspecting

---

the tools Drupal.org provides, starting with the central feature of all Drupal modules: the project page.

Project Pages

Modules, themes, translations, and even Drupal core itself are all referred to as *projects* on Drupal.org. Each project has its own page at *http://drupal.org/project/file _name*, which contains a wealth of information that can be used to evaluate a module's health.

Figure B-3 shows the first part of a module's project page. Here you can find the name of the module's *maintainer* (usually the original author and/or the module's primary developer), the date the project was first created, a description of what the module does, and sometimes a screenshot showing what the module does.

Figure B-3. The project page for the Devel module

The original project creation date can be useful when looking for time-tested solutions (if the module was created in the past week, it's probably best to let it mature a bit before depending on it). But also be aware that some older modules may be legacy solutions that more modern modules deprecate.

Further down, we see the module release table (pictured in Figure B-4), which we discussed briefly in Chapter 2. A plethora of useful information is available here, including the date that the code was last updated; whether the module has "Official releases," which indicate stable releases; links to release notes for each release to tell what bugs were fixed and features were added; and a link to view all releases—even old, outdated ones.

Releases

Official releases	Date	Size	Links		Status	
6.x-2.0-rc2	2008-Aug-21	184.3 KB	Download · Release notes		Recommended for *6.x*	✓
5.x-2.1	2008-Sep-05	174.38 KB	Download · Release notes		Recommended for *5.x*	✓
5.x-1.8	2007-Dec-28	98.21 KB	Download · Release notes		Supported for *5.x*	⚠

Development snapshots	Date	Size	Links		Status	
6.x-2.x-dev	2008-Sep-06	205.07 KB	Download · Release notes		Development snapshot	✗
5.x-2.x-dev	2008-Sep-06	186.12 KB	Download · Release notes		Development snapshot	✗

- **View all releases**

Figure B-4. The module release table for a typical module

This release table, taken from the Date module on September 7, 2008, is indicative of a healthy project. The Date module has stable releases for both Drupal 5 and Drupal 6 (although the Drupal 6 version is only a release candidate, this shows that it is nearing completion and ready for testing). The date on the module's development releases indicates that the code has been updated very recently, which means that the maintainer is actively developing on the project. Clicking on "View all releases" shows releases of this module dating back to Drupal 4.7, and it even has a Drupal 7 development release, although Drupal 7 is currently in active development and is not close to being released yet, as of the current date.

On the other hand, signs that it might be worth looking elsewhere include:

- If there are only development snapshots available and no official releases, or if there is no release table *at all*, this indicates that this module is undergoing development and should not yet be relied upon for production websites.
- If the last updated date of the latest release is several months in the past, this could indicate lack of maintainer activity and interest in the module. It could also mean that you've found an example of a completely perfect module that has no bugs and needs no new features added, but those are pretty rare.

Finally, at the bottom of the project page is an optional list of links, including resources such as a project's external home page, a link to its documentation, or a demonstration site. Presence of these links tends to indicate a maintainer who is passionate about his module, and wants it to be as high-quality as possible.

Also, don't miss the project's usage statistics, which are invaluable in evaluating the popularity of a module in relation to others.

Issue Queues

Development of code in the Drupal community happens in a project's *issue queue*, such as *http://drupal.org/project/issues/3060*, pictured in Figure B-5. The issue queue is a log of bugs, feature requests, support requests, and tasks for a given project that module maintainers use as their public working space. Anyone in the community can log issues against a project, and anyone can provide solutions for them as well.

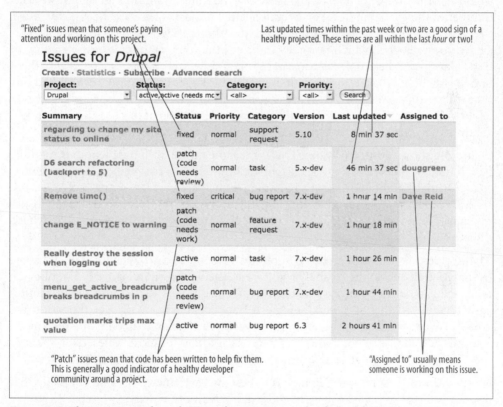

Figure B-5. The issue queue from the Drupal core, an example of a healthy project

You can find an issue queue for a project in several ways. The most common way is simply to start on the project's page. If you scroll to the bottom, you will see a list of links for support, features, etc. The handiest link in that list is the "View open issues" link under the Support section. You can also look at the main list of all issues across all projects at *http://drupal.org/project/issues*, and use the Project drop-down list to select the project you're interested in.

Because issue queues provide an open window into what's happening with development of a given project, being able to "read" an issue queue is an invaluable skill in evaluating a project's health.

For example, most people might logically assume that a project with lots of issues is a poor-quality project, and one with very few issues is a high quality project. While this certainly can be the case, it's worth pointing out that Drupal itself currently has more than 5,000 open issues, and its code is written to a very high standard of quality. More often than not, the number of issues in an issue queue merely indicates the *popularity* of a project, not necessarily a lack of quality.

That said, the specific details of said issues are very important. In Figure B-5, we see a number of things that indicate an overall healthy project. There are a couple of issues that have been marked fixed within the past 24 hours. Two of the issues are also assigned to developers, which normally indicates that they are taking responsibility to find solutions for the problems. Most of the open issues have code associated with them in one way or another: a couple that are ready for larger community review, and one that still needs more work, but is at least the start of a solution. This is indicative of a healthy developer community around the project. Only two of these issues are marked "active," which indicates that they are still awaiting code to fix them.

Figure B-6 shows a different story. This is the issue queue from the Flexinode module, which was the predecessor to the current CCK module. At first glance, it looks similar to the Drupal issue queue that we saw earlier. Sure, there are a few more "active" issues, and none that are currently marked as having been fixed. But there are still a few issues that have some code attached, and even some that are assigned to developers. So what's the problem?

The problem is the "Last updated" column, which indicates when a reply was last posted to the issue. In the Drupal project issue queue, shown in Figure B-5, replies are typically at most an hour or two apart, with some replies as recent as eight minutes ago! This means that at almost any given hour, people from all over the world are constantly contributing to the project. However, the last time that anyone responded to Flexinode's most recent issue was 18 weeks ago, and for most issues, over one year ago. This is a sure sign of an abandoned module whose maintainer has lost interest.

Most modules are somewhere in between these two extremes, with a mix of issues that haven't been looked at in awhile and those that have more activity. Spot-check a couple of issues by clicking them and seeing who's actually responding. Is it the maintainer, specifying what she found when she looked at the problem, or is it other desperate users who are saying, "Yep, I have this problem too. Any ideas?"

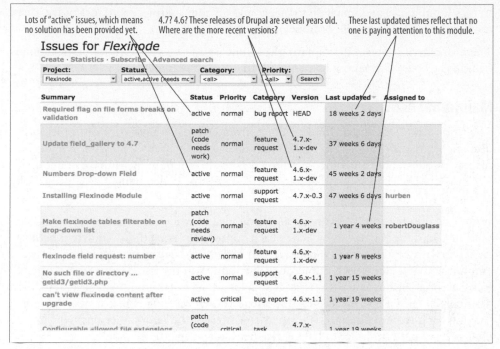

Figure B-6. The issue queue from Flexinode, an example of a project that has been abandoned

Code

All of Drupal's contributed modules are stored in a central code repository at *http://cvs .drupal.org/viewvc.py/drupal/contributions/modules/*, which you can browse through in order to get a sense of how the code looks for a given module prior to downloading it. Obviously, people with a PHP background are going to be able to get more out of this, but in general anyone can spot some basic best practices. Look for clearly written, documented, well-organized code that conforms to a standard coding style. Code that does not meet these criteria is harder to maintain, and harder for other developers to jump in and help with.

The People Behind the Code

Each contributor to Drupal is a unique individual who has his own areas of interest, expertise, background, and motivations for contributing. Some contributors are master programmers who live, breathe, sleep, and eat code. Some are backed by Drupal development and consulting companies, and are paid to maintain their modules. Others are hobbyists who run a fan club site and maintain one or two particular modules that act as the main backbone of their community. Still others help out for the fun of it, because it feels good and they enjoy it. There are those who get code as far as they need it, toss it out there, and move on to bigger and greener pastures. And, of course, there are those who are some, all, or none of the above.

Therefore, a critical piece to evaluating a module is to also learn more about the humans behind the code. Drupal.org has a few useful tools to help.

Maintainer Activity

The first is the "Developers" link at the bottom of project pages (for example, *http:// drupal.org/project/developers/3060*), which takes you to a table, shown in Figure B-7, displaying a list of the individual developers who are maintaining (or have maintained) the project. The data shown here are the *commits*, or code changes to a project, by everyone who has ever had access.

From this information, you can get a general idea of who within the project has been working on it the longest, how active each contributor is, and how much experience each has with a given project's code. A sign of a good, healthy project is lots of recent commit activity, along with numerous contributors in the list if some of the original folks are no longer around. If this list is small, and the last commit was several months ago, particularly if the project's issue queue shows warning signs, it may be worth looking for alternative solutions, or perhaps offering the maintainer payment for the changes you need, in order to help entice her interest again.

Developers for *Drupal*

User	Last commit▼	First commit	Commits
webchick	1 day ago	1 week ago	21 commits
Dries	1 day ago	8 years ago	16220 commits
drumm	1 week ago	2 years ago	1084 commits
Gábor Hojtsy	7 weeks ago	1 year ago	2390 commits
killes@www.drop.org	34 weeks ago	2 years ago	715 commits
Steven	1 year ago	7 years ago	2083 commits
Kjartan	1 year ago	8 years ago	694 commits
Natrak	4 years ago	8 years ago	174 commits
Jeroen	7 years ago	8 years ago	253 commits

Figure B-7. A list of developers for the Drupal project, along with commit activity

User Profiles

Anytime that you see a username on Drupal.org, you can click it to view the user's profile (for example, *http://drupal.org/user/35821*), as shown in Figure B-8. Although there's information here that's typical of any user profile on any site, such as first and last name, a list of interests, gender, and country, there are a few elements that are particularly useful to those looking to find out more about the person behind the code.

The user profile begins with a brief blurb about the user's contributions to Drupal. This typically mentions modules that they have written, various initiatives that the user's a part of, such as the documentation team or site administration team, and other such data. This information can help provide insight as to the person's motivations and background.

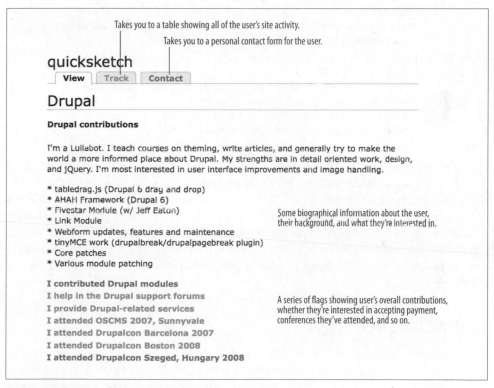

Figure B-8. User profile page on Drupal.org

This information is followed by a series of "flags" that indicate things such as whether the person helps out with documentation, user support, and module development, as well as what Drupal conferences the user has attended. Each flag is a link that displays a list of other users who have that flag checked. A user with many of these links displayed is generally much more tied into the larger Drupal community than one without.

The tabs along the top edge are also very useful. The Track tab shows a list of all of the posts on Drupal.org that the user has created or responded to. This can help gauge his overall involvement in the Drupal community and how active he is, as well as his general attitude towards others.

The Contact tab, if he's enabled it, can be used to contact the user directly via email.

Although it can be tempting to use the Contact form to ask maintainers support questions or to report bugs about their modules directly, this is considered bad form. Time a maintainer spends answering emails is time that is *not* spent further developing the module and helping other users who might have the same problem.

Always use a module's issue queue for reporting problems, as that method allows anyone who uses the module to respond, not just the maintainer, and allows the results to be searched by others. In general, use a maintainer's contact form only for topics that are intended to be kept private, such as requests for hire.

The contact form can also be used to send a general "thanks" for a job well done; most module developers hear only about problems from their users, so it can make a maintainer's day to hear from someone who has nice things to say about the code she received for free.

Further down the profile page, there's an indication of how long the user has been a member of Drupal.org, as well as a list of the projects that the user has committed code to during that time, shown in Figure B-9. Some maintainers have one or two projects listed here, and others have 50 or more. A list consisting of many projects is usually indicative of someone who's been around awhile and likely knows what he's doing. On the other hand, *because* he has been around awhile, he might also be over-extended and trying to do too many things at once, and all of his modules may be suffering as a result.

Getting Involved

By far, the best way to keep up-to-date on what modules are the most useful, and to ensure that those modules do what you need, is to actually get directly involved and help. The Drupal community offers a myriad of ways for *everyone*, from the person who just installed Drupal for the first time yesterday to the person who has been coding since she was in diapers, to give something back.

The "Getting Involved" handbook at *http://drupal.org/getting-involved* is the main "jumping-off" point for ways to get involved in the Drupal project. Here are a few that are suited to nonprogrammers as well:

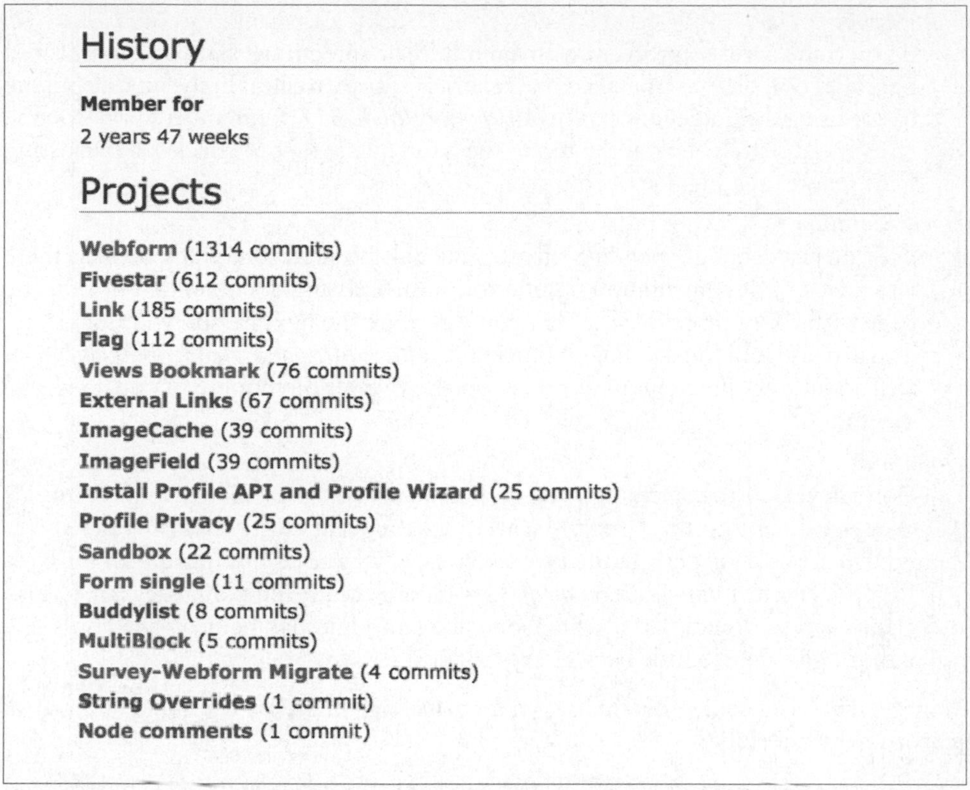

History

Member for
2 years 47 weeks

Projects

Webform (1314 commits)
Fivestar (612 commits)
Link (185 commits)
Flag (112 commits)
Views Bookmark (76 commits)
External Links (67 commits)
ImageCache (39 commits)
ImageField (39 commits)
Install Profile API and Profile Wizard (25 commits)
Profile Privacy (25 commits)
Sandbox (22 commits)
Form single (11 commits)
Buddylist (8 commits)
MultiBlock (5 commits)
Survey-Webform Migrate (4 commits)
String Overrides (1 commit)
Node comments (1 commit)

Figure B-9. Drupal developers have a list of projects they've committed to at the bottom of their user profiles

Issue queue cleanup

While you're evaluating modules, you'll naturally be in the issue queue anyway. Why not take a few extra minutes and look for places you might be able to clean things up? If there are two or more similar issues, mark the higher-numbered one as a "duplicate." See if a bug report is still valid, and if it's not, mark it "fixed." If you see a support request that you know the answer to, answer it. Every minute spent by someone other than the module maintainer on this type of activity is more time that she can spend improving her modules, and so this type of contribution is hugely appreciated by maintainers.

Helping with user support

If you've gotten as far as getting Drupal installed, congratulations! You now officially know enough to help someone else. Head to the Drupal forums or *#drupal-support* on *irc.freenode.net* and look for opportunities to answer other users' questions. You're guaranteed to learn a ton in the process.

Filing issues

If you come across a problem with a module, or something that you think would be really cool, file it as a detailed bug report or feature request in the module's issue queue using the guidelines at *http://drupal.org/node/317*. Remember to click on the "Advanced search" link at the top of the issue queue first to check for an existing issue before creating one of your own.

Documentation

Did you just get done spending a frustrating half-hour on something because there was a lack of documentation or an error in the existing documentation? Edit the page with your corrections, so that you can spare the next person your same fate. You can also join the documentation team at *http://drupal.org/contribute/documen tation/join* to collaborate with others on the overall direction of Drupal's documentation.

Donations

Don't have time to contribute yourself, but have some spare change rolling around? You can donate to the Drupal Association, the legal entity that provides server infrastructure, organizes Drupal conferences, and handles fundraising for the Drupal project at *http://association.drupal.org/donate*. Many individual developers also gladly accept donations. If using someone's module has helped save you some money, give them a little back to say "thanks."

Why get involved? Aside from the "warm fuzzy feeling," there are a number of practical reasons, which include:

- As a general rule, more attention is paid to your support requests, bug reports, and feature requests if you are known to be a contributor to the project.

- Being an active part of the community helps forge relationships, which can lead to clients and employers.

- Being involved can help take months off of your Drupal learning curve by exposing you to discussions and individuals that you wouldn't otherwise have come across.

- You can help shape the exact direction of modules and even the Drupal core itself, so that they meet the requirements for your project.

- It's also really fun! You meet people from all over the world, and get to learn from some of the best and brightest minds out there on web design.

Looking forward to meeting you on Drupal.org!

Summary

The tips and techniques outlined in this chapter can help identify "must-have" modules long after this book is out of date. By assessing things such as how active a project's maintainer is, how large the user community is around a project, and how well-documented and easy-to-read its code is, you can help make smart, future-proof choices on your module selection. And by getting involved directly in the community itself, you can meet the awesome people who make Drupal what it is, and become one of them yourself!

References

Here is a list of the resources referred to in this appendix:

Bug report and feature request guidelines: *http://drupal.org/node/317*

Case studies: *http://drupal.org/cases*

Contribute page: *http://drupal.org/contribute*

Contributed module list: *http://drupal.org/project/Modules*

CVS repository online: *http://cvs.drupal.org/viewvc.py/drupal/contributions/modules*

Developers list for the Drupal project: *http://drupal.org/project/developers/3060*

Documentation team: *http://drupal.org/contribute/documentation/join*

Donate money: *http://association.drupal.org/donate*

Drupal core project issue queue: *http://drupal.org/project/issues/drupal*

Drupal.org forums: *http://drupal.org/forum*

Drupal "Before You Start" forum: *http://drupal.org/forum/20*

Drupal showcase forum: *http://drupal.org/forum/25*

New York Observer case study: *http://drupal.org/node/141187*

Planet Drupal: *http://drupal.org/planet*

Popular Science magazine case study: *http://drupal.org/node/233090*

Sony BMG MyPlay case study: *http://drupal.org/node/241344*

Third-party resources: *http://drupal.org/node/289913*

Modules and Themes Used in This Book

This appendix lists the modules and themes used in each project throughout the book. These are all included with the source code and are listed here for quick reference or if you would like to replicate the chapters without using the source code.

This book was written against Drupal 6.4.

Chapter 1, *Drupal Overview*

Not applicable.

Chapter 2, *Drupal Jumpstart*

Modules:

- Administration menu 6.x-1.1 (*http://drupal.org/project/admin_menu*)
- FCKeditor module 6.x-1.3-rc1 (*http://drupal.org/project/fckeditor*)
- FCkeditor package 2.6.3 (*http://fckeditor.net*)
- IMCE 6.x-1.1 (*http://drupal.org/project/imce*)

Theme:

- Garland (core)

Chapter 3, *Job Posting Board*

Modules:

- Advanced help 6.x-1.0 (*http://drupal.org/project/advanced_help*)
- Content Construction Kit (CCK) 6.x-2.0-rc10 (*http://drupal.org/project/cck*)
- FileField 6.x-3.0-alpha6 (*http://drupal.org/project/filefield*)
- Views 6.x-2.0-rc4 (*http://drupal.org/project/views*)

Theme:

- Wabi 6.x-1.1 (*http://drupal.org/project/wabi*)

Chapter 4, *Product Reviews*

Modules:

- Advanced help 6.x-1.0 (*http://drupal.org/project/advanced_help*)
- Amazon 6.x-1.0-beta3 (*http://drupal.org/project/amazon*)
- Content Construction Kit (CCK) 6.x-2.0-rc10 (*http://drupal.org/project/cck*)
- CSS Injector 6.x-1.3 (*http://drupal.org/project/css_injector*)
- Fivestar 6.x-1.13 (*http://drupal.org/project/fivestar*)
- Search (core)
- Views 6.x-2.0-rc4 (*http://drupal.org/project/views*)
- Voting API 6.x-2.0-beta6 (*http://drupal.org/project/votingapi*)

Theme:

- Nitobe 6.x-1.6 (*http://drupal.org/project/nitobe*)

Chapter 5, *Wiki*

Modules:

- Advanced help 6.x-1.0 (*http://drupal.org/project/advanced_help*)
- Diff 6.x-2.0 (*http://drupal.org/project/diff*)
- Freelinking 6.x-1.6 (*http://drupal.org/project/freelinking*)
- Markdown filter 6.x-1.0 (*http://drupal.org/project/markdown*)
- Pathauto 6.x-1.1 (*http://drupal.org/project/pathauto*)
- Token 6.x-1.10 (*http://drupal.org/project/token*)
- Views 6.x-2.0-rc4 (*http://drupal.org/project/views*)

Theme:

- Barlow 6.x-1.0 (*http://drupal.org/project/barlow*)

Chapter 6, *Managing Publishing Workflow*

Modules:

- Advanced help 6.x-1.0 (*http://drupal.org/project/advanced_help*)
- Trigger (core)
- Views 6.x-2.0-rc4 (*http://drupal.org/project/views*)

- Views Bulk Operations 6.x-1.1 (*http://drupal.org/project/views_bulk_opera tions*)
- Workspace 6.x-1.3 (*http://drupal.org/project/workspace*)
- Workflow 6.x-1.1 (*http://drupal.org/project/workflow*)

Theme:

- Light Fantastic 6.x-1.0 (*http://drupal.org/project/lightfantastic*)

Chapter 7, *Photo Gallery*

Modules:

- Advanced help 6.x-1.0 (*http://drupal.org/project/advanced_help*)
- Content Construction Kit (CCK) 6.x-2.0-rc10 (*http://drupal.org/project/cck*)
- Custom Pagers 6.x-1.10-beta1 (*http://drupal.org/project/custom_pagers*)
- FileField 6.x-3.0-alpha6 (*http://drupal.org/project/filefield*)
- ImageCache 6.x-1.0-alpha2 (*http://drupal.org/project/imagecache*)
- ImageField 6.x-3.0-alpha1 (*http://drupal.org/project/imagefield*)
- Token 6.x-1.10 (*http://drupal.org/project/token*)
- Views 6.x-2.0-rc4 (*http://drupal.org/project/views*)

Theme:

- Ubiquity 6.x-1.x-dev (2008-May-31) (*http://drupal.org/project/ubiquity*)

Chapter 8, *Multilingual Sites*

Modules:

- Book (core)
- Content Translation (core)
- Forum (core)
- Internationalization 6.x-1.0-beta1 (*http://drupal.org/project/i18n*)
- Localization (core)
- Localization client 6.x-1.3 (*http://drupal.org/project/l10n_client*)

Theme:

- Dreamy 6.x-1.3 (*http://drupal.org/project/dreamy*)

Chapter 9, *Event Management*

Modules:

- Advanced help 6.x-1.0 (*http://drupal.org/project/advanced_help*)
- Content Construction Kit (CCK) 6.x-2.0-rc10 (*http://drupal.org/project/cck*)
- Calendar 6.x-2.0-rc3 (*http://drupal.org/project/calendar*)
- Date 6.x-2.0-rc3 (*http://drupal.org/project/date*)
- Flag 6.x-1.0-beta5 (*http://drupal.org/project/flag*)
- Views 6.x-2.0-rc4 (*http://drupal.org/project/views*)

Theme:

- Deco 6.x-1.1 (*http://drupal.org/project/deco*)

Chapter 10, *Online Store*

Modules:

- Content Construction Kit (CCK) 6.x-2.0-rc10 (*http://drupal.org/project/cck*)
- FileField 6.x-3.0-alpha6 (*http://drupal.org/project/filefield*)
- ImageCache 6.x-1.0-alpha2 (*http://drupal.org/project/imagecache*)
- ImageField 6.x-3.0-alpha1 (*http://drupal.org/project/imagefield*)
- Token 6.x-1.10 (*http://drupal.org/project/token*)
- Ubercart 6.x-2.x-dev (2008-Nov-3) (*http://drupal.org/project/ubercart*)

Theme:

- Pixture 6.x-1.1 (*http://drupal.org/project/pixture*)

Chapter 11, *Theming Your Site*

Modules:

- Devel 6.x-1.9 (*http://drupal.org/project/devel*)

Theme:

- Bluemarine (core)

Index

T

t() function, 275
Table of Contents module, 207
Tagadelic module, 269
Talk module, 207
taxes
    online stores, 349, 370
taxonomies
    about, 59–61
taxonomy
    about, 13
    internationalization, 299, 307
    synchronization with nodes, 300
    versus CCK, 96
Taxonomy Redirect module, 269
template files
    theming, 388, 397–408
template variables
    overriding, 411
    theming, 408
test orders
    online stores, 372
test users, 48
text
    formatting in wikis, 183
    translating in user interfaces, 273
text areas, 97
text editors
    theming, 392
text fields, 97
text-to-HTML translators, 76
thanking Drupal developers and maintainers,
    448
Theme Developer module, 393
theme functions, 409
theming, 381–416
    about, 69–75, 382–393
    custom themes, 393
    overrides, 408–414
    template files, 388, 397–408
thumbnails
    generating, 237
time increments, 322
time zones, 318, 324, 426
tokens
    about, 195
    Pathauto, 197
toolbars
    content editing, 76

    FCKeditor, 87
    Web Developer Toolbar, 392
Tracker module, 202–206
tracking
    attendance, 315
    changes in wikis, 184
    editorial workflow, 213
    revisions in wikis, 199–202
    stock in online stores, 350
translation
    content, 274, 279, 286, 293
    installation of, 280
    installation process, 277
    Locale module, 275
    user interfaces, 273, 275, 288
Translation Overview module, 310
Translation Synchronization module, 300
triggers
    assigning, 219
    workflow, 215–220
troubleshooting
    Clean URLs, 253–255
    ImageCache module, 253
    resources, 15

U

Ubercart, 343–353
uninstalling modules, 40
Update Status module, 429
update.php script, 420, 431
updating
    Drupal, 427–435
uploading
    files, 93
    photos, 237, 240–245
URLs
    Clean URLs, 253, 426
    ImageCache module, 253
    images, 248
    and nodes, 13
    views, 119
    in wikis, 185
user interfaces
    translating, 273, 275, 288
user profiles
    about, 48
    on Drupal.org, 447
users
    about, 10

About the Authors

Angela Byron is an open source evangelist who lives and breathes Drupal. She got her start as a Google Summer of Code student in 2005 and since then has completely immersed herself in the Drupal community. Her work includes core coding and patch review, creating and contributing modules and themes, testing and quality assurance efforts within the project, improving documentation, and providing user support on forums and IRC.

Angela is on the Board of Directors for the Drupal Association and is the Drupal 7 core co-maintainer. She helps drive community growth by leading initiatives to help get new contributors involved, such as Drupal's participation in Google Summer of Code and Google's Highly Open Participation (GHOP) programs. She is a sought-after lecturer on many themes, especially the topic of women in Open Source. Angie is known as "webchick" on Drupal.org.

Addison Berry takes part in many aspects of both the Drupal software and community. She contributes patches to core Drupal, maintains several contributed modules, and is active in various mentoring programs such as the Drupal Dojo group and the GHOP program.

Addison is the Drupal project Documentation team lead, helps maintain Drupal.org, and is a permanent member of the Drupal Association General Assembly. She has worked to provide a wide range of video and written tutorials covering all aspects of Drupal from community involvement to code. Addi is known as "add1sun" on Drupal.org.

Nathan Haug is one of the foremost user-interface developers in the Drupal project. His interest in combining design and software implementation led him to undergraduate degrees in both Visual Communications and Computer Science. He developed significant UI improvements for the Drupal 6 release, including Drupal's drag-and-drop implementation and a framework for easy Ajax-like behaviors.

Nathan is considered the leading JavaScript developer in the Drupal project. In 2007, he led a development team at SonyBMG to build a Drupal-based platform for community websites around each of SonyBMG's music artists. He spends much of his time working on popular contributed modules such as Fivestar and Webform, or working to improve functionality in Drupal core. Nate is known as "quicksketch" on Drupal.org.

Jeff Eaton has been building Internet and desktop software for over a decade. He's participated in projects ranging from web portals for communities and nonprofits, to enterprise client-server applications for retail industries and large-scale web applications for companies like Dow AgroSciences and Prudential Real Estate.

In 2005, he began developing solutions based on the open source Drupal content management framework. In the years since, he's become a core developer for the Drupal project, specializing in architecture and API development. In his capacity as a consultant for Lullabot Consulting, LLC, he's helped plan and build the software infrastructure for Drupal sites that have included MTV UK's music portal, SonyBMG's artist site platform, and Fast Company's groundbreaking business networking site. Jeff is known as "eaton" on Drupal.org.

James Walker is Lullabot's Director of Education; he oversees the company's public workshops, seminars, and private Drupal trainings, combining his passion for both technology and teaching. A leader in the Drupal community, James is a founding member of the nonprofit Drupal Association and the Drupal security team. As a long-time member of the Drupal community, James maintains more than a dozen modules and has contributed countless patches to Drupal core.

A longtime believer in Open Source and Open Standards, James has spent years coordinating Drupal's involvement with other communities such as Jabber/XMPP and, most recently, OpenID. An engaging speaker, James is a frequently requested presenter at many types of technical conferences. His humorous and informative lectures have been among the most well-attended at DrupalCons, starting with the first one, four years ago. James is known as "walkah" on Drupal.org.

Jeff Robbins is cofounder and CEO of Lullabot. Jeff started one of the world's first web development companies in 1993 and has developed sites for Ringo Starr, MTV, and New York's Museum of Modern Art. Additionally, Jeff spent most of the 1990s fronting the band Orbit, touring with the Lollapalooza festival, and penning a top-10 modern rock single.

Jeff hosts Lullabot's popular Drupal podcast and has garnered a certain amount of recognition within the community. Additionally, he has contributed many widely used Drupal modules and themes including ConTemplate, LoginToboggan, the Zen theme, and the Theme Developer tool. Jeff is known as "jjeff" on Drupal.org.

Colophon

The animal on the cover of *Using Drupal* is a dormouse. Dormice are part of the *Gliridae* family and originally come from Africa and Southern Europe. There are many species of this rodent, but the most popular and common one on the pet market is the African dormouse. The other known dormice are the "common dormouse" or the "hazel mouse" and most resemble small squirrels. Their name is derived from the French word *dormir*, which means to sleep—significant because dormice hibernate for as long as six months, or longer if the weather is cool, awaking only briefly to eat food they stored nearby. During the summer months, they accumulate fat in their bodies allowing them to hibernate for such long periods of time.

On average, dormice are about four inches long, not including the two-inch bushy tail. They have rounded ears, large eyes, and their fur is thick and soft and reddish brown in color. Dormice have an excellent sense of hearing and use a range of different vocalizations to signal each other. They are very playful, social, and personable animals (more so if you raise them from a young age). Their playfulness consists of flips, climbing rope, and leaping and jumping; they are nocturnal so they play mostly at night. Being left alone may cause them to become stressed and unhappy, as they thrive on interaction with others.

Dormice feed on fruit, insects, berries, flowers, seeds, and nuts, and they are especially partial to hazelnuts. They are unique among other rodents because they lack a "cecum," a pouch connected to the colon of the large intestine, which is used in fermenting vegetable matter. Dormice breed once or twice a year and produce an average litter of four young. Their average lifespan is a somewhat short five years. They are born hairless, and their eyes don't open until about 18 days after birth, rendering them helpless at birth. They become sexually mature after the end of their first hibernation.

The cover image is from an unknown source. The cover font is Adobe ITC Garamond. The text font is Linotype Birka; the heading font is Adobe Myriad Condensed; and the code font is LucasFont's TheSansMonoCondensed.

Related Titles from O'Reilly

Web Authoring and Design

ActionScript 3.0 Cookbook

Ajax Hacks

Ambient Findability

Creating Web Sites: The Missing Manual

CSS Cookbook, *2nd Edition*

CSS Pocket Reference, *2nd Edition*

CSS: The Definitive Guide, *3rd Edition*

CSS: The Missing Manual

Dreamweaver 8: Design and Construction

Dreamweaver 8: The Missing Manual

Dynamic HTML: The Definitive Reference, *3rd Edition*

Essential ActionScript 3.0

Flex 8 Cookbook

Flash 8: Projects for Learning Animation and Interactivity

Flash 8: The Missing manual

Flash 9 Design: Motion Graphics for Animation & User Interfaces

Flash Hacks

Head First HTML with CSS & XHTML

Head Rush Ajax

Head First Web Design

High Performance Web Sites

HTML & XHTML: The Definitive Guide, *6th Edition*

HTML & XHTML Pocket Reference, *3rd Edition*

Information Architecture for the World Wide Web, *3rd Edition*

Information Dashboard Design

JavaScript: The Definitive Guide, *5th Edition*

JavaScript & DHTML Cookbook, *2nd Edition*

Learning ActionScript 3.0

Learning JavaScript

Learning Web Design, *3rd Edition*

PHP Hacks

Programming Collective Intelligence

Programming Flex 2

Web Design in a Nutshell, *3rd Edition*

Web Site Measurement Hacks

Our books are available at most retail and online bookstores.

To order direct: 1-800-998-9938 • *order@oreilly.com* • *www.oreilly.com*

Online editions of most O'Reilly titles are available by subscription at *safari.oreilly.com*

The O'Reilly Advantage

Stay Current and Save Money